D022643

CO

The Future of
Fiscal Federalism

The Future of Fiscal Federalism

Edited by
Keith G. Banting
Douglas M. Brown
Thomas J. Courchene

School of Policy Studies
Institute of Intergovernmental Relations
John Deutsch Institute for the Study of Economic Policy
Queen's University at Kingston

DOUGLAS COLLEGE LIBRARY

Canadian Cataloguing in Publication Data

Main entry under title:

The Future of fiscal federalism

Proceedings of a conference held at Queen's University, Nov. 4-5, 1993.
Includes bibliographical references.
ISBN 0-88911-657-1

1. Fiscal policy – Canada – Congresses. 2. Federal-provincial fiscal
relations – Canada – Congresses.* 3. Canada – Social policy –
Congresses. I. Banting, Keith G., 1947-   . II. Brown, Douglas Mitchell,
1954-   . III. Courchene, Thomas J., 1940-   . IV. Queen's University
(Kingston, Ont.). School of Policy Studies.

HJ793.F87 1994   336.71   C94-931012-3

© School of Policy Studies, 1994

Contents

List of Tables and Figures

TABLES

FIGURES

Acknowledgements

From its inception, this book has been a collaborative enterprise to which a large number of people and institutions have contributed. Its origins lie in a conference on "The Future of Fiscal Federalism" held at Queen's University in November 1993, which attracted academics and policymakers from across the country. The conference was jointly sponsored by the School of Policy Studies, the Institute of Intergovernmental Relations, and the John Deutsch Institute for the Study of Economic Policy. A conference of this size represents a significant financial commitment, and the organizers would like to acknowledge the support received from the Social Sciences and Humanities Research Council, the Department of Finance of the Government of Canada, and the Ministry of Intergovernmental Affairs of the Government of Ontario.

The success of the conference also depended heavily on the organizational skills of Sharon Alton, Jane Hodgins, Art Stewart, and Sharon Sullivan. The preparation of the book itself once again reflects the professionalism of the publication unit in the School of Policy Studies. The editors wish to thank Valerie Jarus and Darrel Reid for the production of camera-ready copy, Marilyn Banting for copy editing, and Gary Leroux for graphic design.

Keith G. Banting
Douglas M. Brown
Thomas J. Courchene

PART ONE

INTRODUCTION

CHAPTER ONE

The Future of Fiscal Federalism:
An Overview

Keith G. Banting,
Douglas M. Brown and
Thomas J. Courchene

INTRODUCTION

Canadians are rapidly approaching a critical juncture in the evolution of their social programs and the system of fiscal federalism that underpins them. Powerful economic and social forces have thrust the reform of social programs to the top of the public agenda. The fiscal crisis facing Canadian governments at all levels, the globalization of economic activity and rapid technological change are generating pressure for a restructuring of core social programs. At the same time, the current system of federal-provincial fiscal arrangements is under intense strain. Warning signs are flashing on all sides: the impending disappearance of the cash payments to provinces under Established Program Financing (EPF) raises questions about the federal role in postsecondary education and health care; the cap on the rate of growth of transfers to the three richest provinces under the Canada Assistance Plan (CAP) has sparked intense anger, especially in Ontario; the ceiling on equalization grants worries those committed to interregional sharing; and the repeated resort to unilateral federal action has eroded the institutions and practices of intergovernmental collaboration. In the view of many commentators, the existing patterns of fiscal federalism are no longer sustainable.

So interdependent are social programs and the fiscal arrangements between federal and provincial governments that it is impossible to reform one without reconsidering the other. Changes in major social programs inevitably trigger adjustments in fiscal relations; and seemingly technical changes in the various formulae embedded in fiscal agreements can have major implications for the long-term development of the Canadian welfare state. What makes the contemporary context so compelling is that both our social programs and fiscal arrangements are under debate at the same time.

Given the centrality of these programs to the well-being of Canadians, it is critical that reforms be accompanied by a wide public debate about their future. This book is premised on the assumption that a close look at the structure of social and fiscal programs in Canada can contribute to such a debate. The chapters and commentaries included here range over a wide area, from the implications of the principles of public finance for the design of fiscal arrangements to the impact of globalization and political change on social policy, from the complexities of Canadian social programs to a comparative perspective on fiscal arrangements in federal states around the world, from the history of Canadian programs to projections about their future. Throughout these wide-ranging perspectives run a set of critical questions. How well suited are our existing social and fiscal programs for the emerging economic and political order? Does "social Canada" need radical change or incremental evolution? What are the appropriate roles of federal and provincial governments in preparing "social Canada" for the late twentieth and early twenty-first centuries? Are our political institutions and processes capable of responding effectively to the challenge?

The purpose of this introduction is to provide a survey of the perspectives explored in the chapters that follow, and to summarize the common threads that run through the book as a whole.

FISCAL FEDERALISM: OVERVIEWS

Part two of the book is devoted to a series of broad overviews of fiscal federalism in Canada. In the first chapter, Robin Boadway and Frank Flatters evaluate the system of fiscal federalism in light of core principles of public finance. In the second chapter, Thomas Courchene reverses the approach by beginning with the structure of social programs appropriate to the new global economic order and then tracing their implications for our fiscal arrangements. Richard Simeon rounds out this part by examining the politics of fiscal federalism, and asking whether we have the institutional and political capacities to fashion creative solutions to our social and fiscal dilemmas.

Economic Principles. Boadway and Flatters address the issue of whether the current system of federal-provincial fiscal arrangements, which took shape at a time when the federation was much more centralized than it is now, meets the economic needs of the federal system we have today. The basic building blocks for their evaluation are five principles of public finance: (a) fiscal efficiency, (b) fiscal equity, (c) the preservation of the integrity of economic union, (d) tax harmonization and (e) the accommodation of spillovers of benefits or costs across provincial boundaries. These principles allow the authors to develop an internally consistent view of Canadian fiscal federalism and how it ought to evolve. For example, the principle of fiscal efficiency leads them to favour provincial design and delivery not only of health, education, and welfare (for which the provinces already have primary responsibility) but also of training and unemployment insurance (which are now either jointly or federally provided). The rationale for the latter has to do with the potential for enhanced integration with provincial welfare and education systems. To the extent that this degree of decentralization leads to differential net fiscal benefits (NFBs) across provinces, which could trigger migration from low-NFB to high-NFB provinces, the solution on fiscal efficiency grounds should be an enhanced equalization program.

While fiscal efficiency can provide support for equalization, it is the principle of fiscal equity or horizontal balance that provide Boadway and Flatters with the real leverage to argue for full equalization of NFBs across provinces. In turn, this objective would call for a "net" scheme rather than the current "gross" scheme in order that the fiscal capacities of the rich provinces were reduced to ensure equality of provincial NFBs. A recurrent theme throughout their chapter is that the more decentralized the federation becomes, the more need there is for effective pursuit of fiscal equity goals by the federal government.

Because of the importance they assign to Ottawa's role in pursuing fiscal equity or redistribution, Boadway and Flatters argue for an enhanced role for the federal government in direct taxation and a devolution of indirect taxation to the provinces. To maintain tax harmonization, the authors would fall back on the use of the federal spending power. Indeed, the federal spending power would also play a critical role in preserving and promoting the economic union, which is a greater challenge in a more decentralized federation, and in providing mechanisms that ensure equitable access to all social programs in the face of spillovers.

Boadway and Flatters give tolerably good marks to the way that the existing system has coped with change, but they also recognize that aspects of the system might be, in the words of their title, in "crisis." One recommendation they offer is to roll CAP and EPF into an expanded equalization program, operated on a net basis — net in the sense that the rich provinces would receive less than under the current CAP and EPF, with the reductions being used to finance equalization transfers to the have-not provinces so as to move the system towards full equalization of provincial NFBs.

In summary, this is an intriguing commingling of centralization and decentralization, with fiscal equity concerns driving the former and efficiency concerns driving the latter.

In his commentary, Fred Gorbet focuses on issues that in his view are underplayed in the chapter by Boadway and Flatters. Foremost among these are the fiscal pressures faced by all governments. He notes that it was not until the second Conservative mandate that transfers to the provinces were frozen or capped. At that point, Ottawa no longer felt politically able to increase taxes to maintain transfers to the provinces when these transfers (cash and especially cash plus tax transfers) were growing at rates beyond all other federal spending. This was doubly the case since the federal perspective was that the provinces were doing a less-than-adequate job of controlling their program spending. Gorbet's main point here is that while equity and efficiency as developed by Boadway and Flatters may imply that the role of federal-provincial fiscal arrangements should increase in relative importance as budgetary responsibilities are transferred to the provinces, it is not clear that concerns about *accountability* point in the same direction. His tentative conclusion in the first part of his commentary is that the issues of affordability, accountability and flexibility will influence future negotiations as much as equity and efficiency concerns.

In contemplating the pattern of change in the future, Gorbet begins from several presumptions: on the transfer side, equalization remains a robust program but neither EPF nor CAP is stable; on the tax side, there is uncertainty about the future of the GST and growing pressure from certain provinces to gain control over the rate and bracket structures under the shared personal income tax. In this context, Gorbet foresees two broad "families of options." The first would involve the continuation of the tax agreements much as today (with perhaps some harmonization of federal and provincial sales taxes), and the evolution of EPF and CAP towards a merged block fund. The second, more radical approach would see the federal government repeal the GST and make up the difference through major cuts to EPF and CAP and increases in income taxes. Transferring the GST to the provinces, as Boadway and Flatters suggest, would roughly match in dollar value the existing levels of cash transfers under EPF and CAP. However, it is uncertain why Ottawa would opt for this when the cash component of EPF is heading towards zero and GST revenues are likely to grow. This is not a challenge in terms of principle, but in terms of practice.

Fiscal and Global Challenges. Tom Courchene also casts social policy and fiscal federalism within a broad framework. However, unlike Boadway and Flatters who approach the issues through a series of principles, he addresses the social envelope in terms of a set of forces that, in his view, will overwhelm the status quo. He begins by arguing that the old social policy paradigm is unsustainable in its own right for a number of reasons: the set of perverse incentives for individuals; the emergence of transfer dependency across the provincial economies; and the increasing intergenerational tug-of-war that has left a wholly inappropriate burden on younger generations. Beyond this, however, there is an entirely new set of forces — globalization and the information/knowledge revolution — that call for a complete reworking of social Canada. Courchene argues that a restructured social envelope has to address a series of challenges: mounting an east-west transfer system over a north-south trading system; recognizing that social policy has a critical role to play in ensuring the successful transition from a resource-based society to a human capital-based society; and accepting that the diverse nature of the several Canadian economies may make federal-provincial asymmetry unavoidable.

Courchene does not view the fiscal crisis as fully exogenous to social policy reform since part of the reason for the debt and deficit mushrooming was and is the unwillingness of government to jettison the social paradigm inherited from the postwar generation. While he has harsh words for some aspects of deficit offloading such as the cap on CAP, he nonetheless views the various freezes, caps and ceilings as an essential catalyst to social policy reform and restructuring. Central to his conception of a new social order is that reform must begin from the bottom up — the time has come to design programs and policies from the vantage point of individual Canadians. Only then should we focus on which level of government should deliver them and how they should be financed. In other words, the federal transfer system should be "derivative" not "determining."

In his comments, Lars Osberg takes issue with several aspects of the Courchene chapter. In particular, he challenges Courchene's use of "transfer dependency." While this term has been in vogue for some time, Osberg argues that it represents a stereotype that is no longer borne out by recent research. Indeed, recent Unemployment Insurance (UI) data for "regular benefits" reveal that Toronto and Montreal have higher UI "dependency" than does Halifax. Osberg is more positive about Courchene's recommendation of a negative income tax for children as one way to address the welfare trap, and he offers some suggestions as to how it might be implemented. Finally, he argues that the returns to restructuring social policy, and particularly to engaging in a substantial training effort, may be low unless there is a demand for trained labour. Thus, one of his priorities is to integrate both the macroeconomic and social dimensions so that they are pulling in the same direction.

Claude Forget is more comfortable with, if not transfer dependency, then at least Courchene's concept that the perverse incentives in the transfer system have generated a "policy induced equilibrium." However, in his comments, he emphasizes the political barriers to change. From his perspective as the head of the Commission of Inquiry on Uemployment Insurance, he believes that in a period of heightened regionalism underscored by recent federal election results, there seems to be no reason why dysfunctional incentives embedded in the transfer system will be amenable to reform. Forget also notes that the unpredictability of federal transfers has always existed, even though the concern about unpredictability is currently heightened. He does not think that the provinces are sufficiently angry to accept lower transfers for more predictability. Moreover, Forget questions whether federal offloading can be linked to the ongoing provincial restructuring: this may have occurred in its own right. His comments conclude with an observation that one reason why Ottawa may engage in reform of welfare, UI, training, and education is that these areas, individually and collectively, are among the most generously funded in terms of international comparisons. Perhaps an option is to generate savings here and convert them to strengthen the federal commitment and predictability with respect to Medicare, which is seen more and more as a defining characteristic of Canada.

Political Challenges. Richard Simeon then provides a more explicitly political overview of the future of fiscal federalism in Canada. Beginning with the proposition that there is a consensus that existing social policies and fiscal arrangements are unsustainable, Simeon questions whether the conditions for a creative or successful resolution exist. He concludes that the political system lacks the institutional capacity to address and manage the challenge.

In developing this conclusion, Simeon offers a series of five institutional or constitutional "trumps" that are likely to frustrate a coordinated, collective effort to address the social and fiscal challenge.

- Constitutional and related issues of national unity tend to trump substantive, functional policy issues;

- Regional distribution of costs and benefits trump other debates on redistribution;

- Fiscal and financial issues trump debate on social policy;

- Intricacies of intergovernmental negotiation trump citizen understanding and politics; and

- Governmental self-interest in seeking to avoid and transfer blame trumps the willingness to share it.

Simeon then elaborates on each of these "trumps," drawing from our past experience, current realities, and future prospects. Compounding all of this is the fiscal burden. Our experience with political federalism has largely been in the context of an expansion of government activities. Now we are embarked on a "federalism of hard times," in which downsizing, restructuring and the avoidance of blame elevate further the power of the respective "trumps."

Is there a way out? One model that Simeon considers, but later rejects, is a version of Breton's competitive federalism, according to which governments act unilaterally in response to economic and social problems. In this model, Ottawa can transfer deficits to the provinces and the provinces react with a wide variety of program changes, restraint measures and increased taxing and borrowing. However, this approach generates serious problems of social cohesion, as would a reliance on disentanglement and a return to a "watertight compartments" approach to federalism. In the final analysis, Simeon opts for a consultative, coordinated approach that recognizes the interdependence and shared nature of the issues, and would involve revitalizing the intergovernmental process and rebuilding the functional linkages between economic and social policy. But overall, Simeon remains more hopeful than optimistic.

In his comments, André Blais endorses many of Simeon's views, but comes away decidedly more optimistic. He sees considerable virtue in competitive federalism and the politics of crisis, which can and frequently do lead to major policy innovations. Indeed, Blais believes that there is a growing consensus among Canadians that the fiscal overhang requires spending cuts. Implicit in his comments is the suggestion that Ottawa can mobilize citizen support for cuts in transfers to provinces provided it also cuts spending in other areas. More generally, Blais offers the suggestion that the time may well be ripe for completely new systems based on principles that appeal to all Canadians.

FISCAL FEDERALISM: THE POLICY SECTORS

Part three directs closer attention to the individual social programs and their relationship with fiscal federalism. Carolyn Tuohy assesses the sources of change in health care, Judith Maxwell addresses the related challenges of postsecondary education and training, and François Vaillancourt deals with the complexities of our income security programs. Arching over these benefits provided directly to individuals is a set of transfers from Ottawa to the provinces: equalization, EPF, and CAP. Ken Norrie's contribution focuses on these federal-provincial transfers, and the appropriate balance between them and direct federal benefits to individuals. Moreover, his chapter sparks a lively debate with his two commentators, and is therefore an appropriate launching point for this section.

Federal-Provincial Transfers. The thrust of Norrie's contribution is that the pre-1977 "balance" or compromise between individual equity and provincial equity is in the process of unravelling. Norrie's solution is for Ottawa to play a greater role in the pursuit of individual equity. This strategy has merits in its own right, but Norrie believes that it will also foster political support for the maintenance of a generous equalization program and therefore of inter-provincial equity as well. This sparks a fascinating debate with David Milne, whose commentary adopts the opposite view.

Norrie develops his conclusion on the basis of a historical and philosophical review of the evolution of federal-provincial arrangements. Before 1977, the equalization program focused on equalizing provincial revenues and therefore achieving regional equity, while the shared-cost programs were designed to provide minimum levels of essential services to all Canadians in the name of individual equity. In Norrie's view, the "curious hybrid of measures" adopted in the 1977 EPF arrangements marked an important watershed. The tax-transfer component of the new EPF arrangements could be seen as enhancing account-ability; but the cash-transfer component, unconditional as it was, lacked any rationale, especially after the 1982 arrangements made it the residual element. Since then, a long series of shifts have eroded both the integrity of the fiscal arrangements and the ability of the federal government to sustain a generous system of intergovernmental transfers.

In searching for solutions, Norrie first considers completing "what we apparently set out to do in 1977 with EPF," namely making EPF and CAP truly unconditional by converting them into further tax-point transfers and embark-ing on an enhanced equalization program. However, he rejects this devolution-ist approach because, among other things, he does not believe that either Ottawa or Canadians generally would long support such large transfers on a purely unconditional basis, that is, without guarantees that programs supporting indi-vidual equity would be maintained. Hence, Norrie is driven in the direction of a larger role for Ottawa in providing individual equity directly. Medicare, where interprovincial spillovers are less, would be devolved to the provinces with enhanced tax room, but funding for postsecondary education and CAP would take the form of federal vouchers, and some version of a refundable tax credit for low-income Canadians. With such anchors securing individual equity,

Norrie believes that Ottawa would also have the political support to pursue interregional equity through a generous equalization program.

Norrie's strategy is reflected by two commentators, although for different reasons. David Milne objects primarily because of his assessment of the political implications. At the "mega-constitutional" level, Milne argues that the federal unilateralism implicit in the approach would be ill-timed given the forthcoming Quebec election and a possible referendum on sovereignty. At the program level, he feels that converting the federal contribution to Medicare into an unconditional tax-transfer is a non-starter because Canadians want to preserve a federal role in defending national goals in health care. More generally, Milne does not agree with Norrie's concern that Ottawa has lost visibility in terms of programs such as social assistance. In general, the "complex interdependence" of the current system is unlikely to give way to strategies for direct federal delivery and disentanglement. According to Milne, the inevitable messiness is best handled by improved institutions for intergovernmental coordination and decision making: "our success or failure in developing and perfecting these intergovernmental institutions and procedures will be a vital part of the story of Canada's unfolding fiscal crisis."

Hobson also rejects Norrie's approach, but on different grounds. He is concerned that reducing the role of intergovernmental transfers in the name of disentanglement and direct federal delivery would increase fiscal disparities between rich and poor provinces. He makes this argument for each component of Norrie's strategy: devolution of full financial responsibility for health care to the provinces, along with the transfer of associated tax room, would erode interprovincial equity; the withdrawal of the federal government from CAP and the introduction of a new federal income-security program would still leave provinces responsible for a residual program of social assistance, with poorer provinces facing greater needs and fewer resources with which to respond; and a shift from the postsecondary component of EPF to educational vouchers would have similar effects. In general, Hobson recommends retaining the existing framework of federal-provincial transfer programs, but making a number of changes to enhance interprovincial equity. The debate between Norrie and his commentators, Milne and Hobson, thus effectively highlights two very distinctive approaches to the future of fiscal federalism in Canada.

Health Care. Health care holds a special place in Canadian political culture, and intense debate swirls around the importance of the federal role in preserving the essential principles of Medicare. The chapter by Carolyn Tuohy investigates these issues by asking a broader question: will the 1990s be "an epoch of fundamental structural change in health care," or will we see a continuation of normal political struggles over incremental change in the distribution of resources within existing programs and institutions.

Tuohy argues that structural change in the health-care system almost always results from "exogenous factors" rather than from powerful interests within the health delivery system itself. However, when episodes of major change are triggered by the broader political system, the resulting policy shifts are heavily influenced by the climate of policy ideas about health-care delivery. Using this basic model, Tuohy provides an insightful analysis of the development of Medicare, and the basic accommodations that were established between the government and private insurers, between the federal and provincial governments, and between the state and the medical profession.

In contemplating the future, Tuohy admits that there are pressures for structural change, and especially for a reduction in the federal role. She suggests that the Reform Party and the Bloc Québécois could play a role in decentralizing social policy "analogous to the role played by the NDP in centralizing it in the 1960s." These political dynamics could be reinforced by the fiscal crisis of the federal government, a general wish for disentanglement, and a desire on the part of provinces to protect themselves from unilateral federal decisions in the future. A decision by the federal government to withdraw from Medicare would create wider opportunities for structural change at the provincial level, and provincial experiments with market forces within a publicly-provided system could generate greater diversity in the types of coverage that Canadians enjoy.

However, Tuohy is sceptical that the future will unfold in this direction. She doubts that the federal government will abandon the Medicare field. More importantly perhaps, she does not believe that a federal withdrawal would, in fact, undermine the current principles that shape health care. Deep public support for the existing model, and the power of organized interests in the delivery system would constrain reform impulses. In fact, Tuohy anticipates a pattern of incremental change, with the greatest activity coming not in the form of user fees but in the de-insuring of some procedures, stronger clinical guidelines, and a growing role for local health authorities in the hospital sector. In the long term, such incremental shifts can become significant. De-insuring services, for example, would expand the scope for private insurance, and over time augment the role of private insurers in Canadian health politics. Nevertheless, for the foreseeable future, Tuohy does not see the politics of fiscal federalism triggering deep structural changes in Canadian health policy.

In his comments, Greg Stoddart presents a less sanguine view of the future, one characterized by "turbulence" and "an atmosphere of exasperation, if not desperation." However, fiscal federalism is implicated in only some of the stresses that he anticipates. For example, he foresees provincial efforts to introduce fees purely to raise revenue, since the demand for health care is very inelastic. Clearly, such efforts would place great pressure on the *Canada Health Act*. Elsewhere, however, fiscal federalism seems less relevant. For example, Stoddart expresses frustration that clinical practice has not evolved in response to research findings about the range of medical procedures that are ineffective or inappropriate. But he calls on health science centres and the self-regulating colleges rather than the federal government to show leadership in moving the system towards "the effectiveness and efficiency frontiers." He also emphasizes the need for new institutions to develop a wider social consensus on which services are medically necessary, but anticipates change at the local level. Difficult decisions about which services will be provided to which groups may well be "dumped to the district or regional level through the creation of new decision-making bodies."

Stoddart is clearly not comfortable by a withering of the federal role. The public, he argues, "wants to preserve a sense (maybe even an illusion) of national unity or identity" through a federal role in health care; and he sees an important role for Ottawa in health promotion through preventive and developmental programs. Nevertheless, he does not seem to be particularly optimistic that the world will unfold in his preferred direction.

Education and Training. "More carrots, please" is Judith Maxwell's plea for education and training. Canada's economic future depends on its becoming a knowledge-based society, in which all citizens participate in a learning culture. However, a learning culture also requires continuous innovation, adjustment, and creativity on the part of educational institutions such as universities and colleges, a dynamic that needs to accelerate despite the decline in financial support from governments. Hence Maxwell's emphasis on stronger incentives to innovation in funding arrangements for educational and training programs.

In this context, Maxwell sees a clear role for the federal government as an agent of innovation. The basic problem, she insists, is that "the federal government has been writing cheques without specifying or monitoring the desired outcomes." Under her dietary regime of more carrots, the federal government would begin to use the leverage implicit in its funding. In the case of post-secondary education, she recommends that the federal government formally relinquish any political credit for the tax points transferred to the provinces, but then transform the remaining cash payments into a more strategic set of transfers: operating grants paid directly to universities, sponsored research grants, reformed systems of student support, and a University and College Innovation Program to reward institutions committed to change. In the case of training programs, the federal government should help to pay for the cost of developing nationwide training standards, and offer to transfer federal activities in training to provinces that have a complete set of standards in place. However, the federal government should also cut funding for training programs in any provinces that are not making clear progress in developing and implementing such common standards.

Given the history of federal-provincial tensions over such strategies, Maxwell recommends abandoning constitutional symmetry and establishing separate arrangements with different provinces. She accepts that Quebec would opt out of the direct payments to universities, and that other provinces might follow suit. If that happens, however, she urges the federal government to insist on a strong innovation program that ensures that federal resources actually promote excellence. In the case of training, asymmetry in the delivery of programs is acceptable as long as common training standards act "as the force that binds the country together and maintains the viability of the economic union."

In his comments, Stefan Dupré supports this combination of assertiveness and asymmetry through his own proposal for "procurement federalism." He argues that Ottawa's capacity to purchase services should be used to reward quality in education and training systems. In the postsecondary education sector, he recommends using the cash portion of EPF to finance the full indirect costs of research that the federal government contracts for in universities. In the case of training programs, he hopes that business and labour representatives on agencies such as the Canada Labour Force Development Board (CLFDB) and the Ontario Training and Adjustment Board (OTAB) will insist that public education institutions face competition from private training schools. Procurement federalism is a potentially powerful instrument of federal assertiveness. For example, the proposal to shift EPF dollars, which currently go to provincial governments, into direct research payments to universities would certainly enhance Ottawa's role in this sector. In the case of training, however, Dupré softens this assertiveness by endorsing Maxwell's call for asymmetric federalism, including the transfer of the federal role in procurement and placement played by Canada Employment Centres to the province of Quebec.

Income Security. The income security sector combines major reform issues and complex intergovernmental relations, which are highlighted in the chapter by François Vaillancourt. The current agenda focuses primarily on income security for the employable population, which is delivered through a complex array of programs by the federal and provincial governments. Seen as a comprehensive system, these programs are bedeviled by differing benefit levels and design features that can inhibit training, mobility, and the transition from welfare to work. Vaillancourt is convinced that program integration and reform requires greater consolidation of authority over unemployment insurance, workers compensation, and social assistance. "One government should be responsible," he argues. Given the distinctiveness of the labour markets in Quebec and the rest of the country, he also suggests an asymmetric response, with Quebec taking responsibility for the programs in that province but a federal agency serving the rest of Canada. Failing that, he suggests general decentralization to the provinces. One major advantage of such a shift, he argues, would be that provinces would have a stronger incentive to ensure that their minimum wages and labour legislation promote higher levels of employment. If decentralization is impossible, Vaillancourt would actually prefer direct federal delivery of income support to individuals, in this case through the abolition of CAP and the transfer of the resources to the Unemployment Insurance program to provide extended benefits for the unemployed.

Finally, Vaillancourt raises a much more radical approach in which existing income transfers would be replaced with a system of Individual Economic Security Accounts. These accounts would represent forced savings by individuals both for old age and for periods of unemployment. Governments, presumably at any level, would be able to contribute directly to an individual's accounts in order to fulfil their redistributive goals and avoid shortfalls. According to Vaillancourt, one of the advantages of such an approach would be to avoid the maze of intergovernmental complexity that characterizes the current system.

In her comments, Susan Phillips takes issue with many of Vaillancourt's recommendations, including his preference for individual savings accounts as opposed to social security. In the domain of fiscal federalism, she is particularly critical of proposals to devolve CAP and perhaps Unemployment Insurance to the provinces at a time when the Canadian economy is undergoing deep restructuring. In her words, "adjustment is predominantly a national issue, and labour markets are becoming more national, not more local." Devolution risks foreclosing the opportunity to focus on the larger forces reshaping the Canadian economy. Concern for gender equity reinforces Phillips opposition to the devolution of CAP. Arguing that a national child-care program is essential to a comprehensive system of family income support, she fears that "if we devolve CAP to the provinces now, it is unlikely that there will ever be a national child-care strategy." Phillips is also sceptical of proposals that would separate support for children from social assistance, with the federal government using CAP dollars to expand child benefits paid directly to families, and the provinces focusing on the welfare needs of adults. Such proposals, she argues, ignore the "social ecology" of family life; the best way to help poor children is "to improve the income, training, and employment prospects of their parents."

Phillips also raises a general issue about the approach to interregional transfers in the Canadian system. Noting that poverty is increasingly an urban phenomenon, concentrated in major metropolitan regions such as Toronto, Montreal, and Vancouver, she argues that the problems of cities need far greater attention. Because our system of fiscal federalism is designed to respond to provinces, not cities, a reconceptualization of the principle of interregional sharing and associated programs is essential. Given the location of the major metropolitan centres, such a shift in emphasis would have radical implications for the system of transfers developed in the last half-century.

A COMPARATIVE PERSPECTIVE

The next section of the book examines Canada's fiscal federalism from a comparative perspective. Richard Bird's chapter surveys the experience of seven developed countries (Austria, Germany, Belgium, Switzerland, Australia, the United States, and Canada) and two developing countries (India and Brazil). His analysis shows that all federal systems face a similar set of issues in designing their fiscal arrangements: the need to redress the "vertical imbalance" between the revenue-generating capacity of the central government and the expenditure responsibilities of the constituent governments; the need for equalization to correct the "horizontal imbalance" of fiscal capacity and expenditure need generated by economic disparity across the units in a federation; and the need for tax coordination among the central and constituent governments. Bird's survey demonstrates that while there is indeed a menu of choice in the experiences of other federations, choosing solutions from abroad needs to be done carefully with due concern for the overall context of the political system. Formulae for fiscal transfers, for example, will be "always and inevitably political," and attention to the rules and process for political decision making in other federal systems is more productive than examining the actual results achieved.

These conclusions are reinforced in Ronald Watts' commentary on Bird's analysis. Watts finds that comparative analysis is undervalued in Canada, arguing that it can be useful in terms of seeing not only what might work better at home, but what would not. The political context of other federal systems is also crucial to effective comparisons in Watts' view. For example, solutions designed to work in a congressional system of separated powers as in the United States or with a distribution of powers that is largely concurrent as in Australia may not work in the Canadian case of a parliamentary federation with a more exclusive division of powers.

Taken together the two contributions raise some important issues about the substance and process of fiscal federalism in Canada. Bird argues strongly that those who would restructure revenues and expenditures to more closely match the two may be on a fool's errand, that all federal systems have a degree of "vertical imbalance" and that in parliamentary federations accountability for expenditures through the legislature means that the fiscal gap need not entail fiscal irresponsibility. On the equalization side, Bird reminds us that regional sharing in federations is more a matter of political values than of economic necessity, and that the important thing is a credible process rather than any specific formula. Bird's chapter hints at, but does not explore in depth, the significance of an asymmetrical approach to tax coordination and harmonization. Canada already presents one of the world's leading examples of such an approach in the differing arrangements for Quebec in tax collection and revenue sharing. How far can such a trend go? The evidence would appear to be that federal systems tolerate considerable asymmetry.

On the process side, Bird and Watts both indicate that there are effective models abroad for improving the intergovernmental machinery to reach political accommodation on fiscal federalism. If, as Watts notes, fiscal relations in Canada are due for a "big bang," are our intergovernmental institutions capable of delivering? The chapter by Simeon and the commentary by Milne cast doubt on the ability of the system to deliver radical results in Canada. Elsewhere coordination is achieved effectively through formal institutions such as Germany's Bundesrat. Given the defeat of the Charlottetown Accord, constitutional amendments to improve coordination on fiscal matters in Canada are not feasible. However, other devices, such as Australia's Commonwealth Grants Commission or India's Finance Commissions might be more readily adapted to Canadian use without constitutional amendment. In any case, Bird, as would Watts, encourages Canadians to continue to examine the underlying political dynamics in other federal systems to understand the preconditions for successful political processes here.

BIG BANG OR QUIET TINKERING

The final section of the book addresses explicitly an issue that emerges earlier in less explicit ways. Is our system of fiscal federalism now so irretrievably flawed that only comprehensive and radical reform will equip Canada for the years ahead? Or, is the basic structure of federal-provincial fiscal agreements essentially sound, and in need of only incremental adjustments to changing circumstances? Are we in for a "Big Bang" or merely "quiet tinkering"? Four commentators address these questions in different ways.

Peter Leslie is convinced that the system indeed needs reform, and thus is not content to characterize the coming process as "quiet tinkering." He prefers the metaphor of "big bang" or — perhaps better — of a "controlled nuclear reaction." Pursuing this latter metaphor, Leslie surveys three risks that must be controlled. The first is the obvious risk to those Canadians directly dependent on the benefits of social programs. To reduce the harm to the beneficiaries, reform must be slow but steady, he argues, and should proceed on the basis of clearly articulated objectives both in terms of the policy goals and fiscal targets. The second risk is deadlock. To avoid this danger, in his view, it is essential to put as many issues as possible on the negotiating table in order to allow maximum room for trade-offs. This has the side risk, of course, of courting agenda overload. The third risk is a familiar one: that of pursuing reform that is neither decentralist enough for Quebec or symmetrical enough for the rest of Canada. Leslie argues for contingency plans to head off the extreme demands on both sides. In particular, he argues for a pre-emptive strike by the federal government to call the bluff of some Quebecers by proposing as one option dramatic asymmetry, whereby Quebec would be responsible for social security but would not receive equalization. Faced with a choice between this option and a more modest asymmetry, Leslie is confident Quebecers will choose the latter, or at least make a more informed choice.

Robert Normand is less sanguine on the prospects for major reform, for a number of reasons. First, in his view it is almost impossible to reform social programs in a period of high unemployment when the recipients feel most vulnerable. Second, he does not interpret the results of the 25 October 1993 federal election as giving a mandate to the Liberals to make major changes that the Conservatives had promised. Third, the fiscal crisis itself allows little room for tinkering; and fourth, the regionalization of the parties in Parliament reduces the ability to reach accommodation. Finally, Normand sees Canada caught in a vicious circle: the federal system is in a mess because we cannot fix anything; and we cannot fix anything because the system is in a mess. In summary, he foresees the usual federal-provincial tug-of-war producing little by way of change. His own prediction is that change will come in the form of federal and provincial legislation to limit budgetary deficits along the lines of the Gramm-Rudman Bill adopted by the U.S Congress. He also proposes a constitutional amendment to make the process of public borrowing more transparent and more difficult.

Katherine Swinton dwells more extensively on process issues in any reform attempt. Unless public interest groups have a role in the process, she is convinced that governments run the risk of massive failure, as in the case of the Charlottetown Accord. In light of that example, she does not give much chance to any reform package that would seek to amend the constitution formally any time soon. In addition, the traditional flexibility and adaptiveness of the constitution which enabled much of the welfare state to be constructed in the first place may now also be constrained by the fiscal limits to the federal spending power, although Swinton does not completely count out reform which hinges on its use. An even more constraining aspect may be the politics of rights — in particular the heightened tendency of interest groups to seek redress through the courts to force the hand of reluctant governments. While litigants have no guarantee of success, Swinton foresees an increase in litigation to force provincial governments to adhere to federal conditions such as those in the *Canada Health Act*, and to extend entitlements through Charter cases and recourse to international covenants. In any case, Swinton warns that a reform process confined to "executive federalism" will not produce public support, and calls for a more open process, and broad public education and debate of the issues.

Finally, John Richards argues for a specific approach to reform. He insists that if the welfare state is to survive, public sector decisionmakers must have the discretion to redesign and restructure programs, including how they are delivered within the public sector. In his view, one of the key obstacles to this flexibility is public sector unions. He goes on to argue for balanced aggregate federal-provincial finances, within a four-year time frame. This can be achieved only by substantially reducing the numbers of persons on the public sector payroll, or the levels of compensation, or both. Moreover, the greatest need for cutbacks is at the provincial and municipal levels, and the federal government should play its role in triggering this process by accelerating the reduction in cash transfers to the provinces.

IN SUMMARY

A number of threads run clearly through the chapters and commentaries in this book, often reflecting the wider public debate over the future of Canada's social and fiscal programs. First, there is widespread agreement here that the status quo is no longer viable. The prescriptions for reform vary widely, but few of our contributors believe that the existing set of programs can meet the needs of Canadians for the rest of this century, let alone the early years of the next.

Not surprisingly, this broad consensus begins to dissolve, however, when attention shifts to prescriptions for change. In the first place, there is debate about the scope and speed of change. On one side are those who see the need for reform or whose analysis points strongly to major change, and who take the view that we must simply "do it." On the other side are those who may share some sense of the urgency but are more pessimistic about the ability of the system to produce change. The debate between Norrie and Milne is an obvious example, but the dichotomy runs through the book more generally. Boadway and Flatters, Courchene, Maxwell, Vaillancourt, Leslie, and Richards also call for determined change, while Simeon, Tuohy, Forget, Normand, and Swinton tend to emphasize the constraints. It is hardly coincidental that in this book it is economists who tend to be optimistic about change, and political scientists and former practitioners who are most sensitive to the constraints. However, this tension undoubtedly reflects a current dilemma of Canadian politics. For many, the need to restructure the role of government and its institutions and programs is clear, but the vested interests in the status quo and the dysfunctional aspects of current institutions and processes get in the way of solutions.

There are also differences in the direction of change charted by our contributors. It is notable, however, that there is substantial support for an active role on the part of the federal government. For some contributors, such as Boadway and Flatters, Milne, Hobson, Stoddart, and Phillips, this activism takes the traditional form of national standards in shared-cost programs. However, there is also considerable interest in direct federal delivery to individual citizens of benefits now funded through federal-provincial programs. Norrie suggests this approach for postsecondary education and income security, although not for health care; Maxwell and Dupré agree for postsecondary education and training; Courchene concurs for child benefits and perhaps postsecondary education; and even Vaillancourt recommends shifting resources from CAP, a shared-cost program, to Unemployment Insurance, an exclusively federal program, if his first choice of decentralization proves impossible. In contrast with this enthusiasm for different forms of federal activism, only Vaillancourt envisages a broad decentralization. This balance undoubtedly reflects the selection of contributors to the book. Nevertheless, it is a reminder that, despite the seemingly overwhelming constraints on the federal government, there are still strong expectations that Ottawa has an active role to play in responding to the economic and social problems that we face.

Another striking thread running through many of the contributions to this book is the acceptance of asymmetry in federal-provincial relationships. For Courchene, asymmetry is the appropriate response to diversity in the pattern of economic and social problems that the regions of Canada confront; but for others, such as Vaillancourt, asymmetry is primarily a response to the distinctiveness of Quebec. Interestingly, several advocates of direct federal delivery, such as Maxwell and Dupré, accept asymmetry as a concomitant of federal activism, although the precise modalities are not worked out here. Their approach undoubtedly reflects the tensions implicit in the wider political economy of Canadian life.

The agenda for the reform of fiscal federalism is clearly a daunting one. As several commentators noted, in an earlier era the issues involved would have been managed — amicably or otherwise — after some months of closed-door intergovernmental negotiation. This agenda, however, coming as it does after the failure of Meech and Charlottetown, and after the scarring effects of the debates over free trade, will not be confined to the backrooms of executive federalism. Too much is at stake for Canadians and for governments alike. The current debate represents a significant opportunity for a new, more open style of politics to respond to issues that touch the core of social Canada. This book is dedicated to the proposition that debate about these issues and opportunities is critical to that process.

PART TWO

OVERVIEWS

CHAPTER TWO

Fiscal Federalism: Is the System in Crisis?

Robin Boadway and Frank Flatters

INTRODUCTION

Canada has one of the most highly developed systems of federal-provincial fiscal arrangements in the world. The essential form of these arrangements has remained unchanged now for several decades. In the meantime, the substantive structure of the federation has undergone major changes, especially in recent years. Put simply, ours has become one of the more decentralized federations. The issue to be addressed in this chapter is whether the current system of federal-provincial fiscal arrangements, which took shape at a time when the federation was much more centralized than it is now, meets the needs of the federal system that we have today. To the extent that this is not the case, we wish to ask how the arrangements might be revised or overhauled.[1]

The term "fiscal arrangements" covers a wide variety of possible dealings between the two levels of government. Our concern will be mainly with two general types of federal-provincial interactions — transfers and tax-sharing arrangements. We do not deal with other forms of economic relations, such as direct regulation of provincial activities by the federal government (which, unlike many other federations, has not been a feature of the Canadian system), or methods of coordinating federal and provincial activities in areas of shared jurisdiction (such as agriculture and immigration), except to the extent that they have implications for financial transfers. This does not preclude investigating possibilities for shared or cooperative decision making over the forms of financial transfers or tax sharing; indeed, in some cases that is almost a necessary outcome.

The chapter proceeds as follows. We begin the next section by outlining our views of the economic role of federal-provincial fiscal relations in a relatively decentralized federation. This will form the basis against which the existing and alternative arrangements will be judged. Next, we recall some of the ways in which the Canadian federation and the fiscal arrangements have evolved over the postwar period. Of particular importance will be three areas in which significant changes have occurred — the relative responsibilities of the two levels of government, the constitution and its interpretations, and federal policy initiatives which have had an impact on federal-provincial fiscal relations. Then we outline some of the main problems with the existing arrangements, as seen by ourselves and by other observers. Finally, we consider options for addressing these problems, some of which have been advocated in the recent literature or in public debate. We stress throughout that the system must be viewed in its entirety since the various components jointly contribute to the objectives of the system as a whole.

Our intent is to present the alternatives in a more or less objective way, although undoubtedly our own biases will creep in. The hope is that the chapter will put some of the key issues into context and serve as a useful background for the more detailed topics to follow in the book.

THE ECONOMIC ROLE OF FEDERAL-PROVINCIAL FISCAL ARRANGEMENTS

The role of federal-provincial fiscal relations depends jointly on the responsibilities that governments at each level are expected to assume, and on how these duties should be divided between levels of government. On neither of these questions is there likely to be strong consensus in Canada. Broadly speaking, those who see a large role for government in addressing the inefficiencies and inequities of the market are likely to expect a great deal from the federal government and to see the system of fiscal relations as an important policy instrument.[2] On the other hand, those who prefer less rather than more intervention by government (say, because they take a cynical view of the efficacy of the public sector, or because they put a low value on equity objectives) are more likely to be content with a highly decentralized federation and a relatively small role for federal-provincial fiscal arrangements. In outlining the economic role of federal-provincial fiscal arrangements in a decentralized federal economy, we leave these as open questions.

The economic case for government intervention is based on equity and efficiency considerations and the failure of the market to attain these goals. We need not review the familiar arguments for and against government intervention. What is relevant here are the particular efficiency and equity issues that arise in a federal economy, and the roles of the federal and provincial governments in addressing them.

Efficiency Issues in a Federal Economy

An efficiently operating economy is one in which the "gains from trade" are exploited to the fullest. A federal system of government gives rise to a number of additional sources of inefficiency which differ from the standard, textbook types of market failure that occur in a unitary state. There are three in particular that are most relevant for our purposes.

Efficiency of the Internal Common Market. To ensure that resources are allocated efficiently across the federation, it is necessary that goods, services, labour, and capital be able to move freely across internal boundaries, and that the market signals which guide these movements not be distorted. In a decentralized federation, there is considerable scope for provincial taxes, expenditures, and regulations to have distortionary effects on the interprovincial allocation of resources.[3] These distortions can be the incidental effects of provincial policies directed at some other goals, or they might result from policies that are deliberately designed to affect the interprovincial allocation of resources. In the first category, differential tax policies and service provision will almost inevitably distort the allocation of resources, especially those that are mobile like capital and some types of labour. In the second category, provinces may attempt to use tax and expenditure policies to attract factors of production to their jurisdiction.[4] Such "beggar-thy-neighbour" policies can give rise to inefficiencies in the internal common market even if all provinces engage in them to the same extent. The maintenance of an efficient internal common market is an important policy objective of the federal government.

Decentralization of Service Delivery. A key issue in any federal economy concerns the degree of decentralization of the provision of goods and services in the public sector. Many economists take the view that decentralization is a valued objective in itself, and ought to be the rule except for specific cases in which there is a sound argument for centralized delivery of a specific public service. This view is based on the notion that decentralization leads to more responsiveness to local preferences and needs, greater political accountability, more efficient administration, induced efficiency through interjurisdictional competition, and greater program innovation. Central provision is called for only in the case of "national" public goods and significant scale economies.

Thus, public goods that serve a local or regional need are best decentralized to the provinces or their municipalities.

A significant proportion of the goods and services that governments provide take the form of *quasi-private* goods and services, that is, goods and services that are private in nature but which are provided through the public sector, typically free of charge. Examples include education, health services, and welfare services. Public provision of these types of goods and services is typically justified on grounds of equity or social insurance, since there is no apparent market failure reason why the private sector could not provide them at least as efficiently.[5] There would seem to be, at best, a very weak case for providing quasi-private public services at the federal level; most economists would argue for decentralized provision. The efficiency argument for federal involvement would have to rest on the existence of significant spillover benefits from provincial activities in these areas. Such spillovers of benefits from the expenditures in one province to the residents of others, if uncorrected, could lead to inefficiencies of provision as well as inefficiencies in the allocation of resources across the federation. Transportation and medical services in one province will benefit travellers from others. Welfare and educational services may benefit persons who are only temporarily in a province. Recognition of this may induce provinces to impose residency requirements which restrict the mobility of labour across provinces, or to tailor their programs to preclude residents of other provinces from migrating to take advantage of them. Thus, there may be national efficiency consequences arising from the decentralized provision of public goods and services which the federal government has an interest in addressing, even though it is not responsible for their provision.

More important for our subsequent discussion is the fact that these quasi-private services fulfil an important equity role in the economy; indeed, they constitute perhaps the main instruments of redistribution available to governments. The discussion of the appropriate federal role in their provision, therefore, might hinge, not primarily on efficiency arguments, but rather on questions of the assignment of responsibility for equity goals. Is vertical equity a matter of national or local concern? Is the reference group for equity considerations the residents of a province or of the entire country?

Fiscal Inefficiency. A final source of inefficiency in a federation that has received considerable attention in the literature derives from the notion of fiscal inefficiency.[6] The idea is that as expenditure and tax responsibilities are decentralized, jurisdictions end up with different abilities to provide public goods and services to their residents.[7] This is because they have different tax capacities, and because they have different needs for public expenditures. The consequence is that provinces are able to provide different *net fiscal benefits* (NFBs) to their residents. The literature has tended to focus on two main sources of NFB differentials (see Boadway and Flatters 1982a). First, differences in source-based tax capacities, such as natural resource endowments, allow different provinces the ability to finance a given level of services at different tax rates. The second source of NFB differentials, which is perhaps less transparent, is that provinces that provide more or less equal per capita service benefits, but finance them with taxes on their residents that are roughly proportional to incomes, provide NFBs that differ across provinces in proportion to residence-based tax capacities. The upshot is that a person of a given income will receive systematically higher NFBs in provinces with higher source-based and residence-based tax capacities.

Differences in NFBs will give an incentive for persons to migrate from low NFB provinces to high NFB provinces; to the extent that they respond, this will result in an inefficient allocation of resources. This provides an efficiency argument for the federal government to take action to eliminate these NFB differentials, a role that will be important in our later discussion. Available evidence suggests that this source of inefficiency may not be empirically very significant. Therefore, the efficiency case for federal government action to reduce or eliminate interprovincial NFBs might not be too compelling.[8] However, as we shall see, the efficiency argument for eliminating NFB differentials can be supplemented by an equity argument.

Equity Issues in a Federal Economy

Much of what governments do addresses primarily redistributive concerns, whether for purely ethical reasons or for more cynical motivations related to political expediency. Therefore, one's view about the role of government in the economy, the degree of decentralization of public sector decision making, and the structure of fiscal arrangements will depend heavily upon one's sense of the importance of redistributive equity as an objective of government policy and one's opinion about how closely government behaviour conforms to benevolence as opposed to expediency. Unfortunately, persons will come to different conclusions about both the properties of society's "social welfare function" and what actually motivates government behaviour.

Two main equity issues arise in federal economies. The first concerns the notional assignment of responsibility for equity; the second concerns the special problem of fiscal inequity which, like fiscal inefficiency, arises whenever budgetary functions are decentralized.

Responsibility for Redistributive Equity. The case for the federal government's assuming a major role in redistribution has a long history in the literature (see Musgrave 1959) and is based largely on normative considerations. The main argument is simply that everyone in the nation ought to "count" equally in the social welfare function; this is taken to be a fundamental implication of citizenship. The relevant social welfare function is considered to be a national one. A second argument is that, because of interregional mobility of factors of production, too little redistribution will be carried out at subnational levels. This is simply an application of the spillovers argument referred to above.

On the other hand, those who argue that responsibility for redistribution ought to be at least partially decentralized do so on two main grounds. The first is that there may be regional preferences for redistribution, or differences in local aversion to inequality, and provinces ought to be allowed to reflect such differences. Lower level governments are felt to be "closer to the people" and hence better placed to meet the particular needs of the poor in their jurisdiction. An extreme version of this argument is that the appropriate "sharing group" or the scope of the social welfare function encompasses only the residents of a province. This is more likely to be the case when provinces are characterized by strong and unique cultural identities. In such circumstances, there might also be far less interprovincial mobility of at least some factors of production, which will also make it easier for provinces to achieve redistributive objectives on their own. The second argument for decentralization of redistributive activities is based on the notion that governments engage in too much redistribution to suit the observer, possibly because much of it is motivated by non-normative concerns. To the extent that resources are interregionally mobile, decentralization will restrain the amount of redistribution undertaken because of competition among jurisdictions and because of economic limitations in the ability to redistribute at lower levels of government.[9]

Of course, this argument is partly an empty one since it is not possible to assign responsibility exclusively to one jurisdiction or another. Virtually everything governments do has redistributive consequences, and that cannot be avoided. Nonetheless, the degree of decentralization of redistribution can be influenced by the extent of decentralization of other functions. In particular, if it is felt that the federal government should play an important role in redistribution, then it should be given access to the policy instruments that are most effective at achieving these goals. This certainly includes direct taxes and their analog on the expenditure side, transfers to individuals. However, as we have mentioned, much redistribution takes place through the provision of quasi-private goods and services, and these are rightly assigned to the provincial level of government on efficiency grounds. To the extent that the federal government has an interest in redistributive equity, therefore, it can only exercise that influence indirectly through its spending power.

Fiscal Equity. The argument for fiscal equity parallels that of fiscal efficiency encountered earlier.[10] In a decentralized federation, provinces will be able to provide different levels of NFBs to their residents. This implies that horizontal equity is violated — otherwise identical persons will be treated differently by the public sector according to the province in which they reside. This is a particular feature of a federation; it will not arise in a unitary state. As with fiscal inefficiency, a federal government which has an interest in national equity will wish to take remedial action to undo these NFB differentials. How that is done is of major consequence to the design of fiscal arrangements. The extent of remedial action that will be required of the federal government to deal with fiscal inequities of this sort will depend on both the degree of variability of fiscal capacities across provinces, and the extent to which fiscal responsibilities are actually decentralized to provincial governments. A federation in which provinces are very homogeneous in their fiscal capacities, or in which provinces have very few fiscal responsibilities is one in which problems of fiscal equity will be of very little significance.

Given these particular issues of efficiency and equity which arise in a federal economy, and which become more important the more decentralized the federation is, what do they imply for the structure of fiscal arrangements? We discuss in sequence the role of intergovernmental transfers and the harmonization of the tax system.

The Role of Federal-Provincial Transfers

The need for intergovernmental transfers arises because of both the various inefficiencies and inequities that arise in a decentralized federation, and the possible imbalances in expenditure responsibilities and revenue raising capabilities. The literature has stressed the following arguments for transfers.

Vertical Fiscal Gap. In virtually every federal economy, the highest level of government collects more revenue than it needs for its own purposes and transfers some to the next level.[11] There are two reasons for this. First, the arguments for decentralizing expenditure responsibilities are much more compelling than for decentralizing taxation. The decentralization of taxation gives rise to inefficiencies in the internal economic union and reduces the ability of the federal government to pursue its equity goals.[12] Second, and perhaps more important, a vertical fiscal imbalance is a prerequisite for the federal government to be able to implement a system of grants to achieve the goals of efficiency and equity in the federal economy. The optimal amount of vertical fiscal imbalance depends on two counteracting forces. On the one hand, a greater imbalance facilitates the role of the federal government in achieving national objectives and enhances the ability to decentralize expenditures to the provinces. On the other hand, the greater the fiscal gap, the less will be the reliance of the provinces on their own sources of revenue, and hence the less may be their degree of political accountability.

Fiscal Efficiency and Fiscal Equity. A key role of federal-provincial transfers is to eliminate, or at least reduce, the NFB differentials which generate fiscal inequities and inefficiencies across provinces; and this role is more important the more decentralized is the federation. This is an interesting instance in economic policy analysis in which efficiency and equity arguments coincide. The importance of these arguments in the Canadian case is substantiated by section 36 of the *Constitution Act, 1982,* which sets out the broad obligation of the federal government to provide equalization so that provinces can offer comparable levels of public services at similar levels of taxation.

The usual prescription is for a set of unconditional transfers that equalize differences in tax capacity across provinces, but which are unrelated to individual provincial behaviour per se, such as tax effort or actual service provision (see Economic Council of Canada 1982). One way to think of the ideal equalization scheme is as one that essentially replicates the financial setting of a unitary state, while at the same time allowing for the benefits of decentralized decision making. In principle, one might also want to take need differences into account.[13] However, it is not at all clear how this could be done properly; nor is it clear that it would make enough difference to be worthwhile. An exception to this might be differences in the need to make transfers (i.e., negative taxes) to low-income persons (Breau Committee 1981). NFB differences arising from this source could be significant across provinces, and could be taken account of by the system of equalizing transfers.

It might be argued that the elimination of NFB differentials could be accomplished by a system of transfers to persons that differed according to province of residence. In principle, there is an equivalence between federal-provincial equalizing transfers and transfers to individuals. However, there is one substantive difference between them: for the provincial public sectors to be equally well off financially, some would have to impose higher taxes on their residents. On the one hand, this has the advantage of imposing more fiscal discipline and accountability on provincial governments. However, on the other, it has the disadvantage of decentralizing the tax system and inducing inefficiencies and inequities on that account.

Interprovincial Spillovers. This is a traditional argument for federal-provincial shared-cost programs. If a province's expenditures give rise to benefits to residents of other provinces, the absence of an incentive to take account of the spillover benefits may be expected to give rise to too low a level of provision. The analog is with externalities in private markets. The remedy is for the federal government to provide the correct incentive by an appropriate matching grant. While this argument is logically correct, it is not clear that it justifies the 50-50 matching grants that have been used in the past. While there are undoubtedly spillover benefits from the provision of welfare expenditures and health insurance programs by each of the provinces, it is unlikely that they are anywhere near the order of magnitude that the matching formula would suggest. The high matching rate may have a better justification as a means of taking differential needs into account across provinces by basing them on actual expenditures. Unfortunately, the adverse incentive effects of doing this are quite high.

Expenditure Harmonization: National Standards. One of the most important reasons for federal-provincial transfers, and one that has been less recognized in the literature, has to do with the fact that in a decentralized federation, the federal government may retain a legitimate interest in the overall design of some provincial expenditure programs for reasons of national efficiency or equity. Again, the more decentralized the federation, the more important this role of transfers might be. This can be accomplished by the exercise of the spending power. The economic justification for using the spending power is that there are national objectives that can be attained by encouraging provinces to incorporate particular federally-defined standards into some of the expenditure programs under their jurisdiction, standards that they would not necessarily have an incentive to meet on their own initiative (but that collectively they might agree with).

There are two main sorts of national objectives for which the spending power might be used. The first concerns the efficiency of the internal economic union. Thus, use of this power to ensure portability or accessibility provisions in provincial programs contributes to the free movement of labour across provinces. The second concerns the federal interest in national equity objectives. Given that a good deal of redistribution is delivered through the provision of public sector goods and services, and that a good deal of this is delivered by the provinces, the spending power is the only instrument by which the federal government may attempt to have national equity standards incorporated into these programs. The use of the spending power to require that certain provincial public services are comprehensive and available to all persons are examples of this. Interprovincial competition could well compromise national standards of equity. The emphasis one puts on the use of the spending power for this purpose will depend upon one's view of the federal role in redistribution.

The exercise of the spending power will require conditional grants, although not matching ones. Given that the conditions may be quite general, the grants could be block grants. It is naturally a matter of judgement as to how extensively the spending power should be used and what sorts of political or constitutional limitations should be placed on its use.[14] The ability to use the spending power in a sense increases the case for decentralizing the provision of public goods and services, since it allows the benefits of decentralization to be achieved without unduly compromising national efficiency and equity. By the same token, the more decentralized the federation, the more important does the spending power become.

In summary, in a decentralized federation, such as that of Canada, federal-provincial transfers play an important role. They allow expenditures to be more decentralized than revenue raising. They allow the federal government to correct the inefficiencies and inequities that result from the fact that decentralization would otherwise lead to differing levels of NFBs across provinces. And, they allow the federal government to exercise some influence over the way in which the provinces design their programs so that national interests are taken into account. Thus, federal-provincial transfers allow decentralization to be done in a way that achieves its benefits without compromising national efficiency and equity goals.

Tax Harmonization and Coordination

Just as the decentralization of expenditures gives rise to inefficiencies and inequities in the federation, so does the decentralization of revenue-raising responsibilities. Therefore, the assignment of tax sources, the division of tax room, and the design of mechanisms for harmonizing taxes should be done so as to allow the benefits of revenue decentralization to be achieved with minimal violation of national efficiency and equity norms.

The principal reason for revenue decentralization is to give the provinces some fiscal responsibility for financing their own expenditures. There are a number of other subsidiary roles that are sometimes alluded to. It allows the provinces to exercise some influence over redistribution and over the tax mix used to satisfy local preferences. It allows them also to use benefit taxation where that may be appropriate (for example, in financing roads out of gasoline taxes or financing health care out of tobacco and alcohol taxes). It may also allow for some coordination between the tax system and certain forms of provincial redistributive expenditures, such as the welfare system.

The main objectives of tax harmonization are threefold. The first is the achievement of efficiency in the internal common market. Differential tax policies across provinces can lead to distortions in the interregional allocation of resources, to wasteful tax competition among provinces, and to excessive use of private sector resources (especially accounting, and financial and management resources), to comply with different tax regimes, and to avoid taxes in high tax jurisdictions. The second objective is national equity, although this is likely to be more contentious. Tax competition can reduce the redistributive content of the tax system, and this may be viewed by some as a disadvantage. As well, different redistributive policies across provinces may detract from national equity goals. This returns us to the question of the appropriate sharing group for the design of redistributive policies. The third main argument for tax harmonization is ease of administration. A harmonized tax system can reduce collection and compliance costs as well as reducing avoidance and evasion.

The goals of tax harmonization can be achieved in a variety of manners. The way in which tax sources are assigned to the two levels of government is important. The general consensus in the economics literature is that the best system is one in which taxes applying on more mobile tax bases (especially capital income) and taxes better able to serve redistributive goals are more centralized.[15] This is generally taken to suggest that taxes on corporations should be highly centralized, followed by taxes on income, and then by general sales taxes, excise taxes, and finally taxes on property.[16] Resource taxation is an interesting case, and one which is relevant for Canada. Since resources are geographically fixed, the efficiency argument for centralizing them is very weak. On the other hand, given the unequal distribution of resources across the federation, decentralization of resource taxes is also likely to lead to significant fiscal inefficiencies and inequities, and to have implications for equalization.

Tax harmonization can be achieved either by assigning to the federal government those bases for which decentralization is very costly, or else, in cases where bases are decentralized or co-occupied, by explicit agreement among governments.[17] In general, however, harmonization is more likely to be achieved for a given tax base the greater is the share of tax room that is occupied by the federal government. In Canada, all major tax bases other than resource and property taxes tend to be co-occupied.[18] Given the extent to which revenue raising is decentralized to the provinces, the federal government cannot be dominant in all of these tax bases. A decision must be made as to which one(s) to dominate. The above arguments would suggest that it is more important to be dominant in the direct than in the indirect tax fields.

With co-occupied tax bases, agreements to harmonize can take a variety of forms. They can be agreements on the base alone (including the allocation of the base among provinces), or on the base and various dimensions of the rate structure. The agreements may or may not include provision for a single tax collecting authority or for collaboration in the auditing function. From the point of view of administrative simplicity, the advantages of a harmonized collection system are many. However, a harmonized collection system need go no further than a single base in most cases.[19] Whether base harmonization is sufficient from an economic point of view is another matter. In the case of a mobile tax base, some uniformity of rates is important to avoid distortions in the common market. If the tax serves a national equity objective, a common rate structure would also be important. The objective of fiscal responsibility for the provinces probably requires in itself little more than the ability of the provinces to select a level of taxes rather than a rate structure.

Symmetric arguments can be applied to the system of transfers to individuals and firms. To an economist, these are equivalent to negative direct taxes so similar arguments about their assignment and the advantages of harmonizing them can be made. Given the mobility of capital, harmonization of subsidies to firms is important. In the case of individuals, mobility is probably less an issue than that of whether to retain control of equity at the federal level.

Finally, it is important to recognize that there is an interrelationship between the division of tax room and the structure of federal-provincial transfers. In a system in which major tax bases are co-occupied, reassigning tax room to the provinces is always a substitute for making explicit transfers to them. It has the advantage of inducing more fiscal accountability at the provincial level. But, it has the disadvantages of increasing NFB differentials, of opening the way for inefficiencies in the internal common market, of reducing the ability of the federal government to achieve national equity objectives through taxation, and to use the spending power for efficiency and equity ends, and of making tax harmonization more difficult to attain.

SOME FEATURES OF THE EVOLUTION OF
THE FISCAL ARRANGEMENTS

The evolution of the Canadian federation and the place of the fiscal arrangements in it has been widely discussed. Useful historical overviews may be found in the recent papers by Leslie (1993) and Norrie (1993), which focus on the fiscal arrangements as a whole. Courchene's (1984) review of the equalization system and its prospects has become a classic in the field. Our purpose here is the more limited one of highlighting some of the salient changes that have occurred in the practice of fiscal federalism in Canada in the past few decades. We group the changes into three main areas — changes in fiscal responsibilities by federal and provincial governments, constitutional changes, and federal government policy changes (Boadway 1992). The ultimate objective is to shed light on how the system of fiscal arrangements, the parts of which were essentially put in place in the 1950s, 1960s and 1970s, stand up to the demands that the principles of fiscal federalism put on them, given the substantial changes in environment that have taken place in the meantime.

Fiscal Decentralization

The prominent characterizing feature of the evolution of the Canadian federation in the postwar period is the gradual but persistent decentralization of fiscal responsibilities from the federal government to the provinces (and their municipalities). Figure 1 depicts program expenditures by the federal government and

FIGURE 1: Government Expenditures (Non-Debt)

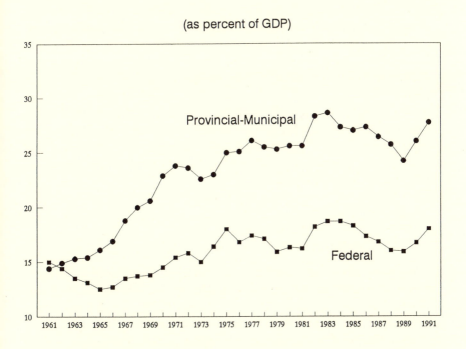

Source: Authors' compilation from Canadian Tax Foundation (various years), *The National Finances*, Toronto: Canadian Tax Foundation.

by the provincial/municipal governments as a percentage of GDP over the period 1961-91. While for the federal government, these barely rose from about 15 percent to about 17 percent over the period, provincial and municipal expenditures were rising from about 14 percent of GDP to over 25 percent. Furthermore, virtually all the rise in federal government expenditures could be attributed to increased transfer payments of various sorts; goods and services expenditures as a percent of GDP actually fell. All categories of provincial and municipal expenditures rose as a percent of GDP. Changes on the revenue side have been equally dramatic. Figure 2 shows federal and provincial own-source revenues as a percentage of GDP over the same period. Federal revenues over the period rose from about 16 percent to about 19 percent of GDP, while provincial revenues went from less than 10 percent of GDP to over 20 percent.

FIGURE 2: Government Revenues

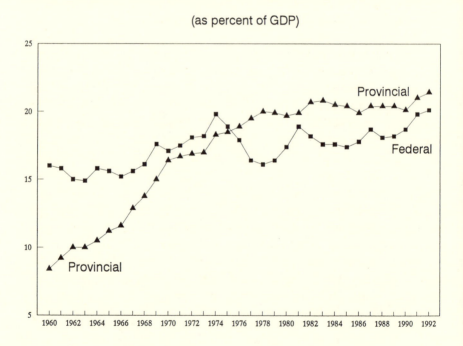

(as percent of GDP)

Source: Authors' compilation from Canadian Tax Foundation (various years), *The National Finances*, Toronto: Canadian Tax Foundation.

Table 1 gives a more direct comparison between the federal government and the provinces for various categories of expenditures and taxes. (Note that these tables do not include municipal expenditures or revenues.) Total federal program spending fell from being twice as large as that of the provinces at the beginning of the 1960s to being the same size at the start of the 1990s. If federal transfers to the provinces are excluded from federal expenditures, the ratio of federal to provincial expenditures falls from about 1.7 in 1961 to just over 0.8 in 1990. The change in the ratio for goods and services expenditures is more dramatic, falling from about 2.5 to only 0.7 over the period. The decline in federal dominance on the revenue side is even more pronounced. The federal government collected almost 2.5 times as much as the provinces from own sources in 1961, but only 1.13 as much in 1990. It raised almost ten times as much direct tax revenue as the provinces in 1961, but only about 1.7 times as much in 1990. Similarly, it collected six times as much indirect tax revenue as the provinces in 1961, but only 1.6 times as much in 1990.

While the provinces' fiscal responsibilities have grown relative to those of the federal government, they have also had to become more financially self-sufficient. Table 2 shows that every province now obtains a smaller proportion of its total revenues from federal transfers than it did two decades ago. However, the decline varies across provinces, as does the extent of reliance on transfers. Thus, at one extreme, Newfoundland's share of revenues obtained from transfers fell from 62 percent in 1970-71 to 44 percent in 1992-93, and that of Prince Edward Island from 62 percent in 1970-71 to 41 percent in 1992-93. At the other end, Ontario's share of revenues from transfers fell from 17 percent in 1970-71 to 16 percent in 1992-93, and British Columbia's from 18 percent to 11 percent. The share in two provinces, Manitoba and Saskatchewan, hardly fell at all. Nonetheless, the differential reliance on federal transfers remains high. This reflects an important characteristic of the Canadian federation — the extent to which it is equalizing across provinces. Indeed, despite the decentralization of fiscal responsibilities to the provinces, and the fact that this might be expected to induce considerable fiscal inequalities among them, the equalization system has succeeded so far in reducing disparities in the fiscal capacities of the provinces to a remarkable degree. Table 3 depicts provincial per capita fiscal capacities before and after equalization for the year 1987-88. How long this equalizing thrust can be maintained in light of current fiscal and political contingencies is an open question.

TABLE 1: Ratio of Federal to Provincial Levels of Activity

	Spending Including Transfers (1)	Spending Excluding Transfers (2)	Goods and Services (3)	Revenue Excluding Transfers (4)	Revenue Including Transfers (5)	Direct Taxes (6)	Indirect Taxes (7)
1961	2.03	1.69	2.48	2.46	1.41	9.51	6.17
1962	1.88	1.59	2.53	2.01	1.25	4.39	4.73
1963	1.75	1.49	2.16	1.95	1.26	4.42	4.56
1964	1.66	1.39	2.07	1.95	1.27	4.37	4.07
1965	1.51	1.27	1.89	1.77	1.19	3.24	4.15
1966	1.43	1.19	1.74	1.65	1.10	2.86	3.61
1967	1.32	1.05	1.52	1.58	0.97	2.66	2.99
1968	1.25	1.01	1.40	1.49	0.94	2.70	2.71
1969	1.22	0.97	1.37	1.50	0.95	2.81	2.44
1970	1.13	0.86	1.09	1.39	0.80	2.51	2.33
1971	1.12	0.83	1.05	1.43	0.78	2.56	2.36
1972	1.15	0.89	1.01	1.43	0.83	2.45	2.27
1973	1.14	0.87	0.99	1.39	0.84	2.31	2.02
1974	1.19	0.91	0.95	1.42	0.85	2.21	1.73
1975	1.19	0.92	0.87	1.36	0.77	2.17	1.76
1976	1.12	0.85	0.89	1.26	0.70	2.05	1.62
1977	1.09	0.85	0.89	1.09	0.62	1.67	1.66
1978	1.12	0.87	0.86	1.03	0.59	1.51	1.95
1979	1.05	0.80	0.79	1.06	0.61	1.70	1.57
1980	1.06	0.84	0.74	1.12	0.67	1.73	1.63
1981	1.08	0.86	0.75	1.21	0.75	1.65	1.59
1982	1.10	0.89	0.76	1.10	0.67	1.62	1.37
1983	1.08	0.86	0.71	1.09	0.62	1.66	1.32
1984	1.15	0.93	0.75	1.10	0.64	1.73	1.34
1985	1.15	0.94	0.78	1.08	0.64	1.68	1.39
1986	1.08	0.88	0.74	1.13	0.69	1.72	1.53
1987	1.08	0.88	0.70	1.15	0.71	1.73	1.58
1988	1.08	0.88	0.69	1.11	0.69	1.61	1.52
1989	1.06	0.87	0.72	1.11	0.70	1.63	1.52
1990	1.01	0.83	0.65	1.13	0.76	1.68	1.59
1991	1.00	0.83	0.70	1.15	0.74	1.44	N/A
Five-year averages							
1961-64	1.83	1.54	2.31	2.09	1.30	5.67	4.88
1965-69	1.35	1.10	1.58	1.60	1.03	2.85	3.18
1970-74	1.15	0.87	1.02	1.41	0.82	2.41	2.14
1975-79	1.11	0.86	0.86	1.16	0.66	1.82	1.71
1980-84	1.09	0.87	0.74	1.12	0.67	1.68	1.45
1985-91	1.10	0.89	0.73	1.12	0.70	1.67	1.52

Notes: Column 1 – Federal spending including tranfers to the provinces/provincial spending.
Column 2 – Federal spending excluding transfers to the provinces/provincial spending.
Column 4 – Federal revenue/provincial revenue excluding transfers.
Column 5 – Federal revenue less transfers/provincial revenue including transfers.
Column 6 – Ratio of personal plus corporate income-tax collections.
Column 7 – Ratio of sales plus excise-tax collections.

Source: Authors' compilation from Canadian Tax Foundation (various years), *The National Finances*, Toronto: Canadian Tax Foundation.

TABLE 2: Proportion of Total Revenues Obtained by Grants

	Nfld.	P.E.I.	N.S.	N.B.	Que.	Ont.	Man.	Sask.	Alta.	B.C.
1970-71	62.2	61.5	47.1	47.3	29.1	17.2	31.7	28.2	23.5	17.6
1971-72	57.2	49.7	46.5	46.3	34.7	20.4	30.5	37.2	22.2	18.8
1972-73	52.3	50.1	42.1	43.4	22.0	19.3	32.3	37.2	20.3	15.7
1973-74	53.9	56.5	47.8	47.8	22.4	18.5	29.8	41.3	16.9	16.2
1974-75	52.0	54.3	45.1	45.7	22.1	17.1	32.7	27.8	17.1	17.3
1975-76	49.4	54.8	47.7	47.5	22.7	21.2	36.5	23.8	13.5	18.5
1976-77	47.9	56.6	46.1	46.5	22.1	22.7	34.0	20.5	13.2	17.9
1977-78	47.2	54.8	46.7	47.6	23.4	17.7	35.3	18.4	9.6	17.1
1978-79	47.8	54.5	47.0	46.3	22.9	17.2	33.9	18.3	9.2	15.7
1979-80	48.1	55.0	46.3	48.2	23.5	17.4	37.1	18.2	8.4	15.8
1980-81	46.8	51.5	45.5	43.5	21.8	17.6	36.4	15.7	7.9	15.2
1981-82	50.5	53.0	49.5	45.5	26.2	18.2	38.4	19.8	11.5	16.2
1982-83	47.2	50.1	42.6	44.4	20.5	15.0	31.1	15.1	6.5	13.9
1983-84	46.6	46.9	42.9	44.1	23.5	17.1	32.6	17.6	9.1	19.3
1984-85	46.7	48.3	39.7	43.4	22.0	16.1	30.4	14.9	10.7	19.3
1985-86	46.5	46.3	38.6	43.6	21.3	16.2	29.1	17.5	9.9	17.2
1986-87	46.9	46.3	38.7	42.8	20.5	14.7	28.1	15.9	14.8	17.1
1987-88	46.2	45.5	38.4	41.3	18.3	14.2	25.0	20.9	14.7	18.3
1988-89	46.7	44.7	21.8	40.9	19.8	12.9	25.9	23.4	16.6	15.3
1989-90	48.6	46.5	38.8	41.0	20.4	11.9	27.7	23.8	15.0	13.6
1990-91	45.6	43.7	36.6	39.8	18.9	11.1	27.9	23.2	14.9	12.3
1991-92	44.5	42.5	36.9	36.6	18.1	11.2	28.5	23.6	11.9	12.5
1992-93	44.2	41.3	37.3	36.4	19.6	15.7	30.0	25.4	14.5	10.8

Source: Authors' compilation from Canadian Tax Foundation (various years), *The National Finances*, Toronto: Canadian Tax Foundation.

TABLE 3: Provincial Per Capita Revenues Before and After Equalization as a Percentage of the National Average for Own-source Revenues, 1987-88

	Nfld.	P.E.I.	N.S.	N.B.	Que.	Ont.	Man.	Sask.	Alta.	B.C.
Before	60	64	76	71	85	108	80	90	146	104
After	98	98	98	98	98	108	98	98	146	104

Source: Boadway and Hobson (1993, Table 4.7).

Constitutional Changes

The Canadian constitution has proven to be extremely flexible and accommodating; for example, it has not precluded the vast decentralization that has occurred over the postwar period. Nonetheless, the constitution remains a legal constraint of sorts, and some of its provisions confer commitments on governments which, even if they are not binding in the legal sense, still have considerable political and moral authority over policymakers.

Some key amendments to the constitution have affected federal-provincial fiscal relationships, beginning with the unemployment insurance amendment of 1940 and the old age pension amendment of 1951, which enabled the federal government to enact two of their largest expenditure programs. The most significant changes occurred with the constitutional amendments contained in the *Constitution Act, 1982*. It contained several provisions with potentially important implications for federal-provincial fiscal relations, of which three are particularly relevant. They are the institution of the *Charter of Rights and Freedoms* (Part I, sections 1-29), the spelling out of federal responsibilities in the areas of equalization and regional disparities (Part III, section 36), and the devolution to the provinces of authority and taxing power over non-renewable resources (section 92A).

The *Charter of Rights and Freedoms* contains at least two sections that may be relevant for fiscal federalism — the mobility rights provision (section 6) and the equality rights provision (section 15). The former provides for the freedom to move among provinces and to pursue a livelihood in any province. In other words, it guarantees the unrestricted movement of labour (subject to the qualification that it may be violated if regional unemployment rates are above the national average), part of what is required for maintaining an effective economic union. The equality rights section guarantees equality before the law without discrimination. The implication of each of these for economic policy has yet to be determined by the courts, but they are potentially important. For example, the equality provision may help define national equity standards, and the mobility provision may restrict provinces in applying discriminatory labour policies.

The non-renewable resource section gave to the provinces the power to regulate and to tax in any manner natural resources within provincial boundaries. In a sense, it simply recognized what had come to be the practice at the time. It is relevant for us because it is undoubtedly one aspect of the federation which is immutable, that is, the provincial ownership and control of resources and the revenues therefrom. One can certainly make strong economic arguments for centralization of ownership and control of resources, and many federations are organized in this way. However, it is not an option open to Canada.

Section 36 ("Equalization and Regional Disparities") contains two parts. In effect, these provisions have two sorts of possible effects on federal responsibilities and obligations. The first part explicitly recognizes the pursuit of equity as a national objective, though one that is shared with the provinces. This is important since, as already mentioned, much of what all governments do has a significant equity dimension. It might be thought of as a justification for federal involvement in provincial programs through the spending power. The second part imposes an obligation of a specific sort on the federal government to pursue equalization objectives. The wording of the provision, if taken literally, would have serious implications not only for the formal equalization scheme itself, but for other major federal-provincial transfers as well.

An important component of federal-provincial fiscal arrangements has been the use of conditional grants by the federal government. Despite the fact that the *BNA Act* gives the provinces "exclusive" legislative responsibility in the areas of health, education, and welfare, the federal government has from time to time used conditional grants to provide an incentive for the provinces to implement programs satisfying specific federal criteria. The constitutionality of such measures has been an issue in the past. However, the federal government has usually been successful in arguing their case, and it seems to be generally agreed now that the use of the spending power by the federal government as a method for providing financial incentives to the provinces is legally acceptable, as long as the federal government does not directly engage in program provision (see Hogg 1985).

The 1982 constitutional revisions could be taken to support and even strengthen this use of the spending power. As mentioned, section 36(1) explicitly recognizes the shared federal-provincial responsibility for equity. As mentioned, it can be argued that public sector provision in the areas of health, education, and welfare have redistributive equity as their ultimate economic rationale. The federal government can now argue that they have an interest in the equitable provision of these services, and since they are precluded from providing them directly, the spending power is the only instrument available for discharging their equity responsibilities. A similar argument might be made with regard to section 36(2). It could be said that the equalization responsibility is fulfilled jointly by the formal equalization scheme, along with the other major transfer schemes discussed below (EPF and CAP). Each of these has an equalizing component, and they complement each other.

The proposed constitutional amendments of the ill-fated Charlottetown Accord of 1992 contained various provisions which would have elucidated and given political direction to federal-provincial fiscal arrangements for the future. There was to be a non-justiciable provision to be added to the constitution which would have described the nature of a commitment in principle of both levels of government to preserving and maintaining "Canada's social and economic union." The social union would include the provision of comprehensive and accessible health care, high quality education and adequate social services and benefits. Section 36 would be amended to include a commitment to ensure that comparable economic infrastructures would be available in all regions. The wording of section 36(2) would be strengthened to commit the federal government to make equalization payments, not just to the principle of equalization. And, a new subsection 36(3) would have been added to commit both levels of government to reducing regional economic disparities. The upshot of these changes to section 36 would apparently have been to strengthen the commitment to fiscal equity and the pursuit of economic opportunity. At the same time, the use of the spending power was to be guided by principles that included a contribution to the pursuit of national objectives, a reduction in overlap and duplication, respecting of provincial priorities and ensuring of equality of treatment of the provinces, while recognizing their different needs and circumstances. As with the Meech Lake Accord, provinces could opt out of national shared-cost programs, provided they carried on a program that met with national objectives. Though the Charlottetown Accord was defeated in the national referendum, its content revealed a significant commitment to the role of the federal government in pursuing national objectives, as well as the need to maintain fiscal equity in an increasingly decentralized federation.

Federal Policy Initiatives

It seems clear that the existing constitution is not a significant constraint on the degree of centralization of economic power. The federal government could exercise potentially significant amounts of financial control through its vast taxing and spending power. And, except for the commitments in section 36 of the *Constitution Act, 1982*, they can also choose to decentralize fiscal responsibilities to the provinces. Thus, federal and provincial financial responsibilities are to a large extent a matter of actual policy decisions. A number of recent policy initiatives have had, or will have, a bearing on the fiscal role of the provinces relative to the federal government and on the fiscal relations between them. In many cases, the effect on federal-provincial fiscal relations is an incidental effect of policies taken with other objectives in mind. Part of our purpose is to point out that the consequences for fiscal federalism are often of a lasting and virtually irreversible nature and, as such, we now have to live with them and adjust our fiscal arrangements accordingly. Each of a number of policy measures is considered separately.

Deficit Reduction Measures. A high priority of the federal government has been the reduction of the budget deficit. In the last several budgets, it has put a substantial part of the burden on reducing expenditures rather than increasing taxes. At the same time, it has taken the position that the part of the budget consisting of transfers to individuals should be protected. That leaves only transfers to governments and business, and expenditures on goods and services as instruments for deficit reduction. Of these, the bulk of the burden was put on transfers to the provinces, including limits on both EPF transfers for all provinces and CAP transfers for the three "have" provinces.

Whatever its merits from a fiscal management point of view, the use of transfers to the provinces for deficit reduction purposes has longer term effects on the structure of federal-provincial fiscal relations.[20] One is that the reduction in federal-provincial transfers and the resultant increase in provincial tax requirements shifts the balance in taxing power from the federal to the provincial governments. Furthermore, this shift may be largely irreversible. The ability of the federal government to take a lead in maintaining a system of harmonized direct taxes across the two levels of government depends upon the share of the tax room it occupies. As the provinces occupy a larger and larger share of the income tax room, the pressures for fragmenting the system increase.

Another effect is that the reduction in federal-provincial transfers reduces the ability of the federal government to achieve national objectives through the use of the spending power. As long as the EPF grant is financed by a combination of tax point transfers and cash transfers, as in the current system, reductions in the cash transfer component will ultimately leave the federal government with little spending power clout.

Introduction of the Goods and Services Tax. The GST was introduced for reasons that had little to do with federal-provincial fiscal relations. But it too may have a lasting incidental impact. Most economists would agree that, as an indirect tax system, the GST is basically well-conceived. However, from a federal-provincial fiscal relations perspective, it has some drawbacks. The main one is that, if the evidence from other countries is anything to go by, it is likely that the direct-indirect tax mix of the federal government will gradually change in favour of the indirect. This implies a reduction in federal share of occupancy of the income tax fields. This will compound the strains put on the system of income tax harmonization and further reduce the ability of the federal government to achieve its national equity goals.

It is true that the federal government could buy harmonization with the provinces in the indirect tax field using the GST. However, such harmonization will be far from perfect. A fully harmonized GST involving the federal government and the provinces would be hard to achieve. It is simply too difficult to operate a multi-stage tax in a multijurisdictional system of government. The problem is that the system of crediting becomes difficult to administer when intermediate sales go through more than one jurisdiction. Perhaps the best that can be done is to have the provinces retain a single-stage system, with that stage being harmonized as closely as possible with the GST, as has been done with Quebec. The main disadvantages of single-stage taxes documented by the federal government (bias in favour of foreign goods, and taxation of business inputs) would continue to apply at the provincial level.

The real problem is that, given the degree of decentralization of the fiscal system in Canada, it is simply not possible for the federal government to dominate both the direct and the indirect tax fields. A choice must be made. We would argue that the case for harmonization and a strong federal presence favour federal government concentration in the direct tax field. From this point of view, the introduction of the GST could be seen as a retrograde measure. This was recognized by the Carter Commission some 25 years ago whose advice was that the federal government turn over the indirect tax fields to the provinces and concentrate on income taxation. This would accord with the traditional textbook assignment of tax bases in a federation (McLure 1983). The indirect taxes presumably would not be harmonized among the provinces, and a multi-stage tax would not be used. These disadvantages are outweighed by having a more harmonized income tax system.

The Operation of the Tax Collection Agreements. The basic form of the Tax Collection Agreements has been in place since 1962. The only major change occurred in 1972, when the federal government began allowing the provinces to introduce tax credits to be administered by the federal government. To be admissible, these credits were supposed to satisfy three criteria. They had to be administratively feasible, must not erode the essential harmony and uniformity of the tax system, and must not jeopardize the functioning of the internal common market. When the Tax Collection Agreements were first entered into, the federal government was dominant in the income tax fields. As the provinces have become more important users of income tax, the system has come under increasing strain. The signs of the strain are several. One province (Alberta) has withdrawn from the corporate Tax Collection Agreements. Others have studied the option seriously (Ontario in the case of the personal income tax, and British Columbia for the corporate tax), and have so far declined to take action despite dissatisfaction with their inability to pursue independent tax policies. The use of tax credits has increased rapidly at both the personal and corporate levels. Some of these credits seem clearly to affect the allocation of capital across provinces, such as venture capital and stock savings programs and various tax credits under the corporate income tax. The principle of a common base has even been eroded, as Alberta, Manitoba, and Saskatchewan received permission to introduce flat taxes on bases different than federal taxable income (i.e., net income).

The tension seems to have arisen because of unilateral federal control over both the base and rate structure of the income taxes. This leaves open to the provinces only the ability to choose the level of rates and the use of credits for provincial policy purposes. As the provinces become more important in the income tax fields, these tensions are bound to increase. Studies in Ontario and British Columbia have recommended that provinces be given a greater role in any changes that involve the base and rate structure, and discussion papers of the federal government and the provinces have proposed changing the form of the Tax Collection Agreements to allow provinces more discretion over their rate structures (see Boadway, Cromb and Kitchen 1989; Clarkson Gordon 1988; Canada 1991). All have recognized that the Tax Collection Agreements have served the federation well. Indeed, the Canadian system has been cited as a model for tax harmonization in the European Economic Community.

Structural Changes in EPF and Equalization. The structures of both the EPF and equalization systems have undergone some significant changes that have influenced their effectiveness. In the case of the EPF, the major structural change resulted from the *Canada Health Act*, 1984. This Act reaffirmed the requirement that had existed since the mid-1960s that to be eligible for the full amount of the federal transfer in support of health expenditures, a province had to maintain a publicly-administered health insurance system which was comprehensive, accessible, universal, and portable. However, it also introduced penalties for provinces whose health-care systems engaged in extra-billing and user charges. The imposition of these additional conditions has been a matter of some controversy. Those who oppose them argue that the provision of health services is clearly a provincial responsibility, and that the full decentralization of health care is likely to lead to more efficient provision through interprovincial competitive pressures. Those who argue in favour of the use of the spending power in the health-care area do so on the grounds that health care is fundamentally an instrument for the pursuit of equity, and the use of the spending power is the only means by which the federal government can achieve national standards of equity in health care. Clearly the matter goes beyond purely economic considerations and involves value judgements about equity versus efficiency. It is not surprising that economists disagree on the matter. It does seem quite clear, however, that from a constitutional point of view, the use of the spending power in this way is legitimate.[21]

The periodic budgetary reductions in EPF cash transfers will make it more difficult for the federal government to maintain effective national standards in health care. Since the inception of EPF in 1977, there have been a number of instances in which the size of the transfers has been reduced, and these have all been felt on the cash transfer side. In 1982, there was a reduction of the equivalent of two personal tax points which had originally been used to compensate for the so-called revenue guarantee in the 1972 tax reform. This may or may not have been justifiable in terms of the revenue guarantee itself, but one result was a reduction in the size of the cash transfer. In 1984 and 1985, the notional postsecondary education component was restricted to increases of 5 and 6 percent respectively as part of the anti-inflation policy of the time. (This component is notional only since there are no restrictions on its use.) In 1986, the growth of EPF transfers was reduced from the rate of growth of GNP to that rate less two percentage points. Then, in the budgets of 1990 and 1991, the per capita amount of EPF transfers was frozen and extended three years beyond.[22] Once the freeze is over, the growth of EPF per capita transfers will be restricted to the rate of growth of GNP less 3 percent. The consequence of these reductions is that the cash component of EPF is becoming less and less important relative to the tax transfer component, and will disappear altogether in the near future (though that day has been postponed by the recession). It could be argued that, once the federal government eliminates cash transfers and requires the provinces to increase their tax room, it will be difficult to reverse the process. While the federal government has stated that it will find other ways to penalize provinces who fail to meet the full criteria set out in the *Canada Health Act*, it is not at all clear how this can be done. The other major grant schemes (equalization and CAP) are negotiated separately with their own objectives in mind. And, equalization applies only to some provinces.

The equalization system itself has undergone some fundamental revisions. Prior to 1982, the system used the so-called national-average standard for determining equalization payments to the have-not provinces. That is, the entitlement was calculated to bring the tax capacity of the have-not provinces up to that of the national average. Oil and gas revenues were not fully equalized. However, as the Economic Council of Canada (1982) argued, given the provincial property rights over natural resources, this was not an unreasonable situation. In 1982, the formula was changed in several significant ways to reduce the financial commitment of the federal government and to ensure that Ontario did not become a have-not province. The national-average standard was changed to a five-province standard (Ontario, Quebec, Manitoba, Saskatchewan, and British Columbia). Oil and gas revenues were included fully in the formula; but, since Alberta was not part of the standard, they were, in effect, largely unequalized. Also, in 1987, the rate of growth of the total equalization transfer was capped at the cumulative rate of growth of GNP.

International Developments. Changes in the international climate facing the Canadian economy may influence the development of fiscal relations within the federation. In particular, they may increase the constraints faced by policy-makers. For example, the growing internationalization of capital markets constrains the ability of governments, both federal and provincial, to impose taxes on capital income. With highly open capital markets, rates of return on capital are largely predetermined internationally. This implies that the ability to extract taxes from capital income is severely limited. In an economy such as Canada's, the taxation of corporate income is to a considerable extent dictated by foreign tax crediting arrangements in creditor countries, especially the United States.[23] One of the main roles of the corporate tax has become to facilitate a tax transfer from foreign treasuries to Canada by exploiting the ability of foreign corporations to obtain credits for taxes paid in Canada. This implies that our corporate tax structure is constrained to be similar to that in the United States.

At the same time, because of the allocation formula used to allocate corporate income tax revenues among provinces, there is an incentive for provinces to engage in tax competition. Under the tax crediting system which operates internationally, there is little gain to provinces from trying to attract capital from abroad via corporate tax incentives for the reason mentioned above; they will simply reduce the size of the transfer from foreign treasuries without affecting the incentive to invest. However, with the allocation formula used for provincial tax collections, provinces can succeed in attracting capital from neighbouring provinces by offering more attractive tax treatment. The total amount of provincial taxes that domestic firms are liable for depends upon in which provinces their profits are earned. If a province lowers its tax rate (or provides an investment incentive), this will provide an incentive for domestic firms to relocate their activities there, but it should not affect foreign firms because of the crediting arrangement. This means that there is an incentive for provinces to engage in interprovincial beggar-thy-neighbour policies, even though such an incentive does not exist at the federal level. This observation has implications for the ideal assignment of taxes and income tax harmonization.

Future Policies. It is difficult to predict what policy initiatives will occur in the future. However, speculation is not entirely idle. One possibility is in the area of social policy. It seems clear that a major rationalization here is on the policy agenda, and will incorporate a number of programs such as welfare, unemployment insurance, and training. Since these policies overlap federal and provincial jurisdictions, their implications for federal-provincial fiscal relations cannot be ignored. Another possible area concerns public sector infrastructure investment which has surfaced during the 1993 election campaign as a possible policy direction. Such a program almost necessarily involves the use of the federal spending power which, to be effective, requires federal transfers to the provinces (and municipalities). There may well be other major policy initiatives, such as environmental or energy policy measures, which will affect federal-provincial fiscal arrangements. Since all of these things involve federal funding to some extent, the additional strain imposed on existing fiscal arrangements in an era in which decentralization has already evolved a long way will be considerable. It is not clear that the system of federal-provincial fiscal arrangements that has evolved over the period can be sustained without major rethinking. In that sense, the answer posed in the title to this paper would be affirmative.

PROBLEMS WITH THE EXISTING FISCAL ARRANGEMENTS

The basic structure of the existing fiscal arrangements has been in place for 25 years, and some of the key components go back to the early postwar period. Yet, as we have seen, the nature of the federation has changed significantly in the meantime. In particular, it has become much more decentralized. The question becomes, in light of all these changes that have occurred, do the fiscal arrangements now serve the purposes for which they are intended?

The theory of fiscal federalism suggests that the role of federal-provincial fiscal arrangements should increase in importance as more budgetary responsibilities are transferred to the provinces.[24] In a sense, the sensible and unobtrusive use of various components of the fiscal arrangements allows the full benefits of the decentralization of public service provision to be achieved without compromising the efficiency and equity of the internal common market. In particular, judicious use of the fiscal arrangements serves to offset the inefficiencies and inequities that inevitably arise as a result of the decentralization of functions, to facilitate coordination among governments on both the expenditure and tax sides of their budgets, to allow for differing degrees of decentralization of taxes and expenditures, and to enable the federal government to retain some means by which it can achieve national efficiency and equity goals in areas otherwise within provincial responsibility. Although we have stressed that the fiscal arrangements must be seen as a whole, in this section we look at each of the major components individually with a view to pointing out how their structures might have become dated given the evolution of the Canadian federation.

Equalization

The main purpose of the equalization system has been to address the fiscal inefficiencies and inequities that arise in a decentralized federation, that is, to meet the principles enunciated in section 36(2) of the *Constitution Act, 1982*. The task becomes greater the more decentralized is the federation. At the same time, the political basis for equalization may diminish with decentralization, as many commentators have pointed out (see, e.g., Courchene 1991). This is almost certainly the case as decentralization has been accompanied by the freeing of trade and the transfer of deficits to the provinces, in some cases selectively to the better-off provinces. Others are better able to comment on the political economy of equalization. The perspective we adopt here is that of the economist to whom the principle stated in section 36(2) is grounded in the traditional fiscal efficiency and equity arguments of the theory of fiscal federalism, arguments that have become part of the standard analytical baggage of the discipline (see Atkinson and Stiglitz 1980; Wildasin 1986).

We have already described how fiscal equity and efficiency in a federation are jointly achieved by a system of federal-provincial transfers which fully eliminate differentials in NFBs across provinces.[25] In principle, this is not easy to achieve in any precise manner since NFB differentials can arise in a variety of different ways, depending on the nature of functions undertaken by government, and also on the extent to which provincial government budgets are redistributive. However, given the stylized facts of the Canadian federation, and some reasonable assumptions about the way in which the provinces behave, a good case can be made for assigning to the equalization system the principal task of equalizing *tax capacities* across provinces.[26] The equalization system can be judged primarily on these grounds, while recognizing that other components of the system may also contribute to the overall equalization objective, including the need to take account of other sources of NFB differentials.

Judged from the perspective of the objective of equalizing tax capacities, the difficulties with the equalization system as it has evolved have been well documented, and we need do little more than recount them here (see Courchene 1984; Bird 1990):

- Since the system is a "gross" scheme rather than a "net" one, the have-not provinces are equalized up, but the have provinces are not equalized down. Furthermore, since the federal government finances the scheme, and since it does not have access to some of the revenue sources which cause significant differentials in tax capacity, the degree of implicit equalization operating through the financing of the system through general revenues is limited.

- The use of a representative five-province standard (RFPS) rather than a representative national-average standard (RNAS) makes it impossible to ensure that NFB differentials are properly eliminated. In principle, this could go either way since both the best-off and the least well-off provinces are missing from the standard.

- One of the most important sources of tax capacity differentials, resource revenues, is very inadequately treated by the equalization system on several grounds. For one, since Alberta is left out of the five-province standard, a substantial part of the oil and gas revenues go unequalized. Given that this constitutes one of the most unequally distributed tax bases, this is a significant shortcoming. By the same token, resource revenues accruing to the have-not provinces are effectively fully equalized; indeed, given that the equalization system is based largely on a system of production tax revenues (rather than rents), equalization systematically discriminates against high-cost producers leading to a situation in which more than 100 percent equalization is imposed on the have-not provinces' oil and gas revenues. Of course, it can be argued using notions of provincial property rights (what the Economic Council referred to as "narrow-based horizontal equity") that only partial equalization of resource revenues is called for; even that would be more than the present system allows for. At the same time, there are some other sources of resource revenue which also go fully or partially unequalized; examples include hydro-electric rents as well as forestry rents, both of which are dissipated in forms other than equalizable tax revenues.

- The federal government's lack of direct access to some of the resource revenue bases which generate NFB differentials has led it to pursue alternative policies to spread the benefits of the resources around the federation, some of which have been clearly sub-optimal. Examples include the National Energy Policy as well as bilateral revenue-sharing agreements.

- In each five-year fiscal arrangements period since 1982-83, there has been a ceiling on the growth of equalization payments. Thus, for the 1987-88 to 1991-92 period, total equalization payments were not allowed to exceed those of 1987-88 augmented by the rate of growth of GNP over the same period. This ceiling, which is essentially arbitrary, especially in light of federal policies to rapidly decentralize a number of important social programs in recent years, became binding in 1988-89, reducing still further the ability of the scheme to achieve full equalization of tax capacities.

- It has also been argued that, by focusing entirely on tax base equalization, other important sources of NFB differentials have been neglected. An often mentioned example of this is the failure to take account of "negative" tax liabilities (i.e., transfers) in the equalization program. We shall return to this when we discuss other components of the system.

These shortcomings in the equalization system imply that it is imperfect when judged against the ideal of full equalization of tax capacities. Despite this, the system does not perform all that badly. Calculations have shown that the RFPS standard has in recent years led to the equalization of the have-not provinces to close to 98 percent of what would be achieved by the RNAS. Whether this would remain to be the case in future years when the ceiling bites more and more, and when (if) resource revenues increase remains to be seen. Of course, the equalization up of the have-not provinces is only one side of the picture. Since the equalization system does not apply to the have provinces, they remain above the national standard. Interestingly enough, in the late 1980s, while Alberta's tax capacity was over 45 percent above the national average, those of the other two have provinces, British Columbia and Ontario, were each above the national average by less than 10 percent (see Boadway and Hobson 1993, Table 4.7, p. 124).

It is worth stressing that our discussion has been premised on the notion that both the economic objectives of the equalization system and the constitutional "commitment" found in section 36(2) can largely be addressed by a system that fully equalizes the tax capacities of the provinces. This policy prescription rests on a set of assumptions about the way in which provincial governments exercise their taxing and expenditure responsibilities that not all observers will agree upon. However, the prescription does have the advantage that it is well-founded in theory. It does put the onus on detractors to be as precise in defending alternatives, including lesser forms of equalization.

Two final points might be made about the equalization system. First, it should be clear that in a system of equalization in which tax capacity is the focus of redistribution across provinces, the degree of decentralization of revenue-raising capacity is an important determinant of the extent of required equalization. To take the extreme case, if taxation remained centralized while expenditures were being decentralized, so that all provincial expenditures were financed from federal-provincial transfers, the transfer system would need only to be a system of equal per capita grants.[27] It is only as taxes are decentralized that differential tax capacities become important. Recognition of this makes clear the complementary relationship that should exist between the EPF and equalization systems. Although it was conceived on political grounds, it is fortuitous that EPF was designed to be an equal per capita grant. Now that the relation between EPF and equalization is clear, opportunities for making that relationship more explicit can be exploited in redesigning the system. We return to this theme in the next section.

Second, our presumption has been that federal-provincial transfers are the appropriate vehicle for addressing NFB differentials across provinces. Some observers have suggested that the task could also be achieved by a system of transfers to individuals.[28] This would require a set of transfers to individuals which differ according to province of residence. Such a system is presumably feasible to operate, although it is more complicated than making grants to the provinces and possibly induces incentive effects on individuals which are a lot more transparent than with grants to the province. From the point of view of the proponents of the system, it has the advantage that provinces are forced to decide to tax back the grant from their residents thereby inducing more political accountability. By the same token, one of the key features of the literature on the assignment problem is that the case for decentralizing expenditures is greater than that for decentralizing taxes (the fiscal gap argument). A scheme of transfers to individuals would increase the need for provincial tax collection, thereby leading to increased possibilities for inefficiency in the internal common market and making tax harmonization more difficult to achieve. As well, the dual system of federal taxes and transfers to individuals and subsequent provincial tax back of the transfers leads to a double tax distortion which could otherwise be avoided.

Established Programs Financing

When EPF was instituted in 1977, it was conceived as an equal per capita transfer to the provinces, though with some general conditions attached with respect to health-care expenditures. As such, it had the potential to perform a couple of important functions as a component of the fiscal arrangements. We have already mentioned that its per capita structure fortuitously rendered it a useful component of the equalization system. At the same time, it also provided a vehicle with which the federal government could exercise its spending power for the purposes of maintaining efficiency in the internal common market and pursuing national equity goals as eventually outlined in section 36(1) of the *Constitution Act*. In fact, the implementation of the spending power was restricted to setting out the criteria that provincial health insurance plans must satisfy. However, EPF was a vehicle that, in principle, could have been used more widely for spending power purposes in other areas.

The fact that part of the transfer took the form of a transfer of tax points to the provinces has had a number of consequences, probably unforeseen or at least unconsidered, which have gradually eroded the usefulness of the scheme, both as an adjunct to equalization and as a block grant with general conditions attached. The mere fact that half of the initial transfer took the form of a transfer of tax points meant that there was a more or less gratuitous shift in income tax room from the federal government to the provinces. While this may have been conceived as a way of inducing more political accountability into the system, it is not clear that any real economic objective was served. It has essentially contributed to the gradual shift in income tax room in favour of the provinces, a shift that is hard to reverse and which many would argue has now reached the point where the harmonization of the income tax system is under threat. This is discussed further below.

Perhaps the more important consequence of implementing part of the EPF transfer in the form of tax room arises from the fact that the cash component is calculated as a residual. That is, for each province, the EPF cash transfer is the total EPF entitlement less the value of the tax transfer to the province, suitably equalized. This has two general types of effects. The first one, which is of lesser importance, is that since the value of an equalized income tax point can differ across provinces, so can the cash transfer. More important, since the growth rate of the aggregate cash plus tax point transfer has been directly tied to the growth of GDP, the growth of the cash component will differ from the rate of growth of EPF to the extent that the tax point transfer does. While the growth rate of EPF was set at that of GDP, this was not a great problem, since the growth in value of the tax points was not much different. However, given the various budgetary restrictions that have been placed on EPF subsequently, the growth in tax room has been and will continue to outstrip the EPF entitlement, with the result that the cash component will gradually be eroded. It has been calculated that under the present regime of a freeze in EPF per capita transfers until 1994 followed by a restriction in the growth rate to the growth rate of GDP less 3 percent, the cash component will disappear early next century. In the case of Quebec, cash transfers will disappear before that, owing to the fact that a higher proportion of the EPF transfer takes the form of tax points. That would obviously spell the end of the system.

Given that the tax transfer is water under the bridge, it is not at all clear that it ought still to be considered a federal-provincial transfer at all. For all intents and purposes, the tax transfer has become part of the provinces' tax room, probably irretrievably so. Thus, it is not clear why the magnitude of the notional tax transfer ought to be a determining factor in calculating the cash owing to the provinces.

Quite apart from its magnitude and the division of the transfer into cash and tax transfer components, the structure of the EPF system itself has led to some controversy. Very few observers would disagree with the principle of EPF being an equal per capita transfer, that is, with the "equalization" component of the transfer. However, the use of the EPF system as a means of imposing federal conditions on provincial health insurance programs has been more controversial. In particular the strictures against user fees and extra-billing have been viewed by some as unilateral federal intrusions into the specifics of program design. This has led to a fear that the federal government could use its spending power to the same effect in other areas in the future. Hence, during the constitutional debate, many persons called for putting varying degrees of constitutional limitation on the federal government's use of the spending power; even the federal government's own proposals did so.

Canada Assistance Plan

CAP is the only major federal-provincial shared-cost program left. It combines conditionality with a 50 percent matching rule. The major question here concerns the justification for the matching rate, given the obvious adverse incentives that it provides to the provinces. In principle, there are a number of justifications that might be given for using a matching formula, though not necessarily at such a high rate. The first is the standard textbook argument concerning spillovers. Given the potential mobility of welfare recipients, the benefits of one province's welfare system spill out into other provinces. The spillover benefits may also include elements of altruism towards the welfare recipients of other provinces. In the absence of some such incentive, provinces would tend not to take these spillover benefits into account. While this might be true in theory, it is highly dubious that the order of magnitude of the problem is such as to call for a 50 percent matching rate. Another related argument is that interprovincial competition on the expenditure side would compete away welfare benefits to the collective disadvantage of all provinces. Again, it is not clear that the appropriate remedy is a matching formula of anywhere near this magnitude.

Another argument views the CAP system as contributing to the equalization objective. If one views welfare payments and services as being essential public services, then it is certainly true that provinces encounter different expenditure obligations in providing these services. Thus, equalization of NFBs requires some equalization on the expenditure side, something that the equalization system does not do. One way to equalize expenditure needs is to base payments on actual expenditures. While this has a greater ring of plausibility than the spillover or interprovincial competition stories, it is questionable why expenditure-based equalization has to be accomplished through a system of matching grants, with its associated incentive effects, as opposed to a scheme based more on expenditure needs, suitably measured.

Finally, it could be argued that the sharing by the federal government of the costs of welfare services could be justified by recognizing that the levels of expenditures on welfare are partly a consequence of macroeconomic policies which are the responsibility of the federal government. Whether this could be used to justify the 50 percent matching rate is questionable.

Apart from the issue of the use of matching rates, there is also a question as to the appropriateness of the conditions attached to CAP, and the role of the federal government in imposing them. Some have argued that the type of conditions attached to the use of CAP funds, such as the requirement that they be based on the needs of welfare recipients, have induced the provinces to design welfare programs that pay undue attention to incentive effects and to the working poor. Others might argue that, given the generally perceived inadequacy of income support programs and the lack of coherence among the various components, such as welfare, unemployment insurance, and the tax system, the federal government could be much more imaginative in its use of the spending power in this area.

Finally, there has been some concern recently with the federal government deficit-reduction measure to restrict CAP transfers selectively to the better-off provinces. Not only was this done with little overall rationale in mind other than budgetary expediency, it was also viewed by the provinces as violating what they saw as an implicit contract. Again this issue found its way into the constitutional debate, with demands that some restriction be placed not only over future new uses of the spending power, but also on the federal government's ability to back out of existing spending power policies unilaterally.

Tax Harmonization

Tax harmonization is an important and integral part of the fiscal arrangements, though it is not always recognized as such. The extent of harmonization of Canada's tax system has been enviable when compared with other federations with a comparable degree of decentralization of fiscal responsibilities. The harmonization takes place largely through the Tax Collection Agreements, and is largely confined to the income tax system. There is virtually no harmonization of either indirect taxes or of other direct taxes, such as those on resources. This has been viewed by economists as less of a problem since the major benefits from tax harmonization come from tax bases that are more mobile, especially capital income (see Boadway and Bruce 1992). Thus, though harmonization of the federal GST and the provincial retail sales taxes might be desirable from the point of view of compliance and collection costs, the economic advantages are limited relative to the income tax, especially that applying to corporations.

From this perspective, there is some concern that the system of harmonization is becoming increasingly eroded and in danger of collapsing. For one thing, the deviations from the common base and rate structure are increasing rapidly as provinces enact more and more tax credits and exemptions, and as the federal government begins to allow major deviations like the flat rate tax in the Prairie provinces. Also, as we have mentioned, the combination of increased provincial reliance on own-source revenues as a result of federal deficit-cutting through the transfer system and the likely changes in the federal and provincial government tax mixes as a result of the introduction of the GST are likely to lead the provinces to occupy an even larger proportion of the income tax room. This, in turn, is likely to cause further provincial discontent with the federal role in the Tax Collection Agreements, a discontent that has already surfaced, at least in the western provinces.

OPTIONS FOR THE FUTURE

We began this chapter with the observation that, while the Canadian federation has undergone major structural changes, especially with respect to the degree of decentralization of fiscal responsibilities to the provinces, the basic form of intergovernmental fiscal arrangements has remained remarkably stable. This could be an indication that the fiscal arrangements are incredibly robust and adaptable to changing economic circumstances. But it could also be the case that the system has been pushed beyond the point where further minor adjustments and tinkering can make any useful contribution to our fiscal structure. According to this latter view, major reforms in the system of intergovernmental fiscal arrangements are long overdue.

The range of possible options for the future is obviously very broad. We begin our consideration of these possibilities with a review of some of the proposals that have appeared in recent discussions. This review is not intended necessarily to be complete, representative, or even fair to those who have put them forward. Our primary purpose is only to illustrate the types of options that have been presented.

Review of Options Under Consideration

Equalization. In the view of some, equalization has become an excessive financial burden to the federal government and, in light of the continuing decentralization of fiscal responsibilities to the provinces, it no longer serves a legitimate national function. Moreover, considerations of equity at a national level are becoming increasingly irrelevant as a guide to policy design. The sorts of proposals that follow from these considerations are several.

One far-reaching proposal is that the goals of fiscal equalization be abandoned by the federal government and that they be assumed, on a voluntary basis, by the provinces.[29] Under such an arrangement, the "have" provinces would transfer fiscal resources directly to the "have-not" provinces, according to measures of fiscal capacity and/or need. This proposal would have the additional advantages of turning equalization into a truly net scheme, and of eliminating the costs that arise under the current scheme which only equalizes the poor provinces up, and which requires the federal government to impose additional tax burdens even on the citizens of poor provinces in order to finance equalization.

The fundamental problem with schemes such as these arises from the fact that the amount of equalization that is required on the basis of the equity and efficiency considerations increases with the degree of decentralization of fiscal responsibilities to the provinces. It is unlikely that provincial governments, responsible only to the residents of their own provinces, would agree to voluntary transfers of the sort that are called for under current circumstances. It is only a federal government, which is responsive to a national constituency, that would be able to sustain a commitment to equalization which is anything like the one we have today. Some people might argue that provinces would voluntarily commit themselves to such a scheme on the principle of social insurance — rich provinces who give today might become recipients tomorrow when their fortunes take a turn for the worse. But this assumes that, say, Newfoundland and Manitoba are equally likely to be "have" provinces in the near future. We would argue that provincial governments would be very unlikely to sustain, on a voluntary basis, even equalization programs that are much less generous than the one we have today. We cannot conceive that they would be able to commit themselves to the sort of transfers required under the current degree of decentralization of fiscal responsibilities. This, of course, would be viewed by some — those who do not recognize a constituency for equity at the national level (and maybe the provincial level as well) — as another advantage of the decentralization of responsibility for equalization to provincial governments. More generally, this raises again the fundamental problem with equalization in a highly decentralized federal system. The greater the degree of decentralization, the greater the amount of equalization that is called for; but the smaller might be the sense of national community and hence the ability of a federal government to maintain a consensus in favour of equalization. While decentralization increases the economic need for equalization, it might diminish the political will to deliver it, as Leslie (1993) has argued.

There have been a number of other suggested changes to equalization which might be better put in the category of "tinkering" rather than making fundamental changes. This is not to say that they would not necessarily have significant financial implications for the provinces. But they do not represent significant changes in the philosophy or the basic system of equalization. For example, there has been considerable discussion at a political/journalistic level of what have been arbitrary decisions about which provinces to include in calculating "national average" indicators of fiscal capacity, or which provinces to exclude on an *a priori* basis from being possible recipients of equalization. And there has been similar discussion of the details of measuring fiscal capacity for particular revenue sources.

In addition, Norrie (1993) and Usher (1993) have made more substantial suggestions for changes in the nature of the equalization formula. Norrie, for instance, has proposed that the formula be changed to one that is based more directly on simple macro-indicators of interprovincial income differences. Usher has also suggested that such a simple macro-indicator (provincial per capita income) be used, not so much to determine the amount of equalization, but rather to set limits on the amount of fiscal equalization undertaken by the federal government. Usher suggests that equalization payments called for under the current equalization formula be made only to provinces whose per capita incomes fall below 90 percent of the national average. Both of these proposals seem to be based on a perception of equalization as a tool for redistributing income among individuals, rather than correcting for real income differences that arise as a by-product of the decentralization of fiscal activities to provincial governments. In other words, although these might appear to be simplifications of the current equalization formula, they actually deny the basic economic rationale that underlies the system of equalization as it has developed in Canada and is described in section 36(2) of the *Constitution Act, 1982*. Furthermore, in the case of Usher's proposal at least, the magnitude of the financial implications for the federal government and for particular provinces are potentially quite large. To proceed with these sorts of proposals without a clearer exposition of their economic rationale, relative to that of the current system whose rationale is widely accepted, would be unwarranted, to say the least. Our own view is that fiscal equalization is a poor instrument for dealing with any issues of interpersonal equity other than those arising from interprovincial NFB differentials.

EPF, CAP and Cost-Sharing. As with equalization, proposals for reform of these shared-cost programs have ranged from those calling for relatively minor adjustments to the existing system to those that would imply very significant changes in their nature. The major structural reforms suggested by some would require considerable recentralization of fiscal responsibilities in the Canadian federation; while those proposed by others would imply significantly greater degrees of decentralization.

The minor amendments usually suggested are in the nature of proposals to eliminate some or all of the arbitrary adjustments and restrictions imposed by the federal government in recent years. These would include removal of the caps on overall growth and on the amounts that particular provinces are deemed to be eligible to receive. Even less radical are suggestions simply to slow down the rate at which the cash component of EPF is being phased out.

Those with a more centralist view of the role of different governments in these major social programs might suggest not only a reassertion of federal expenditure responsibilities, but also a harder line by the federal government in restricting the options available to the provinces with respect to program design and delivery.[30] An even more centralist approach is to suggest that the federal government withdraw from EPF and CAP and replace some or all of these transfers to the provinces with direct transfers to individuals, thus completely bypassing the provinces in the affected areas.[31] By so doing, the federal government would immediately assume a major, if not dominant, role in areas that traditionally (and constitutionally) have been treated as primarily provincial responsibilities in Canada. Leslie (1993) also suggests a major reassertion of federal responsibility with respect to the financing of social programs, although he does not make very specific proposals as to how this should be accomplished.

The opposite, decentralist, approach, would be to hasten the exit of the federal government from the financing and/or control of social programs. Norrie, for instance, suggests that this be done with respect to health expenditures. No clear economic rationale is provided for distinguishing so sharply between education and health with respect to the extent of centralization of fiscal responsibility and program delivery.[32] Bird (1990) and Hobson and St.-Hilaire (1993) recommend that CAP contributions be eliminated and replaced by an expenditure-based equalization program.

As discussed earlier, the real issue here is the extent to which one buys arguments about either interprovincial spillovers or the importance of the internal common market as providing an efficiency argument for federal involvement; or about the national level as representing the appropriate sharing community with respect to concerns of vertical equity, and therefore providing an equity argument for a federal role in these programs, as suggested by section 36(1). A point worth emphasizing, and one stressed in the fiscal federalism literature, is that a judicious use of the spending power allows one to achieve the abundant advantages of decentralization without sacrificing national efficiency and equity objectives. The key is to find that balance between legitimate federal concerns and overintrusive intervention.

Tax Sharing and Harmonization. There has been surprisingly little discussion in the literature on the issues related to the sharing and harmonization of taxes between the federal and provincial governments. The Carter Commission perceptively recommended nearly three decades ago that the federal government abandon the sales tax field to the provinces and concentrate its efforts solely on direct taxation, using equity as its justification. In his summary of a set of studies prepared for the Ontario Economic Council, Hartle (1983) discussed the need for greater provincial influence over tax structure decisions in order for the Tax Collection Agreements to remain palatable for the provinces. At the same time, he pointed out the dangers in terms of administrative and compliance costs, and more importantly, the threat to the internal common market, that would result from a collapse of the Agreements and the adoption of "go-it-alone" policies in the income tax field by the provincial governments. Boadway (1992) and Ip and Mintz (1992) provide an overview of the arguments presented in the section on the evolution of fiscal arrangements, which rank the various tax fields in increasing order of need to centralize and coordinate — from capital and personal income taxation, to general sales taxes and excises, and finally resource and property taxes.

Decentralization versus Recentralization. Underlying much of the discussion on each of the issues dealt with here are often significant differences in views concerning the appropriate degree of decentralization in the Canadian federation. Those with a strongly decentralist view are often willing to see further erosion of equalization at the federal level, and would certainly agree with proposals that would decrease its total cost to the federal government. They would encourage the federal government to loosen its financial involvement with, and any strings it attaches to, provincial expenditures in social policy areas. And they would be willing to continue to decentralize responsibility for revenue raising and the tax structure to the provinces.

As we pointed out earlier, the appropriate design of the system of federal-provincial fiscal arrangements certainly does depend on the degree of decentralization of various fiscal responsibilities in the federation. Our own approach for the purpose of this chapter is to take the degree of decentralization as more or less given, and not to make major proposals in that regard.[33] Given that, we ask what sorts of adjustments might be called for, on the basis of basic economic principles outlined and discussed in earlier sections, in the current system of fiscal arrangements. In other words, the system of fiscal arrangements is viewed, not as an end in itself, but rather as a tool for accommodating and making workable the more fundamental goals and characteristics of the federal system. From our discussion here and earlier it will be easy enough to infer many of the adjustments that might be required in the event of further changes in the nature of the federation. The remainder of this section outlines what we perceive to be some of the major options for fiscal arrangements that accord with the basic economic principles we have discussed and which will meet the basic needs of the federal system as it now stands.

Minimal Requirements for Fiscal Arrangements

We begin by outlining what we view as the principal "minimal requirements" of a system of fiscal arrangements in the Canadian federal system. These derive from the basic economic principles outlined in earlier sections, and their application to the Canadian system as it is today. There are five requirements that we feel are worth repeating here.

First, in light of the high degree of fiscal decentralization on both the tax and the revenue side, and the size of the interprovincial disparities in fiscal capacities, it is essential, on grounds of economic efficiency and fiscal equity, for the federal government to continue to operate an effective equalization program. To repeat, increased decentralization of fiscal responsibilities makes equalization *more*, not *less* important. This will require not only a continuation of the commitment to equalization, but also a resolve to remedy some of the major flaws in the current system.

Second, there must be effective mechanisms and procedures for dealing with the shared responsibility between the federal and provincial governments for delivering programs aimed at achieving redistributive equity. We take it as given that social programs will continue to be an area of shared responsibility. When the major shared-cost programs were introduced in the 1960s, there was little question that the federal government played the major rule in the "negotiations" over program design. But the cost-sharing formulae almost guaranteed that provincial spending would grow until budgetary pressures forced the federal government to take corrective action and begin to off-load financial responsibilities onto the provinces. This necessarily increased the powers of the provinces in these fields. As a result, there is now considerable tension over the relative roles of the two levels of government. What is necessary at this time is to devise some mechanisms for a true sharing of responsibility. The provinces need room to experiment with alternative modes of program design and service delivery. At the same time, in order to meet national equity needs, and also to prevent decentralized decisions of provincial governments from causing undue harm to the Canadian common market, the federal government must continue to play a national role.

The final three "minimal requirements" are somewhat related to the second one. First, to the extent that provincial, or shared federal-provincial, activities involve significant spillovers of benefits or costs across provincial boundaries, there must be some mechanism for the federal government, or some other institution, to ensure that these effects are taken into account. Second, there must be sufficient capability at the federal level, and/or some other form of institutional arrangement, to protect the integrity of the economic union. And third, there must be continued harmonization of tax systems across the country. This is especially important with respect to taxes on corporate and personal incomes. Each of these considerations becomes more important the greater is the extent of decentralization of fiscal responsibilities to the provinces.

The Scope for Federal Action in Achieving Them

In order to operate an adequate equalization program at the federal level, the federal government must have access to sufficient revenues to finance the payments to the have-not provinces. In light of the considerations outlined in our discussion of tax harmonization, it would be preferable for the federal government to retain maximum revenue-raising powers in the income tax fields. Given the degree of fiscal decentralization that has already occurred, it is probably unrealistic for the federal government to contemplate remaining dominant in all major tax areas. If a choice had to be made about whether (a) to cede further income tax room to the provinces and expand its role in the sales tax area, and (b) the opposite, i.e., maintain its share of income tax room and let the provinces expand their role in sales taxes, the federal government ought to choose the latter. The introduction of the federal GST could be thought of as retrograde from the viewpoint of the fiscal arrangements.

In order to maintain a federal presence for equity and efficiency reasons in the social program area, it is essential for the federal government to retain some spending power. This cannot, however, be absolute. As mentioned above, some mechanisms for joint power sharing need to be developed. The old systems of cost sharing, subject to federal standards, are not necessarily the optimal way of achieving this goal.

Possible Modest Changes

Is it possible to remedy the major problems with the existing system of fiscal arrangements through a number of relatively modest changes? The answer to this question depends in part on the semantic issue of what sorts of changes are considered "modest," and what would make them "major." Some of the existing problems arise from initial flaws in program design. For instance, the equalization program was never designed as a truly net scheme. While this might not have been too great a problem when provincial fiscal responsibilities were much smaller than they are now, the current magnitude of the equalization program makes them more significant. But many of the other problems arise from the (generally unilateral) imposition by the federal government of ad hoc adjustments in light of underlying systemic changes, and from short-term political or economic expediency. The result is that the current system of fiscal arrangements is very difficult to justify on the basis of any underlying economic principles. In that sense, what is clearly required now is a rethinking, and, where necessary, a redesign of the fiscal arrangements in light of the economic goals they are meant to achieve. We would say, therefore, that any changes that are made should certainly be the result of a *major rethinking* of their purposes and their actual effects. Major changes in program design should not be ruled out.

It is useful to begin by pointing out a number of relatively modest changes in programs that could result in considerable improvement in the arrangements as they now stand. The first of these changes would be to remove the arbitrary caps and exclusions that have been placed on levels and/or growth rates of transfers to the provinces, individually or in aggregate. Some of these "modest" changes would, of course, have significant effects on the federal budget. The correct response to these implications is not to shy away from the changes, but rather to search for other, less arbitrary, ways of dealing with these budgetary effects. Another useful change would be for the federal government to cease the practice of including in what is termed the federal contribution to EPF the tax points that have been transferred to the provinces. By transferring the tax points, the federal government unburdened itself of this share of responsibility for EPF programs. Therefore, these revenues are now the responsibility of the provinces and are no longer, in any sense, a "federal contribution." In the absence of spending caps, this change would have no substantive implications. However, as long as the government imposes limits on the growth of federal EPF contributions, this suggested change would slow down the rate of decline of "real" federal contributions — i.e., what the federal government refers to as EPF cash transfers.

Major Reforms

As we have seen from the earlier discussion, a wide variety of major reforms to the current fiscal arrangements could be imagined. In many cases, however, it is our impression that the changes that have been suggested do not make a coherent package in light of the underlying economic goals of these arrangements. And in other cases, they rest on the assumption of the need for a major change in the degree of centralization of fiscal responsibilities in the federation. What we would like to suggest here is simply a few major reforms that could be justified on the basis of the economic principles we have outlined earlier, and are generally consistent with what we perceive to be the current extent of decentralization. In the event of significant changes in the degree of decentralization, there would have to be corresponding changes in the fiscal arrangements. Such adjustments should be determined on the basis of the economic purposes of the arrangements.

Rationalize EPF and CAP Financing, and Turn Equalization into a Net Scheme. The equalization has never been a net scheme. That is, while it provides transfers to have-not provinces, it only "equalizes down" from the rich provinces to the extent that federal taxes to finance these transfers fall relatively more heavily on the residents of rich provinces than on those of poor ones.[34] There are a number of ways in which this deficiency could be corrected. One, as has been mentioned earlier, would be to have the equalization program operated solely by the provinces, so that all transfers to the poorer provinces would be financed by provincial taxes levied by the rich provinces. The amount of taxes to be collected in each of the rich provinces, in an ideal scheme, would be determined in exactly the same manner as the transfers to each of the poor provinces. We have already described our reservations about the viability of a provincially operated equalization program. The same effect could be achieved, however, by several types of federally run schemes. The first possibility would be one in which the federal government financed equalization transfers to the have-not provinces by a special levy on the federal income tax in the non-recipient provinces, where the tax rate in each of the latter jurisdictions varied with their fiscal capacities as measured by the equalization formula. In other words, in order to finance equalization payments to the poor provinces, residents of the rich provinces would pay a province-specific surcharge on their federal income tax.

An alternative is one that would not only deal with some of the problems we have alluded to with the current equalization program, but also rationalize the EPF and CAP schemes. First, as suggested earlier, tax points that had been transferred to the provinces no longer would be counted as part of the federal

EPF contribution. Second, the total amount of the federal transfers to the provinces under these two programs would be aggregated into a single transfer program. This aggregate amount would then be adjusted up or down for each province according to the full amount of their equalization entitlement, positive or negative. In effect, CAP and EPF would be rolled into an expanded equalization program which would be operated on a net basis. The have provinces would end up with smaller federal EPF and CAP contributions, with the reductions being used to finance equalization transfers to the have-not provinces. CAP transfers would no longer be determined by a cost-sharing formula, which, as we have already pointed out, cannot be justified on the basis of any compelling economic argument. As discussed by Bird (1990), they could either be allocated on a simple equal per capita basis, or on the basis of some index of expenditure need in the area of welfare payments and services. This arrangement would make it even more important for the federal and provincial governments to work out an arrangement for both levels of government to exercise their legitimate voice in program design and implementation. Presumably the federal government would have to retain some spending power to withhold funds from provinces who do not meet what are determined to be legitimate national needs. Whether, and if so, under what conditions, the federal government would be permitted to exercise this power unilaterally is something that would need to be discussed.

Reassign Tax Room. It could well be argued on the basis of current thinking about tax harmonization that, given the high degree of decentralization of fiscal responsibilities in the Canadian federation, the federal government is playing too large a role in the sales tax field, and too small a role in income taxes. There could be little justification for the scale to be tipped any further in this direction. And, if there were an opportunity to consider a major realignment in the assignment of tax responsibilities, it might be argued that the federal government should get out of the sales tax field, ceding this area to the provinces, and occupy a much greater share of the income tax.

Also important is the share of the overall tax room occupied by the federal government relative to the provinces. To maintain an effective equalization system, as well as to be able to exercise responsibility for national equity and efficiency objectives through the spending power, it is essential that the federal government have access to sufficient financial resources. It is our view that, as a result of the steady erosion over the past several years, the federal government is perilously close to having insufficient tax room to carry out its national responsibilities. Unfortunately, this cannot be remedied by unilateral action alone. It would seem to be necessary for both levels of government to collaborate in any major realignment of the tax room between the federal government and the provinces.

New Mechanisms for Joint Federal-Provincial Decision Making. There can be little doubt that key reasons for the somewhat ad hoc current state of federal-provincial fiscal arrangements are that the federal government has often acted unilaterally and for reasons of short-term expediency in making program adjustments, and there is no national institution charged with systematic analysis and consideration of alternative arrangements. Furthermore, in areas of shared responsibility, especially in the area of social programs, there also appears to be a similar lack of joint analysis and decision making. If these allegations are true, and if it is felt that these are significant deficiencies in the current system, then alternatives should be explored, along the lines, say, of the Australian Grants Commission, for introducing institutions for joint analysis and decision making in the area of federal-provincial fiscal arrangements. Such a body would meet regularly in order to consider the state of these arrangements, and to prepare proposals to be considered on a regular basis before the expiry of any particular set of fiscal arrangements.

Extending Grants to Training and Unemployment Insurance, and Decentralizing Them. A somewhat more ambitious change would involve not only the fiscal arrangements but also the division of expenditure responsibilities between the federal government and the provinces. One example of such a change which would appear to be consistent with the general principles we have enunciated above would be to turn over to the provinces responsibility for labour training as well as unemployment insurance on the grounds that they are services that can be delivered more efficiently at the provincial level and that this would allow for coordination of these programs with provincial welfare and education schemes. The latter would result in a rationalized scheme and would eliminate the adverse incentives that provinces are said to face in terms of exploiting the federally-funded unemployment insurance system. Parenthetically, this would also eliminate the temptation that the federal government might have to use these programs as instruments to address regional inequalities. However, the federal government would still retain an interest in ensuring that the programs were designed so as to be consistent with maintaining the efficiency of the economic union and with national equity standards. That is, they would wish to maintain some national standards while at the same time reaping the efficiency benefits of decentralized service delivery. This might be done by retaining some tax room and using it to provide block funding to the provinces with general conditions attached, that is, by using the spending power.

CONCLUSIONS

We have by no means covered all the options that might be considered as suitable ways of renewing the fiscal arrangements. However, we hope we have given a flavour of what in our view are the shortcomings of the existing arrangements, and of the desirable features that a renewed set of arrangements should satisfy. Our basic message is that the federation has evolved into a relatively decentralized one, and that must be recognized when thinking about the fiscal arrangements. Decentralization has its virtues in terms of improving the efficiency with which public services are delivered. At the same time, decentralization increases the need for fiscal arrangements to address the various national inefficiencies and inequities that inevitably accompany decentralization. Fiscal realities suggest that one cannot hope for a major reinjection of federal funding to the provinces. Within these constraints, we must look for a set of federal-provincial fiscal arrangements that allow the federation to take full advantage of the benefits of decentralized decision making and service delivery, but do so in a way that does not compromise the efficiency or equity of the internal economic union.

We would be remiss if we did not acknowledge that the system has served us extremely well in the postwar period. The way in which we have accomplished decentralization while maintaining basic norms and mechanisms for achieving national objectives is a model compared with many other federations. Those that have decentralized have often done it with little regard for the inefficiencies and inequities that result. More often, federations have been too reluctant to decentralize. However, our system is not perfect. The equalization system has well-known warts. The spending power has at times been used too intrusively (some would say in the case of the *Canada Health Act*) and at others too reluctantly (education?). The need for renewal of the existing arrangements is a good opportunity to move the system in the direction of perfection.

NOTES

We are grateful to Leah Anderson for the research assistance she provided and to Paul Hobson for discussions on many aspects of this chapter. Valuable comments were also made on an earlier draft by Travis Armour, Roderick Hill, Wade Locke, and Dennis Stang.

1. We concentrate almost exclusively on fiscal relations between the federal and provincial governments, thus excluding the territories and the municipalities from the discussion. Nonetheless, some of the same issues apply to relations involving these other governments, and some of the same remedies apply as well. In addition, we do not consider other emerging forms of government in Canada such as aboriginal self-government.

2. Nationalists in Quebec would be an important exception to this generalization. An important subset of this group sees a significant role for government in the economy, and sees the provincial government, and not the federal government, as performing it. According to this view, the federal government should leave as much tax room as possible for the province to be able to carry out its functions.

3. Of course, federal government policies may also interfere with the efficiency of the internal common market. We do not address this problem since it is not of direct concern for fiscal arrangements.

4. The same policy instruments could also be used to discourage unwanted factors, like unskilled labour, from entering a province.

5. For more detailed discussion of the rationale for public provision of quasi-private services, see Boadway (1992); and Boadway and Bruce (1993).

6. The concept of fiscal efficiency is discussed in detail in Boadway and Flatters (1982b). The notion goes back to Buchanan (1952); and Scott (1952).

7. The literature has also stressed the possibility of a fiscal externality in an economy with local public goods; see Flatters, Henderson and Mieszkowski (1974). The argument here focuses more on an economy in which provincial expenditures are on quasi-private goods and services, which seems to be the more relevant case.

8. Representative empirical evidence may be found in Winer and Gauthier (1882); and Day (1992). The implications of the Winer-Gauthier study for the welfare cost of fiscal inefficiency has been analyzed by Watson (1986).

9. Others might argue that decentralization may lead to more redistribution because interest groups are more likely to capture provincial governments than the federal government.

10. It also has lengthy historical antecedents: see particularly Buchanan (1950) and the application to Canada in Graham (1964); and Boadway and Flatters (1982a).

11. This is also true at lower layers of the federation, as well as in unitary states with respect to municipalities.

12. There might also be stabilization reasons for the federal government retaining more tax room than is necessary for its own expenditure purposes.

13. By the same token, it might be argued that cost differences might be taken account of in equalizing grants. However, this can lead to inefficiencies in provision, particularly in reduced incentives for economizing on the costs of providing public services at the provincial level.

14. It might be noted in passing that from the point of view of the arguments given here, the simultaneous recognition of the role of the federal government in maintaining the internal economic union and the virtual gutting of the federal spending power which formed part of the federal government's constitutional proposals of 1992 were mutually inconsistent.

15. Those who would down-play the federal redistributive role, or the redistributive role of government more generally, would not be persuaded by the latter consideration. But the importance of mobility of the tax base can be derived from efficiency considerations alone.

16. See Boadway (1992); Dahlby (1992); and Ip and Mintz (1992) for discussions of the assignment of taxing powers.

17. Harmonization may also be achieved to some extent without formal agreement, simply by competition among governments (see Boadway and Bruce 1992).

However, evidence from various federations suggests that the extent of such harmonization is not likely to be great.

18. We are ignoring customs duties since they are not an important revenue-raising device.

19. An exception to this, discussed further below, is that harmonization of a multi-stage tax (VAT) in a federation is difficult even if rates and rate structure do not differ across jurisdictions.

20. A more detailed discussion of the consequences for federal-provincial fiscal relations of the recent budgetary measures may be found in Boadway (1989; 1992).

21. The Canadian Medical Association apparently feels the same. The court action that they had initiated to challenge the constitutionality of the *Canada Health Act* was dropped.

22. CAP transfers to the three have provinces were also unilaterally restricted to increases of 5 percent, a move that was upheld by the Supreme Court of Canada.

23. This is discussed fully in Boadway, Bruce and Mintz (1987). There is a sizable literature on the issue of why creditor nations offer tax credits since it apparently involves a pure loss of revenue to them. The issue is yet to be resolved.

24. This was one of the themes to come out of the economic analysis that accompanied the constitutional reform initiatives of 1992; see the discussion in Boadway, Courchene and Purvis (1991).

25. Again, we find it most useful to think of the role of equalizing transfers as essentially preserving the financial characteristics of a unitary state, while at the same time allowing for the advantages of decentralization.

26. Basically, what the argument presumes is that provincial public services take the form of quasi-private goods and services, that these goods and services are provided on a roughly equal per capita basis, and that residence-based taxes are roughly proportional. This leads to a system in which all tax sources, residence-based and source-based alike, should be fully equalized according to standard principles of efficiency and equity (see Boadway and Flatters 1982a).

27. Some federations come much closer to this form than the Canadian one, though they do not always implement their transfers in an ideal way. Mexico is a good example, as is Indonesia, both of which are much more centralized on the expenditure side as well. Germany is another example, given its relatively centralized tax collection machinery.

28. For example, François Vaillancourt has stressed this to us in conversation.

29. This is one of the suggestions put forward for consideration, and later rejected, by Norrie. The proposal for a provincially-run equalization system has been made most forcefully by Hobson and St.-Hilaire (1993), though their objective is not to gut national equity but to foster it. They would convert the EPF program entirely to tax points but earmark those tax points to be used for equalization purposes among the provinces.

30. This is one of the "straw men" suggested by Norrie (1993). He ultimately rejects this approach as being unrealistic in face of current fiscal realities.

31. Norrie makes this suggestion with respect to postsecondary education and welfare, but not health, which he would leave entirely to the provinces (1993).

32. Another of Norrie's "straw men," which is similar to one of Leslie's as well, is a suggestion that the federal government remove itself from the social policy field entirely, and decentralize the financing of these programs to the provinces by vacating more tax room.

33. Parenthetically, it might be worth mentioning that we see no convincing *economic* argument against an asymmetric arrangement for Quebec, for example, along the lines of the opting-out provisions of the Meech Lake or Charlottetown Accords. Nor do we see an asymmetric division of powers as being an essential obstacle, provided there is adequate account made for the ability of the federal government to foster national efficiency and equity objectives through the spending power.

34. In fact, because the scheme is not a net one, the federal government has in the past sometimes resorted to ad hoc policy changes designed to shift real incomes from the have provinces to the have-nots. Examples include bilateral energy revenue-sharing arrangements (see Boadway, Flatters and LeBlanc 1983) and the National Energy Policy itself (Boadway and Hobson 1993).

BIBLIOGRAPHY

Atkinson, A.B. and J.E. Stiglitz (1980), *Lectures on Public Economics*, New York: McGraw Hill.

Bird, R.M. (1990), "Federal-Provincial Fiscal Arrangements: Is There an Agenda for the 1990s?" in *Canada: The State of the Federation 1990*, ed. R.L. Watts and D.M. Brown, Kingston: Institute of Intergovernmental Relations, Queen's University.

Boadway, R.W. (1989), "Federal-Provincial Fiscal Relations in the Wake of Deficit Reduction," in *Canada: The State of the Federation 1989*, ed. R.L. Watts and D.M. Brown, Kingston: Institute of Intergovernmental Relations, Queen's University, 107-135.

_____ (1992), *The Constitutional Division of Powers: An Economic Perspective*, Ottawa: Economic Council of Canada.

Boadway, R. and N. Bruce (1992), "Pressures for the Harmonization of Income Taxes Between Canada and the United States," in *Canada-U.S. Tax Comparisons*, ed. J.B. Shoven and J. Whalley, Chicago: The University of Chicago Press.

_____ (1993), "The Government Provision of Private Services," mimeo.

Boadway, R.W., N. Bruce and J.M. Mintz (1987), *Taxes on Capital Income in Canada: Analysis and Policy*, Toronto: Canadian Tax Foundation.

Boadway, R.W., I. Cromb and H. Kitchen (1989), "The Ontario Corporate Tax and the Tax Collection Agreements," Toronto: Ministry of Treasury and Economics.

Boadway, R.W., T.J. Courchene and D.D. Purvis (1991), *Economic Dimensions of Constitutional Change*, Kingston: John Deutsch Institute for the Study of Economic Policy, Queen's University.

Boadway, R.W. and F.R. Flatters (1982a), *Equalization in a Federal State*, Ottawa: Economic Council of Canada.

_____ (1982b), "Efficiency and Equalization Payments in a Federal System of Government: A Synthesis and Extension of Recent Results," *Canadian Journal of Economics*, 15, 4: 613-633.

Boadway, R.W., F.R. Flatters and A. LeBlanc (1983), "Revenue Sharing and the Equalization of Natural Resource Revenues," *Canadian Public Policy*, 9, 2: 174-180.

Boadway, R.W. and P.A.R. Hobson (1993), *Intergovernmental Fiscal Relations in Canada*, Toronto: Canadian Tax Foundation.

Buchanan, J.M. (1950), "Federalism and Fiscal Equity," *American Economic Review*, 40: 583-599.

_____ (1952), "Federal Grants and Resource Allocation," *Journal of Political Economy*, 60: 208-217.

Canada. Department of Finance (1991), *Personal Income Tax Coordination: The Federal-Provincial Tax Collection Agreements*, Ottawa: Department of Finance.

Canada. Parliamentary Task Force on Federal-Provincial Fiscal Arrangements, Breau Task Force (1981), *Fiscal Federalism in Canada*, Ottawa: Supply and Services.

Clarkson Gordon (1988), "The Feasibility of a Self-Administered Income Tax System for British Columbia," mimeo, Toronto: Clarkson Gordon.

Courchene, T.J. (1984), *Equalization Payments: Past, Present and Future*, Toronto: Ontario Economic Council.

_____ (1991), "Canada 1992: Political Denouement or Economic Renaissance?" in *Economic Dimensions of Constitutional Change*, ed. R.W. Boadway, T.J. Courchene and D.D. Purvis, Kingston: John Deutsch Institute for the Study of Economic Policy, Queen's University, 45-69.

Dahlby, B. (1992), "Taxation under Alternative Constitutional Arrangements," in *Alberta and the Economics of Constitutional Change*, ed. P. Boothe, Edmonton: Western Centre for Economic Research.

Day, K.M. (1992), "Interprovincial Migration and Local Public Goods," *Canadian Journal of Economics*, 25: 123-124.

Economic Council of Canada (1982), *Financing Confederation: Today and Tomorrow*, Ottawa: Supply and Services Canada.

Flatters, F., V. Henderson and P. Mieszkowski (1974), "Public Goods, Efficiency, and Regional Fiscal Equalization," *Journal of Public Economics, 3*, 2: 99-112.

Graham, J.F. (1964), *Intergovernmental Fiscal Relationships*, Toronto: Canadian Tax Foundation.

Hartle, D.G. (1983), *A Separate Personal Income Tax for Ontario: An Economic Analysis*, Toronto: Ontario Economic Council.

Hobson, P.A.R. and F. St.-Hilaire (1993), "Rearranging Federal-Provincial Fiscal Arrangements: Toward Sustainable Federalism," Montreal: Institute for Research on Public Policy.

Hogg, P. (1985), *Constitutional Law of Canada*, 2d ed., Toronto: Carswell.

Ip, I. and J. Mintz (1992), *Dividing the Spoils: The Federal-Provincial Allocation of the Taxing Power*, Toronto: C.D. Howe Institute.

Leslie, P. (1993), "The Fiscal Crisis of Canadian Federalism," in *A Partnership in Trouble: Renegotiating Fiscal Federalism*, ed. P.M. Leslie, K. Norrie and I. Ip, Toronto: C.D.Howe Institute.

McLure, C.E.R. Jr., ed. (1983), *Tax Assignment in Federal Countries*, Canberra: Centre for Research on Federal Financial Relations, Australian National University.

Musgrave, R.M. (1959), *The Theory of Public Finance*, New York: McGraw Hill.

Norrie, K. (1993), "Intergovernmental Transfers in Canada: An Historical Perspective on Some Current Policy Issues," in *A Partnership in Trouble: Renegotiating Fiscal Federalism*, ed. P.M. Leslie, K. Norrie and I. Ip, Toronto: C.D. Howe Institute.

Scott, A.D. (1952), "Federal Grants and Resource Allocation," *Journal of Political Economy*, 60: 534-538.

Royal Commission on Taxation (1966), *Report* (The Carter Report), Ottawa: Queen's Printer.

Usher, D. (1993), "A Proposal to Make Equalization Payments More Equalizing and Save the Federal Government Three and a Half Billion Dollars," mimeo.

Vanderkamp, J. (1986), "The Efficiency of the Interregional Adjustment Process," in *Disparities and Interregional Adjustment*, ed. K. Norrie, Toronto: University of Toronto Press.

Watson, W.G. (1986), "An Estimate of the Welfare Gains from Fiscal Equalization," *Canadian Journal of Economics*, 19, 2: 298-308.

Wildasin, D.E. (1986), *Urban Public Finance*, Chur, Switzerland: Harwood Academic Publishers.

Winer, S.L. and Gauthier, D. (1982), *Internal Migration and Fiscal Structure: An Econometric Study of the Determinants of Interprovincial Migration in Canada*, Ottawa: Economic Council of Canada.

Comment: Is There a Crisis?

Frederick W. Gorbet

Robin Boadway and Frank Flatters provide an excellent canvass of the principles and issues involved in assessing federal-provincial fiscal relations. Indeed
the breadth of their chapter has left me searching for ways that I could add value
to their discussion. I concluded that I would try to amplify their ideas by
providing the perspective of one who has not delved as deeply into the history
or theoretical framework for fiscal federalism, but who, on the other hand, got
to play a part in a number of significant decisions that are having and will
continue to have profound effects. If you like, you can call this the view from
ground level rather that 30,000 feet.

Let me divide my comments into three parts: broad factors that have shaped
and will continue to shape the context for bargaining over fiscal arrangements;
some specific comments on programs; and some thought-starters on directions
for change.

THE CONTEXT FOR BARGAINING

First, and most important, the system is under considerable stress today, in my
view, not so much because of the decentralization noted in the essay, but rather
because of the fiscal pressures all governments are facing. The remarkable
growth in provincial spending and taxing emphasized in the chapter makes a
review of the adequacy of federal fiscal relations desirable, but it is the fiscal
pressures that give the issue urgency.

It is interesting to note that attempts to deal with the federal deficit over the
1984-92 period divide into two rather distinct subperiods with respect to the
fiscal transfers. From 1984-88, during the Conservatives' first mandate, transfers to the provinces were barely touched. There was a deliberate attempt, for

a lot of reasons, to try to deal with the problem without cutting transfers. As a result, while all program spending grew by 3.6 percent per year, on average, from 1984-85 to 1989-90, cash transfers to the provinces grew by 4.5 percent per year (and cash and tax transfers grew by 6.5 percent per year).

Even in the first budget of the second mandate, the government opted for very significant tax increases rather than focusing on transfers to provinces. It was only in 1990, when it became clear that the tolerance for tax increases had been reached if not exceeded and that significant further spending cuts would require cuts to transfers, that the first Expenditure Control Program was introduced, freezing EPF transfers and reducing the growth rate of CAP in the non-equalization-receiving provinces.

I recount this brief history for two reasons. First it is important to understand the fiscal consequences of the status quo. The last renewal of the equalization program was for two years only. The program expired on 31 March 1994 and at that date payments will cease to flow if no legislative action is taken. The EPF and CAP restraints are also legislated. If no action is taken, the controls on EPF and CAP transfers expire on 31 March 1995. At that time, EPF returns to a GDP-3 percent formula and CAP snaps back to a 50 percent cost-sharing ratio in Ontario, Alberta, and B.C. The status quo would result in increased federal expenditures for CAP in the "have provinces" of $2-3 billion in 1995-96, and this would grow as EPF requirements increased in subsequent years. These federal spending pressures provide an impetus to serious bargaining, and they assure that affordability will continue to be as important as equity and efficiency in the future bargaining context. Subsequent to preparation of these remarks, the Equalization Program was renewed for five years. EPF and CAP are being reviewed with legislation expected in the fall of 1994.

Second, it is important to recognize that there is an accountability issue that is central to fiscal federalism and that is not given as much attention as it deserves in the Boadway-Flatters chapter. Put simply, the federal government in 1990 reached the point where it no longer felt politically able to increase taxes to maintain transfers to the provinces. This political reality was reinforced by the federal perspective that the provinces were doing a less than adequate job of controlling their program spending, particularly in comparison to the restraint that had been exercised at the federal level. (For example, from 1984-85 to 1989-90, federal program spending grew by 3.6 percent per year, while provincial program spending grew by 6.7 percent per year. Provincial growth rates ranged from 4.3 percent annually in Alberta, to 9.7 percent annually in Ontario.)

Boadway and Flatters argue that the "theory of fiscal federalism suggests that the role of federal-provincial fiscal arrangements should increase in importance as more budgetary responsibilities are transferred to the provinces" (p. 50). While equity and efficiency considerations may lead to that conclusion, particularly in a comparative static framework, it is not clear that concerns about accountability support such a view. There are two dimensions of the accountability issue that need to be considered. The first is the practical political issue I just raised. When one government gets credit for spending and another gets chastized for taxing, there is a political disequilibrium that cannot long be sustained. As well, however, there is the economic issue of whether the allocation of resources between private goods and public goods is optimal when the political accountability for spending and taxing decisions becomes separated. The focus on efficiency in the chapter is almost entirely in the context of the efficiency of the common market, rather than efficiency of resource allocation between public and private goods. Is part of our deficit problem because we have more pubic goods than we are willing to pay for? And is the blurring of the link between spending and taxing part of the reason why?

The final point I want to make about the future bargaining context concerns the issue of flexibility versus certainty. It is important to recall that the fiscal transfers are federal programs, authorized by federal statute. This is true of equalization, notwithstanding section 36 of the constitution, and it is true of CAP, as the Supreme Court confirmed. The same is not true, however, with respect to the federal-provincial Tax Collection Agreements. These are agreements in the true sense of the word; the provinces have the constitutional right to be in the field and it is in their interest to remain in the agreements only so long as the benefits they feel they get outweigh the costs.

The provinces have made it clear that they are looking for greater certainty with regard to future transfers, and they were quite keen to be able to constitutionalize agreements — a proposal that was accepted by the federal government in the Charlottetown Accord. The defeat of the Accord will not diminish their desire for certainty over funding and Prime Minister Chrétien suggested during the campaign that the new government would wish to provide this certainty in whatever new transfer arrangements it introduced.

An important contextual issue will be how to balance the certainty provinces want with the ability to make changes if circumstances change. It will be equally important to recognize that certainty is also valuable with respect to tax harmonization and as transfers take on more of the characteristics of agreements, it will be useful to keep in mind the possibility of developing a more explicit linkage between transfer agreements and tax harmonization agreements.

To recapitulate, affordability, accountability, and the need to balance certainty against flexibility will influence future negotiations as much as efficiency and equity concerns.

COMMENTS ON PROGRAMS

Let me now make a few comments on specific programs, in the context of the Boadway-Flatters observations. With respect to transfers, I agree completely with their analysis with regard to equalization. It has worked remarkably well. It continues to be necessary to the federation we have developed and, while it is under some stress because of the operation of the ceiling, it is much more robust than either EPF or CAP. It should be maintained and strengthened as the foundation of a reformed fiscal arrangements system.

In my view, neither EPF nor CAP is stable in its current structure. As reforms are considered, the issue of conditionality with respect to the programs these transfers fund will have to be addressed head on. Concerns about the erosion of the power to enforce the *Canada Health Act* as the cash portion of EPF disappeared were taken very seriously by the last federal government and I believe that they have been dealt with in a more definitive way than suggested by Boadway and Flatters through amendments to the *Fiscal Arrangements Act* that allow the withholding of funds from any federal transfer to a provincial government (including CAP or equalization) if the conditions of the *Canada Health Act* are breached and if there is inadequate cash flowing under EPF to support the necessary withholding. Having said that, however, I do believe as we move forward we will have to be more imaginative in the ways by which we seek to impose conditionality on provincial discretion for program delivery.

The chapter makes much of the importance of the spending power as a tool for achieving "the abundant advantages of decentralization without sacrificing national efficiency and equity objectives" (p. 62). My sense is that it will be a long time, if ever, before the fiscal situation of the federal government permits the kind of use of the spending power that we have seen in the past. The federal role in establishing and maintaining national standards (loaded as that phrase is), will in future rest less on coercion and more on leadership and consensus building in an effort to develop standards that are truly national, rather than federal — not an easy exercise, and possibly not achievable, but certainly one worth striving for.

With regard to the tax side, I have three brief comments. First, adopting the GST is characterized as "retrograde" inasmuch as it reflected a choice to replace a sales tax with a sales tax, rather than ceding the room from the manufacturer's sales tax to the provinces in return for income tax points that could make up the

$15-16 billion shortfall. I doubt whether this would have been possible. It certainly would have been an interesting negotiation with Alberta. In any event, the new government is committed to removing the GST so we are likely to have a chance in the near future to see if a trade-off of sales tax room for income tax points is a starter.

My second comment is with respect to income tax and the debate now going on regarding tax on income rather than tax on tax. It would be a serious mistake to underestimate the strength of conviction on the part of the western provinces, and Ontario, that they need and deserve more flexibility than the current agreements permit. There is a point at which they will withdraw and collect their own taxes, as Quebec does, if they cannot get this flexibility within the agreements. From a federal perspective, the ultimate trade-off in managing this issue is not between more or less harmonization within the agreements, but rather between allowing enough flexibility to convince provincial governments that it continues to be in their own interests to remain within the agreement and being so rigid that the agreement self-destructs. The frontiers are being pushed, as Boadway and Flatters note, and they will continue to be pushed in the coming years. This will not be an easy negotiation!

A final point with respect to tax is to note the very real pressure to deal with the deductibility of provincial payroll and capital taxes. This is not noted in the chapter but it continues to be an important federal-provincial harmonization issue that I believe the new government will have to address.

DIRECTIONS FOR CHANGE

I think that federal-provincial fiscal arrangements will dominate the policy agenda for the life of the next government. The system is not yet in crisis, but it is headed that way. It will have to change, and change will have to be major. Modest changes, such as those set out in the chapter, are unlikely to be practical because the resources to finance them are unavailable. The system is going to have to be reformed within a constrained resource envelope that is consistent with restoring fiscal balance. The fiscal positions of all governments ensure that there will be little, if any, generosity in the negotiations and they are likely to be acrimonious and driven by narrow perceptions of self-interest. The existence of two powerful regional parties in Parliament, vying with each other for the role of official opposition, can only exacerbate the difficulty of finding broad national consensus on these issues.

It will be important in these negotiations that all issues — transfers, taxes, program design, and possibly even budget making and debt financing — be on the table together to maximize the room to manoeuvre and the trade-offs that can be made. The issues that will drive the process will be the imminent expiry of equalization, together with the government's search for new tax options to replace the GST. But lurking in the background, not too far away, will be the expiry of the controls on EPF and CAP in early 1995 and the federal fiscal burden that will entail, and the unfinished business with respect to tax on income and deductibility of capital and payroll taxes.

It is difficult to speculate, but I could see the negotiations developing in a way where there would be two broad families of options on the table. Each one would have as its centrepiece a strengthened equalization system, which I would hope would operate on a net basis. One family of models would see intergovernmental tax arrangements carry on much as today. There would be some degree of harmonization of the federal and provincial sales taxes: ideally the development of a truly national sales tax with one base, one rate, one administration and audit system, and an agreed formula to share the revenues. It is difficult to see how you get there from here, but it is not a bad model for the new government to aim for. In this world, federal non-equalization transfers (EPF and CAP) would continue but I think would evolve towards a merged block fund. Growth of the fund would be determined by affordability considerations; distribution would most likely be on an equal per capita basis and conditions would apply.

There would be a search, hopefully with some success, for mechanisms to provide certainty (at least for a fixed period of time) and cooperation in establishing national standards. This will be tricky without opening up the constitution again, but worth considering carefully because we will probably be in a constitutional round again in any event before this government's mandate expires.

The second broad family of models would be more radical. If there is no provincial willingness to cooperate in retooling the GST, the federal government could decide to deliver on its promise to repeal the GST by vacating the field and making up the revenue loss by some combination of transfer payment cuts and income tax increases. In 1992-93 cash transfers for CAP and EPF totalled about $16.4 billion, about $1 billion more than the revenue raised by the GST. Withdrawing from CAP and EPF totally would raise two very serious concerns: how would efficiency and equity standards be developed and enforced; and what would future flows mean for the federal fiscal position, given that EPF cash is slated to decline anyway and GST revenues would grow over time. Both of these concerns would militate against an absolutist application of this kind of scenario, but these concerns might be minimally satisfied by combinations of GST withdrawal, major cuts to EPF and CAP with residual amounts being delivered as an equal-per-capita block fund, and income tax increases. In this scenario, the government would have to do some hard calculating, hard thinking and hard bargaining. But it is not a scenario that I would rule off the table.

Let me conclude by providing a capsule commentary on where the players are likely to come from:

The equalization-receiving provinces and particularly Quebec will stress horizontal equity and progressivity. In discussions over the past two years, Quebec more than other provinces has recognized the reality of the federal fiscal position. Their thrust has been to import equalization principles into EPF and CAP so that as transfers become more limited they get distributed more and more on the basis of need.

Alberta and B.C. have consistently stressed accountability and visibility as a basis for replacing transfers with greater income tax room. I expect they will continue to do so.

Ontario has been increasingly preoccupied with its share. This is a relatively new development and will have very real and substantial implications for the next round of negotiations. Ontario has also been a leader in the quest for certainty, in direct response to the federal changes to CAP, though this is something that is shared by all provinces.

Ontario's position is likely to be even more complex in light of its large deficit problem, the reality of a provincial election in 1995 at the latest, and the relative strength of the Ontario caucus in the Liberal government.

The federal government's position so far has been driven primarily by affordability and accountability, although there is obviously a continuing concern to protect the ability to enforce standards that will contribute to efficiency and equity. How the new government will determine the trade-offs that have to be made among these considerations is as yet unclear.

CHAPTER THREE

Canada's Social Policy Deficit: Implications for Fiscal Federalism

Thomas J. Courchene

INTRODUCTION

Social Canada may not be in free fall but it is certainly facing tough and uncertain times. Part of this relates to the emerging range of unmet needs on the social policy front but part, also, reflects the fact that the existing set of programs is being pared back. This is troubling many Canadians, particularly those who view the social programs as an integral part of the glue that binds us together as a nation. Intriguingly, some of these challenges to the existing social policy environment relate to the social envelope itself, namely the inability of the system to evolve and to transfer resources *within* the envelope from low-priority areas to high-priority areas (Courchene 1993*a*). But the bulk of the challenges comes from outside the social envelope.

One strand of this external pressure arises from globalization and the knowledge/information revolution, and the resulting need for the social envelope to make the transition from a resource-based conception to a human-capital-based conception. Another strand relates to the ongoing fiscal crisis. To the extent that the rest of the economy has begun to make this transition away from a resource-based economy, it has done so by running up the government debt-GNP ratio to 100 percent and by exposing Canada to a 40 percent net foreign debt to GNP ratio. These two strands are related in the sense that one can mount a case that much of the debt accumulation is a result of a last-ditch and ultimately futile attempt on the part of governments at all levels to defend the last generation's social-regional policy and spending conception in the face of the emergence of a new socio-economic paradigm (see Courchene 1993*a*; Lipsey 1993). This harkens back to the statement by Saskatchewan's Roy

Romanow that "we can't afford any sacred cows or we risk losing the herd." Whatever the cause of this fiscal profligacy, the current reality is one where the social envelope is being squeezed.

Yet a dedicated exercise focused only on reducing costs on the social policy front is equally futile because under such a scenario "Canada begins to look more like the United States" (Maxwell 1993). Restructuring, rather than simply paring, has to be the order of the day because in a knowledge era social policy is progressively indistinguishable from economic policy and, hence, integral to regaining our competitive edge. In his recent Benefactors Lecture for the C.D. Howe Institute, Richard Harris (1993) provides a convenient summary of these issues. Harris notes that there has been a fundamental shift in Canada's wealth generation process — away from resource capital and towards physical and especially human capital. He then notes that although we ran up our debts and deficits within a framework in which our "national collateral" was resources, the national collateral that now has to service this indebtedness is increasingly our human capital base. I would add that part of the reason why employment growth will likely be frustratingly slow and that we will be operating below our potential is that, in key areas, this new collateral is sadly lacking.

In brief (and subject to a couple of critical caveats detailed at the end of this introduction), this is the imperative for restructuring social programs and their relationship with the economic order. Or, in the words of the title, this is Canada's social policy deficit. However, restructuring becomes incredibly complicated because of the way in which our federation addresses the division of money and power. In terms of the latter, both levels of government are involved in virtually every aspect of the social envelope. In terms of the former, the existence of both vertical and horizontal fiscal imbalances implies that these imbalances have to be addressed via a system of intergovernmental grants. And these financial transfers have taken on a life of their own, both analytically and politically, frequently quite independently of their "bridging" role.

For a contribution to a book *The Future of Fiscal Federalism*, it has taken me a long time to get around to mentioning the fiscal arrangements. This is by design. Canadian scholars in economics and political science have made significant contributions to the international literature on intergovernmental relations, both financial and political. Nonetheless, the approach I shall adopt is that the time has finally come to abandon this top-down approach to social policy (in both jurisdictional and fiscal terms) in favour of working from the bottom up. Specifically, in full appreciation of the fiscal crisis on the one hand and the emerging social policy needs on the other, the fundamental social policy issue becomes: what constellation of programs and incentives are appropriate from the vantage point of individual Canadians in order that they can become productive citizens in this new global order? Then, and only then, should we pose the subsidiary questions: Which level of government should deliver these programs or services? and How should they be financed? In other words, the real problem is, in the first instance, to restructure social Canada, not to restructure the fiscal arrangements. Finding a solution to the latter may not address the former. This is a tall order and I am sure in what follows I shall violate these precepts on more than one occasion. Nonetheless, as we approach the millennium, these principles constitute the appropriate starting point: with the erosion of the fiscal surplus from resources, we no longer have the luxury of harbouring a vision of social Canada where most of the fruits are dissipated in a self-serving tug-of-war between governments.

The chapter proceeds as follows. Part two focuses on those aspects of the old paradigm that are no longer sustainable or economically viable: incentive incompatibility, the entrenched degree of provincial economic disparities, and the intergenerational tug-of-war. However badly the existing social policy envelope performs in terms of the old paradigm, it is woefully off-side in terms of the new socio-economic order. Thus, part three highlights selected features of the globalization and knowledge/information era and the challenges posed for social policy. To this point in the analysis, the emphasis is on restructuring, not on the paring down of the social envelope. Part four then turns to the fiscal squeeze on social Canada, where the focus is on the system of federal-provincial transfers and deficit shifting. In part five, I address the relationship between social policy restructuring and the fiscal transfers, and argue that there have been some salutary effects of deficit shifting. Parts four and five then address, in more detail, selected aspects of horizontal and vertical imbalance in the federation. The final section attempts to draw together the various strands of the analysis in terms of the imperatives for our new social order. The emphasis here is that in the first instance pride of place must go to restructuring the social programs and not to reworking the fiscal arrangements. In other words, social policy ought to be about people, not about governments.

Two Neglected Areas

In approaching the restructuring of social and economic policy, I shall be focusing primarily on integrating the social sphere into the economic and political spheres. This neglects the other direction and, in particular, the integration of the economic sphere with social priorities. The most glaring omission here is the conduct of macropolicy. I take it as axiomatic that the best social-policy environment is a high-employment economy. Moreover, the gains from social policy restructuring will be reaped largely within a growing economy. Apart from the inappropriateness of fiscal policy over the 1983-89 boom (on which I assume there is mainstream consensus), the key issue here is whether the Bank of Canada's single-minded pursuit of zero inflation in the same time frame as the introduction of the Free Trade Agreement (FTA) and the Goods and Services Tax (GST) as well as the global recession has levelled such a blow to social Canada directly (in terms of unemployment) and indirectly (through the ballooning of deficits and debt from both interest rate charges and from the collapsed economy; and through the consequent ratcheting down of intergovernmental grants and cuts across the social envelope), that social policy restructuring is rather futile until the economy is more robust. There is, of course, another side to this issue, namely that with inflation now laid to rest and private sector restructuring largely behind us, Canada is poised to take full advantage not only of the FTA but as well the emerging consumerism in South Asia and Latin America. Recently, this debate has been cast in terms of goals and instruments: with governments targeting on deficit reduction and the Bank focusing on inflation control, who is concerned about employment (see Fortin 1994; Scarth 1994). In other words, what is the appropriate third instrument: the exchange rate or some version of an incomes policy? While these issues are critical to social Canada, they are way beyond the bounds of this chapter. More importantly, however, they do not, in my view, argue for a delay in terms of rethinking and restructuring social policy in part because restructuring is at the very least a medium-term process. Likewise, the evidence that UI beneficiaries would opt for work if work were available (Phipps 1993) does not constitute evidence against welfare or UI "traps," in part because it leaves "work" undefined. (In particular, for at least one single mother in Ontario, welfare was deemed preferable to a $41,000 government job!) The key point here is that while the demand side is obviously critical, it will receive scant attention in what follows.

The second omission relates to the nature of, or rather the philosophy underpinning, the conception of our industrial structure. Is Anglo-American capitalism capable of producing and utilizing a highly-skilled labour force? Why is it that the English-speaking industrial economies lag so far in apprenticeships and the emphasis on technologists? Why did the leveraged buyouts of the 1980s, replete with their destruction of many "heritage" firms, not spread to Japan and continental Europe? Must we blindly follow the U.S. conception of anti-trust and merger laws? These important issues have not really been addressed in Canada. But they should be, because skills upgrading will work best within a system that attempts to increase productivity through technical change and the utilization of a labour force with a higher skill mix rather than via the commodification of labour, i.e., competing with the "bottom end" of the labour market (Myles 1991, p. 363). While I have attempted to detail some of these issues elsewhere (Courchene 1992), the area is basically unresearched. Essentially, the notion is that the commercial/industrial side of the economy ought to incorporate, wherever feasible, the social policy goals and aspirations of Canadians. For example, apart from the chartered banks, the one institution in Canada that has taken low-skilled Canadians and turned them into technologists or skilled workers is the military. Might we not consider a training role for the military as we struggle to upgrade our skills and human capital? As noted, this line of analysis will also not be pursued further in what follows.

THE UNSUSTAINABILITY OF THE OLD ORDER

The claim that the existing social envelope is unsustainable is hardly novel. As early as the mid-1970s, analysts were expressing concern about the nature of the incentives within programs such as UI and welfare and their likely impact on labour market re-entry, regional economic adjustment and the inevitable drift towards what has since come to be referred to as "transfer dependency" for individuals, families, regions and entire provinces. However, these concerns fell largely upon deaf ears with the result that, as years and generations passed, the incentives in the system came more and more to influence and eventually to dominate the socio-economic environment. As importantly, whole industries (e.g., large parts of tourism) have arranged themselves to mesh with the incentives in the social envelope. While many of the early examples of the negative spillovers associated with the operations of social Canada were drawn from Atlantic Canada, these phenomena now apply across the country. Witness the recent attempt by Bell Canada to shorten its work week to four days and to have UI, after a waiting period, pick up the tab for the fifth day. Who's next? Will the 1994 version of Ontario's "social contract" replace the "Rae days" with "UI days"? To be sure, the UI authorities have rejected the Bell request, but the fact that Bell would contemplate such a strategy reveals the pervasiveness of the transfer mentality.

Thankfully, expressing concern about these perverse incentives is now no longer limited to economists and policy analysts. As Premier Frank McKenna noted at the 1993 Couchiching Conference:

> Welfare was never meant to be a way of life, but it becomes so for thousands of Canadians. And we do them a disservice by allowing it to spread from one unsuspecting generation to the other. Canada is the only country that I know in the world that offers such generous programs that there is absolutely no incentive in return to divert yourself towards education or training. Passive assistance programs grind away at our ability to move our province forward and they are destroying those that they meant to help. Maintaining a culture of cradle-to-grave dependency is no longer viable. (p. 21)

The premier expresses even more concern when it comes to UI:

> I think that a lot of Atlantic Canadians would now tell you ... the truth is that the generosity of Canada has in many ways been the principal impediment to our growth. In Atlantic Canada, we've been the victim of your generosity.... Unemployment insurance was reformed so that not only were people out of work able to obtain unemployment to fill in the gaps, but that everybody who could get 10 weeks of work would be able to draw unemployment for the rest of the year.... I inherited the province in 1987 where we had 128 fish plants, every one of them geared to work 10 weeks, because that's all they needed. (pp. 20-21)

What the 10/42 system implies is that working for $5,000 for ten weeks (or $500 per week) will generate close to $12,000 in UI benefits over the rest of the year. Thus, the societal cost of these ten-week jobs is more than twice as much again as the private cost. Recently, in what the *Toronto Star* (1993) referred to as "a kind of Canadian milestone," Statistics Canada reported that in two New Brunswick counties, 100 percent of two-earner households accessed UI at some time during 1992 and also noted that the ratio was well above 90 percent for many other counties in Atlantic Canada. More anecdotally, when I toured Gaspésie in the mid-1980s as part of a regional development project, there was "evidence" of a rash of small ($1,000 and $2,000) loans from the caisses populaires supposedly to help "buy" the required ten-week jobs. This is rational, indeed income-maximizing, behaviour on the part of each individual but at the societal level it is part of what has come to be referred to as "transfer dependency" and, as already noted, it is not limited to the have-not provinces. This is poor economic policy, it is poor social policy and it is making all of us poor!

The aggregate data on UI appear to indicate that benefits increase in each recession, but then do not fall back much in succeeding booms. For example, both 1980 and 1989 had annual unemployment rates of 7.5 percent. Yet UI benefits (in constant dollars) were almost 70 percent greater in 1989 (with the average weekly benefit level only 6 percent higher in constant dollars). In other words, what begins as an increase in benefits triggered by an increase in unemployment (i.e., what begins as a *stabilization* initiative) becomes converted into part of the overall *redistribution* system. That the welfare and UI systems serve to trap individuals should not come as a surprise once one recognizes that, from their inception, these programs embodied a passive income-support rather than an active re-entry mentality. As the Economic Council of Canada (1992) pointed out, the perceived role for welfare at its inception was largely one of addressing the concerns of the disabled and other unable-to-work Canadians whereas the role for UI was conceived largely to mop-up any cyclical unemployment. In other words, full employment was the order of the day and these programs were designed to cater to the permanently unemployable (welfare) or the cyclically unemployed (UI). There was no provision for the possibility of structural unemployment. This mentality probably explains, but does not condone, the existence of essentially confiscatory tax rates in the transition from these programs to employment at the minimum wage. It is intriguing that we Canadians have been willing to levy 100 percent tax rates (and, for welfare, more than 100 percent because one loses associated benefits like free drugs, etc.) in the transition from welfare or UI to work, whereas we would never contemplate levying such confiscatory taxes on the rest of Canadians. And then we express surprise (indeed, often, "blame the victim") when Canadians react to these confiscatory taxes exactly as the rest of us would react! In any event, what happened is that, over time, an increasing number of welfare and UI beneficiaries have come from the able-to-work category (i.e., as a result of "structural" changes in the economy). Except in circumstances such as the 10/42 syndrome, the social programs do not entice Canadians into their web, but once there, the incentives certainly serve to "trap" them into the system.

All of this speaks to two aspects of unsustainability, one related to individuals and one related to regions.[1] The first is the economic and moral bankruptcy of imbuing the social envelope with a set of incentives that makes it very difficult for rational citizens to pursue avenues that will make them better off over time. These incentives were off-side even in the context of a resource-based economy, but they are exacerbated dramatically in a knowledge/information era (see part three below). The second aspect relates to the unsustainability arising from the gradual entrenching of transfer dependency and the declining economic viability of Canada's provincial and regional economies. This aspect merits further attention.

TABLE 1: Provincial Income Disparity Relatives, 1991 (Relative to the National Average)

| | Y/P | E/LF | LF/P | Y/E | PI/P | PDI/Y | PDI/P | PDI^1/P | AHE^1 | Transfer to Persons Wages and Salaries | | $T+S+G^2$ Wages and Salaries | |
| | | | | | | | | | | Absolute | $Relative^3$ | Absolute | $Relative^3$ |
	(1)	(2)	(3)	(4)	(5)	(6)	(7)	(8)	(9)	(10)	(11)	(12)	(13)
Nfld.	.65	.91	.83	.87	.76	1.25	.81	.83	.92	.57	2.21	1.04	1.57
P.E.I.	.64	.92	.96	.72	.76	1.25	.79	.81	.80	.48	1.87	1.17	1.78
N.S.	.78	.98	.92	.87	.83	1.09	.85	.85	.92	.34	1.32	.94	1.43
N.B.	.76	.96	.88	.88	.80	1.10	.83	.84	.87	.39	1.53	.90	1.36
Que.	.91	.98	.97	.96	.94	1.01	.92	.93	.96	.30	1.18	.78	1.09
Ont.	1.09	1.01	1.04	1.04	1.10	1.00	1.09	1.09	1.04	.21	.83	.56	.85
Man.	.86	1.02	.97	.87	.86	1.06	.91	.92	.90	.29	1.15	.83	1.26
Sask.	.80	1.03	.96	.82	.82	1.06	.82	.86	.91	.36	1.41	1.08	1.64
Alta.	1.15	1.02	1.06	1.06	1.01	.88	1.01	1.03	1.01	.20	.81	.62	.94
B.C.	1.05	1.00	1.01	1.03	1.04	1.00	1.04	1.06	1.05	.25	.98	.58	.88
Canada	1.00	1.00	1.00	1.00	1.00	1.00	1.00	1.00	1.00	.26	1.00	.66	1.00
High/Low	1.80	1.13	1.28	1.47	1.45	1.42	1.38	1.35	1.31	N/A	2.73		2.09

Notes:
- PI and PDI represent Personal Income and Personal Disposable Income respectively.
- The product of columns (2), (3) and (4) may not equal columns (1), because figures have been rounded to two decimal places.
- PDI^1 equals PDI after the allocation of the federal deficit across provinces (by provincial shares of federal taxation).

1. AHE equals average hourly earnings (fixed-weighted), from Table 19 of *Provincial Economic Accounts.*
2. T+S+G/W+S = Transfers plus Subsidies plus Government expenditures on goods and services, as a percent of wages and salaries (W+S).
3. The relatives in column (11) are not identical to those that would derive from column (10), because the calculations in (11) are based on four rather than two decimal places. This observation also applies to columns (12) and (13).

Source: Statistics Canada (1992).

Provincial Disparities

Table 1 presents data relating to provincial-income- disparity "relatives" for 1991. The first four columns are the components of an identity:

$$\frac{Y}{P} \equiv \frac{Y}{E} \cdot \frac{E}{LF} \cdot \frac{LF}{P} \tag{1}$$

where Y/P =   gross domestic (provincial) product per capita;

       E/LF = the employment rate, where E is employment and LF is the labour force. This equals unity minus the unemployment rate;

       LF/P = the labour force as a proportion of total population. Essentially, this is the product of the participation rate, LF/LFA (where LFA is the labour-force-age population) and the dependency ratio, LFA/P (where the differences between LFA and P relates to those not of labour-force age, i.e., children and elderly).

       Y/E = gross provincial product per employed person, E (where Y/E is derived residually).

Newfoundland has a Y/P ratio of only 65 percent of the national average (or only 55 percent of Alberta's Y/P) because its ratios for columns (2) through (4) are also well below the national average. After the operation of the transfer system, however, Newfoundland's relative disparity improves to 83 percent of the national average (column 8). As the last row of the table indicates, the high-low ratio drops from 1.80 for Y/P to less than half (i.e., 1.35) for PDI[1]/P. Some details relating to the operations of the transfer system appear in the last four columns of the table. For example, the ratio of transfers and government expenditures as a percent of wages and salaries exceed 100 percent in New-foundland, P.E.I., and Saskatchewan (column 12) and would include more provinces if the wages and salaries component of G were removed from the denominator in columns (12) and (13).

Were one to go into more analytical detail relating to the methodology underpinning Table 1 (Canadian Labour Market 1990; Courchene 1994), I think that the following observations/implications could be drawn:

- The degree of regional disparity evident in Table 1 is not new. As the CLMPC analysis indicates, these disparities have long been with us. To be sure, there has been some convergence, but the CLMPC chalks this up to the increasing role of government in the postwar period (1990, p. 36). On the other hand, two provinces (P.E.I. and Newfoundland) now have levels of Personal Income greater than GDP and this was not true in the early 1980s. What else has altered is that Saskatchewan and Manitoba now appear to have entrenched themselves in the "have-not" group, whereas a decade ago Saskatchewan was in the "have" group in the sense of being ineligible for equalization.

- Analytically, it is hard to escape the conclusion that the operations of the interprovincial and interpersonal transfer system have generated a "policy-induced equilibrium" in terms of the provincial characteristics relating to unemployment and output.

- A comparison with the Australian data (Courchene 1993b; 1994) indicates that the disparities across Australian states reveal almost no divergence in unemployment rates (E/LF) and overall participation rates (LF/P). And in terms of income per capita, the Australian high-low ratio is 1.30 compared with 1.80 for Canada. The comparable Australian data is reproduced as an Appendix to this chapter). While much more research needs to be done to draw firm conclusions from a Canadian and Australian comparison, it is instructive to note that, on the one hand, Australia has a commitment to equality and to an equalization system that is at least on par with Canada's but, on the other, it has no equivalent to our unemployment insurance program (see the Appendix) and very little in the way of explicit regional policy. In any event, the Australian data indicate that regional transfer dependency does not automatically follow from the pursuit of a generous social contract which, in turn, lends support to the argument that Canadian provincial/regional disparities reflect a policy-induced equilibrium.

- One can debate whether this pattern of provincial disparities was sustainable within "old Canada," namely within the framework where we were resource rentiers and running an east-west economy behind tariff walls. As I later will argue, this old Canada is gone and the issue of sustainability has come to the fore.

- Complicating all of this is that the industrial heartland is now reeling. To be sure, the collapse of the centre embodies a significant cyclical component, but the forecasts are for a low-employment-growth recovery.

If they have not yet done so, the have-not provinces should view all of this with alarm. The underlying issues here transcend the viability and affordability of the interprovincial/interregional transfer system; with Ottawa's unilateral fiscal hit on Ontario under the Canada Assistance Plan, issues relating to "willingness" and "desirability" of the existing transfer system are not far from the surface.

Intergenerational Economic Cleavages.

Not too long ago our collective wisdom predicted a rosy future for Canada's younger generations. Their cohorts were relatively small so that what awaited them was higher-than-normal wages and employment prospects. The exact opposite is now turning out to be the case and while this too reflects, in part, the cyclical downturn, the expectation is that lower wages and employment prospects will more likely be their fate.

To be sure, this challenge is not unique to Canada (Courchene 1993*b*). U.S. Senator Daniel Moynihan has noted that this is the first generation of Americans where the elderly are better off than the young. This observation may not carry fully over to Canada, but the trend is certainly in this direction. (See the paper by Vaillancourt in this volume.) This is disturbing because the ongoing under-funding (in terms of skills formation) of our youth is occurring in precisely the time frame when we all recognize that human capital formation and skills development are the key to their and our continued economic prosperity. But this is not the end of the story since the massive debt overhangs imply that we are also saddling the young with a very substantial negative fiscal dowry. In an era where the elderly will be more numerous and more wealthy, this is a recipe for disaster. In a thought-provoking book, *Selfish Generations?*, New Zealander David Thomson (1991) argues that the welfare state in his country has been hijacked by a single cohort — the soon-to-be goldenagers. Likewise, this scenario may not apply fully to Canada, but the message is clear. If, in a knowledge-intensive world, we underinvest in the young and at the same time burden them with paying the bills for our past and current consumption then we should not be surprised if, when their interests vest, they opt to renege on the intergeneration transfers that underpin aspects of our social contract.

To illustrate aspects of the underlying issue, allow me to focus on two specific examples. The first relates to the entitlement nature of our society and it involves my own sector, the universities. Tenured faculty (largely males) in virtually all universities have either instigated or supported a policy of prefer-ential hiring for women and minorities. The result is massive intergenerational discrimination of young (white) males by older tenured males. This is done in an incredibly clever and politically-correct way; young males cannot hope to advance their own interests because this means arguing against restoring gender balance. Moreover, this approach directs attention away from the real issue — tenure. In this Charter era, there is neither rhyme nor reason for tenure. Ten-year (not tenure) contracts, with provisions for renewal, would be far more appro-priate. Yet we in the academy are attempting to use the Charter to lobby for extending our entitlements even further through elimination of mandatory retirement. Thus, while the private sector is restructuring to stay alive, the university sector is intent on preserving and extending sinecures and in the process ensuring that the current generation of university students is deprived of full access to state-of-the-art ideas. Without too much difficulty, this inter-generational entitlement warfare can be extended to the rest of the public sector.

The other example relates to the operations of the Canada Pension Plan (and the QPP as well, but I will focus only on the CPP). A recent study from the Centre of Public Sector Studies of the University of Victoria by Lam, Prince and Cutt (1993) notes that the contribution rates of 1990 could support an annual CPP payment of $1,464 if one assumed an average life span of 80 years. But the 1990 CPP for a person with average income was $6,675, for an annual shortfall of $5,211 per pensioner. The authors calculate the equilibrium contribution rates required to finance the existing pension levels in real terms is in the order of 16 percent. (Note that the equilibrium contribution rate would be reduced to 8 percent if CPP assets were invested at average rates of return obtained by private sector funds rather than turned over to the provinces at federal government bond rates.) Thus, whereas most of my generation will receive our CPP on the basis of a contribution rate in the range of say 3.6 percent to 5 percent, the next generation can look forward to a 16 percent contribution rate for the *same real benefit levels*.[2] But this is not the end of the story. With the spotty employment record of many of the young generation, it is likely that a goodly number of them will end up qualifying, at retirement, for more like one-half of a full CPP. As I have indicated elsewhere (1994), this will not mean one additional cent for the future pensioner living in Ontario because the entire half-CPP will be taxed away by GIS and Ontario's GAINS. This is a ticking societal time-bomb. It borders on the immoral, let alone on the inequitable. We are depressing the *current* income prospects of the young with these incredible payroll taxes with little to look forward on their part in terms of *future* (retirement) income benefits.

As noted earlier, this is a recipe for reneging on the implicit intergenerational social contract or, alternatively, for a dramatic opening of our borders to young immigrants who will share in the task of providing entitlements to the older generation. More to the point, this is yet another aspect of the unsustainability of the existing social envelope.

This focus on aspects of non-viability of our social policy framework has been cast largely, but not entirely, in the context of "old Canada," i.e., without reference to the sweeping nature of changes in the society and economy arising from globalization and the information/knowledge revolution. In this "new Canada," the challenges to the social-policy status quo are magnified dramatically, as the next section demonstrates.

THE NEW GLOBAL ORDER

With globalization and the knowledge/information revolution, the world is in the throes of one of its epic transformations. The knowledge/information revolution will have impacts on the role of human capital not unlike the impact of the industrial revolution on the role of physical capital. Figures 1 and 2 attempt to distill the range of influences on the social envelope of globalization and the knowledge/information revolution respectively. Lest readers tend to assign undue credence to material embodied in tables, I have subtitled both Figures with a subjective *tour d'horizon*.

The thrust of these Figures is that sustainability and competitiveness in this new global order requires nothing less than a wholesale rethinking not only of the social envelope but of the relationship between the individual and the state. As noted in Figure 2, this ought to spell the end of "geography" as a defining principle in the federal government's approach to political economy. While there is obviously a role for an equalization program (which I interpret to be part of "people prosperity"), the federal government should remove all "equal-izing" aspects from other programs.[3] That is, we should put all the equalization into one explicit program. To the extent that "place prosperity" is pursued, this should be advanced by provincial governments (as recommended by the Macdonald Royal Commission), subject to some agreed-upon definitions of an internal economic and social union.

In the previous section, the restructuring focus related largely to the fact that aspects of the old order were becoming increasingly unsustainable. The essence of the message in Figures 1 and 2 is quite different — a new vision of social policy is essential in order for Canada to regain its competitive edge as well as to ensure that all Canadians have the opportunity to develop their human capital potential so as to become effective citizens in the new global order. In other words, straightforward paring down of the existing social envelope cannot be the end of the story: a restructured social envelope is of the essence in an era where knowledge and information are at the cutting edge of competitiveness. As Figure 2 suggests, social policy is, in key areas, becoming indistinguishable from economic policy.

A related thrust (which appears in the lower part of Figure 2) is that this new social order may well involve a reshuffling of powers, *de facto* or *de jure*. In particular, since Canada's competitiveness is in the balance, it is only natural that there will be national, if not federal, dimensions to those social programs that relate to competitiveness, regardless of what the constitution may say. Whether this national or federal dimension will be one of leadership

FIGURE 1:   Globalization and Social Policy: A Subjective *Tour d'horizon*

A: General Implications

- At its most basic level, globalization is the internationalization of production. Even at this level, it represents a severe challenge to social policy because welfare states in all countries were geared, incentive-wise, to their respective national production machines. What is the optimal nature of the social policy envelope when production is international?

- It is the international private sector that is globalizing, not the international public sector. Thus, economic space is transcending political space. In countervail fashion, some functions of the economic nation state are being passed upward (FTA, NAFTA, Europe 1992, Bank for International Settlements).

- Power is also flowing downward both to citizens (Figure 2) and to international cities since it is largely via the latter that "institutions" are globalizing. The European regional science literature now focuses on the "regional-international" interface and not only the national/international interface, i.e., economic regions are cross-cutting traditional political boundaries.

- Globalization as represented by free trade pacts has other social-policy implications. With freer markets, delivering social policy via cross-subsidization is more difficult. Distributional (i.e. tax-transfer) instruments, not allocative instruments, must now deliver social policy. This is a welcome development.

- Relatedly, with the spread of FTAs, whether in Europe or America, social policy issues are coming under the rubric of competition policy — hence, the increasing use of the term "social dumping."

B: Canadian Relevance

- As trade increasingly flows north-south, Canada will cease to be a single economy, but rather a series of north-south, cross-border economies. What will then bind us east-west is more of a social policy railway than an economic policy railway. The emerging challenge is how to mount an east-west transfer system over an increasing north-south trading system.

- In particular, the political economy of transfers will alter. When the second-round spending effects of equalization and interregional transfers tend to go south, rather than back to the "golden triangle," how will this alter Canadians' (or Ontarians') taste for transfers?

- In an increasing number of areas, a central vision emanating from the centre will no longer be acceptable — the regions will be too economically diverse in that the requirements for a Great Lakes economy like Ontario will differ from those for a Pacific Rim economy like British Columbia. Part of the solution will likely be one or all of greater decentralization, greater asymmetry and greater east-west flexibility (including wage flexibility).

FIGURE 2:   The Information/Knowledge Revolution and Social Policy:
             A Subjective *Tour d'horizon*

- The informatics revolution is inherently decentralizing in that individuals can now access, transform, transmit and manipulate data and information in ways that governments at all levels are powerless to prevent. This will make old-style governance more difficult for governments of all stripes.
- With knowledge at the cutting edge of competitiveness, aspects of social policy become indistinguishable from economic policy. Regardless of what the constitution may say, it is inconceivable that the federal government will be relegated to the sidelines in terms of social policy if national competitiveness is at stake.
- Drucker's predictions (1986) are holding up well — the manufacturing sector is becoming uncoupled from the resource sector (i.e., GNP is becoming less raw-material intensive) and, within manufacturing, production is becoming uncoupled from employment. The latest version of the latter is the prediction for a low-employment-growth recovery.
- Despite our generous resource endowment, Canada cannot avoid making the transition from a resource-based economy and society to a knowledge-based economy and society. Further success in the resource areas will progressively require the application of knowledge and high-value-added techniques.
- The middle class in this new era will include versions of technologists and information analysts. But we don't do this. We remain a professional society (as do most Anglo-American countries). Hence, the disappearing middle class. Social policy has a critical role to play in this inevitable shift from boards and mortar to mortar boards.
- In tandem with globalization, the knowledge/information revolution is altering much of the old order:
  - interregional transfers will have to tilt from "place prosperity" to "people prosperity." To the extent that place prosperity remains important, it ought to be a provincial not a federal matter.
  - there is emerging the notion of a global "maximum wage" for certain activities. Wages beyond this maximum wage will shift the activity offshore. As Drucker (1993) notes, this is a powerful argument for "contracting out," i.e., to enhance the productivity of these activities.
  - This is turning the original *BNA Act* on its head. Some of the line functions like forestry, fishing, mining, and energy can and probably should be devolved to the provinces (in any event they will continue to be driven by global imperatives) and some of the traditional provincial areas such as education and training will have to take on national, if not federal, dimensions. Since not all provinces will be able or willing to take down these areas, asymmetry will likely increase.
  - We will witness, if we are not already witnessing, an exciting and, to some, a bewildering set of provincial experiments across the full range of the social envelope. Ottawa's role is to provide the framework within which this experimentation can take place and to ensure that there is information with respect to the successes and the failures. In the same way that Saskatchewan's experimentation led to Medicare a quarter of a century ago the ongoing process is, Schumpeterian-like, creating or re-creating key elements of our new social order.

(i.e., standards, portability etc.) or whether it will involve a legislative role will depend on a range of issues dealt with later in this paper.

To this point in the analysis, there has been no explicit mention of "cutting" social programs. Rather, the emphasis has been on restructuring. However, the ongoing reality is one of squeezing the social envelope by means of a series of caps, freezes, and ceilings to the set of federal-provincial transfers. This is the focus of the next section.

FISCAL FEDERALISM

Table 2 presents estimates of the annual and cumulative "losses" arising from federal "offloading" with respect to EPF and CAP over the period 1986-87 to the present and, indeed, to 1994-95. This table was compiled by the Canadian Teachers Federation and I selected it, rather than others, because of its higher values for deficit offloading. The table assumes as the benchmark the regime in place as of 1985-86. The estimated "losses" result from any and all changes to EPF and CAP since then. For EPF, these changes include the shift from GNP growth as the escalator to GNP – 2 percent, then GNP – 3 percent and finally the freeze on EPF (except for population growth) from 1990-91 through to 1994-95. On the CAP side, the critical change was of course capping the growth of CAP transfers at 5 percent for the three have provinces, Ontario, British Columbia, and Alberta.

The cumulative "losses" for EPF are nearly $27 billion, spread across provinces on roughly an equal-per-capita basis. The CAP "losses" total $8.5 billion, with Ontario bearing $6.8 billion, B.C. bearing $1.5 billion with a quarter-billion loss for Alberta. Were one to add the equalization program to Table 2, this would add another $3 billion or so to the "losses" for the have-not provinces, largely as a result of the application of the equalization ceiling in 1989-90 ($1.4 billion) and 1990-91 ($1.1 billion), based on Department of Finance numbers.

Given that the resulting grand total is somewhere in the range of $40 billion, what is one to make of these numbers? The first general point is that they are wholly arbitrary in the sense that the benchmark is arbitrary. For example, were one to benchmark the table in the early 1950s (i.e., *before* the devolution of income tax points), the cumulative totals through to 1994-95 would clearly be hugely *positive*.

Another approach to benchmarking would be to include as "losses" only those shortfalls resulting from arbitrary federal actions *within* any given five-year fiscal arrangement period. Implicitly, at least, this appears to be the approach adopted by Boothe and Johnston (1993). The argument here would be

TABLE 2: Downloading Federal Deficits: Estimated Losses ($ Millions) in Federal Transfers to the Provinces and Territories, 1986-87 to 1994-95[p]

Year		Nfld.	P.E.I.	N.S.	N.B.	Que.	Ont.	Man.	Sask.	Alta.	B.C.	Yuk.	N.W.T.	Canada
1986-87	EPF	$ 7.1	$ 1.6	$ 10.9	$ 8.9	$ 81.5	$ 113.6	$ 13.3	$ 12.6	$ 29.6	$ 36.0	$ 0.3	$ 0.7	$ 315.9
	CAP	-	-	-	-	-	-	-	-	-	-	-	-	-
1987-88	EPF	15.0	3.4	23.2	18.9	174.5	245.3	28.6	26.9	62.9	77.4	0.6	1.4	678.2
	CAP	-	-	-	-	-	-	-	-	-	-	-	-	-
1988-89	EPF	23.9	5.4	37.0	30.0	279.0	396.2	45.5	42.6	100.3	125.2	1.1	2.2	1,088.4
	CAP	-	-	-	-	-	-	-	-	-	-	-	-	-
1989-90	EPF	33.9	7.7	52.8	42.7	398.1	570.0	64.6	59.8	144.2	181.2	1.5	3.1	1,559.6
	CAP	-	-	-	-	-	-	-	-	-	-	-	-	-
1990-91	EPF	67.8	15.5	106.9	86.2	811.4	1,172.3	129.8	118.6	297.5	379.2	3.2	6.7	3,195.0
	CAP	-	-	-	-	-	389.5	-	-	0.0	36.2	-	-	425.7
1991-92	EPF	90.0	20.4	142.6	116.1	1,099.0	1,629.0	172.4	156.5	403.4	524.9	4.5	9.5	4,368.1
	CAP	-	-	-	-	-	1,166.4	-	-	41.5	142.4	-	-	1,350.3
1992-93	EPF	100.4	22.5	159.7	129.5	1,232.5	1,835.7	192.2	173.9	455.5	597.9	5.2	10.8	4,915.7
	CAP	-	-	-	-	-	1,714.8	-	-	63.6	306.3	-	-	2,084.7
1993-94	EPF	103.0	23.1	164.0	132.9	1,269.6	1,904.3	196.9	177.4	473.4	622.1	5.4	11.2	5,083.4
	CAP	-	-	-	-	-	1,700.0	-	-	66.7	506.8	-	-	2,273.5
1994-95	EPF	111.3	25.1	178.4	144.1	1,384.9	2,094.2	214.7	193.2	521.8	684.3	6.0	12.2	5,570.1
	CAP	-	-	-	-	-	1,785.3	-	-	70.0	532.2	-	-	2,387.5
Total 1986-87 to 1994-95														
	EPF	552.5	124.7	875.6	709.1	6,730.5	9,960.3	1,058.0	961.4	2,488.7	3,228.2	27.8	57.7	26,774.5
	CAP	-	-	-	-	-	6,756.1	-	-	241.8	1,523.9	-	-	8,521.8

[p] Projected

Notes:
1. EPF: Established Programs Financing. The figure includes both health and postsecondary education and is the sum of both cash and tax points. Losses in EPF are calculated using 1985-86 as the base year. Cumulative losses due to restraints prior to 1986-87 are not included.
2. CAP: Canada Assistance Plan. This was capped at 5 percent for Ontario, Alberta, and British Columbia for 1990-91 to 1994-95 inclusively.
3. Totals may not add up due to rounding.
4. Nominal GNP growth was assumed to be as follows: 1993: 5.7 percent and 1994: 6.0 percent.
5. The federal share of total CAP shareable expenses were assumed to be constant from 1992-93 to 1994-95 for Alberta and from 1993-94 and 1994-95 for Ontario and British Columbia.

Sources: Department of Finance, Established Programs Financing, relevant issues. Department of Finance, unpublished information. Statistics Canada, Population Projections 1990-2011 Based on Recent Changes in Fertility Levels and Revised Immigration Targets, December 1991, unpublished information. Various Ministries of Treasury and Economics, unpublished information. Conference Board, *Provincial Outlook*, Winter 1993.

Reproduced from CTF (1993, Table 10).

that the parameters for each five-year set of arrangements are "negotiated" and that offloading should be defined by federal arbitrary changes within the five-year term that depart from these negotiated agreements. It is probably not necessary to add that this interpretation would not sit well with the provinces.

A third way to approach these numbers is to exclude as "losses" those shortfalls that are not the result of arbitrary initiatives. Arguably, this would exclude equalization payments, since the provision for the equalization ceiling was introduced in 1982-83, although it only became binding during the 1987-92 fiscal arrangements period.[4] While on the subject of equalization, one might note that the reason that the ceiling became binding in the 1989-91 period had more to do with what was happening in Ontario (spiralling revenues as a result of the prolonged boom and some major tax hikes) than what was happening in the have-not provinces.

A fourth general point that one might make in the context of Table 2 is that the provinces could not have expected to have avoided the federal government's deficit concerns. The issue would then become one of whether the treatment of EPF, for example, was more stringent than the federal government applied to those areas of social policy under its own jurisdiction. On this score, Ottawa was reasonably consistent:

- the indexation of family allowances was reduced to inflation minus 3 percent in 1986. Now that family allowances have been folded into the new child tax credit (1993), this tax credit will also be subject to indexation only by the amount of inflation over 3 percent. Note that this is more restrictive than a GNP – 3 percent escalator;

- While Ottawa had to abort its attempt to partially index OAS/GIS in 1989, it introduced a full clawback of OAS for the elderly rich;

- UI maximum benefits were reduced in 1990 from 46-50 weeks to 35-50 weeks and the qualifying period was increased from 10-14 to 10-20 weeks. In 1993, UI maximum benefits were reduced from 60 percent to 57 percent of insurable earnings. By itself, this latter measure is a 5 percent reduction (on a continuing basis) in what UI benefits would otherwise have been.

Given that all the "losses" arising from EPF in Table 2 relate to decreases in the EPF escalator (i.e., a move towards partial indexation), this was not all that different from Ottawa's moves towards partial indexing for some of its own programs. Indeed, while the EPF freeze embodies *zero* indexing, the fact that GNP has not exceeded 3 percent recently implies that the effective impact is not much different than that which would have prevailed under a continuation of a GNP – 3 percent escalator.[5]

Boothe and Johnston (1993) also adopt this framework and define off-loading as decreases (in percentage terms) in transfers to the provinces that exceed decreases in Ottawa's other programs. They introduce a further twist: transfers to the provinces should be defined only to include the cash component, since the tax-point components are in effect provinces' own revenues.[6] Under this combined approach, Boothe and Johnston still find that there has been considerable offloading, but at a much reduced rate than would be obtained from a Table 2 methodology.

My fifth general comment on Table 2 relates to the Canada Assistance Plan. Not since the National Energy Program has there been a federal initiative as destructive to the integrity of federal-provincial fiscal relations as the cap on CAP. One can visualize what may have triggered this. Ontario was embarking on a substantial enriching of its welfare system and unless Ottawa took some counter initiative it would be dragged along for half the cost in the very time frame that it was pursuing (at least rhetorically) deficit control. Including all three have provinces within the cap provides some "rationale" for the measure,[7] but it is evident that the real target was Ontario (and the figures in Table 2 bear this out). The dollars involved are very substantial. Indeed, the annual shortfall this year is not far off the province's savings from the imposition of its "social contract."

More importantly, this does not auger well for the future of the fiscal arrangements. Ontario is already on record as warning Ottawa that a failure to restore Ontario to parity with the rest of the provinces could "dissipate" the support for equalization and the interregional transfer system generally (Ontario 1992). This could be a tall order, given that achieving parity for the three have provinces, at least under existing arrangements, will involve over $2 billion annually in additional transfers (see the CAP total for 1993-94 in Table 2). While some of the Liberals elected in the Toronto area argued during the campaign for a restoration of the old CAP arrangements, it is difficult to envision this as a Liberal priority, given that it would absorb the entire "savings" from the helicopter contract cancellation within three years. More on the CAP dilemma later.

Summarizing to this point, while the data in Table 2 are correct in a technical sense, they probably exaggerate federal offloading in the broader political economy context. On the other hand, the above comments relating to alternative interpretations of the numbers probably go too far in the direction of minimizing the impact. While there is probably no consensus or middle ground here, it must certainly be the case that there has been substantial federal offloading. More-over, the issue relates not just to the dollars involved but as well to the arbitrary and sudden nature of these federal initiatives. Provincial finance ministers are

DOUGLAS COLLEGE LIBRARY

left with precious little in the way of lead time to adjust to these negative fiscal shocks. Note also that this deficit shifting and lack of lead time also applies to a broader range of federal fiscal hits than those associated with federal-provincial transfers. For example, Ottawa's decision to clawback OAS payments for the elderly rich represents a significant tax loss to the provinces. This is so because under the old system OAS payments were part of income for tax purposes and the provinces received something like one-third of the total taxes raised against OAS incomes. Under the new system, the clawback goes to Ottawa and, once fully clawed back, OAS ceases to be part of income. Given that future retirees will at the same time be more numerous and more wealthy, this will represent a progressively more significant provincial fiscal hit. One can, of course, point out that since OAS payments come from Ottawa, it does make sense that the clawback should also go to Ottawa and not be shared with the provinces. In a sense, the logic here is impeccable. But the political economy is quite different: these and other sorts of "sweeteners" to the provinces were part and parcel of the system that led to our shared personal income tax system, one that is at the same time both harmonized and decentralized and generally held up as a model system for a decentralized federation.

Generalized offloading (directly through transfer caps and freezes or indirectly by removing sweeteners such as the previous treatment of OAS and family benefits) could well lead to a fraying of the Tax Collection Agreements and a tendency for other provinces (or groups of provinces) to follow Quebec in establishing a separate personal income tax system, or at least to insist on a switch from the current "tax on tax" approach to a "tax on base" approach which would allow rate and bracket freedom for the provinces' share of the joint personal-income-tax system. (This point is also made in the contribution by Gorbet in this volume). Cast in this somewhat broader framework, the issue of generalized offloading is more than a social policy issue for the provinces. It is a fiscal integrity and fiscal autonomy issue.

Pursuing this latest theme, were one discussing federal transfers a few years ago, the key issue would have been one of sorting out the implications that would arise when the cash component of EPF fell to zero. Because Quebec opted to receive an extra 8.5 personal income tax points in lieu of cash transfers for hospital insurance, Quebec's cash was expected to fall to zero sometime in the mid to late 1990s. The severity of the recession (and, in particular, the collapse of personal income) probably means that the zero-cash-transfer eventuality has been pushed into the millennium. Nonetheless, the combination of a shift to a "tax on base" approach coupled with a receipt of an additional 8.5 personal income tax points (i.e., parity with Quebec)[8] has surfaced as a desirable option for the provinces, on both fiscal autonomy and predictability grounds.

THE TRANSFER/RESTRUCTURING NEXUS

Now that I have focused in turn on the restructuring imperative and, albeit briefly, on the fiscal-federalism or deficit-shifting developments, it is appropriate to explore the relationship between the two.

To begin, I think that I am on rather safe ground by asserting that fiscal stringency will continue to be the order of the day. Indeed, the projected fiscal deficits for this fiscal year for both Ottawa and Queen's Park are already recognized as being far too optimistic and, since the forecasting error arises largely because of a revenue shortfall, this presumably carries over to the other provinces as well. With a year or so remaining in terms of the EPF freeze, the provincial finances are bound to be under continued and even enhanced pressure. This, then, is the backdrop to the discussion of the relationship between fiscal federalism and social policy restructuring.

Let me now shift to more shaky ground and proclaim, subject to an important caveat to be aired later, my personal support, thus far at least, for the ongoing degree of fiscal stringency embodied in the federal-provincial transfers (although not necessarily for the form it has taken, especially in terms of CAP). My rationale here is related in part to a recent article by Chandler (1993). She notes that the private sector has spent most of the last decade engaged in dramatic restructuring. To a degree, the federal government has also got into the game by restructuring aspects of both the economy (e.g., the FTA and the GST) and its own fiscal house (e.g., personal and corporate tax reform, the GST, expenditure control). Chandler's answer to her implicit question, "Guess who's turn it is now?" is, not surprisingly once one poses such a question, "the provinces." The catalyst for this provincial restructuring is, of course, the fiscal crisis:

> The severity of the recession, combined with the restructuring in the private sector and restraints on federal transfers, dealt a heavy blow to provincial governments. Tax revenues fell way shy of expectations, and the cost of providing welfare and other social services soared, with the result that provincial deficits ballooned. The combined provincial deficit rose from $4.8 billion in 1989/90 to $24.7 billion in 1992/93. The combined provincial debt has risen in tandem, from $119 billion in 1989/90 to $186 billion in 1992/93. (Chandler 1993, p. 3)

In the face of such a fiscal crunch, the obvious, indeed rational, first response by the provinces will be to appeal to Ottawa to ratchet up transfer payments. Were Ottawa to cave in, the result would be to forestall meaningful restructuring. After all, the provincial public sectors spent the decade of the 1980s believing themselves largely immune from the traumatic dislocations taking place in the private sector. How many IBMs and GMs must be brought to their knees before the provinces begin to question the effectiveness and efficiency of the university sector (particularly Nova Scotia with its dozen or so institutions), or of the university/community college interface (e.g., Ontario, where they exist as two solitudes) or of the transition from school to work (in all provinces)? Restructuring is inevitable and essential, and I view the pressure coming from the federal-provincial transfer system as both message and messenger in this process. This said, however, there is a limit in terms of how far Ottawa can push the provinces. Surely, all governments should now realize that a strategy of fundamental restructuring must dominate an offloading strategy.

This last concern relates to the above-mentioned caveat, namely the possibility that the fiscal overhang at the provincial level will lead primarily to social policy cost-cutting rather than fundamental restructuring. What happened in the private sector in the 1980s may be instructive here. The early 1980s restructuring agenda was essentially aborted because of the combination of (a) the booming U.S. domestic economy reflecting Reagan's "military Keynesianism" (tax cuts and defence expenditures); (b) the fall in the Canadian dollar to the low 70 cent range; and (c) the willingness of the Americans to tolerate massive balance-of-payments deficits. In tandem, these factors restored *temporary* viability to our industrial status quo. However, when the restructuring finally came, it was nothing short of brutal since it involved not only this foregone or aborted restructuring but as well the adjustment to the FTA and to the macro parameters (the GST and the pursuit of zero inflation which sent the dollar up to 89 cents). That it would have been preferable to pace this adjustment more evenly over the decade is, I think, not in doubt, but it is somewhat irrelevant from the vantage point of 1993. Even were one to argue that the fiscal crisis for the provincial sector is roughly analogous to an 89 cent dollar for the private sector, there are at least two differences between the provincial and private sector restructuring processes that generate cause for concern. The first is that there are no markets as such in the provincial public sector and, as economists, we know very little about the "triggers" and processes of major institutional change. I doubt that political scientists know much more, but hopefully they do. Second, and relatedly, because of the jurisdictional overlap in the social envelope, no amount of fiscal squeezing of the provinces can generate meaningful restructuring unless Ottawa is also willing to commit itself to major structural initiatives. To be sure, Ottawa has introduced some welcome changes in family benefits and elderly benefits, but thus far it has been singularly unwilling to make meaningful structural changes to the critical area of UI and its relationship to welfare, training and labour force re-entry. If this continues to be the framework within which the federal government is exerting fiscal pressure on the provinces, then there is a danger that the result will be social policy erosion rather than social policy restructuring. Indeed, I will go much further here: this is unconscionable behaviour[9] on the federal government's part because pressuring the provinces on the fiscal front without at the same time recognizing that Ottawa itself holds the key to unlocking the system in a manner consistent with the dictates of a global/information society will inevitably lead to a grinding down of social Canada and an acceptance, willy nilly, of an American vision and version of social policy.

This critical caveat aside, it is instructive to focus on what is in fact occurring at the provincial level. While cost-cutting is now the order of the day, most of these initiatives also embody aspects of "creative destruction" or restructuring across a very wide range of policies. Quebec is, I think, the acknowledged leader here, whether in terms of a holistic approach to health and welfare or in terms of creative approaches (including wage supplementation) to the welfare-work transition. This should not come as a surprise, since this province has, since 1976 and probably since 1960, embodied a vision of a society where fiscal, cultural, financial, and even economic policy has been geared to weaning itself from dependency on Ottawa. Note that in this process, it still makes eminent sense for the province to ensure that it gets (more than?) its fair share of any federal favours and largesse. In its quest for greater control over "social Quebec," I think that the province is helped substantially by having its own income tax system which, because of its additional tax-point transfers, accounts for roughly one-half of income taxes paid by Quebecers. Control over the parameters of an income tax system is a powerful device for coordinating and integrating the social envelope. This is not meant as an argument for extending the Quebec approach to other provinces, especially since Quebec is marching to the beat of a different drummer. But it may be a strong argument for granting the provinces greater flexibility under the existing shared personal income tax (Courchene and Stewart 1991).

Quebec aside, virtually all provinces have embarked on significant initiatives that fall somewhere between cost-cutting and restructuring: Alberta's stripping away of parliamentarians' pensions and its rather draconian across-the-board expenditure cuts and controls; Saskatchewan's closing of 52 hospitals, one of which was never opened; Ontario's "social contract," following upon somewhat similar controls over the civil service in Newfoundland, etc. Some of this is clearing restructuring — for example, implicit in the social contract legislation is that the combination of wages/job security has placed civil servants in a privileged position vis-à-vis the private sector. And Saskatchewan's hospital closings can hardly fall solely in the cost-cutting category. Were the truth to be told, most should never have been opened. Perhaps this is why Romanow's popularity still remains in the 40 percent range.

However, it is New Brunswick that, thus far at least, has taken the lead in terms of overall restructuring. Among the features of "NB Works," as the program is called, is the shift from passive income support towards what the Europeans would call an "active society" — education, training, etc., that comingles UI/welfare/training, Ottawa and New Brunswick, and the public and private sectors. The other major initiative on the horizon is Ontario's "Turning Point," namely the blueprint for a fresh approach towards welfare which foresees both workfare and a shift towards a negative-income-tax approach for children of low-income families.

I revert back to rather safe ground in suggesting that these initiatives represent but the tip of the iceberg in terms of what one can expect in the future. More to the point, however, the system is embracing a mentality that recognizes the inevitability, even desirability, of fundamental restructuring. In this sense, off-loading has been successful and the time has come for governments to abandon their internal tug of war and jointly embark on the restructuring imperative. How might the fiscal arrangements, and particularly the set of federal-provincial transfers, fit into all of this? In order to address this, it is useful to take an analytical view of these transfers.

INTERGOVERNMENTAL TRANSFERS AND HORIZONTAL/VERTICAL IMBALANCE

Given the unconditional nature of EPF, equalization and, for the three have provinces, parts of CAP as well, these transfers are no longer closely related to the financing of the social programs.[10] Rather, they are best viewed as measures designed to mitigate the vertical and horizontal imbalances in the federation. Since these transfers for 1992-93 range from $994 per capita in Alberta to $2,276 in P.E.I., one could argue that $994 represents the per capita transfer directed towards restoring vertical imbalance with the excess for any province representing the contribution towards restoring horizontal imbalance.

The rationale for these vertical transfers is to ameliorate the situation where the provinces' share of overall expenditures exceeds their share of overall revenues. A secondary role for these transfers (though important in the eyes of many Canadians) is to allow the federal government to exert some "national" control over the social envelope, e.g., portability, preservation of the economic union, the *Canada Health Act* requirements. However, there are alternative ways to address this vertical imbalance issue.

At one end of the spectrum would be the elimination of the vertical imbalance by transferring additional tax points to the provinces. Several analysts have proposed that the cash component of EPF (or at least that associated with health) be converted to a tax-point transfer. In the limit, one could conceive of the disappearance of federal-provincial cash transfers, except for the equalization program.

At the opposite end of the spectrum, one can envisage sorting out vertical balance by an enhancement of Ottawa's expenditure responsibilities. This approach, too, has some adherents: elsewhere (1993a) I have argued that Ottawa could replace CAP transfers with a direct negative-income-tax-type transfer to children and could convert the PSE component of EPF to a system of portable PSE vouchers to students.

The middle ground here would be to perpetuate the existing set of transfers, albeit with some changes in the direction of enhancing their predictability both within and between the five-year agreements.

How ought one to choose among these alternatives? My position on this issue is that the time has finally come to rethink and restructure the social programs from the perspective of those who may have to fall back on them, that is from the vantage point of individual Canadians and not from the vantage points of the various governments. What this means is that fiscal federalism issues must become *derivative, not determining*, in terms of the future of the social programs.[11] The remainder of the chapter is directed towards elaborating on aspects of this option. Prior to addressing the many issues involved in such an option, I want to devote some time to the issues relating to horizontal imbalance, i.e., to the equalization program.

EQUALIZATION AND THE SOCIAL ENVELOPE

Section 36(2) of the *Constitution Act, 1982* enshrines the principle of equalization. However, Canada's approach has been to embody equalization in a whole range of programs in addition to the formal equalization program. There are significant and highly distorting equalization components in UI, in terms both of qualifying weeks and benefit weeks. The equal per capita nature of EPF transfers embodies significant equalization because, for example, the costs of delivering health care is significantly more expensive in Ontario than in some other provinces. With the cap on CAP transfers to the have provinces, this program has now been effectively "equalized." I support the Ontario position (Ontario 1992) that all the equalizing aspects of federal-provincial or interprovincial transfers should be combined into a *single* equalization program. Beyond this, there should be no special "geography" or "place-prosperity" aspects to the range of other interregional and intergovernmental transfers.

Turning now to the formal equalization program, there are both equity and efficiency arguments underlying the system. An impressive theoretical literature on these issues now exists, thanks in large measure to Queen's economist Robin Boadway and his colleagues (e.g., Boadway 1992; Boadway and Flatters 1982; Boadway and Hobson 1993). The simplest version of the model begins with the notion that an individual's comprehensive income or benefits is the sum of his/her net private sector income or benefits and net public sector benefits (or NFBs, net fiscal benefits). On efficiency grounds, one would want to ensure that individuals in different provinces who have similar net private sector benefits (or, for simplicity, similar wages) also have similar NFBs. Suppose that this is not the case and, in particular, suppose that residents in a resource-rich province have larger NFBs than residents in other provinces because resource royalties accrue (untaxed by Ottawa) to the province which can then be used to finance the province's expenditures. Given that what matters to individuals is overall or comprehensive income, it would be rational for an individual to migrate to this province at a lower level of net private benefits (a lower wage rate) provided that this was more than compensated by the increase in NFBs. Such migration would be output-diminishing since the individual would be moving to a lower wage (productivity) job. In the literature, this is referred to as rent-seeking or fiscally-induced migration. An equalization program can help equate net fiscal benefits across provinces and, therefore, be efficiency enhancing. Alternatively, under the assumption that provincial ownership of resources is triggering the differential net fiscal benefits, these NFBs could be eliminated if the resource revenues were included (imputed) as income for personal income tax purposes.

There is also a "fiscal equity" rationale for equalization which would require full equalization of NFBs over all provincial revenue sources (broad-based horizontal equity) or full equalization of NFBs over all non-resource-based revenues and only a portion of resource revenues (narrow-based horizontal equity) (Boadway and Hobson 1993, chap. 4). While I support the efficiency rationale for equalization, I have considerable trouble with this "fiscal equity" approach because it seems to impose a unitary-state vision on a federal system. I would rather cast the equity case in terms of either or both a "federal rationale" or a "citizenship (nationhood) rationale."[12] In any event, the constitution now requires us to provide equalization so as to ensure reasonably comparable levels of public services at reasonably comparable rates of taxation. The concerns that I wish to air relate not so much to the theoretical principles as to the manner in which we have applied them in the existing equalization formula. In particular, the notion that the analytics of equalization means that all provinces' revenues should be brought up to the national average level, let alone the level of the top province as is frequently argued, is not correct once one broaches Canadian reality.

Most of the issues I want to raise relate in one way or another to the "standard" for equalization. When equalization was first introduced in 1957, provincial revenues were brought up to the level in the two wealthiest provinces. In 1962 the standard became the national average level, but in 1964 it reverted back to the top two provinces. With the introduction of the comprehensive program in 1967, the national average again became the standard, up until 1982 when the current "five-province" standard was introduced. Most of these changes had to do with the role and impact of resource rents in the system. If this book had been produced in the mid-1980s, there would have been an argument on behalf of the have-not provinces that the five-province standard was inappropriate because it resulted in a lesser amount of equalization than would arise under a national average standard. This is not a big concern today because the five-province and national-average standards are essentially identical. If they diverge again, this issue will surely come to the fore once more.

A more important issue relating to the standard is that there are recurring pressures for equalization to embody both "needs" and "costs." In principle, this is the correct approach. In practice, however, the manner in which some have-not provinces tend to phrase the argument is, in my view, quite inappropriate. This issue arises most frequently in terms of the Canada Assistance Plan. Specifically, given that, say, Newfoundland has a very high unemployment rate, should not this be factored into its level of transfers (either in equalization or in CAP by, for example, having more than 50 percent cost sharing)? My answer here is probably "yes." Newfoundland's per capita CAP transfers are roughly $250. This does seem inadequate to accommodate an unemployment rate in the high teens. But the growth of welfare spending in Newfoundland in the 1980s has been the lowest of all the provinces, in large measure because the province has been able to channel much of its potential welfare burden onto the UI program. The *net* inward flow of UI benefits to Newfoundland in 1991 was roughly $750 million, or about $1,300 per capita. By all means let us take account of "need" in the equalization formula, but we must then *net away* funds from *all* other transfer programs specifically designed to address aspects of this need.[13] It is precisely because we tend to focus program by program, without taking an overall perspective, that the overall transfer system has given rise to aspects of transfer dependency in the first place.

A related issue has to do with introducing "costs" into the equalization formula. We know that, in general, the costs of providing most public services are higher in, say, Ontario than in many other provinces; physician fee schedules are higher; university salaries tend to be higher, particularly for the top echelon of universities; average wage levels for civil servants are higher, etc. Most of this arises because of "capitalization"; the higher incomes in Ontario are capitalized in the value of land, services, etc. Recall that the Americans do not have an equalization program and one of the rationales for its non-existence is that income differences across states are "capitalized," so that there is nothing to equalize, as it were. Hence, one of the leading federal scholars in the U.S., Wallace Oates (1972) is able to claim that equalization programs are a matter of "taste," not of "principle." While I do not accept Oates' view of equalization (and, more importantly, nor does our constitution), it is nonetheless the case that as between P.E.I. and Ontario the impact of capitalization is such that arguments to the effect that equalization must bring P.E.I.'s revenues up to the national average (or the top province, as is favoured in some quarters) in order to provide "reasonably comparable" level of services is not correct. It is a matter of taste, not principle.

Another aspect of the equalization literature is that the appropriate form of equalization ought to be constituted on a "net" rather than a "gross" system, where "net" in this context relates to direct transfers of revenue from have provinces to have-not provinces (as in the German equalization system) and where "gross" refers to the existing system where equalization payments are made from Ottawa's general revenues with no attempt to reduce *actual* revenues accruing to have provinces. Once again, I have no problems with a "net" equalization system and indeed my article with Glen Copplestone (1980) was, I think, the first time that the possibility of an interprovincial revenue-sharing pool for equalization was aired in the Canadian context. What I do have problems with is the notion that the appropriate role of a "net" system is to bring the "rich" provinces down to the level of the "poorest" province (or bring the poorest up to the richest) in terms of access to per capita provincial revenues. This conception of equalization is clearly implicit, if not explicit, in the Boadway *et al* theoretical literature. Setting aside once again whether the concept of horizontal equity underpinning this body of analysis is an appropriate one for a federal nation, the substantive application issue is that this equality of per capita revenues is not called for in practice, as some of the above argumentation was designed to demonstrate.

None of this is intended to downplay the critical role that equalization plays in our system. But it should sound a warning that we might recoil a bit from our national proclivity to equalize here, there, and everywhere. Indeed, we have now reached a point where the existence of equalization payments themselves have been capitalized in land, labour, services, etc. of the have-not provinces.

Not to put too fine a point on this, my view is that we do too much equalization now, not too little.

TOWARDS A NEW SOCIAL ORDER

The socio-economic climate is ripe for meaningful social policy reform since the existing system is grinding down under the combination of the debt/deficit burden and competitive pressures. In a sense, change is no longer the issue. Rather, the issue is a choice between erosion and restructuring. And, to repeat a theme of this chapter, this restructuring must be undertaken from the perspective of citizens, not governments. However, any restructuring agenda must deal with the perennial federal complications on the economic and political fronts. Among the complications, I would include the following:

- Ottawa is likely to achieve fiscal flexibility sooner than the provinces, unless Ottawa expands the transfer system. Along with this flexibility, it is probably the case that Ottawa is poised for some major initiatives in the social policy area. As I argued earlier, now that knowledge is at the core of competitiveness, it is inconceivable that Ottawa will not want to play a leading role in this area. Moreover, an initiative on the apprenticeship front was a key plank in the Liberal's platform. It will not take long for the Liberals to realize that the obvious source of funding for apprenticeship and training is from a major restructuring of the social programs. And as we now know, the former Tories had a blueprint for social policy reform at the ready. Pressures are clearly building in the Ottawa corridors for major restructuring.

- Some provinces are in such dire economic straits that they are probably not far away from inviting Ottawa to take over areas such as welfare. Hence, these provinces would presumably welcome a federal initiative.

- So would most Canadians who, on the issue of restructuring, are well ahead of their political leaders.

- But there are also some provinces who would vigorously resist, and even challenge in the courts any federal intrusion in areas under provincial jurisdiction.

- In some areas like training and apprenticeship, there may be a middle ground: devolution from both Ottawa and the provinces to local boards composed of labour, business, provincial, and federal representatives.

- In other areas, however, asymmetrical solutions will be inevitable. This harkens back to something along the lines of my "concurrency with provincial paramountcy" proposal during the constitution debates (1991). For example,

Ottawa could step in and rationalize the UI/welfare subsystem, but then be willing to let provinces take back the area under some considerations such as respecting the economic and social union. This would be *symmetry in principle* but likely *asymmetry in practice*. I think that the time has come to recognize that asymmetry in practice has always existed and to view some potential further asymmetry in practice as a solution rather than a problem. We cannot expect Ontario to do only what P.E.I. either wants to do or is able to do. Nor can we expect Ottawa to lie dormant unless it obtains the approval of Quebec and Alberta. Some version of concurrency with provincial paramountcy is needed to break through this jurisdictional logjam.

- If we embark on such a restructuring, the likelihood is that the present set of federal-provincial transfers would have to be reworked in a manner consistent with the social policy reform. It is in this sense that I argued earlier that the transfers ought to be viewed as derivative.

Most of the above points relate to process, not to substance. Part of the reason for this is that it is not at all obvious that there even exists an "optimal" social restructuring. Because of this, there is an argument for some degree of flexibility in any new restructuring so that the system can evolve in ways that make sense for the various cross-border economies. Nonetheless, I think that we have to begin to "think the unthinkable" in terms of proposals that are placed before Canadians for debate and discussion. For example, the typical reform proposal for UI is to return it to insurance principles that apply identically across the country. But why not go the further step and ask whether or not both UI and welfare can be replaced by some version of a negative income tax? This would certainly alter what would be appropriate in terms of the fiscal arrangements! Likewise, why not consider ways in which our two subsystems for the elderly (OAS/GIS and CPP/QPP) can be combined into a single program? (See Hamilton and Whalley 1984.)

Perhaps not fully consistent with the above proposals, but certainly also worth placing on the restructuring agenda is the suggestion of converting CAP into some version of a negative income tax for children. This would not be like the existing child tax credit because it would begin to be clawed back at a much lower income level. While my intent here is not to argue for any particular proposal, I do want to direct some attention to this one. There has been much discussion in policy circles to the effect that Ottawa could look after the income-support or social insurance programs for unemployed employables while the provinces would look after the "unable-to-work." However, the line between the two will inevitably be very fuzzy, with the likely result of yet another jurisdictional quagmire. Making Ottawa responsible for the welfare of children (to go along with its responsibility for goldenagers) cuts through all of this much more cleanly. The provinces would focus on all adults and, within this context, one could contemplate an integration of the existing UI and welfare programs in ways that provide incentives for training and labour-force re-entry. (Note that under some version of opting out or concurrency with provincial paramountcy, this approach need not differ from the approach in the previous paragraph for those provinces that wish to exercise their paramountcy.) One potential advantage to this approach is that because all children would be treated equally, this proposal would restore the "Ontario deficit" that currently besets the Canada Assistance Plan.

The reader will recognize that in arguing for converting CAP to a negative income tax for children I have violated my earlier enunciated principle, namely that the fiscal transfers ought to be derivative, not determining. The correct approach would be to focus on the restructuring imperative related to welfare. If, as I suspect, the result will be that some separate provision has to be put in place for children, *then* the conversion of CAP into an NIT for children becomes a potential instrument.

One can add many more proposals to this agenda — a tax-point transfer for Medicare, a voucher system for PSE, etc. And readers will have their own proposals. My role here is not to opt for a particular form of restructuring, only to present the case for a restructuring imperative. Since most of these proposals represent substantial restructuring, they will need adequate lead times and in some cases the provision for transitions. In turn, this implies that we must engage in this societal debate now, while we may still have a window of opportunity, rather than later when any restructuring in all likelihood will be driven by the international capital markets.

Prior to concluding, I want to devote some attention to where and how pressures for fundamental restructuring may come to the fore. Simeon (this volume) argues that there is a set of "trumps" that are characteristic of our federation: regional politics trumps other dimensions of distribution; fiscal federalism trumps social policy; the intergovernmental dynamics trumps citizen politics, etc. These are the sorts of insights that we have come to expect from Simeon. However, while they certainly applied to the old order, we are now in a new paradigm — fiscally, socio-economically, and in terms of the citizen-state relationship. The game has changed; to mix the metaphor, kings, queens, and even pawns can now check-mate any trump.

To sustain such an argument, I need to identify some restructuring dynamics that can finesse the powerful cards that federalism in all its forms (constitutional, regional, intergovernmental) has always held. Let me suggest three.

The first has already been alluded to, namely that in this globalization/ knowledge/fiscally-constrained era, Ottawa will recognize that social envelope restructuring holds the key to regaining our competitive edge. Short of a dramatic economic recovery, this option easily dominates (initially at the conceptual level and then on the political level) the alternatives of embracing the U.S. social envelope or turning the task (via inaction) to the gnomes of Zurich. Therefore, expect a new dynamic from Ottawa.

The second way in which federalism or jurisdictional deadlocks can be finessed is through provincial initiatives.[14] Typically, one associates this with the demands from Quebec or perhaps Ontario now that it is likely to play a more assertive role in the wake of the CAP fiasco. This is clearly possible. But it does not address Simeon's "regional politics trumps other dimensions of distribution." Consider, therefore, the following avenue. Implicit, even explicit, in Premier McKenna's Couchiching address was the fact that the days of the status quo on the New Brunswick social envelope front are numbered. Transfers of the existing magnitude will not be sustainable economically or politically. NB Works was the initial response. The obvious next step is a joint Maritime or perhaps Atlantic initiative which would involve a total reorganization of the social envelope and which could involve regional control of the existing level of net transfers under UI, to be phased out gradually over, say, a ten-year period to the non-place-prosperity level of UI prevailing elsewhere. The rationale for this would be two-fold: to devise a more rational approach to the UI/ welfare/training subsector and to forestall some pre-emptive strike by Ottawa on UI. Would Ottawa refuse such a package? Negotiate perhaps, but refuse, no. Therefore, with somewhat less likelihood, expect a new dynamic from the provinces.

The third dynamic is at the same time more speculative and less likely, namely that citizens in one or more of the provinces will find their services reduced to a level where they will ask Ottawa to step in on their behalf. The extreme case here would be one where the capital markets require a federal guarantee on the province's bond offering, i.e., the province runs into the proverbial "debt wall." Since it is inconceivable that Ottawa would provide such a guarantee, we will be in for major institutional change and restructuring. But pressures will build up well before this bankruptcy point. Federal transfers can maintain revenues per capita, but they cannot prevent a run-up in expenditures or an outflow of people, both of which will complicate the servicing of the existing debt levels. One hopes that one is wrong here, but this harkens back to the earlier comment that some provinces are probably willing right now to transfer areas like welfare to the federal government.

To be sure, given that unsustainability of the old paradigm and the unmet challenges of the new socio-economic order represent the underlying thrusts of much of the above analysis, it may well be the case that this perspective leads me to place too much emphasis on the restructuring imperative and too little on the entrenched constitutional-political-intergovernmental-regional dynamics that have been the hallmark of Canadian federation. Or, in economists' jargon, this vantage point may lead me in the direction of falling back on "heroic" assumptions. But I adhere to the proposition that heroes are not so much born as cornered. Canada is cornered!

IMPLICATIONS FOR FISCAL FEDERALISM

Prior to concluding, it is appropriate to redirect attention to the theme of this book, namely the implications for the future of fiscal federalism. In the world sketched out above, federal-provincial transfers would be derivative, not determining. Currently they play more of a determining role. In effect, they drive much of social Canada. We tend not to speak of a welfare problem but rather about a CAP problem. Likewise the challenges relating to health tend to be framed in terms of an issue of EPF or the *Canada Health Act*. These were the instruments that were critical to delivering the social infrastructure and policies associated with the old paradigm. Redesigning these federal-provincial transfers is not the same as restructuring social Canada.

This does not in any way downplay the critical importance of the federal-provincial financial interface in any restructured system. But it may be a quite different interface. For example, both structure and magnitude of federal-provincial transfers would presumably be very different under a scenario where UI and welfare were replaced by some version of a negative income tax or a guaranteed annual income. This more fundamental rethinking of social Canada will become more difficult if, in the first instance, reform initiatives are focused on the fiscal arrangements. The thrust of this chapter has been that the time has come in terms of fiscal, economic, and social considerations to engage in this more fundamental restructuring. And the way to do this is to begin by asking ourselves what constellation of policies makes sense from the perspective of individual Canadians and their families, not what makes sense for governments.

In all of this, however, there is one aspect of the existing set of fiscal relations that must survive in one form or another, namely the preservation and enhancement of the economic and social union. Currently, the spending power plays a critical role in this process. Preserving the integrity of the personal income tax system (e.g., the prohibition of beggar-my-neighbour tax provisions) is accomplished largely through the exercise of the federal spending power. So are the provisions relating to portability and the lack of residency requirements on the social union front. Were the ideal social policy restructuring to involve further asymmetry or further decentralization, the case for an effective social and economic union would presumably become all the stronger. To be sure, the exercise of the spending power is not the only way to deliver a social and economic union: I have long adhered to the principle that for programs to be national they need not be central. But until other effective provisions are put in place to guarantee the internal socio-economic market, Ottawa should not abandon the leverage associated with the exercise of the spending power.

CONCLUSION

In an era where fiscal deficits are dominating the economic landscape, one can, as the title suggests, speak meaningfully of a social policy "deficit." Intriguingly, the two sorts of defects are related since, as noted earlier, the failure to undertake social policy reform in the 1980s contributed to the running up of fiscal deficits. Now the shoe is on the other foot; fiscal deficits are wreaking havoc with the social programs. However, simple cost-cutting on the social policy front merely widens the social policy deficit or deficiency in the important sense that a restructured social policy envelope is crucial to our longer-term prosperity. In the broader context, the message here is that social policy restructuring is the order of the day and that the fiscal arrangements must be reworked to accommodate the new social policy order. Indeed, this restructuring will likely have significant implications for other aspects of fiscal federalism which have not been touched upon in this chapter, such as the assignment of tax powers. For example, the jurisdiction that is ultimately in charge of overseeing the transition from welfare/UI to work should probably have considerable control of, or flexibility within the personal income tax since this is an obvious integration and reconciliation vehicle for the subsystem.

Nonetheless, whatever the imperatives for the medium term, I suspect that in the immediate future it is inevitable that "tinkering" of some sort will be the order of the day when it comes to the fiscal arrangements, in part because some decisions have to be made within a matter of months. We will be very poorly served by our political class if they view this tinkering as anything other than a temporary and stop-gap measure on the road to addressing the real challenge — restructuring social and economic policy to render it consistent with globalization and the knowledge/information revolution. To be a Canadian in the new millennium must mean that all citizens have full opportunities to develop and enhance their human capital. Thankfully, there is no trade-off here — this is good economic policy and good social policy. But getting there will be tough because the required decision making will likewise be tough. Unlike private sector restructuring, there is precious little that individual Canadians can do, acting in their own spheres, to bring about this new social order. Thus, my advice to like-minded Canadians is to maintain pressure on our political class and perhaps even to adopt the admittedly irreverent slogan that appears daily on the masthead of the *Whitehorse Star* — *Illegitimus non carborundum.*

Appendix
State Income Disparities in Australia

Table A.1 presents data on regional disparity relative for the Australian states in the same time frame (1991) and on more or less the same basis as Table 1 (in the text) for Canada. The first four columns of Table A.1 are fully comparable with the corresponding columns of Table 1. Columns (5) and (6) of Table A.1 are closely, if not fully, comparable with columns (6) and (7) of Table 1. HDI stands for Household Disposable Income and is the Australian counterpart, at least as far as I can ascertain, to our Personal Disposable Income. The last column of Table A.1 is AWE (average weekly earnings) which is a proxy for the Table 1 entry AHE (average hourly earnings).

The message in the text is that state regional disparities in Australia embody much less disparity then in Canada. This is obvious. What is not so obvious is why this is the case. The text argues that part of this is probably attributable to the fact that there is little in the way of specific regional policy on the part of the Australian government. Indeed, there is no UI program, as such, in Australia. What they call "unemployment benefits" (administered centrally) are really what we would call welfare.

Since this comparison between Australia and Canada is somewhat peripheral to the main message of the paper, I shall leave it to the reader to make the relevant comparisons. However, I would add three observations. First, it appears that Australia has avoided the regional transfer dependency that is evident in Canada, even though Australia holds equity and equality in at least as high a regard as do Canadians. Second, Australia appears to be suffering from "national" transfer dependency in the sense that what was once the highest income per capita economy has now fallen to the high teens or low twenties in terms of income per capita rankings among developed nations. Canada has managed to retain its overall income per capita ranking. Finally, the comparison of Table 1 and Table A.1 requires much more research before one can draw meaningful conclusions. Somewhat more in the way of comparative analysis appears in Courchene (1993b), but these tables represent a puzzle that clearly requires more research.

TABLE A.1: Regional Disparity Relatives (Australia 1991)

	(1) Y/P	(2) Y/E	(3) E/LF	(4) LF/P	(5) HDI/Y	(6) HDI/P	(7) A.W.E.
New South Wales	1.035	1.047	1.008	0.981	1.035	1.018	1.022
Victoria	1.053	1.051	0.991	1.010	.0984	1.043	1.008
Queensland	0.888	0.891	0.989	1.008	1.001	0.891	0.931
South Australia	0.883	0.889	0.990	0.974	1.048	0.926	0.952
Western Australia	1.037	1.020	0.981	1.036	0.858	0.889	1.005
Tasmania	0.810	0.850	0.982	0.970	1.061	0.859	0.968
Australia	1.000	1.000	1.000	1.000	1.000	1.000	1.000
High/Low[1]	1.300	1.240	1.030	1.070	1.240	1.210	1.100

Notes: [1]For the six states.

Sources: ABS, *The Labour Force, Australia* (July 1991), 6203.0; *Australian National Accounts, 1990-91, State Accounts, 5220.0; Estimated Resident Population by Sex and Age, States and Territories of Australia* (June 1990 and Preliminary June 1991), 3201.1; *Distribution and Composition of Employees, Earnings and Hours, Australia* (May 1991), 6306.0.

NOTES

This chapter draws heavily on my forthcoming C.D. Howe monograph on social policy. I would like to thank Paul Boothe for valuable comments on an earlier draft.

1. Note that at this juncture, the issue relates to *structure, not to dollars*. Indeed, it might be best to view all of this under the assumption that the dollars dedicated to the social envelope remain fixed. Later, I shall drop this assumption.

2. Recently, an alternative approach to the CPP has been floated in the policy arena, namely increasing the retirement age to 70. This will serve to keep contribution rates down, but it will discriminate against younger Canadians since this age increase will have a substantial lead time associated with it.

3. There will still be regional redistribution in many of the social programs. For example, a UI program with identical qualifying weeks and with benefit weeks based on these qualifying weeks would still generate greater benefits in high-unemployment areas. This is appropriate. The reference in the text is intended to remove any specific regional provisions built into programs such as UI. Note also, that there will always need to be "emergency" measures, such as the grain subsidy and the "cod moratorium." What is disturbing here, however, is the lack of sunset or phase-out provisions to ensure that such stop-gap measures do not end up as yet another feature of our "permanent" redistributive system.

4. The equalization ceiling is "rebased" in the first year of each five-year period (i.e., equalization is set equal to formula entitlements for this first year). Thus, the ceiling can only be binding for the remaining four years of each five-year agreement. For these four years, equalization in aggregate cannot exceed the cumulative rate of growth of nominal GNP from the base (initial) year. If it is in excess, the reduction in equalization entitlements is an equal per capita decrease for all recipient provinces.

5. This is not quite correct because the definition of GNP for EPF purposes is a three-year moving average ending with the current year. Thus, even though GNP fell below 3 percent almost immediately after the freeze was in effect, the three-year GNP average would have exceeded 3 percent at least for the first year of the freeze. However, all of this ignores the symbolic impact of a freeze.

6. Note that the contributions by Boadway and Flatters and especially that by Dupré (both in this volume) also take issue with including tax points as part of the EPF transfers. It is true, of course, that these tax points are now part of the provinces' own revenues. However, one has to separate the value of these tax points in the hands of the provinces from the notional role that they play in the EPF program. At the very least, a fuller analysis would have to focus on the 1977 arrangements themselves and on the critical 1982 arrangements which introduced an overall ceiling to EPF and converted the cash component into a residual transfer (see Courchene 1984).

7. One way of interpreting the cap on CAP is that it "equalized" the CAP transfers — it tilted payments away from the "have" provinces, while leaving the system untouched for the have-not provinces. Some provinces, Quebec in particular, had argued that the growth rate of overall federal-provincial transfers was larger for the have than for the have-not provinces in recent years. Ottawa may have been responding to these concerns. However, given that per capita CAP transfers for

1992-93 to Quebec were $335 compared with, say, $233 for Newfoundland and only $183 for Saskatchewan, it is difficult to see where or why Quebec had much to complain about.

8. Actually, these 8.5 PIT points relate only to EPF. Quebec also receives another 5 PIT points under CAP and yet another 3 for various other programs for an overall transfer of 16.5 PIT tax points. Thus, full parity with Quebec probably means 16.5 tax points, not only the 8.5 associated with EPF.

9. One might argue that Ottawa's behaviour is unconscionable in another sense — it was its inability to put its own fiscal house in order during the 1980s boom that has precipitated the existing fiscal havoc. As argued in the introduction, a major part of this fiscal profligacy represented a futile effort to adhere to an outdated and outmoded social policy paradigm.

10. EPF transfers are unconditional in that they can be spent as the provinces please. However, provincial spending on health (from whatever revenue source) must satisfy the requirements of the *Canada Health Act.*

11. Thankfully, I am not alone in arguing for this refocus — see Boothe and Reid (1993).

12. The "federal" rationale for equalization payments relates to the proposition that equalization is the cornerstone of a meaningful federal system. For any constitutional assignment of powers to be meaningful, provinces must have the financial capacity to fulfil these responsibilities. The "citizenship" rationale has to do with the notion that Canadians, wherever they live, ought to have access to certain basic economic and social rights — rights that ought to attend Canadian citizenship, as it were. Since some of these rights fall under provincial jurisdiction, it is imperative that provinces have funds adequate to provide them. While there are aspects of equity associated with both these rationales, they are distinct from the horizontal equity notion underlying the NFB conception. Indeed, under either the federal or nationhood rationales, the first-best solution is an equalization program, whereas under an NFB formulation the first-best solution really is a set of differentiated transfers to individuals. One arrives at a set of equalization payments only as a second-best solution. It is in this sense that I argue that the concept of "fiscal equity" as reflected in the NFB conception is essentially alien to a federal system. For more detail, see Courchene (1984, chap. 3).

13. Or more correctly, net away all funds that flow in because of specific "place-prosperity" features of other programs.

14. The ideas in this paragraph and the following one are the result of a conversion with Fred Gorbet about our respective conference papers. Needless to say, Gorbet may not be in agreement with the way I have distilled some of these ideas.

BIBLIOGRAPHY

Boadway, Robin (1992), *The Constitutional Division of Powers: An Economic Perspective*, Ottawa: Economic Council of Canada.

Boadway, Robin and Frank Flatters (1982), *Equalization in a Federal State*, Ottawa: Economic Council of Canada.

Boadway, Robin W. and Paul A.R. Hobson (1993), *Intergovernmental Fiscal Relations in Canada*, Toronto: Canadian Tax Foundation.

Boothe, Paul and Barbara Johnston (1993), *Stealing the Emperor's Clothes: Deficit Offloading and National Standards in Health Care*, Commentary 41, Toronto: C.D. Howe Institute.

Boothe, Paul and Brad Reid (1993), "An Overview of Fiscal Federalism," in a paper presented at the Conference on the "Future of Fiscal Arrangements in Canada," University of Alberta.

Canadian Labour Market and Productivity Centre (1990), "A Review of Regional Economic Development Policy in Canada," *Quarterly Labour Market Productivity Review*, (Fall): 23-34.

Canadian Teachers' Federation (1993), background material for a seminar on "The Impact of Federal Economic Policies on Public Education and Teachers," Ottawa: June 20-22.

Chandler, Teresa (1993), "Restructuring: The New 'R' Word," in *CABE News*, Canadian Association for Business Economists (Fall).

Courchene, Thomas J. (1984), *Equalization Payments: Past, Present and Future*, Toronto: Ontario Economic Council.

_____ (1991), *The Community of the Canadas*, Reflections Paper 8, Kingston: Institute of Intergovernmental Relations, Queen's University.

_____ (1992), "Mon Pays, c'est l'hiver: Reflections of a Market Populist," *Canadian Journal of Economics*, 25, 4 (November): 759-791.

_____ (1993a), "Path-Dependency, Positive Feedback and Paradigm Warp: A Schumpeterian Approach to the Social Order," in *Income Security in Canada: Changing Needs, Changing Means*, Montreal: Institute for Research on Public Policy.

_____ (1993b), "Globalization, Institutional Evolution and the Australian Federation," forthcoming in a conference volume from the Federalism Research Centre, Canberra ACT, Australia.

Courchene, Thomas J. and Arthur E. Stewart (1991), "Provincial Personal Income Taxation and the Future of the Tax Collection Agreements," in *Provincial Finances: Plaudits, Problems and Prospects*, ed. Mel McMillan, Toronto: Canadian Tax Foundation.

Courchene, Thomas J. and Glen H. Copplestone (1980), "Alternative Equalization Programs: Two-tier Systems," in *Fiscal Dimensions of Canadian Federalism*, ed. Richard Bird, Toronto: Canadian Tax Foundation.

_____ (1994), *Social Canada in the Millennium*, Toronto: C.D. Howe Institute.

Economic Council of Canada (1992), *The New Face of Poverty: Income Security Needs of Canadian Families*, Ottawa: Supply and Services Canada.

Drucker, Peter F. (1986), "The Changed World Economy," *Foreign Affairs* (Spring): 3-17.

_____ (1993), *Post-Capitalist Society*, New York: Harper Bros.

Fortin, Pierre (1994), "Slow Growth, Unemployment and Debt: What Happened? What Can We Do?" in *Stabilization, Growth and Distribution: Linkages in the Knowledge Era*, ed. Thomas J. Courchene, Bell Canada Papers, vol. 2, Kingston: John Deutsch Institute for the Study of Economic Policy, Queen's University.

Hamilton, Colleen and John Whalley (1984), "Reforming Public Pensions in Canada: Issues and Options," in *Pensions Today and Tomorrow: Background Studies*, ed. David Conklin, Jalynn Bennett and Thomas Courchene, Toronto: Ontario Economic Council.

Harris, Richard (1993), *Trade, Money, and Wealth in the Canadian Economy*, Benefactors Lecture, 1993, Toronto: C.D. Howe Institute.

Lam, Newman, Michael Prince and James Cutt (1993), *Reforming the Public Pension System in Canada: Restrospect and Prospect*, Victoria, B.C.: Centre for Public Sector Studies, University of Victoria.

Lipsey, Richard (1993), "Wanted: A New Social Contract," *Policy Options/Options Politiques*, 14, 6 (July/August): 5-9.

Maxwell, Judith (1993), "It's Time to Rethink the Social Role of Government," Keynote address to the Canadian Pension Conference, Montreal (8 June).

McKenna, Frank (1993), "Transcript of Speech by the Honourable Frank McKenna on Education to the Annual Couchiching Conference," mimeo (5 August).

Myles, John (1991), "Post Industrialism and the Service Economy," in *The New Era of Global Competition: State Policy and Market Power*, ed. David Drache and Meric Gertler, Montreal and Kingston: McGill-Queen's University Press.

Norrie, Kenneth (1993), "Intergovernmental Transfers in Canada: An Historical Perspective on Some Current Policy Issues," in *A Partnership in Trouble: Renegotiating Fiscal Federalism*, ed. P.M. Leslie, K. Norrie and I. Ip, Toronto: C.D. Howe Institute.

Oates, W.E. (1972), *Fiscal Federalism*, New York: Harcourt Brace Jovanovitch.

Ontario (1992), "Financing Canada's National Social Programs: The Need for Reform," paper released at the First Ministers' Conference, March.

Osberg, Lars (1993), "Integrating Social and Economic Policy Micro Transitions and Macro Policy in a Federal State," *Income Security in Canada: Changing Needs; Changing Means*, Montreal: Institute for Research on Public Policy.

Phipps, Shelley (1993), "Does Unemployment Insurance Increase Unemployment," *Canadian Business Economics*, (Spring): 37-50.

Scarth, William (1994), "Alternative Assignments of Policy Instruments to Macroeconomic Goals: Comment," in *Stabilization, Growth and Distribution: Linkages in the Knowledge Era*, ed. Thomas J. Courchene, Bell Canada Papers, vol. 2, Kingston: John Deutsch Institute for the Study of Economic Policy, Queen's University.

Statistics Canada (1992), *Provincial Economic Accounts: Annual Estimates, 1981-1991*, Catalogue 13-213, Ottawa: Supply and Services Canada.

Thomson, David (1991), *Selfish Generations? The Aging of New Zealand's Welfare State*, Wellington: Bridget Williams Books.

Toronto Star (1993), "Villages make UI a Way of Life," 6 September, A.8.

Comment: The Nature of Dependency

Lars Osberg

There are a great many insights and observations in Tom Courchene's chapter — some I agree with heartily and some I disagree with. Since a commentary should be somewhat shorter than the original paper, I will select one aspect of the chapter I dislike and one aspect that I like, and make a general, overall comment.

The aspect that I dislike is the use of the term "dependency." This term is used repeatedly and has been used and re-used in the broader public discussion until it has become a cliché. However, the phenomenon which the term seeks to describe is rather vague and all-embracing, and the evidence that is cited is often entirely anecdotal. In fact, the term "dependency" has two quite distinct meanings and the debate on "dependency" has become sloppy and misleading because people often shift back and forth between these two meanings, without realizing the transition.

The term "dependency" is sometimes used in the accounting sense of "being reliant on," as indicated by the fact that a relatively high percentage of total income comes from a particular income source. In the accounting sense, senior citizens are highly "dependent" on unearned income in transfer payments and pensions, while the Alberta government is heavily "dependent" on transfer payments from oil companies. Dependency, in this sense, is an *ex post* accounting relationship which describes income flows. Since this conference has already heard numerous comparisons between Atlantic Canada and the rest of the country, and since unemployment insurance has often been mentioned, I could not resist the temptation of preparing Table 1. In order to maintain comparability, Table 1 compares urban areas only and it is notable that in the

TABLE 1: 1992 Unemployment and Unemployment Insurance Dependency

	Halifax	Toronto	Montreal
Unemployment Rate (%)			
Age 15-24	15.4	19.1	18.0
Age 25-44	8.9	11.0	12.6
Age 45+	7.7	8.1	11.4
Total	9.9	11.5	13.1
Labour Force (000's)			
Total	166.8	2,005.2	1,585.6
Population >15 Years of Age	246,200.0	2,890,900.0	2,469,900.0
UI Claimants			
Number	11,594.0	161,472.0	136,356.0
% of Labour Force	7.0	8.1	8.6
% of Population	4.7	5.6	5.5

Note: Regular benefit claimants only.

Source: Author's compilation

accounting sense, Halifax had in 1992 a *lower* rate of "dependency" on unemployment insurance than either Toronto or Montreal.

However, the term "dependency" is also often used in a behavioural sense to evoke images of addiction, false reliance on transfers and bad behaviour induced by the presence of transfer mechanisms. Observed outcomes are in this context, interpreted as voluntary choices and evidence on *ex post* accounting flows is used to justify the presumption of behavioural impacts from the presence of transfer payments. The Courchene chapter, like much of the literature in this area, shifts back and forth between the accounting and the behavioural interpretation of dependency, often without any apparent realization of the transition.

It is often hard to penetrate this dialogue with empirical evidence since "dependency" in the behavioural sense is vaguely specified, and it is an easy slide from stereotypes and anecdotes to macro data on accounting flows between provinces and broad generalizations about the psychological attitudes of entire regions of the country. Courchene's chapter, for example, discusses a hypothetical example of a worker who is employed for ten weeks and on unemployment insurance for 42 weeks. This sentence is followed by the statement that in two New Brunswick counties 100 percent of two-earner households accessed UI at some point during 1992 and the ratio was above 90 percent in "many" other counties. The paragraph concludes with the statement "this is transfer dependency." Although the insinuation is clear, no attempt is made to ascertain whether the average duration of unemployment insurance receipt was two weeks or 20. There is no attempt to examine whether similar concentrations of unemployment insurance receipt could be found elsewhere (e.g., in east end Montreal) and there is no consideration of whether individuals "chose" in any sense to become unemployed.

For the record, however, ten-week workers are a very small proportion of total employment. Christofides and McKenna (1992) report that nationally, ten-week jobs were 2.19 percent of all jobs in 1988. Green and Riddell (1993, Table 6) report that in high-unemployment local labour markets the number of 10-13 week jobs were 2.44 percent of total jobs. Since some fraction of these jobs were followed by a return to school or a short duration spell of unemployment, the stereotypical "10/42 worker" is necessarily a smaller percentage of total employment. The continued reappearance of this stereotype in the public debate indicates the important fact that anecdotes have a far greater political and social impact than their numerical importance would warrant.

It is observably the case that people and governments in Atlantic Canada, and in depressed regions of the country generally, receive transfer payments. However, before those accounting flows are transmuted into a broad, overall behavioural assertion of "dependency," the mechanisms of presumed behavioural change should be specified. *Which* program is affecting *what* behaviour? *Who* is doing *what* differently? *How much* does behaviour actually change in response to program changes?

As it stands, the "dependency" argument is often used in a vague, overall macro sense, but is it individuals, firms or governments that are supposed to be behaving differently? The recent literature on unemployment insurance is far more uncertain about the behavioural impacts of UI than the literature of the early 1970s (see Osberg 1993). Is it being suggested that equalization payments to provincial governments are altering the wage elasticity of labour supply of individuals? Are firms supposed to be less profit-maximizing because provincial governments have additional revenue? Why is it that additional revenue in equalization payments to Saskatchewan induces "dependency" while additional revenue in oil royalties to Alberta does not? Economists have long argued that decisions are influenced by prices at the margin, and federal transfer payments such as equalization and EPF are unconditional — how is it that these transfer payments are supposed to influence provincial government priorities?

On the other hand, if one prefers broader generalizations, should Canadians be using the evidence of Table 1 to support a whole new series of anecdotes about lazy residents of Toronto and Montreal, living a life of leisure on unemployment insurance? I think not, because Table 1 really indicates the disproportionate impact of the 1990-93 recession on Toronto and the longer term structural problems of the Montreal economy. As Sharpe (1994) has shown, two-thirds of the job loss of the 1990-93 recession was concentrated in metropolitan Toronto. (On the other hand, Montreal has had higher unemployment than Halifax since the late 1970s.) The serious point to make is that the demand side of labour markets is crucial to our understanding and interpretation of accounting data on unemployment insurance flows.

A second point to emphasize is the sharp divergence between urban and rural labour markets in many parts of Canada. Atlantic Canada's rural problems are not unique. Although fishing villages in Atlantic Canada have been dramatically affected by the collapse of the east coast fishing industry, the broad employment trends in farming, forestry, and mining are similar across Canada. And although the problems of Algoma Steel may be relatively new, while those of Sydney Steel are long-standing, they are very similar. The greater relative importance of the rural, resource-based economy in Atlantic Canada heavily influences interprovincial statistical comparisons, but the fundamental structural problem is rural-urban, not interprovincial, in nature.

One thing that I agree with strongly in the Courchene chapter is the emphasis on knowledge and information as being the cutting edge of international competitiveness and his statement that a well-educated labour force is essential for future prosperity. Intergovernmental transfer payments are crucial to maintaining accessibility of education. In discussing educational attainment, it is essential to distinguish carefully between stocks and flows. As Table 2 indicates, there has been a dramatic change in recent years in the Grade 12 retention rate in Nova Scotia. However, the educational characteristics of the labour force stock are still dominated by the older cohorts of workers who entered the labour force during a period when educational attainment was much lower. In the mid-1960s two-thirds of Grade 7 students in Nova Scotia dropped out before Grade 12 — these people are now in their mid-40s and will continue to be in the labour force for about the next 20 years. As Table 3 indicates, the educational attainment of Atlantic Canadians differs dramatically by age cohort, and older cohorts have a relatively low attendance rate at university, compared to the national average. However, since Courchene's chapter points out the necessity for reformed social policy to emphasis the development and enhancement of human capital potential, it is worth recognizing that the recent dramatic increase in educational attainment in Atlantic Canada has produced a rate of university attendance among 20-24 year olds that is *higher* than the national average.[1]

TABLE 2: Nova Scotia Department of Education Provincial Retention Rates*

Grade 12		Grade 7		Retention Rate (%)
Year	Enrolment	Year	Enrolment	
1992	12,881	1987	13,678	94
1991	12,165	1986	13,981	87
1990	11,578	1985	14,099	82
1989	11,662	1984	14,450	81
1988	11,834	1983	14,927	79
1987	11,408	1982	14,576	78
1986	10,972	1981	14,999	73
1985	10,777	1980	15,372	70
1984	11,376	1979	15,794	72
1983	11,691	1978	16,826	69
1982	11,637	1977	18,360	63
1981	10,910	1976	18,832	58
1980	10,742	1975	19,003	57
1975	9,817	1970	18,417	53
1970	8,860	1965	17,111	52
1965	5,315	1960	16,146	33

*Retention rates may be over-estimated as there is no record of the number of students returning to grade 12 after dropping out for a period of time. During downturns in the economy, more students are likely to return to school.

Source: Author's compilation.

TABLE 3: Percentage of Population Years 15 and Older Who Have Attended University

Age Group	Nfld.	N.S.	N.B.	P.E.I.	National
			(percent)		
All>15	16.4	20.9	17.9	20.7	20.8
15-19	10.0	9.1	10.2	12.3	5.5
20-24	31.9	34.7	33.0	35.7	29.9
25-34	20.5	27.1	22.1	24.9	26.3
35-44	19.4	26.8	21.8	27.4	27.9
45-54	14.4	19.1	16.7	18.8	21.7
55-64	7.5	13.1	10.8	13.4	13.3
65+	4.9	10.1	8.0	9.7	9.8

Source: Census of Canada, 1991. Cat. No. 93-328 pp. 24-29.

It is clear that the governments of Atlantic Canada have delivered substantially more educational services to their population in recent years. Clearly, intergovernmental transfer payments are a crucially important part of the revenues of the provincial governments in Atlantic Canada, from which educational expenditures are financed. Although it is hard to know for certain the counterfactual case — what quantity and quality of educational services provinces would have been able to deliver in the absence of federal transfer payments — my suspicion is that money matters. The educational system has managed to deliver a relatively high level of accessibility and quality, even in some of the poorest rural areas of Atlantic Canada. I do not see how this would have been possible in the absence of intergovernmental transfer payments and I think that such investment in education is highly desirable, on both equity and efficiency grounds. In all our talk of fundamental reforms to intergovernmental transfer payments we should, therefore, remember that there really is a baby in this bathwater.

As to transfer payments to individuals, one of the proposals in the Courchene chapter that I do like is his suggestion for a negative income tax for children. The chapter does not provide many details and one has to recognize that such a program will be inserted into an economy, and a society, undergoing very rapid change. The high rate of divorce and remarriage (as well as more informal mergers and dissolutions of households) means that the membership of family units changes continually. Increasingly sophisticated managerial strategies for the "just in time" hiring of labour and an increased casualization of the low wage labour force means that *individual* income flows have also become highly variable. As a result, a negative income tax scheme which requires people to qualify *ex-ante*, *before* they receive benefits would face very high administrative costs, because individual children will be continually moving into and out of eligibility. Since it is essential for income to arrive *in time* to pay for the groceries, a negative income tax scheme, to be useful, must have fairly frequent payments. There are, therefore, substantial administrative advantages to delivering the guarantee level of a negative income tax for children as a demogrant and taxing back any excess payments through an existing mechanism such as the income tax system. An effective negative income tax for children would, therefore, be very similar to the recently abolished family allowance system, although presumably considerably larger in value.

My most general comment on the Courchene chapter is that although I found it relatively easy to agree with the need to "restructure" social policy in some general sense, I found very few details. I agree that changes must always be made in social policy because social problems are always changing. I agree that it is increasingly necessary to recognize the linkages between economic and social policy. However, I am left wondering what exactly is meant by "restructuring."

Furthermore, I would argue that one cannot realistically consider restructuring social policy without paying some attention to the macroeconomic context. In many ways, redesigning unemployment insurance and social assistance in the middle of a recession is like redesigning bathing suits in January. Although little harm is done by conceptual redesign (indeed one must plan ahead if new bathing suits are to be delivered in July) people will resist wearing new bathing suits right away — and their resistance is entirely reasonable, if, in fact, the lake is frozen.

If continued high unemployment means that jobs are not, in fact, available there is little point in reforming social policy to "increase incentives" to accept (non-existent) jobs. Without a demand for trained labour, there are few payoffs to increasing the supply of training. A balanced reform of social policy must recognize the crucial importance of the demand side of labour markets, and the role of macroeconomic policy in influencing aggregate demand.

NOTE

1. Although, during the school year, Nova Scotia attracts a substantial inflow of out-of-province students, the census data on which Table 3 is based measures population as of 1 June, and records residence as "place of normal residence."

BIBLIOGRAPHY

Christofides, L.N. and C.J. McKenna (1992), "Employment Tenure in Canada," paper prepared for the Canadian Employment Research Forum conference, 5-7 March, mimeo, University of Guelph.

Green, D.A. and W.C. Riddell (1993), "Qualifying for Unemployment Insurance: An Empirical Analysis," Discussion Paper 93-33, Vancouver: Department of Economics, University of British Columbia.

Osberg, L. (1993), "Unemployment Insurance and Unemployment — Revisited," Working Paper 93-04, Halifax: Department of Economics, Dalhousie University.

Sharpe, A. (1994), "The Rise of Unemployment in Ontario," in *All for Naught: The Unemployment Crisis in Canada*, ed. L. Osberg and B. MacLean, Kingston: McGill-Queen's University Press.

Comment: The Constraints on Change

Claude E. Forget

Tom Courchene's central point seems to be the following. Canada along with many other countries but perhaps more acutely than some, is confronted with a new economic and social paradigm: globalization, the knowledge-based economy and all that. Much of our current economic and particularly social policies is embedded in a system of federal-provincial fiscal transfers. Can those fiscal transfers, and hence relevant economic and social policies, be restructured to fit the new paradigm? That is the central issue raised by Courchene.

The first part of his presentation is devoted to these social policies and fiscal transfers said to be non-viable or non-sustainable. A powerful set of misguided incentives is described through its impact on individuals, regions, and the balance between the young and the old. From my own perspective, it is hard to disagree with the characterization by Courchene of those impacts as a "policy induced equilibrium in terms of the provincial characteristics relating to unemployment and output." The additional point is made that bad as they have been, those impacts look even worse from the vantage point of the emerging economic and social paradigm. However, their characterization as non-sustainable is unfortunate as its suggests some sort of natural equilibrium process whereby the adverse effects of the existing incentives on the economy and those, in turn, on the public finances would naturally lead to a reform of fiscal transfers.

At the time of my work on unemployment insurance, I used to think that the dysfunctional incentives inherent in that program were corrupting our political process. With the benefit of hindsight, I would now reverse the order of causality: our political system itself reaches a position of equilibrium by generating such dysfunctional incentives. In a period of heigthened regionalism underscored by the recent federal election results, there seems no reason to believe that dysfunctional incentives embedded in net fiscal transfers to a number of regions can be successfully challenged.

In his second section, Courchene describes how some $40 billion cumulatively have been cut back from fiscal transfers since 1986-87. Whether or not this is in line with Ottawa's cutbacks in its own programs is, in my opinion, a rather moot point. Those federal savings account for much less than half of the total increase in provincial debts over the period.

At this point, Courchene indulges in a digression that has little to do with his main point. He is concerned that federal unilateral actions with regard to fiscal transfers have destroyed the mutual trust between provincial and federal governments a phenomemon much in evidence for instance in regard to the CAP payments to Ontario subjected by Ottawa to a unilateral ceiling. However, it has long been known that the relationship between giver and recipient is not an equal relationship and that transfer payments from Ottawa to the provinces are not based on a contractual relationship, the commonly used expression "federal-provincial agreements" being just a public relations face saver for the provinces. Provinces never complained about the unpredictability of federal moves when grants were on the increase, the question is: Are they sufficiently miffed with that unpredictability now that grants are decreasing that they would be prepared to forego some transfers in favour of greater certainty? My guess is that it is not very likely. Also bear in mind that it is not a question that is up to Ottawa to settle or even agree to with the provinces, as the constitution itself would have to be amended to provide for binding intergovernmental agreements.

Be that as it may, the real question is not whether or not provincial governments are happy with their relationship with Ottawa, but whether the scaling back of federal payments to provinces is leading to a mere erosion or to a restructuring of social policies. Courchene presents some examples of provincial initiatives at restructuring public policies in Quebec, Saskatchewan, Ontario, and New Brunswick. However, he does not make clear whether Ottawa is necessary to the process. It is not even clear whether provincial experiments in restructuring are triggered by federal offloading. Given the nature of the examples quoted, the answer is: probably not.

The next and last section of Courchene's chapter is devoted to exploring ways in which what he calls horizontal transfers could be limited. That they should be is something that he supports and which is hardly in any doubt. The increasing number of recipients and the decreasing surplus from which those transfers are financed make that inevitable. What is important to know is rather whether the dysfunctional incentives inherent in the "welfare-UI-training-education" nexus are at the top of the list of items that will be modified if and when horizontal transfers are scaled down. Here Courchene does not take us very far, but we can collect a number of throw away sentences that provide a glimpse of his thinking on this issue.

- Ottawa is unwilling to act on the UI front taken in isolation;

- Ottawa desires to be active on the nexus described above but taken as a whole;

- Ottawa's initiatives in that regard can be expected to be welcomed by some provinces;

- However, in other provinces and notably Quebec, this will be vehemently rejected hence the likelihood of an asymmetrical outcome.

Interesting as it is to speculate about these various propositions, no evidence is produced to support any of them, and therefore it is legitimate to doubt whether indeed the financial need to reduce transfers will lead as a matter of priority to a restructuring of the incentive systems present in the welfare to education nexus.

I would add that perhaps the strongest incentive for Ottawa to act and articulate strong initiatives (including wholesale delegation to the provinces) relating to that nexus just could be the realization that all those programs, that is to say welfare, UI, training, and education, singly and collectively are among the most generously funded in Canada as compared to almost all OECD countries. The issue for Canadians here is not to spend more but to spend more smartly. Indeed, savings can be made by Ottawa out of these programs that could be far more politically rewarding if reinvested, assuming tax reduction is not on the agenda, in strengthening federal commitment and funding predictability with regard to our national health system seen more and more as a defining characteristic of Canada.

CHAPTER FOUR

The Political Context for Renegotiating Fiscal Federalism

Richard Simeon

INTRODUCTION

The chapters in this book have underscored the magnitude and intractability of the current issues in fiscal federalism. There is a consensus among commentators, and perhaps even among governments, that the existing arrangements are unsustainable. In this chapter, I will address the political and institutional context within which fiscal arrangements and the associated issues of managing public debts and deficits and the future of social policy are to be debated and discussed. To what extent do we have the political will and the institutional capacity to decide these issues effectively? "Effectiveness," of course, has different meanings for different authors: for some the central priority is restraining debts and deficits, for others it is preserving the social safety net and for yet others it is integrating social, educational, and other policy areas with policies for growth and competitiveness. I will take effectiveness to mean achieving some degree of coordination between the different levels of government, making tough decisions to manage the deficit and ensuring that the costs of that are fairly distributed, and establishing a policy framework in which we can build the linkages between fiscal arrangements and social policy and other policies aimed at economic restructuring, such as workforce training. This is the basic policy challenge for the country, to which all governments must contribute. Effectiveness in the federalism context also means the ability to minimize interregional and intergovernmental conflict and to maximize the responsiveness of the intergovernmental process to citizen concerns.

My central argument is that we are faced with some profound dilemmas. On the one hand, the problems of debt, deficits and the future of social policy face the public sector collectively, as a whole. The national deficit is a function of both federal and provincial taxing and spending. Governments are interdependent, so that initiatives taken at one level have immediate consequences for the other. The programs available to citizens, and the tax burdens to pay for them, are a combined product of what all the governments do. This suggests that any re-thinking or restructuring of public finances or the welfare state which is to meet the needs of citizens requires a coordinated effort with all the governments working together.

But on the other hand many factors stand in the way of such collective effort. If the policy imperative calls for a coordinated approach, seeing the public sector as a whole, the political imperatives render that extraordinarily difficult to achieve.

This may be too pessimistic a conclusion. There is indeed a general consensus that something must be done, and the fiscal crisis no doubt concentrates the minds of those involved. Governments at both levels now appear to be making concerted efforts to curb spending and "rationalize" expenditures. The initial exchanges between the provinces and the new federal government have been characterized by relative harmony and goodwill, along with a sense that "we are all in it together." The Liberal Party's "Plan for Canada" promises close coordination and cooperation with the provinces (Liberal Party of Canada 1993) — as, indeed, all new governments do. Nevertheless, it is hard to believe that the conditions for a creative or successful resolution exist. The system lacks the institutional capacity to address and manage the challenge.

That difficulty can be summed up in a number of propositions which I will explore in this chapter.

First, in federal-provincial relations, the constitution and related issues of national unity tend to trump or dominate debate on substantive, functional policy issues.

Second, questions about the regional distribution of costs and benefits tend to trump debate in terms of alternative aspects of distribution.

Third, fiscal and financial issues tend to trump debate on social policy.

Fourth, the intricacies of intergovernmental negotiation tend to trump citizen understanding and participation and blur accountability.

And finally governmental self-interest in seeking to avoid and transfer blame usually trumps willingness to share it. This is especially true in the current context when the task is clearly to make very difficult decisions with strong distributional implications, both regionally and intergovernmentally.

We are only just becoming familiar with the federalism of restraint, the federalism of hard times. It is likely to be very different from the competition and conflict associated with the federalism of growth, which characterized the period between the 1960s and 1980s. Then the governmental competition was over the expansion of government activities and the competition for credit. Today it is about downsizing, restructuring and the avoidance of blame.

Let us explore each of these dilemmas.

PRIMACY OF THE CONSTITUTION

First, ever since the 1960s, the high politics of the constitution, and the associated debates about the character and structure of the Canadian political community, have dominated federal-provincial relations. We have practised what one might call "constitutional federalism." Specific policy issues have been subordinated to the more symbolic politics of identity, and the federalism of community has dominated functional approaches to federalism. None of the major rounds of constitutional debate since 1970 have focused primarily on designing institutions to render the division of powers more coherent. Where division of powers issues have been debated — as in the debate over the spending power, or the proposals of the Allaire Report (for the best summary, see Russell 1993) — the discussion has focused more on the implications for community, than on the functional policy consequences. The constitutional amendments of 1982 barely touched on the division of powers — except for a clarification of provincial jurisdiction over resources. The Meech Lake Accord referred only to the federal spending power and constitutionalizing agreements concerning immigration. The Charlottetown Accord dealt with a longer list of division of powers issues, but that discussion too was not approached with a view to exploring the most appropriate sharing of responsibilities from a policy perspective. We may now be paying a high price for this.

For a blessed brief period following the defeat of the Charlottetown Accord, it appeared that through exhaustion if nothing else, we had removed the symbolic, community, constitutional issues from the table. We could turn our attention from the crowded constitutional agenda to the shared policy problems, and from constitutional "fixes" to the informal mechanisms of adaptation in fiscal arrangements and intergovernmental cooperation. But clearly this was a temporary respite. The election of 25 October 1993 and its aftermath, seem certain to pull us back to the constitution and to the debate about the future of the federation.

The election result can be seen as the dropping of the second shoe after the Charlottetown referendum of October 1992. It signalled the continuing rejection by many citizens of politics as usual. The counter-elites who masterminded the attack on Charlottetown have now achieved massive representation in the House of Commons. The differences between Quebec and the rest of

Canada which were papered over by the referendum result have now achieved renewed salience. Thus Quebec, which voted NO in the referendum largely because it gave Quebec too little recognition of its distinct status, has struck back by electing enough Bloc Québécois MPs to form the Official Opposition. Many "rest of Canadians," notably but not only in the west, who apparently voted against the Accord largely because it gave too much to Quebec and too little to them have struck back by electing an almost equal number of Reform Party MPs.

Throughout the last 30 years, despite the obvious differences in emphasis between Liberals and Conservatives, two broad alternatives for accommodating French-English differences have been put forward — renewed federalism on the decentralist model and national bilingualism, combined with multi-culturalism. The new Liberal government clearly falls squarely within this framework. Nevertheless, the strength of the Bloc Québécois and the Reform Party reveals the fragility and lack of consensus on both these models. Significant proportions of Canadians outside Quebec reject both constitutional recognition of Quebec as a distinct society, and official bilingualism (Stark 1992; Adams and Lennox 1990). In Quebec, majority opinion ranges from a federalism that recognizes its distinct status, through various forms of sovereignty (Stark 1992; Dion 1992) Indeed, it would appear that each successive round of constitutional negotiations has peeled back the onion to reveal the underlying differences about the nature of the Canadian political community more sharply. The divisions have become more polarized.

The election result has ratchetted up the stakes one more notch, as each side of the debate now has a major regionally based political party to speak for it; and as two of the three parties which shared the earlier consensus (the Conservatives and the NDP) have been decimated. Moreover, of course, the election result has placed this debate at the heart of national politics, in Parliament. Reform is in Parliament in part to challenge both the commitment to official bilingualism and recognition of Quebec as a distinct society, emphasizing instead provincial and individual equality. And the Bloc is in Parliament to show that federalism cannot be renewed and cannot meet Quebecers' aspirations. As we saw in the election campaign, there was a kind of dynamic interaction between them. More support for the Bloc in Quebec reinforced Reform's pledge to stand up to Quebec; more support for Reform showed Quebecers how little they could expect from renewed federalism.

What are the implications of these developments? In some ways, it could be argued, the effects may be positive. Legitimate and widespread opinions once suppressed, muted or papered over have been democratically expressed and brought out into the open. So there may be a new kind of honesty to the process.

Moreover, the debates will no longer go on mainly in the elitist confines of federal-provincial negotiations, or the Cabinet and caucus room; instead they will take place in public parliamentary sessions, for all to see. If the result is failure, so be it, and let the chips fall where they may.

There is a lot to be said for this view. But it illustrates an old dilemma: processes that meet the democratic criterion of openness may fail on the criterion of the ability to manage or resolve conflict and to find compromise. If it is positive to get the disagreements out on the table, the problem remains of how to put the pieces back together.

It is hard to predict how the new Parliament will play out, or what the consequences of the federal election will be for the next Quebec election, to be held by the fall of 1994. It may be that all parties will tacitly agree to put the constitutional issues aside. It may be that participation in Parliament will bring both the Bloc and Reform into the traditional politics of accommodation. It may be that having made their point in electing the Bloc, Quebec voters will opt for federalist Quebec Liberals in the provincial election. Or that if they elect the PQ, they will reject sovereignty in a subsequent provincial referendum.

But none of this is certain or even likely. Bloc and Reform are more likely to continue to play off against each other. The very fact that the Liberal government holds a majority, rather than minority, may strengthen this tendency, since both Bloc and Reform can indulge these regionalist impulses without fear of actually bringing the government down. The Liberal government will be caught in the middle: any concessions to Quebec to undermine the Bloc will fuel Reform sentiment; refusal to do so will fuel the Bloc. Every government decision will be intensely scrutinized for its distributional consequences, as we have seen already with concessions on agriculture within the GATT, and with the decision to terminate the previous government's helicopter program.

It is also possible that the presence of the Bloc as the Official Opposition will add fuel to the growing recent tendency in the rest of Canada to say: "Let Quebec go."

However it develops, the effect of the election is that in one form or another, the constitutional or national unity issue is or soon will be back on the table. The dangers are that fiscal possibilities will be assessed and interpreted in terms less of their ability to meet the substantive policy problems than in terms of their likely implications for the coming Quebec election and the future of national unity; and that the energies and attention of policymakers will be diverted to the constitution. Once again, the constitution is likely to trump functional federalism.

REGIONAL POLITICS TRUMPS OTHER DIMENSIONS OF DISTRIBUTION

A number of years ago, Edwin R. Black pointed out that in Canada, issues of distribution which in other advanced countries might be played out in terms of class or economic sectors, in Canada are played out in terms of distribution across provinces and regions (Black 1975). Again, the results of the election will reinforce this tendency because of the prominence of the two regionalist parties, and because of the relative weakness of the Liberals in some regions — though this regional imbalance is far less marked than in most of the Trudeau years. All federal proposals will be scrutinized and attacked on the basis of regional balance sheet calculations of relative gains and losses. The politics of regional jealously is likely to be exacerbated by the nature of the choices that have to be made. Assuming those choices will inevitably involve reductions rather than increases in transfer payments and regional development spending, then what we will see is not that some are gaining relative to others, or even than some are gaining while others are losing, but rather that *all* will be losing. Every province and region will have grievances against the centre. Following the election of the Parti Québécois in 1976, there was a flurry of "balance sheet federalism," in which various governments purported to demonstrate how they lost and others gained in the distribution of federal revenues and spending (Leslie and Simeon 1977). In 1993, the Ontario government began what may be a new round of such efforts with the publication of a similar set of studies demonstrating unfair treatment of Ontario (Ontario Ministry of Intergovernmental Affairs 1993). Again, this does not augur well for a rational or coherent addressing of the problems, or for the ability to build consensus around fiscal arrangements and social policy.

This may have especially important implications for the long-term future of equalization. What is likely to be most threatened in the politics of the zero-sum is the commitment to sharing and redistribution, or what Peter Leslie calls the "sharing community" (Leslie 1993, pp. 3-9). There may be much less willingness to see this as an essential part of the Confederation bargain, especially in a province like Ontario, which is increasingly preoccupied with its own problems, increasingly linked economically to the United States rather than to other Canadian provinces, and increasingly has a population whose experience of Canada is not rooted in the traditional Canadian emphasis on region and language.

FISCAL FEDERALISM TRUMPS SOCIAL POLICY

Fiscal federalism is simultaneously concerned with two sets of issues. On the one hand, it is concerned with revenue sharing and intergovernmental transfers, which in turn then are linked to the economic issues of macroeconomic policy, debts, deficits, and the like. But on the other hand it is about social policy: about the amount and quality of the health care Canadians receive, about our social welfare systems, and about postsecondary education. Each perspective tends to raise a different set of conceptual issues; each engages a different set of interest groups; each has a different policy network associated with it; and each engages different sets of government officials — finance and treasury on one side, ministries of health, education, and welfare on the other. Hence a debate in one policy network about the future of fiscal federalism is likely to be very different from a debate about the welfare state which might take place in another network.

Since in Canada, federal-provincial cooperation in social policy has been expressed in terms of financial instruments — EPF, Equalization, CAP — the treasury and economics network has tended to dominate. The social policy network has played a subordinate role, especially in a period of restraint. We see this in the design of such programs as EPF. This transmuting of social policy into fiscal arrangements has frustrated full debate about national social policy, and effectively excludes from the discussion groups and agencies in the social policy network.

This tendency for the fiscal horse to drag the social policy wagon is undoubtedly exacerbated by the current fiscal crisis. The danger is that the finance and treasury agencies which are likely to drive the renegotiation process will do unnecessary damage to our social policy framework, and fail to explore creative reform of the social policy system.

Clearly, in the current context, when we need both to deal with debts and deficits and to re-think our social policy system, we must bring these two networks together. We cannot discuss fiscal policy without thinking about social policy — and vice versa. This is difficult enough to do *within* a level of government; it is even harder to do when we must simultaneously bridge across levels of government. Thus we have to ask whether there is a mismatch between the institutional machinery and the way in which the issues are structured.

THE INTERGOVERNMENTAL DYNAMIC TRUMPS
CITIZEN POLITICS

The dominance of the intergovernmental forum, and the transmuting of social into fiscal policy creates enormous frustrations for citizens in understanding, and therefore contributing to the process. There are the familiar problems identified by Smiley (1979) and others: the secrecy of the intergovernmental process, the arcane and esoteric language of fiscal and intergovernmental issues replete with their formulae and assumptions. As a Quebec journalist wrote in 1966, "The holy spirit seems to have a marked horror for those mortal men who occupy themselves with fiscal arrangements" (In Simeon 1972, p. 66). Where, as in our federal system, governments spend money which they have not taken responsibility for raising; and spend money over whose use they have no control, accountability is attenuated.

Perhaps more fundamentally, the dominance of fiscal and intergovernmental perspectives draws a dark veil between cause and consequence in public policy. It is not easy for citizens to perceive the link between a development in the fiscal arena and the real world policy implications. To take a hypothetical example, if a potential client visits a rehabilitation centre in Toronto and finds the doors locked, how is he or she to link that to a federal "cap on CAP" a few years earlier. The complexities and intricacies of intergovernmental relations are at war with the transparency necessary for effective policy debate at the level of the public.

More generally, the ability of intergovernmental processes to work out effective arrangements in the current context is seriously undermined by the delegitimation of executive federalism that occurred during the constitutional process. There remains little citizen confidence in these mechanisms. Citizens have traditionally been even more excluded from fiscal federalism debates than they have from the constitution. Yet, especially in this round, the results will have consequences at least as great for many of the groups that mobilized around the constitution as the constitution itself had. Continued exclusion will further contribute to the delegitimation of the intergovernmental system. This too undermines the institutional capacity of the system to make the very hard decisions that now face it. Indeed, another consequence of our preoccupation with the constitution in recent years — and of the very personal way in which Prime Minister Mulroney approached it — is an undermining and deterioration of the intergovernmental machinery, and of the functionally-oriented trust relationships among officials which make it work effectively (Dupré 1985). To rehabilitate intergovernmental relations is a daunting task, given the disrepute into which this process has fallen. Thus what we might call the democratic deficit and the performance deficit reinforce each other.

GOVERNMENTAL SELF-INTEREST TRUMPS COLLECTIVE APPROACHES

Finally, to return to my starting point, while it is obviously true, and recognized by all the governments that they are all in this together, and that the issues of debts and deficits are a collective problem which neither level can solve alone, the fact of the matter is that each government is primarily concerned with its own bottom line. Each seeks to minimize its losses and maximize its gains. There are few incentives or rewards for doing anything else. So each seeks to maximize its revenues, while transferring as many costs as possible to other levels. The result is a kind of cascading of the fiscal burden, from Ottawa to provinces, and from provinces to municipalities and other transfer agencies and ultimately to the citizen. Again, this is not propitious for a coherent or cooperative resolution of the issues.

CONCLUSION

Thus to repeat the central point: the current politics of federalism and of intergovernmental relations reduces our capacity to deal with the financial crisis and to re-think our social policy. My suggestion is the same as that recently advanced by David Cameron: that federalism, in the context of restraint, may have an "obstructive capacity" (1993, p. 9) — getting in the way of resolution of crucial issues. It may be a system that works well in good times, but is less well-equipped to deal with the bad times. This analysis may be too pessimistic. There do seem to be a number of areas where there are mutual incentives to agree — for example, in more integration of the federal and provincial sales taxes, or in some common approach to borrowing. The "Liberal Plan for Canada" does pledge a commitment to intergovernmental cooperation, and "working together" with the provinces in many areas (1993). Yet there is no escaping the zero-sum character of what happens to federal transfers.

Given the need for coordination and integration of the fiscal system and associated social policies, what alternatives are available? One model has been proposed by Albert Breton (1985). His "competitive federalism" would achieve coordination by having each government look to its own powers and taking its own decisions, reacting and adjusting to the actions of other governments and to its own economic and political environment as it sees fit. Ottawa has considerable flexibility in this regard. The major elements of fiscal federalism

— CAP, equalization and EPF — represent the exercise of the federal spending power. There is no legal barrier to unilateral federal reduction of these transfers. The Canada Assistance Plan is the most vulnerable, because the federal transfer is entirely in the form of cash. That is also true for equalization, though it may receive at least some symbolic protection through section 36 of the *Constitution Act, 1982*. EPF consists of a combination of cash and tax transfers, but here federal leverage is limited because of the declining proportion of cash. Similarly, it is also conceivable that Ottawa could bring substantial pressure to bear on provincial policy choices through altering the conditions attached to the transfers, as was done with the *Canada Health Act, 1984*.

Faced with budget crises, provinces also have considerable freedom to act alone, whether through expenditure cuts, increased taxation, borrowing or policy change. Existing program conditions place relatively few constraints on provincial experimentation in this area.

This process has, of course been proceeding. While the provinces were largely protected from federal restraint measures between 1984 and 1988, the first term of the Mulroney government, since 1988 a wide range of limits and caps have been applied to federal transfers. For their part, provinces have responded to these developments, and to changes in their revenue and expenditure situations with a wide variety of program changes, restraint measures and increased taxing and borrowing.

There is little doubt that the federal measures have been a strong stimulus to more aggressive provincial restraint measures. Perhaps then, the Breton model is the correct approach.

However, it has high costs, not only for the governments involved, but also for citizens. Unilateral federal limits on transfers have obviously contributed to the ballooning of provincial deficits and the accompanying debt, which the smaller, economically weaker, provinces have much more difficulty financing. Unlike the federal debt, most provincial debt is held abroad (Mendelson 1994). We risk repeating the situation of the 1930s, in which some provinces teetered on the brink of bankruptcy. Similarly, leaving the governments on their own risks unrestricted competition for revenues and the break down of the tax collection agreements which have provided considerable harmony in the taxation system. Thus, there are dangers in unrestricted fiscal free-for-all. More generally, unilateral, competitive federalism fails to deal with the linkages between federal and provincial policies. For example, it is now conventional wisdom that unemployment insurance (federal) must be more tightly integrated with education (provincial) and welfare (shared). Similarly job creation is now tightly linked to education. No government alone possesses the instruments and powers to attack any of the issues on the current policy agenda. And efforts to do so may play havoc with coherence of programs at the other level. Thus, unvarnished competitive federalism, despite its attractions, is not a desirable model.

A second model which has achieved much attention is to seek savings, transparency, and a closer link between programs and costs by a program of rationalization of federal and provincial responsibilities through disentanglement. While there may be much potential here, the record offers little optimism for the achievement of major change. Governments have advocated "disentanglement" since the 1970s. The clarifications of the division of powers in the Charlottetown Accord ostensibly were designed to entrench provincial paramountcy in a number of fields, but instead ended up setting out a bewildering array of new intergovernmental agreements. Similarly, the Charlottetown provisions on the economic union and trade and commerce increased rather than decreased overlap and interdependence. These results illustrated that most policy areas do indeed have both federal and provincial dimensions, and that both orders of government are loathe to give up their policy levers or to concede leadership to the other. There is indeed, much room for rationalization through informal transfers of responsibility. But there will be no return to an earlier model of the federalism of watertight compartments.

Indeed, the emphasis on federal-provincial agreements underlines the need for the third model: a return to functionally-based collaboration. Given the existing roles of government and the present financial arrangements, it seems to me we must try to convince governments to adopt a cooperative approach, and to recognize the interdependence and shared character of the problems they are facing, however difficult that is.

The critiques of such an approach are well-known (Breton 1985). There is the danger, on the one hand, that governments may constitute an "elite cartel," cobbling together agreements that meet their own institutional needs, but which pay little heed to broader citizen concerns. This is the criticism of the Meech Lake process. There is, on the other hand, the risk of deadlock, paralysis and inability to agree. These risks increase the more the intergovernmental arena is seen as the formal decisionmaker; effective action by any government is then held hostage to intergovernmental agreement.

We need, therefore to seek a middle ground, between the uncoordinated independent action of governments which seek to relieve their own budgetary crisis by dumping the problem onto others and the requirement of joint decision making in order to get anything done. The Royal Commission on the Economic Union and Development Prospects for Canada distinguished four levels of federal-provincial interaction — autonomous, independent action by each government; consultative processes to exchange information and provide opportunities for persuasion, pressure and influence; coordination, in which governments would seek agreements on broad policy objectives, implementing them independently; and joint decision making in which formal, binding commitments are made (Royal Commission 1985, p. 261). As I have argued, neither the first nor the last is acceptable in light of current challenges. The emphasis must be placed on the consultation and coordination parts of the spectrum.

Even that is no panacea and will be difficult to achieve. In order to do so, it is first necessary for governments to recognize that this *is* a set of collective, shared problems, and that unilateral solutions are likely to cause more problems than they solve. We urgently need to reorient our thinking about federalism from the constitutional/community axis to a more functional, policy-oriented perspective. One might hope that the gravity of the issues and the pressure of public opinion will bring this about. We then need to develop mechanisms, both within governments and between governments, which recognize the interaction of fiscal federalism and social policy, and social policy and economic policy, rather than keeping them separate. This suggests that participation at the intergovernmental table should not be limited to finance and treasury ministers and officials. We also need to recognize the need for more transparency in these relationships, so that citizens can see and understand the linkage between fiscal arrangements and social policy. And we need to provide greater opportunity for citizen groups to inject their views into the intergovernmental process. Proposals to open up the budget process might help here. Another model is the 1981 parliamentary enquiry — the Breau Task Force — (Canada 1981) which provided the first public forum for extensive interest group commentary on fiscal federalism. However, it was flawed by its being a federal government vehicle designed largely to make the case against the provinces in fiscal matters. A better model might be some form of enquiry which was jointly sponsored by the 11 governments. Following the Supreme Court decision on CAP, we also need to develop some rules for the conduct of the "dis-spending power." As the Liberal program states, there is a need to ensure at least some predictability and stability for each level of government as it plans its own responses to the new challenges (1993, p. 21). We need to ensure that provinces are not vulnerable to arbitrary or capricious cuts, while at the same time accepting that ultimately, these are federal spending powers for which Ottawa must be responsible to Parliament. Perhaps one model might be binding five-year agreements. Changes within those periods could be made only with some level of intergovernmental consensus. Finally, I think to revitalize the intergovernmental process, rebuilding the functional linkages in economic and social policy which have fallen into disrepair in the past few years of constitutional high politics.

In the longer run, we also need to consider some broader changes, including a re-thinking of federal and provincial roles and responsibilities in these linked areas of public finance, social policy, and economic policy. In the short run, however, as governments grapple with the enormous problems of dividing up the pain of deficit reduction and policy restructuring, the prospect is for more rather than less conflict. No simple set of institutional fixes gets us around the tensions associated with the politics of restraint and cut-backs. And we are left with the dilemma that just as our continuing constitutional, regional, and linguistic conflicts have got in the way of a coherent approach to the practical issues, so failure to deal with them effectively will exacerbate those same fundamental conflicts about the very future of Canada.

BIBLIOGRAPHY

Adams, Michael and Mary Jane Lennox (1990), "The Public's View of the Canadian Federation," in *Canada: The State of the Federation 1990*, ed. R.L. Watts and D.M. Brown, Kingston: Institute of Intergovernmental Relations, Queen's University.

Black, Edwin R. (1975), *Divided Loyalties: Canadian Concepts of Federalism*, Montreal and Kingston: McGill-Queen's University Press.

Breton, Albert (1985), "Supplementary Statement," in Royal Commission on the Economic Union and Development Prospects for Canada, *Report*.

Cameron, David (1993), "Take It or Receive It from the Top," paper prepared for IPAC Conference on "Decentralization and Power Sharing: Their Impact on Public Sector Management," 8 October.

Canada. Parliamentary Task Force on Federal-Provincial Fiscal Arrangements, Breau Task Force (1981), *Fiscal Federalism in Canada*, Ottawa: Supply and Services Canada.

Dion, Stephane (1992), "Explaining Quebec Nationalism," in *The Collapse of Canada?* ed. R. Kent Weaver, Washington, DC: Brookings Institution.

_____ (1993), "La Secession du Québec: Evaluation des probabilités après les élections fédérales du 25 Octobre, 1993," paper presented at a conference, Center for Research on North America, Autonomous Nationale University of Mexico, 12 November.

Dupré, Stefan (1985), "Reflections on the Workability of Executive Federalism," in *Intergovernmental Relations*, ed. Richard Simeon, Toronto: University of Toronto Press.

Leslie, Peter M. (1993), "The Fiscal Crisis of Canadian Federalism," in *A Partnership in Trouble: Renegotiating Fiscal Federalism*, ed. Peter M. Leslie, Kenneth Norrie and Irene Ip, Toronto: C. D. Howe Institute.

Leslie, Peter M. and Richard Simeon (1977) "The Battle of the Balance Sheets," in *Must Canada Fail?* ed. Richard Simeon, Montreal and Kingston: McGill-Queen's University Press.

Liberal Party of Canada (1993), *Creating Opportunity: the Liberal Plan for Canada*, Ottawa: Liberal Party of Canada.

Mendelson, Michael (1994), "Fundamental Reform in Fiscal Federalism," in *Fiscal Federalism for the 21st Century*, ed. S. Torjman, Ottawa: Caledon Institute.

Ontario. Ministry of Intergovernmental Affairs (1993), *The Distribution of Federal Spending and Revenue by Province: Implications for Ontario and Other Provinces,* study prepared for the Ministry by Informetrica, Ltd.

Royal Commission on the Economic Union and Development Prospects for Canada, Macdonald Commission (1985), *Report,* Vol. 3, Ottawa: Supply and Services Canada.

Russell, Peter (1993), *Constitutional Odyssey: Can Canadians be a Sovereign People?* Toronto: University of Toronto Press.

Simeon, Richard (1972), *Federal-Provincial Diplomacy: The Making of Recent Policy in Canada,* Toronto: University of Toronto Press.

Smiley, D.V. (1979), "An Outsider's Observations of Federal-Provincial Relations Among Consenting Adults," in *Confrontation or Collaboration: Intergovernmental Relations in Canada Today,* ed. Richard Simeon, Toronto: Institute of Public Administration of Canada.

Stark, Andrew (1992), "English-Canadian Opposition to Quebec Nationalism," in *The Collapse of Canada?* ed. R. Kent Weaver, Washington, DC: Brookings Institution.

Comment: The Politics of Fiscal Federalism

André Blais

Richard Simeon makes the following arguments:

1. Canadian fiscal federalism is facing tough problems.
2. Solving these problems requires the political will and the institutional capacity to achieve some degree of coordination between the different levels of government.
3. The structure of the political debate in Canada, the focus being on constitutional issues and questions of regional distribution, does not facilitate the achievement of such coordination.
4. The present political context just seems to aggravate these difficulties.

Let me briefly react to these points. I will elaborate somewhat more on the last.

TOUGH CHOICES

I would certainly not dispute the fact that governments face tough choices. The federal deficit is a very serious problem. The federal government will have to cut spending even more in the coming years, and transfers to the provinces will have to be reconsidered.

INSTITUTIONAL CAPACITY AND COORDINATION

I am a little more skeptical here of Simeon's emphasis on coordination. First, while I would agree that it is preferable to have *some* degree of coordination, I also see many virtues in competition among governments. We obviously need a mixture of competition and coordination. Second, I am not convinced that institutional capacity is the crucial factor. Major policy innovations tend to occur in times of crisis, and as we are presently in a crisis situation, politicians might be forced to bring about substantial changes to the way Canadian fiscal federalism works. More on this below.

THE CONSTITUTIONAL AGENDA

There is no doubt that much of fiscal federalism, and federal politics more generally, has been driven by the constitutional (and regional) agenda. But this has not prevented the Conservatives from adopting some bold and innovative policies, most especially the Free Trade Agreement (FTA) and the Goods and Services Tax (GST), despite the fact that both these polices had very substantial constitutional and regional implications. The point here is that I am not convinced that fiscal federalism has performed that poorly in the past. In fact if we were to compare Canada with the United States, perhaps we would conclude that Canadian fiscal federalism is a small success, and that part of the success should be imputed to our obsession with the constitution.

THE NEW POLITICAL CONTEXT

Simeon believes that it will be extremely difficult to renew fiscal federalism, because constitutional and regional preoccupations will remain at the forefront. In fact, things will get even worse, as the presence of the Bloc and Reform will ensure that "all federal proposals will be scrutinized and attacked on the basis of regional balance sheet calculations of relative gains and losses."

There is much truth in these assertions. But this is not the whole story. It is also a fact that the Bloc and Reform cannot afford to be catering solely to regional interests. Certainly Lucien Bouchard and Preston Manning also want to be perceived as *responsible* politicians who are able to overcome narrow regional perspectives.

There is another new dimension of the political context whose consequences are, in my view, insufficiently explored by Simeon. That is the fact that Canadians have been sensitized to the seriousness of the deficit. On the one hand, Canadians have told parties that jobs are more important than the deficit. However, in making up their minds on this priority issue, the great majority of Canadians have come to recognize that the deficit is also more serious than they thought. There is now a near consensus that there is a fiscal crisis, that something has to be done about it, and that something is spending cuts.

I would argue that this crisis situation gives the Liberals some room for manoeuvre. Canadians will, I think, understand that the federal government might have to reduce tranfers to the provinces to the same extent it cuts its spending in other areas.

It is also in times of crisis that existing ways of functioning get questioned and that new approaches get considered. Gorbet has indicated in his comments that the status quo is not the reversion point, since the existing system of transfers will expire. This seems to be a ripe moment to establish a completely new system, and to build that new system on broad principles that appeal to all Canadians. These principles would have to compete with regional sensitivities; but I believe that, in times of crisis, Canadians would support a system of fiscal transfers with a clear political and philosophical rationale.

PART THREE

POLICY SECTORS

CHAPTER FIVE

Social Policy and Equalization: New Ways to Meet an Old Objective

Kenneth Norrie

INTRODUCTION

The brochure that sets out the program for this conference states that, "We are approaching a critical juncture in the evolution of fiscal federalism." Few would disagree with this view as it applies to fiscal transfers under the Established Programs Financing (EPF) arrangements for health care and postsecondary education, and those under the Canada Assistance Plan (CAP) for social assistance. Jurisdictional disputes and issues of program design have never been far from the surface in these cases, and recent constitutional initiatives and federal budgetary measures have brought these debates to the fore.

These same observers would almost certainly agree, however, that the comment does not apply with equal force to the third pillar of Canadian fiscal federalism, the equalization program. The principle of unconditional transfers to have-not provinces, based on indices of relative fiscal capacity and funded out of federal government general revenue, seems firmly ensconced. Criticisms of this program, such as they are, generally focus on the suitability of the five-province standard, the ceiling on entitlements, and a number of minor design flaws.

Indeed, some authors see equalization as the key to reform of the other programs (see Richards 1992; Cousineau 1992; Boadway and Hobson 1993; Hobson and St-Hilaire 1993; Hobson 1993). Briefly, the argument runs as follows. A convincing case can be made, on efficiency grounds, for full and final devolution of responsibility for social programs to provincial governments. There is a fair element of interregional redistribution implicit in EPF and CAP transfers, however, which would be lost if these programs were simply ended. This trade-off between efficiency and interregional equity could be avoided, the argument goes, if the equalization program were modified and expanded to offset these effects.

I shall argue in what follows that this proposal, while logically appealing, rests on two untested propositions. First, it is not clear that devolution will increase the efficiency of social program delivery. Second, the federal government may be more constrained in its ability to expand the equalization program than is realized. I suggest instead a set of arrangements that constitute a new way to meet a long-standing federal government policy objective: a parallel commitment to individual and regional equity.

FISCAL FEDERALISM TAKES SHAPE

The federal and provincial governments began immediately after World War II to put together the complicated series of intergovernmental fiscal arrangements that would come to define postwar Canadian federalism. The major components of this system are familiar: the cost-sharing arrangements in health, post-secondary education, and social assistance, together with an equalization program. Since the degree of substitutability between shared-cost programs and equalization is at issue, it is important to understand the origin and subsequent evolution of this set of measures (see Norrie 1993; Leslie 1993).

Shared-Cost Programs

The first example of shared-cost programs in the postwar period was the National Health Grants of 1948, wherein Ottawa provided matching grants to the provinces for a variety of health-care services. Nine years later, the *Hospital Insurance and Diagnostic Services Act* was passed, and by 1961 all provinces had plans covered by the legislation. Under this Act, Ottawa agreed to pay to each province annually an amount equal to 25 percent of the average per capita cost of hospital services in Canada plus 25 percent of the per capita cost of hospital services in that province, this sum multiplied by the province's population.

Medical insurance was next. The federal government responded to pressures for a national insurance scheme by introducing the *Medical Care Act* in 1966. By 1971 all provinces were part of the scheme, and by 1972 both territories were covered as well. The Act specified that each province was to be in charge of designing, implementing, and administering its own medical insurance plan. As long as the plan met four general conditions — comprehensive in terms of medical coverage, universal in its coverage, publicly administered, and fully transferable among provinces — it would be eligible for federal funding amounting to 50 percent of the national per capita cost of medical insurance, this figure multiplied by the province's population.

The first major initiative in postsecondary education came in 1951 when Ottawa instituted a series of cash grants to universities. This assistance was altered significantly as part of the 1967 fiscal arrangements legislation. Direct cash grants to universities ended, and the funds went instead to provincial governments. The federal contribution to each province was set at 50 percent of the operating costs of its postsecondary educational institutions. A portion of this transfer came via an abatement of personal and corporate income tax. The residual amount was in the form of a cash transfer.

Ottawa was involved in a number of cost-sharing ventures with the provinces in the social assistance field prior to 1966. In that year, these programs were consolidated under the Canada Assistance Plan (CAP). Under the plan, the federal government undertook to pay 50 percent of each province's expenditure in meeting the basic requirements of recipients of aid. The only conditions were that the programs be directed to families and individuals in need, and that there not be unreasonable residency requirements.

In modern textbook terms (Boadway and Hobson 1993), one can offer two rationales for these federal government transfers. First, to the extent that provincial government expenditures on health, postsecondary education, and social assistance programs spill over into other jurisdictions, federal transfers improve efficiency by providing a subsidy for the benefits received by non-residents. Second, to the extent that government expenditures on social policy are intended to be redistributive, federal cost-sharing grants contribute to national equity by ensuring some minimum standard of uniformity among individual Canadians.

It is difficult to gauge how relevant the spillover argument may have been at this time, but the federal government grants certainly had important inter-regional equity implications. Interestingly, however, these effects differ notably among programs. The formulae used to determine the transfers for hospital and medical insurance meant that the programs were implicitly equalizing as long as low-cost jurisdictions were also relatively poor ones. The arrangements for the other two programs were less implicitly equalizing. The 50-50 cost-sharing of postsecondary education expenditures meant that the more a province spent in this area per capita, the higher was its per capita federal grant.[1] The per capita value of the federal transfer for social assistance could vary significantly as well. The redistributive effect could, in principle, go either way. For given benefit rates, provinces with high social assistance requirements would receive extra federal funding. This feature would favour the less-advantaged jurisdictions. To the extent that benefit rates were more generous in richer provinces, however, the redistribution would be reversed.

Equalization

The federal government's concern for interregional equity went beyond transfer programs for health, postsecondary education, and social assistance. Significantly, however, this commitment took quite a different form. When the system of tax-sharing replaced that of tax-rentals in 1957, Ottawa introduced a formal equalization scheme intended to even out the resulting fiscal disparities among provinces. Provinces whose fiscal capacity fell below a certain standard were entitled to receive equalization payments.[2] The transfer in each case was equal to the per capita amount needed to bring the province up to the standard, this sum multiplied by the province's population. The payments, then as now, were made out of federal general revenues, and were intended to be purely unconditional transfers.

The terms of the equalization program were adjusted several times in the ensuing years. Natural resource revenues were introduced into the tax base in 1962, and in 1967 the standard became the average national per capita yield from each of 16 separate tax sources. Each province's fiscal capacity was now compared, tax by tax, against this standard. If the per capita yield on the first tax category was higher, a negative entitlement on that tax category resulted. If the per capita yield from that source was below the national average, a positive entitlement resulted. If the sum of the entitlements over the 16 tax categories was positive, the province received an equalization payment equal to this shortfall multiplied by its population. If the sum was negative, the province's entitlement was set at zero.

Remarks

Like the shared-cost programs, equalization acted to redistribute income interregionally, but, significantly, the rationale for doing so was quite distinct. Federal grants to provincially-designed and administered social programs were intended to provide a measure of equality among individual Canadians. Thus it made sense to base the federal transfers on provincial government expenditures in these areas, and to attach broad conditions to them. Equalization payments, on the other hand, were meant to offset disparities among provincial governments, with no concern as to how these funds were used. Thus it made sense to base the transfers on provincial government revenues, and to make them entirely unconditional.

The force of this distinction is underscored by considering that, if inter-regional redistribution were the main policy objective at this time, Ottawa could simply have offered a larger share of equalized tax revenue to the provinces, and not bothered with grants tied to specific provincial government expenditures. Put differently, while the shared-cost programs were generally equalizing in nature, their primary purpose was to provide minimum levels of essential services to individual Canadians. The Rowell-Sirois Commission explained the unconditional nature of equalization payments, which it called national adjustment grants, with the now-famous phrase "A province ... may, for example, starve its roads and improve its education, or starve its education and improve its roads" (Royal Commission 1940, p. 84). Perhaps out of concern that provinces might actually starve education, shared-cost programs in key social services for individual Canadians were developed in tandem with equalization.

THE 1977 EPF ARRANGEMENTS

The equalization program gained immediate acceptance, but the cost-sharing arrangements met with some resistance from the outset. The federal-provincial discussion and negotiation that ensued brought about, in 1977, an important change in Canadian fiscal federalism. These arrangements were widely applauded at the time, but in retrospect they appear as a curious hybrid of measures, responsible for the quandary that we find ourselves in today.

Forces for Change

The first concern with the shared-cost programs was political in nature. Some provinces, Quebec in particular, objected to the federal government playing an active role in areas that they saw as falling under exclusive provincial jurisdiction. To meet this objection, Ottawa introduced a technique known as "opting out." Under it, a province could decline to participate in a federal government program, and instead receive additional tax points to finance a program of their own creation. The practice was formalized in 1965 under the *Established Programs Financing (Interim Arrangements) Act*. All provincial governments were given the opportunity to take tax points instead of cash grants in a number of social policy areas. Quebec opted for the tax points in all cases, but no other province expressed any interest in the option.

The second concern was fiscal. The federal government soon learned what it meant to make open-ended spending commitments to programs over which it had little direct control. In response, it began to implement a series of ad hoc adjustments. The 1972 *Fiscal Arrangements Act* placed a ceiling on the annual increase in grants for postsecondary education, and in 1975 officials announced a ceiling on health-care expenditures. These actions are the first examples of what was to become an important irritant in later years, namely a unilateral change in federal government spending commitments for shared-cost programs.

The third concern was with the efficiency of program delivery. Some observers argued that minimum national standards for social policy were inappropriate because preferences with respect to social policies varied by region. By putting conditions on its grants, Ottawa was imposing an inappropriate mix of social programs on Canadians, and was discouraging the experimentation and innovation that would improve the efficiency of these programs over time. Provincial governments were more aware of local preferences, or at least more likely to uncover them through experimentation. Thus, it was argued, they should be free to tailor social policies to what they perceived were the best interests of their own residents.

Other observers pointed to the potential for resources being mis-allocated due to the fact that, with cost-sharing, provincial governments could provide $1 worth of social programs for less than $1 of their own-tax revenue. In the cases of social assistance and postsecondary education, for example, provinces were effectively spending 50 cent dollars. This feature was less true for the health and hospitalization grants, since the size of the federal transfer to any province depended on more than just the amount of spending on these programs in that province. Simple economic theory suggested that, faced with distorted relative prices of this magnitude, provincial governments were likely over-spending on social policy, and underspending in other areas.

The EPF Arrangements

The *Federal-Provincial Fiscal Arrangements and Established Programs Financing Act* was unveiled in 1977 as a response to these concerns. Ottawa maintained its commitment to health and postsecondary education, but altered the manner in which it supported them. Henceforth, its contribution to these two very different programs, with their distinct shared-cost funding histories, was to be made in the form of a block grant. The grant was to be paid in two parts. The first portion consisted of an annual cash payment to each province, equal to 50 percent of the average per capita federal contribution to health and postsecondary education in 1975-76, this figure multiplied by that province's population. The base grant was to be escalated each year by the rise in per capita GDP averaged over the preceding three years. The other part of the federal contribution involved a transfer of personal and corporate income tax points to the provinces. Practically, this provision meant that Ottawa reduced its tax rates by these amounts, leaving room for the provinces to increase theirs.

The cash transfer portion of the new arrangements retained the equalization feature that was implicit in the earlier cost-sharing arrangements for hospital and medical insurance. The tax point portion of the transfer did not have this same property, however, given the differences in provincial fiscal capacities. This effect was offset to some extent by making the transferred tax points subject to equalization. Thus, poorer provinces received the value of their tax points plus an additional cash transfer, referred to as associated equalization. Some inequality remained, however, since the tax points transferred to the richer provinces were not equalized downwards to the national standard.

The Canada Assistance Plan was not altered at this time, although there was some discussion about treating it in a parallel fashion to health and post-secondary education. For whatever reason, it remained a straight cost-sharing formula. The federal government remained committed to cover 50 percent of the social assistance costs each provincial government incurred, subject to some general conditions. The grant to each province under this program thus continued to depend on the case load and the generosity of the provincial scheme.

Remarks

In retrospect, the mix of cash and tax transfers adopted in the 1977 EPF arrangements was a curious hybrid of measures. As noted above, there is a clear, if controversial, rationale for the conditional grants that were in place until 1977. National social programs can be justified to the extent that they offset important interprovincial spillovers from social policy expenditures. More importantly, by bringing about minimum national standards in these program areas, they reflect a commitment to national equity.

There is also a clear, if equally controversial, rationale for the tax transfers that were part of the 1977 arrangements. Tax transfers are consistent with the view that efficiency is better served if provinces are free to design and administer social programs as they see fit. The argument is a simple one of accountability. With tax transfers, the government that spends is also the government that taxes. The opportunity cost of each $1 spent on social programs is clear to voters, who can therefore be expected to choose more wisely the amount of government spending they wish to see.

There is no obvious rationale, however, for the cash portion of the federal contribution. As lump sum transfers, they could no longer be used to ensure a minimum national standard of social services. To the extent that the cash transfers were used in that manner anyway, as in the case of the *Canada Health Act* some years later, there was little point in altering the form of the grant in the first place. If they were not intended to be so used, it is legitimate to ask why the entire contribution did not take the form of an equalized tax point transfer, to enhance political accountability.

It might be argued that cash transfers were retained to provide a degree of interregional equity that tax point transfers could not, even when equalized. But if equalization was the dominant motive, why choose to transfer tax points at all, and why leave the Canada Assistance Plan with a different, and less obviously redistributive, funding formula? Why not rely entirely on purely unconditional cash transfers for all programs? Once tax transfers are introduced, it is fair to ask why there must be a greater degree of equity among provinces with respect to social policy than there is for other expenditures. If the equalization formula is adequate for all other provincial government responsibilities, why is it deficient in these specific instances? If the answer is that these expenditures are somehow more fundamental, we are back to the case for minimum national standards, and hence shared-cost programs.[3]

This curious choice of a mixture of grants and tax transfers in the 1977 EPF arrangements explains the nature of much of the debate on fiscal transfers since. Both those who saw the arrangements as preserving a role for the federal government in social policy formation, and those who saw them as removing Ottawa from this field completely, were disappointed by the subsequent experience with this hybrid arrangement.

FISCAL FEDERALISM TODAY

The 1977 arrangements were no sooner in place when the federal government began adjusting the terms and extent of its commitments. The cumulative effect of these adjustments has been to bring the arrangements for EPF and CAP to the point where it is legitimate to refer to them, as the program brochure does, as "under immense strain." The equalization program faced its own set of pressures, and the formula was adjusted accordingly. The issues surrounding the future of this program are quite different, however.

The EPF Arrangements

The EPF arrangements were altered in 1982 to take the form that is still in effect today. Each province is entitled to receive an annual transfer equal to the product of a uniform basic entitlement[4] and its population. The entitlement is paid in two parts. Federal authorities first calculate the value to each province of the tax points transferred to it in 1977, plus associated equalization where relevant. This amount is then recorded as EPF tax transfers. The second part of the transfer is a cash payment. It is equal to the difference between the province's total entitlement and the estimated value of the tax transfer plus any associated equalization. Cash payments are a residual amount in effect.[5] They have no independent base as they did between 1977 and 1982.

The intent in 1982 was to escalate the basic entitlement each year by the average of the change in GDP over the last three years. As the federal government budget situation worsened, however, this provision was altered. Payments deemed to be owing to postsecondary education (an hypothetical figure given the nature of the grant) were limited to 6 percent growth in 1983-84 and 5 percent growth in 1984-85. In 1986, Ottawa lowered the escalator on the basic entitlement to two points below the growth rate of GDP (GDP less 2) for 1986-87 and subsequent years. In the 1989 budget, the escalator was reduced by another percentage point, effective for 1990-91. In the 1990 budget, the basic EPF entitlement was frozen for two years at the 1989-90 per capita figure. The next year the freeze was extended to 1994-95.

This freezing of the basic entitlement has an important implication for the future of the programs covered. With the per capita entitlement frozen, the only growth in federal contributions to established programs comes from population growth. The value of the tax points transferred in 1977 continues to grow, however, meaning the residual cash portion is declining. Eventually, if the freeze is extended long enough, the cash contribution will fall to zero. This situation will occur first in Quebec because it has more tax points to begin with, the result of an earlier opting-out arrangement. Cash transfers will be effectively zero for Quebec before the end of this decade, and for the other provinces soon thereafter.

The Canada Assistance Plan

The Canada Assistance Plan escaped federal budget austerity scrutiny until 1990. In that year, Ottawa announced a ceiling of 5 percent growth on the total amount it would transfer under CAP in the next two fiscal years to those provinces not receiving equalization — B.C., Alberta, and Ontario. This limit was extended to 1994-95 in the 1991 budget. British Columbia challenged the initial action, and the B.C. Court of Appeals ruled in its favour in June 1990. This decision was overturned by the Supreme Court of Canada in August 1991, clearing the way for the federal government to impose its spending ceilings.

This ceiling has no effect as long as social assistance expenditures in each of the three have provinces rise by 5 percent or less each year. The federal contribution remains at 50 percent of total provincial outlays. If provincial expenditures rise by more than 5 percent annually, however, whether due to a rising case load or a more generous benefit structure, the federal share falls. The result is that the marginal dollars spent on social assistance are purely provincial ones. The federal government cannot influence these expenditures in any way, for better or worse, since it has no fiscal levers left.

The other implication of the ceiling is that the further Ottawa's share of CAP expenditures falls below 50 percent, the less likely it is that the cost-sharing arrangement will ever be reinstated. The reason is that the snap-back required to bring Ontario back into the program will be too large for the federal authorities to manage. This temporary budget measure will almost certainly become a permanent feature.

Equalization

The equalization program came under considerable pressure during the 1970s as a result of the energy crisis (Courchene 1984). The huge increases in resource revenues in the western provinces, Alberta in particular, increased equalization entitlements substantially. After a series of ad hoc adjustments, in 1982 the base for calculating equalization entitlements was changed from a national average to a five-province standard. Alberta was omitted from the base to remove the energy revenue distortion, and the Atlantic provinces were removed as an offset. There were further adjustments to the number of taxes represented, and to the revenue guarantees.

A cap was placed on the program at this time whereby total federal payments for equalization could not rise above the 1982-83 figure by more than the increase in GDP. This ceiling became binding late in the decade, and the equalization formula in effect became irrelevant. The recipient provinces complained of an equalization shortfall, equal to the amount they would have received under the formal program less the amount they would receive as a result of the cap. Total payments were "re-based" in late 1991 in response, which solved the problem for the time being.

EPF AND CAP: IS FURTHER DEVOLUTION THE ANSWER?

If EPF and CAP are under "immense strain," what is to be done? As noted in the introduction to this chapter, one prominent view is that we should finish what we apparently set out to do in 1977 with EPF: make the fiscal transfers truly unconditional, and extend equalization as needed to maintain interregional equity. The validity of this view depends crucially on the strength of two key assumptions: devolution is efficiency-enhancing, and the federal government's ability to provide equalization funds is essentially unconstrained.

What Would Further Devolution Involve?

Health and postsecondary education are the most obvious candidates for further devolution. The minimum solution in these cases is to do absolutely nothing. The federal government presence is rapidly winding down at any rate, and soon there will be little or no cash transfers left. At this point, the programs will be purely provincially funded since Ottawa clearly cannot take back the tax points transferred in 1977. With no federal government leverage remaining, the provinces will be able to administer these programs as they wish.

Most proponents of this view, however, envision that, upon withdrawing, Ottawa will also turn over to the provinces all the fiscal resources it currently devotes to social policies. One way to do this is to make the cash transfers purely unconditional; that is, to drop any pretence that they are destined for particular uses by the provinces, or that they can be used to influence provincial policies. Cash grants would still go to zero over time, but at least the provinces could use them to ease the transition.

Generally, however, the devolution scenario envisions the federal government transferring to the provinces enough personal and corporate income tax points to replace the current cash transfers. This adjustment would take place in two steps. First, the nine provinces would receive the points that Quebec already has by virtue of earlier opting-out arrangements. Then, all ten would receive whatever tax room was left to reduce the cash entitlement to zero. In the interests of maintaining equity among provinces, these tax transfers would be equalized as was done for the tax points that were transferred in 1977.

Even with associated equalization, however, this action would increase the degree of fiscal disparity among provinces since the formula does not equalize the rich provinces downward. Hobson and St-Hilaire (1993) would avoid this outcome by having the federal government cede the value of the EPF cash transfers in the form of a tax abatement rather than actual tax transfers to individual provinces. Thus Ottawa would declare that a certain portion of its revenue base was reserved for established programs. The revenue it collected from this base would be distributed to the provinces much as EPF cash is currently. The advantage over the present arrangement, presumably, is that Ottawa would lose its ability to vary the size of the cash transfers for budgetary reasons.

Federal withdrawal from the Canada Assistance Plan could be accomplished with an EPF-type procedure. First, a figure would be chosen to represent the national average per capita federal government contribution to CAP programs. The next step would be to calculate the number of tax points needed to generate this sum, and reduce the federal rate accordingly to make the room available to the provinces. This tax transfer would be equalized, as in 1977. Since the per capita value of the cash transfer for CAP varies by province, it may be necessary to consider special transitional arrangements for provinces whose per capita revenue will fall under the new arrangement.

Devolution of CAP through tax transfers is subject to the same comment that applies to the idea of converting EPF cash to tax transfers. The end result may not be as fully equalizing as the current arrangement. Boadway and Hobson (1993) and Hobson and St-Hilaire (1993) suggest a way around this objection. Social assistance liabilities should be viewed as negative tax liabilities, with transfers to provinces rolled into the equalization formula. A provinces with an above-average social assistance liability and a below-average revenue capacity would receive equalization payments on both counts. A province with an above-average social assistance liability and an above-average revenue capacity, however, would not receive transfers until the former amount began to exceed the latter amount.

A decade or more of work on social policy makes clear that it is impossible to talk about reforms to CAP without mentioning unemployment insurance. If this connection is acknowledged, and if CAP is to be completely devolved to the provinces, it is logical to presume that the recommendation of the devolutionists is that unemployment insurance would be as well.[6] Provinces would be free to structure their program as they wished, to set contribution and benefit rates, and to integrate unemployment insurance and social assistance.

How would unemployment insurance be funded in this event? Presumably, in keeping with the efficiency perspective that informs the devolution argument more generally, each plan would be self-financing, with the provincial government (or governments if the smaller provinces decided to coordinate actions) alone responsible for any differences between claims and employer-employee contributions. In the interests of not restricting interprovincial labour mobility, there would be some provision for migrants being able to draw the benefits for which they were entitled while seeking work in another province.

The present unemployment insurance scheme acts to redistribute income among regions (Reid and Snoddon 1992; Leslie 1993), so any move to devolve responsibility for it would have to take this effect into account. Presumably, contribution rates and benefits would be adjusted in each region until the plans became actuarially sound. Boadway and Hobson (1993) argue that any such devolution would have to be accompanied by associated equalization payments to equalize the abilities of provincial governments to contribute to the plans.

Is Devolution Efficiency-Enhancing?

The traditional argument as to why devolution is thought to be efficiency-enhancing presumes that social policy preferences vary sufficiently by province or region, and that regional governments are more likely to be aware of these differences, and will therefore tailor policies accordingly. National standards, however general, are inefficient because they impose the same mix of policies on all Canadians, regardless of preference. A variant of this argument says that even if preferences do not vary in this manner, there are dynamic efficiency gains from freeing provinces to experiment with respect to new ways to deliver social policies. National standards are inefficient in this view because they discourage this process of innovation.

This argument is most compelling in the case of health insurance. However important Ottawa's involvement was in getting hospital care and medical insurance schemes established initially, these programs are now established in the true sense of the term. On a more positive note, health care is also the example that best fits the public choice model of competitive federalism. The challenge of containing costs may be best met by encouraging the experimentation and innovation that come with decentralized control. The one important national standard from an economic point of view, that of portability, can be fairly easily achieved through interprovincial coordination.

In other areas, the efficiency argument is less convincing. It is at least arguable that spillover effects and externalities are important in these cases. Provincial governments have little incentive to plan their social policies with the residents of other jurisdictions in mind. Postsecondary education is often cited as an example of an activity particularly prone to this consideration. Educated workers are more mobile interprovincially, so are likely to receive their training in one province and spend their working lives in others. Social assistance is another example. Unemployed workers frequently move among provinces in search of jobs, or back to their home province when laid off.

One might argue that the costs of spillovers of these types normally are not large enough to offset the efficiency gains from further decentralization. Alternatively, to the extent they are important, they can be countered by a zero-sum system of interjurisdictional transfers. But consider what this latter recommendation means in practice. Provinces such as Alberta would make payments each year to those such as Newfoundland, as compensation for the educational expenses embodied in interprovincial migrants. B.C. would bill Alberta each year for part of the cost of social assistance for its out-migrants that end up on B.C. welfare rolls. The difficulty of making this type of calculation, not to mention enforcing the actual payment, is obvious, as the recent exchange between Premiers Harcourt and Klein over bus tickets to Vancouver for Alberta welfare recipients well illustrates. Thus if spillovers are a problem in fact (and on this point we badly need better information), there is certainly cause for concern.

There is also a logical problem with the argument for devolution with full equalization. The rationale for transferring tax points to the provinces rather than cash is the simple public finance principle of accountability. Governments will be better policymakers if they are forced to raise taxes commensurate with their program expenditures. Any political benefit they derive from introducing a new program will have to be set against the political price that comes with higher taxes. This discipline is missing if governments are spending funds that another government has raised. If this principle is sufficient to justify tax transfers, however, it is fair to ask why it does not apply with equal force to equalization payments, especially as these transfers will grow significantly under the devolution scenario.

Will the Equalization Transfers be Forthcoming?

Efficiency considerations aside, the devolutionist proposals presume that equalization and equalization-type transfers can be extended as required to meet equity objectives. Is this faith justified?

If the interpretation of the historical development of Canadian social policy given above is at all credible, it is wrong to think that the federal government's commitment to equalization is invariant to the associated set of social and economic union policies. Voters may well support transfers aimed at providing basic social services to individual Canadians, yet balk at transferring the same amount of money unconditionally to provincial treasuries.

It is legitimate to question, therefore, whether the political consensus for a national equalization scheme can hold in the face of further devolution. Unconditional cash transfers would increase under the devolution scenario, and they would be more visible with the presence of the Bloc and the Reform Party in the House of Commons. It is entirely possible that a point would be reached where the federal government loses political legitimacy with the voters. Ottawa taxes individual Canadians, bearing the political costs as it should. It then transfers the revenue on an unconditional basis to other governments, who get the political credit for the services provided. It is easy to see why provincial governments like this system. It is more difficult to see why any federal politician would countenance it for long.

Political will aside, there is another reason to question whether the federal government should be left with responsibility for equalization under the devolution scenario. Provinces are certain to seek more control over personal income taxes in order to integrate postsecondary education and training, unemployment insurance, and social assistance programs. This change would force the federal government to rely relatively more on sales taxes and other such revenue sources. Since these taxes tend to be more regressive, the equity basis of a national equalization scheme becomes suspect.

These considerations suggest that one implication of the devolution of social policy may well be the sacrifice of some of the interregional income redistribution that is contained in the current transfer programs. This outcome could be avoided, however, if responsibility for equalization could be shifted to the provinces. Ottawa would wind down the equalization program. In its place, richer provinces would make direct fiscal transfers to poorer ones. There is some recent theoretical work (Dahlby and Wilson forthcoming; Burbidge and Myers 1992; Snoddon 1993) on interprovincial equalization schemes, and there are a number of proposals as to how such a system might operate in practice (Helliwell and Scott 1981). The first step in all of them is to decide upon a representative provincial fiscal base, much as is done now. Provinces with a fiscal capacity above this figure would contribute some portion of their surplus to an equalization fund. Those with capacities below this level would draw from the fund. Net payments would be zero.

This type of scheme is consistent with the public choice principles that are advanced to support devolution of social policy in the first place. Residents of the richer provinces would get to decide each election how much they are willing to contribute annually in the way of unconditional transfers to other provincial governments. If it is important to have questions of intraprovincial redistribution settled within each province, as the proponents of devolution insist, surely it is equally important to have interprovincial sharing handled in the same manner.

A PREFERRED APPROACH

If one accepts that the time for cost-sharing ventures in social policy is past, and if one is reluctant to accept a greater degree of interregional inequality, and if one is sceptical that an interprovincial equalization scheme would ever see the light of day, what option is left?

One solution is to retain a federal presence in social policy, but alter its form. Fiscal transfers should go directly from the federal government to individual Canadians. This is hardly a novel idea. In its most general form, cash transfers to individuals have been the staple recommendation for decades of economists working in the social policy field. The idea received considerable airing in Canada in the 1980s, in accounts that went beyond general arguments in support of the idea to quite detailed recommendations as to how to proceed with particular schemes (Royal Commission 1985; Commission of Enquiry 1986; Courchene 1987). The perception at the time was that Canada was not ready for radical reform of this type. Maybe now it is an idea whose time has come.

Direct grants to individuals have three important advantages over transfers to provinces. First, they remove the efficiency problems that come with the separation of taxation and expenditure responsibilities. Provincial governments would not be financing programs with revenue they have not collected, which public choice theory suggests should lead to a more efficient set of policies. Second, the federal government would not have a major problem of political legitimacy, since it would be providing visible benefits to Canadians with the taxes it levies. With its legitimacy enhanced, the national equalization program is more secure. Third, direct grants to individuals can be the first step in a move towards a more efficient and effective system of social support measures.

How would this reform of the transfer system proceed? The first two steps are purely bookkeeping ones. First, the federal government should acknowledge that it no longer controls the tax points it transferred to the provinces in 1977 as part of the EPF arrangements. This step reduces the reported federal contribution considerably, but these are fictional transfers in any case. Second, it should formally separate the EPF cash transfers into the two basic components of insured health services and postsecondary education. They are distinct programs, with very different objectives, and they should be treated as such. For want of any more logical division, the proportions can be the ones used to allocate cash and tax transfers between the programs currently.

We acknowledged above that there is little compelling case for a continuing federal government role in health-care administration. Thus the next step is to compensate the provinces for the fact that henceforth they will be solely responsible for this activity. The federal cash transfer for insured health services for 1992-93 is estimated to be $6.2 billion (Canadian Tax Foundation 1992, 16:18). This sum would be turned over to the provinces, in exchange for which the provinces take over sole authority for health-care services. The transfer would be by means of extra tax points rather than cash transfers, for reasons spelled out above.

The case for a continued federal presence in postsecondary education rests on two assumptions: there are important spillover effects in this area due to interprovincial mobility, and provinces are not likely to act to offset them through a system of transfers. The form of federal assistance must be altered, however. The current transfers would be redirected from provincial governments directly to students. This objective can be achieved by means of educational vouchers, or as additional tax credits for tuition and other expenses.

Students would be free to use this assistance at the (accredited) institution of their choice. The provinces would cut back their contributions to universities and other institutions by an equivalent amount, and allow tuition fees to rise.

This approach has several advantages over the present one. The more direct link between supply and demand for education should encourage a more flexible and responsive educational system. Further, spending and taxing responsibilities would be more properly aligned. Provincial governments would no longer be spending revenue raised by Ottawa. Conversely, the link between the federal government's taxation and spending in this area would be more obvious, thereby enhancing its political legitimacy.

The Canada Assistance Plan can be transformed in a similar manner. The basic idea would be to convert the present cost-sharing arrangement with the provinces into a system of direct grants (or refundable tax credits) to individuals. Ideally, this change would be part of a more encompassing reform that would replace the current hodge podge of income support and supplementation programs with a basic guaranteed annual income scheme. Part of the attraction of this innovation is that it would allow some badly needed parallel reform of the unemployment insurance system. The scheme itself could revert to basic insurance principles, while the income support component would be shifted to the guaranteed annual income.

There are several variants of such schemes in the recent Canadian literature. The Macdonald Commission recommended first that the unemployment insurance scheme operate more like an actual insurance program. This goal would be accomplished by reducing the benefit rate, raising the entrance requirements, tightening the link between the maximum benefit period and the minimum employment period, and removing regional differences. The Commission argued as well for a transitional adjustment assistance plan designed to allow Canadian workers to adjust to changing opportunities in the labour market. Finally, it advocated a guaranteed annual income scheme to be known as the Universal Income Security Program (UISP).

The Forget Commission focused mainly on reforms to the unemployment insurance system, but its recommendations were premised on there being in place a comprehensive program of income support and supplementation. Courchene also makes his recommendations for reform of UI in the broader context of changes in job creation and adjustment enhancement, and changes to what he calls the family benefits package. He favours an incremental approach to reform, largely because of the monumental federal-provincial bargaining and consultation that would precede it. But, as noted above, we no longer have this luxury of time.

The proposals by the Macdonald Commission, the Forget Commission and Courchene differ in detail, but they all bring the same advantages. They are less costly to administer than current schemes, they are less demeaning for recipients, and they remove the worst of the perverse work incentives. Provinces could supplement the basic income support with schemes of their own design and funding, so the proposals do not run afoul of jurisdictional concerns. An important ancillary benefit is that these changes make it possible to undertake some badly needed reform of the UI system. Equally important from the perspective of this paper, a system of direct grants to families and individuals brings with it enhanced accountability by provincial governments, and renewed political legitimacy to the federal government.

The mention of increased visibility for the federal government returns to a theme that has run throughout this chapter. Ongoing support by Canadians for purely unconditional interregional income redistribution, such as that achieved through the current equalization program, requires that the federal government have a legitimate and independent role in the federation. Without some enhancement of Ottawa's political role, there is every chance that the federation will alter in ways that even the most ardent proponents of devolution will come to regret.

CONCLUSION

This paper has argued that the future for social policy reform in Canada lies in devising new ways to meet an old objective. The old objective is the balance between a commitment to individual equity and to regional equity that characterized the system of intergovernmental fiscal relations that developed after World War II. This balance was tilted seriously in 1977, and it will be lost entirely if the federal government continues to withdraw from social policy formation. The new ways to meet the old objective are federal government transfers for postsecondary education, training, and social assistance that go directly to individual Canadians. There are direct benefits to such a scheme, and there is one important associated benefit, the maintenance of a national equalization program.

NOTES

1. This feature was offset somewhat by introducing a supplementary provision whereby any province could, if it wished, receive a flat grant of $15 per capita, accelerated annually by the rate of growth of postsecondary education expenditures.

2. Defined in 1957 to be the average per capita yields from personal and corporate income taxes and succession duties in the two richest provinces.

3. Cash transfers might be justified if one could show that there was a vertical fiscal gap evident at this time. This argument is difficult to make for Canada at any time in the post-World War II period, however, and is particularly difficult to make in this decade.

4. Defined as the national average federal contribution to established programs in 1976.

5. As Hobson and St-Hilaire note this change in the funding arrangements for EPF made the federal contributions fully equalizing (1993).

6. Thus Boadway and Hobson write, "It would make more sense if both unemployment insurance and welfare were delivered at one level of government, and the provincial level would be the appropriate one." (1993, p. 153)

BIBLIOGRAPHY

Boadway, Robin W. and F.R. Flatters (1982), "Efficiency and Equalization Payments in a Federal System of Government: A Synthesis and Extension of Recent Results," *Canadian Journal of Economics*, 15: 613-633.

Boadway, Robin W. and Paul A.R. Hobson (1993), *Intergovernmental Fiscal Relations in Canada*, Toronto: Canadian Tax Foundation.

Breton, Albert (1985), "Supplementary Statement," in Royal Commission on the Economic Union and Development Prospects for Canada, Macdonald Commission, *Report*, Vol. 3, Ottawa: Supply and Services Canada, 486-526.

Burbidge, John B. and Gordon M. Myers (1992), "Redistribution Within and Across the Regions of a Federation," Working Paper Series, McMaster University .

Burns, R.M. (1980), *The Acceptable Mean: The Tax Rental Agreements, 1941-1962*, Canadian Tax Foundation.

Canadian Tax Foundation (various years), *The National Finances*, Toronto: Canadian Tax Foundation..

Commission of Enquiry on Unemployment Insurance, Forget Commission (1986), *Report*, Ottawa: Supply and Services Canada.

Courchene, Thomas J. (1979), *Refinancing the Canadian Federation: A Survey of the 1977 Fiscal Arrangements Act*, Toronto: C.D. Howe Institute.

_____ (1984), *Equalization Payments: Past, Present and Future*, Toronto: Ontario Economic Council.

_____ (1987), *Social Policy in the 1990s: Agenda for Reform*, Toronto: C.D. Howe Institute.

Cousineau, Jean-Michel (1992), "Social Security and the Division of Powers in Canada," in *Delivering the Goods: The Federal-Provincial Division of Spending Powers*, ed. Jean-Michel Cousineau, Claude E. Forget and John Richards, Canada Round, No. 12, Toronto: C.D. Howe Institute, 77-92.

Dahlby, Bev and L.S. Wilson (forthcoming), "Fiscal Capacity, Tax Effort, and Optimal Equalization Grants," *Canadian Journal of Economics*.

Economic Council of Canada (1982), *Financing Confederation: Today and Tomorrow*, Ottawa: Supply and Services Canada.

Guest, Dennis (1980), *The Emergence of Social Security in Canada*, Vancouver: University of British Columbia Press.

Helliwell, John and Anthony Scott (1981), *Canada in Fiscal Conflict*, Vancouver: Pemberton Securities.

Hobson, Paul A.R. (1993), "Current Issues in Federal-Provincial Fiscal Relations," in *Canada: The State of the Federation 1993*, ed. Ronald L. Watts and Douglas M. Brown, Kingston: Institute of Intergovernmental Relations, Queen's University.

Hobson, Paul A.R. and France St-Hilaire (1993), "Rearranging Federal-Provincial Fiscal Arrangements: Toward Sustainable Federalism," Montreal: Institute for Research on Public Policy.

Leslie, Peter M. (1993), "The Fiscal Crisis of Canadian Federalism," in *A Partnership in Trouble: Renegotiating Fiscal Federalism*, ed. P.M. Leslie, K. Norrie and I. Ip, Toronto: C.D. Howe Institute.

Moore, A. Milton, J. Harvey Perry, and Donald I. Beach (1966), *The Financing of Canadian Federation: The First Hundred Years*, Canadian Tax Foundation.

Norrie, Kenneth (1993), "Intergovernmental Transfers in Canada: An Historical Perspective on Some Current Policy Choices," in *A Partnership in Trouble: Renegotiating Fiscal Federalism*, ed. P.M. Leslie, K. Norrie and I. Ip, Toronto: C.D. Howe Institute.

Perry, J. Harvey (1989), *A Fiscal History of Canada — The Postwar Years*, Toronto: Canadian Tax Foundation.

Reid, Bradford and Tracy Snoddon (1992), "Redistribution Under Alternative Constitutional Arrangements for Canada," in *Alberta and the Economics of Constitutional Change*, ed. Paul Boothe, Edmonton: Western Centre for Economic Research, University of Alberta.

Richards, John (1992), "Suggestions on Getting the Constitutional Division of Powers Right," in *Delivering the Goods: The Federal-Provincial Division of Spending Powers*, ed. Jean-Michel Cousineau, Claude E. Forget and John Richards, The Canada Round, No. 12, Toronto: C.D. Howe Institute.

_____ (1994), "A Few Suggestions for the Redesign of Intergovernmental Transfers," (manuscript).

Royal Commission on Dominion-Provincial Relations, Rowell-Sirois Commission (1940), *Report*, Ottawa: Supply and Services Canada.

Royal Commission on the Economic Union and Development Prospects for Canada, Macdonald Commission (1985), *Report*, 3 vols., Ottawa: Supply and Services Canada.

Smiley, Donald V. (1963), *Conditional Grants and Canadian Federalism*, Toronto: Canadian Tax Foundation.

Snoddon, Tracy R. (1993), "Voluntary Transfers in a Model With Majority Voting and Local Public Goods," mimeo, University of Alberta.

Splane, Richard (1987), "Social Policy-Making in the Government of Canada" and "Further Reflections: 1975-1986," in *Canadian Social Policy*, ed. Shankar A. Yelaja, Waterloo: Wilfrid Laurier University Press, 224-265.

Comment: Political Constraints on Fiscal Federalism

David Milne

This collection boasts a wonderful blend of economists, public finance specialists and political scientists gathered together to tackle important questions about the future of Canada's fiscal arrangements. In this case, I am joined by two economists — one presenter and one commentator — who are attempting to speculate on the future of Canada's equalization program, especially in the light of the changes that may arise in other intergovernmental fiscal arrangements. As a political scientist, I know that my principal job will be to test the political dimensions of these ideas and proposals, but I must admit to feeling some initial reticence about what political science may actually have to offer to this discussion.

On re-reading Richard Bird's recent piece on future fiscal arrangements, I was, however, again reminded about how central political science is to this whole question. The reasons are quite simple:

> Federal-provincial fiscal arrangements are much more than an economic issue. How financial and administrative responsibilities are allocated between governments is a central political question. The answer to this question reflects a country's style, its concerns, and its goals. (1990, p. 109.)

> A federation is inherently a political creation with primarily political objectives, and its fiscal arrangements must be viewed within this political framework. (1990, p. 129.)

And just as fiscal arrangements in the past were the product of larger political, social, and economic forces, so future fiscal arrangements will be "set outside the narrow parameters of public finance." Ultimately, Bird argues the arrangements may come down two critical factors: "who determines the [future] rules of the game and how are these rules changed: all else follows" (1990, p. 129.)

Now if we are to bear in mind this wise advice, and apply it to the paper at hand, what should we say? Of course, there still remains a major question mark on the future of Quebec in Canada, a matter that Bird thought central to any filling in of answers on future fiscal arrangements. The recent election of the Bloc Québécois as Official Opposition in Parliament has only served to increase uncertainty on that score. Nor has the question of addressing the forces of regionalism found resolution either with the Charlottetown Accord or the future fate and agenda of Preston Manning and his Reform Party. But at least some things are clearer from the 1993 federal election about the strength and alignment of political forces and how they are likely to be brought to bear on the fiscal proposals in Kenneth Norrie's chapter. In short, what will those who set the future fiscal rules have to say and what changes will they permit?

With the uncertainty surrounding the current political landscape and the high political stakes in yet another renewal of the old battle of Quebec separatism-Canadian unity, it would seem likely that federal leaders who set the fiscal rules would wish to approach the question of sharing money cautiously, postponing any decisive action at least until after the unfolding of an election or referendum in Quebec. In any event, such an interval would provide Ottawa with an opportunity to launch consultative vehicles and generally encourage public discussion of the question of reworking fiscal arrangements, including social programs and unemployment insurance, without exposing the advocates of federalism to risk in what will be the second major debate by Quebecers over their political future in less than a generation. Certainly, we cannot reasonably expect a stable set of financial arrangements until this mega-constitutional question is again faced. Moreover, given the strength of devolutionist thinking in Quebec, the west, and elsewhere, it seems scarcely reasonable to see this as a time for a vigorous reassertion of the federal spending power in provincial areas of jurisdiction.

If this is so, I think the government of Canada would be most unlikely to adopt Norrie's proposals for changing Established Programs Financing. Adopting a student voucher system instead of transfers to provinces for postsecondary education, for example, would virtually guarantee a vicious showdown with Quebec and many other provinces on one of the most sensitive of provincial jurisdictions — and this at precisely the point when the federal Liberals are engaged in fending off a two-front war in Parliament with Quebec sovereignty and western regionalism. It would also almost certainly constitute a serious blow to the Chrétien government's efforts to present a new Liberal face to Canadians, since adoption of former Prime Minister Trudeau's old pet student voucher scheme to circumvent provinces would reinforce the claim that Chrétien is indeed "yesterday's man." Moreover, it is not at all clear that precipitate action on this front would be much welcomed by the client groups caught in the middle of the intergovernmental crossfire, namely the post-secondary educational institutions themselves. In any event, while it is certainly true that innovation and diversification is needed in Canada's postsecondary educational system, we may be entitled to wonder whether an effective and enduring solution can really be purchased by the application of this simple market expedient.

Political pitfalls of an even more serious kind await a federal government that would seek to follow Norrie in jettison any federal role in defending national equity goals in health care, leaving the field entirely to the provinces. While I am hardly a booster for the politics of the *Canada Health Act* as practised by Trudeau,[1] it is obvious that Canadians at large do regard the maintenance of these goals within our public Medicare system as — to steal a tarnished phrase — a "sacred trust." Certainly public concern goes much further than the mere issue of portability, to comprehensiveness and accessibility of health care. For that reason, no government in Ottawa whatever its partisan stripe could politically countenance any such withdrawal, even if personally inclined to do so. Rather the federal challenge will be to find ways of providing sufficient flexibility and incentive within the terms of the *Canada Health Act* to permit provinces to achieve needed economies and innovation. In short, the challenge will be to find a way to marry the advantages of a genuine decentralization of program design and delivery within a system of general national equity goals.

It is worth underlining too that any proposed federal transfer of tax room to the provinces for health care (in the order of $6.2 billion in 1992) will merely increase the provinces' stake in the direct tax field, and potentially raise risks to harmonization of the tax system and to the economic union.[2] Moreover, this decentralization of taxing would also seem to put additional pressure upon the equalization program just when the strains on Canada's notion of the "sharing community" may be at their most severe.

The preference for transfers to persons rather than to governments continues in Norrie's suggestions respecting the Canada Assistance Plan. Here, too, direct grants to individuals, perhaps in the form of a guaranteed annual income, are proposed as a means of securing federal visibility, currently lost in the existing CAP fiscal arrangements. While it is true that the federal government has frequently complained of its lack of visibility in these and other social policy expenditures, this case has often been much exaggerated. The fact is that, despite the arcane nature of the intergovernmental fiscal arrangements, neither the Canadian public nor the social policy community and interest groups have failed to recognize the important federal role in social policy; indeed, outside

Quebec, people have consistently looked to the federal government for leadership in this area, even when the jurisdiction is provincial and when federal financial contributions towards the maintenance of social programs are declining.

But apart from Ottawa not needing (nor wanting) enhanced visibility for expensive social costs during a period of restraint, the proposal is unlikely to proceed for at least two additional reasons. The first is that the impediments of federalism are likely be as effective a conservative force against dramatic policy innovation as they have been in the past.[3] The second is that Ottawa would have to worry about its ability to manage and fund a guaranteed annual income scheme over the long haul. After all, if it is unable to afford its part of the existing *cost-shared* arrangements for social assistance under CAP, what confidence can one have in Ottawa's capacity to assume the function on its own through a guaranteed annual income scheme?

Kenneth Norrie's chapter shows a commendable resistance to the messiness and apparent disorder of Canadian federalism and a desire to tame and discipline it with the application of relatively straightforward rules or doctrines. It is, of course, always tempting to see the problems in our current fiscal arrangements resolved forthrightly by the assignment of a clear division of responsibility based on a public choice model of federalism, but the stubborn reality of shared jurisdiction and interdependence resists such appealing solutions. Disentanglement strategies are not easy to execute nor to maintain.

In my view, complex interdependence over budgetary and fiscal relations among governments in Canada is likely to continue. In short, fiscal federalism will resist neat compartmentalization. It is for that reason that I am inclined to accept scholars such as Robin Boadway and Frank Flatters in their arguments in this collection for better institutions for intergovernmental coordination and decision making. That was also the thinking behind the ill-fated Council of the Federation proposal in the September 1991 federal proposals. One way or another, our success or failure in developing and perfecting these intergovernmental institutions and procedures will be a vital part of the story over Canada's unfolding fiscal crisis.

Now, oddly enough, Norrie's chapter has relatively little explicitly to say about the future of equalization. Neither the problem of the ceiling on the equalization program, nor the widening disparities in fiscal capacity among provinces, nor the question of a net scheme get treated. And while his proposed changes to Established Programs Financing arrangements would substantially negate the *implicit* elements of equalization in these current arrangements, his proposals do not address this erosion of equalization nor estimate its consequences. Certainly, there is no reason to suppose that a system of transfers to individuals would itself actually compensate for or even address this notion of equity in the federation.

The ideological rationale underlying Norrie's preference for "transfers to persons" may also deserve more careful scrutiny. He wishes his proposals to be seen as an attempt to "rebalance" fiscal arrangements following the confusions and disorder flowing from the 1977 changes to Established Programs Financing. In effect, his proposals for transfers to individuals would allegedly preserve an "old objective of a balance between a commitment to individual equity and to regional equity." To make this claim, equalization is cast wholly into the "regional equity" category; shared-cost social programs, since they are conditional upon provincial expenditures for certain purposes, are placed in the box of "individual equity" because "their primary purpose was to provide minimum levels of essential services to individual Canadians." But this distinction does not hold up. Not only is Norrie forced to acknowledge a substantial redistributive and equalizing role in these arrangements (hence, they cannot be programs exclusively devoted to individual equity), but federal conditionality permitted considerable variation in levels of public service in these programs. Since federal payments were linked to provincial expenditure decisions, it could hardly have been otherwise.

Moreover, the problems of maintaining this distinction are just as problematic with the equalization program. First, it is worth pointing out that equalization speaks to a notion of *provincial* equity, not regional equity. It aims to give each province the requisite financial means to meet its constitutional responsibilities. Moreover, equalization, although unconditional, has always aimed at equalizing the provision of basic public services for individual Canadians. That is self-evident in our constitution in the language of section 36 on equalization and regional disparities where the commitment is to "promoting equal opportunities for the well-being of Canadians" and "providing essential public services of reasonable quality to all Canadians." Equalization payments are specifically aimed at ensuring that "provincial governments have sufficient revenues to provide reasonably comparable levels of public services at reasonably comparable levels of taxation." Individual equity for all Canadians is inextricably linked with that of provincial equity. It would seem artificial to attempt to separate them.

It is time to remind ourselves once again that fiscal arrangements after all arise as products of politics; they are not constructed on clear and distinct rules of logic, equity, or economic theory. For that reason, I hesitate to accept the claim that Norrie's proposals merely retrieve a logic allegedly lost in the fateful changes to the established programs financing arrangements in 1977. In my view, the proposals signal rather a preference to depart from the intricate workings of cooperative federalism and to move towards federal unilateralism and selective disentanglement. While Ottawa unilaterally retreats from any role in health care, it proceeds with bold new programs over the heads of the provinces in postsecondary education and income security. Decentralization in one direction, centralization in two others. In the end, however, it remains unclear how these decisive steps would help resolve the complicated and unavoidably *shared* patterns of intergovernmental interdependence for these and related policy areas — or, for that matter, why and how they are thought necessary to shore up federal legitimacy and equalization itself.

While there are undoubtedly many changes coming in Canada's social programs that will require a restructuring of fiscal arrangements, the complexity and interdependence of the whole system of arrangements does not really permit fast unilateral solutions. Neither a course of simple devolution nor centralism will do. Instead, a decent respect for the genuine complexity of the fiscal system is called for. Nor are the answers to the problems of Canada's debt and economy easy or obvious. Under these circumstances, even if Canada were not facing an ongoing national unity crisis, it would be reasonable to expect federal politicians to take time to experiment with many new ideas and arrangements rather than boldly charting a wholly new system for the future. For policy rationalists in a hurry, this sounds maddeningly conservative. But perhaps that is why, for the most part, "big bang" is reserved for physics.

NOTES

1. See my critique of this feature of Trudeau's federalism (Milne 1986, pp. 181-184).
2. See Boadway and Flatters, in this volume, for expressions of concern on this score.
3. See Banting for a classic statement of the conservative influence of federalism upon Canadian social policy (1987).

BIBLIOGRAPHY

Banting, Keith G. (1987), *The Welfare State and Canadian Federalism*, Kingston and Montreal: McGill-Queen's University Press.

Bird, Richard M. (1990), "Federal-Provincial Fiscal Arrangements: Is There an Agenda for the 1990s?" in *Canada: The State of the Federation 1990*, ed. Ronald L. Watts and Douglas M. Brown, Kingston: Institute of Intergovernmental Relations, Queen's University, 109-134

Milne, David (1986), *Tug of War: Ottawa and the Provinces under Trudeau and Mulroney*, Toronto: Lorimer.

Comment: New Versus Old Instruments

Paul A.R. Hobson

One of the numerous contributions of Kenneth Norrie's chapter is that it draws attention to the importance of discussing the various elements of federal-provincial fiscal arrangements as a package, as does the chapter by Boadway and Flatters (this volume). The central message appears to be that a wholesale devolution of social policy to the provinces would so seriously undermine the legitimacy of the federal government as to put in jeopardy the essential feature of Canada as a sharing community. Rather, it is argued, the federal role in delivery of social policy needs to be recast, placing a greater emphasis on transfers paid directly to persons.

Correctly, the chapter identifies the principle of equalization as the foundation on which Canada's "national" social programs rest. Equalization as presently structured, however, cannot be relied on alone to achieve the goal of fiscal equity. The chapter by Boadway and Flatters has discussed this thoroughly. To reiterate, what this would require in the extreme is the full equalization of provincial fiscal capacities (more or less, depending on adjustments for need and/or cost differences). The fiscal equalization program, however, raises fiscal capacities in the have-not provinces to a level somewhat below the corresponding national average. Even after equalization, there remains a significant degree of fiscal disparity between the have and have-not provinces. Thus, the devolution of responsibility for financing social programs to the provinces along with an accompanying transfer of tax room would simply exacerbate the problem.[1] It would also place upward pressure on levels of equalization payments, possibly further straining the level of political commitment to maintaining a system designed around unconditional cash transfers to recipient provinces.

In these comments, I want to make three main points, all of which promote federal-provincial fiscal disentanglement but are consistent with the goal of promoting fiscal equity, and none of which involve any increased equalization commitment on behalf of the federal government:

- EPF cash contributions to the provinces should be replaced with a tax abatement to the provinces (i.e., Norrie's proposal that there should be a simple transfer of tax room in place of the "health-care component" of the EPF transfer should be rejected).[2] EPF cash would henceforth grow in step with the income tax base. Associated revenues would be distributed across provinces so as to preserve the equal per capita nature of EPF inclusive of the value of the existing EPF tax points.

- CAP (or its successor after income security reform) should be replaced with a block funding scheme, distributed across provinces so as to fully equalize (standardized) per capita social assistance liabilities.

- The federal government should not replace the "postsecondary education component" of EPF and contributions to social assistance payments under CAP (or its successor after income security reform) with direct transfers to individuals. (i.e., Norrie's proposals along these lines should be rejected.)[3]

EPF AND THE POSTWAR DEVOLUTION OF INCOME TAX ROOM TO THE PROVINCES

It is useful to think about the evolution of federal-provincial cost-sharing arrangements in the social policy field as transfers in lieu of the return to the provinces of income tax room ceded under the Wartime Tax Rental Agreements. Over the immediate postwar period, the system of tax rentals evolved into a system of tax abatements accompanied by explicit equalization payments. When it was first introduced in 1957, the standard for equalization was per capita revenues in the two richest provinces. As a result, income tax abatements made to the provinces at that time were, in effect, equal per capita revenue transfers.

The process of actually returning income tax room to the provinces began with the 1962 *Federal-Provincial Fiscal Arrangements Act*. In part, this was designed to promote a greater degree of accountability at the provincial level as the provinces clamoured for increased access to income tax revenues to meet rapidly rising expenditures on social programs in the areas of health, education, and welfare. The 1962 arrangements also included a proposal to adopt a national average standard for equalization. This was to be accompanied by the inclusion of 50 percent of natural resource revenues among the revenue bases eligible for equalization. While revenue neutral at the time, this posed a problem as to how to effect any further devolution of income tax room without widening fiscal disparities between the have and have-not provinces.

By retaining its dominance in the income tax field, the federal government had been able to achieve a variety of social policy goals through the use of the spending power. In practice, cost-sharing arrangements in the areas of hospital insurance, health care and postsecondary education were tied to national average per capita expenditures and amounted to specific purpose, equal per capita transfers.[4] The genius of EPF, introduced in 1977, was that it permitted the replacement of these earlier cost-sharing arrangements with a further devolution of income tax room to the provinces that was, in effect, fully equalized. This was accomplished by augmenting the (equalized) value of the EPF tax points with a cash component. This further devolution of tax room in 1977 had the effect of placing the other provinces on a more equal footing with Quebec, which had secured additional tax room for itself under earlier opting-out provisions. In addition, it should be recalled that a portion of the earlier postsecondary education transfer had been in the form of a tax transfer.

When viewed in the context of the postwar devolution of income tax room to the provinces, then, there is no implication that somehow "there must be a greater degree of equity among provinces with respect to social policy than there is for other expenditures." (Norrie this volume, p. 162). Rather, the equal per capita nature of EPF was consistent with the objective of not further widening the degree of fiscal disparity across provinces, i.e., promoting the goal of fiscal equity. Fiscal equalization alone (as presently structured) cannot accomplish the goal of fiscal equity; equal per capita transfers such as those under EPF complement the fiscal equalization program in levelling fiscal capacities between the have and have-not provinces.

WHAT TO DO ABOUT EPF?

The problem with EPF was that the per capita total transfer was designed to grow in line with per capita GDP, a growth rate that was less than the rate of growth of the personal income tax base. In addition, various federal budget measures, including the five-year freeze on per capita entitlements beginning in 1990-91, further reduced that rate of growth. Thus, whatever the effective transfer of tax room was in 1977, the associated number of tax points has been severely eroded since then. This has been a significant cause of the widening fiscal imbalance between the federal government and the provinces.

This erosion in the effective number of EPF tax points could be halted by a simple but clear division of federal income tax revenues. The federal government would cede a negotiated fraction of its income tax revenues to the provinces in the form of a tax abatement. The value of this tax abatement would grow in line with the income tax base, in step with the value of the existing EPF tax points. The tax abatement would then be distributed across provinces on a residual basis, much like the existing EPF cash component, thus preserving the equal per capita — cash plus tax — feature of EPF (Hobson and St-Hilaire 1993).

The issue is, therefore, really one of disentangling the EPF cash component from the federal government's budgetary decisions. It is a question of how to halt the further erosion of the tax points effectively transferred in 1977, tax room to which the provinces might legitimately lay claim. This cannot be accomplished through a direct transfer of additional tax points to the provinces without sacrificing fiscal equity.[5] It can, however, be done by instead following the proposed tax abatement procedure. In effect, the procedure ensures a fully equalized transfer, with all provinces implicitly equalized to the national average.

RECASTING CAP

The determination of provincial fiscal capacities for equalization purposes fails to take into account "negative" tax liabilities in the form of transfers to persons, such as those made under provincial welfare programs. To some extent CAP provides an offset for this since provinces are, in principle, reimbursed for 50 percent of social welfare expenditures. Thus, in principle, those provinces with relatively high social welfare liabilities — per capita social welfare expenditures — receive proportionately more by way of transfer. In practice, however, provinces differ in terms of "need" (the number of welfare recipients per capita) and "generosity" (expenditures per recipient) in respect of welfare programs. Moreover, those provinces with below average fiscal capacities have less ability to spend on social welfare yet, typically, they exhibit greater need.

From the perspective of the have provinces, the cap on CAP first imposed in the 1989 budget has limited growth in entitlements to a maximum of 5 percent per annum. This has resulted in federal transfers falling significantly below the 50 percent level around which the program was designed. Indeed, at the margin, welfare expenditures in the have provinces are simply not cost-shared once the growth ceiling has been passed. Provinces are not equal in terms of their eligibility under CAP.

It is difficult to predict the outcome of the federal initiative on income security reform in Canada. One possible scenario is that responsibility for income security — including unemployment insurance — may be devolved completely to the provinces. At the very least, this would require the transfer of associated payroll and income tax room to the provinces. The provinces would then be in a position to develop more integrated approaches to delivery of income security (e.g., the Newfoundland guaranteed annual income proposal). The problem would be accommodating what would inevitably be a widening gap in fiscal capacities (after equalization) between the have and have-not provinces, one element that would be essential to ensuring reasonably comparable levels of income security across provinces.

An alternative scenario, seemingly preferred by Norrie, would be some form of guaranteed annual income scheme delivered by the federal government, with the provinces, presumably, left with responsibility for making cash transfers to those who are not caught in the income security net. To the extent that this suggests an increased federal presence in the income security field, it seems improbable that it would be adopted without some accommodating transfer of tax room from the provinces to the federal government. Moreover, it suggests either an accompanying transfer of responsibility for welfare services or a separation between responsibility for income assistance (primarily at the federal level) and responsibility for welfare services (at the provincial level). Certainly, a case might be made for maintaining a decentralized delivery system for welfare services.

As long as there remains a role for the provinces in delivery of social welfare, the case can be made that some form of cost-sharing arrangement is justified. Hobson and St-Hilaire propose a block grant scheme that is equalized for differences in need across provinces (1993). Under their scheme, the total federal commitment would be based on a fixed percentage, say 50 percent, of standardized provincial social welfare expenditures across all provinces. Each province's equal per capita entitlement would be adjusted according to a built-in equalization formula, based on the difference between its per capita liability and the corresponding national average. The net effect would be a system of differential cost sharing: those provinces with above average need would receive in excess of 50 percent cost sharing; those with below average need would receive less than 50 percent cost sharing. The associated equalization scheme would operate separately from fiscal equalization; since it simply acts to redistribute a given pool, there would be no additional cost to the federal treasury.

TRANSFERS TO GOVERNMENTS OR INDIVIDUALS?

The main thrust of Norrie's reform proposals is to substitute transfers to individuals for existing transfers to governments (education and welfare) and for the federal government to withdraw from health care with an accompanying transfer of tax room. The problem with a simple transfer of tax room has already been discussed. As an option, it inevitably carries with it the implication that the degree of fiscal disparity between the have and have-not provinces will be allowed to increase. In principle, a federally administered guaranteed annual income scheme would reduce the pressure on provincial welfare programs and obviate the need for a significant portion of transfers currently made under CAP. There would still be a case, however, for cost-sharing arrangements associated with remaining provincial social welfare expenditures — that is, there would still be a place for transfers to the provinces in respect of social welfare expenditures, although the levels would be much lower than at present and the way in which the monies are distributed across provinces might take a different form.

What of the option of replacing the "postsecondary education portion" of the EPF transfer with a system of educational vouchers? The logic of substituting transfers to individuals for transfers to governments is based in what Boadway describes as "the false dichotomy between place prosperity and people prosperity." Again, the combined effect of fiscal equalization and EPF is to reduce the degree of fiscal inequity in the system. To follow Norrie's proposal would therefore increase the degree of fiscal inequity between the have and have-not provinces. In turn, this would result in a greater degree of horizontal inequity across provinces associated with the federal personal tax-transfer system. A uniform federal personal tax-transfer system will only be horizontally equitable if all sources of fiscal inequity through provincial budgets are first eliminated.

As noted in the Boadway and Flatters contribution, fiscal equity (and fiscal efficiency) may be promoted through a federal personal tax-transfer system which discriminates against those provinces with above average fiscal capacities. That is, such a system could, in principle, substitute for a system of equalization payments designed to eliminate differences in net fiscal benefits (NFBs) across provinces. The federal rate structure would vary by province; tax rates would be higher (and subsidies lower) in those provinces with relatively high levels of NFBs. In practice, however, such a system would be complex, difficult to administer, and politically destructive.

Since the fiscal equalization program does not operate as a net scheme, fiscal disparities remain between the have and have-not provinces. The disparity in fiscal capacities is reduced under EPF as an equal per capita transfer since it is a "fully equalized" transfer. Anything that increases the degree of fiscal disparity will increase the degree of horizontal inequity in the system. Replacing the "postsecondary education component" of the EPF transfer will increase the extent of horizontal inequity associated with the federal personal income tax structure.

CONCLUSION

The interplay among the three major federal-provincial transfer programs is a significant component of the federal commitment to equalization enunciated in section 36(2) of *The Constitution Act, 1982.* While that principle is certainly addressed by the fiscal equalization program, it is also addressed significantly by EPF as structured. Equally, CAP (or its successor following income security reform) partially addresses the problem associated with the asymmetric treatment of personal taxes and personal transfers under the fiscal equalization program, a recognized deficiency of the program. There is an important role, then, for maintaining transfers to governments: fiscal equity in the federation is a necessary condition for there to be overall horizontal equity.

Much of the disenchantment with federal-provincial fiscal relations in Canada at the present time arises from a poorly defined allocation of federal revenues between federal programs and transfers to the provinces under EPF and CAP. It is possible to achieve a greater degree of fiscal disentanglement without sacrificing the principle of fiscal equity (or fiscal efficiency) within the same general framework as the existing system. Indeed, within the same general framework, there can be improvements in program design that will enhance their functioning by equalizing for differences in need as regards the delivery of social programs at the provincial level. Thus I do not accept Norrie's conclusion that the form of the federal presence in funding social programs must be altered. Moreover, to do so along the lines he proposes would increase fiscal inequity in the system as well as introduce an element of horizontal inequity into federal transfers, to the detriment of residents of the have-not provinces in particular.

NOTES

1. Technically, a transfer of tax room occurs when the federal government alters its rate structure such as to open up tax room to be filled by the provinces with no net increase in the burden on taxpayers.

2. A tax abatement involves the transfer to a province of a fixed proportion of income tax revenues collected by the federal government within that province.

3. As Norrie observes, it is difficult to attach much other than symbolic significance to the terms "health-care component" and "postsecondary education component" of EPF.

4. Thus, for example, hospital insurance grants (25 percent national average per capita + 25 percent actual per capita), medical insurance (50 percent national average per capita), and even the university grants (minimum 50 percent national average) were all (more or less) equal per capita revenue transfers and with relatively few strings attached.

5. In principle, this could be avoided by a change in the equalization standard, say to a top-two-province standard. Alternatively, voluntary interprovincial equalization might be relied on. However, neither option would be likely to find much political support.

BIBLIOGRAPHY

Hobson, Paul A.R. and France St-Hilaire (1993), *Reforming Federal Provincial Fiscal Arrangements: Toward Sustainable Federalism*, Montreal: Institute for Research on Public Policy.

CHAPTER SIX

Health Policy and Fiscal Federalism

Carolyn Tuohy

In order to understand the evolution of public policy regarding health care in Canada, and to speculate about its future development, it is useful to distinguish three dimensions of policy. A dimension which I will call "distributional" policies relates to the allotment of tangible benefits across various interests in society. A second dimension, which relates to issues of identity, status and belief, is the "symbolic" dimension of policy. The third dimension is "structural" — it relates to the allocation of positions of influence in the making and implementation of policy.[1] These dimensions are not mutually exclusive — a given policy may well have distributional, symbolic, and structural implications. But policies differ in the level of their distributional, symbolic, and structural content.

This chapter focuses primarily on the distributional and structural dimensions of policy, although I will make some reference to symbolic dimensions as well.

The central argument advanced here can be summarized simply. Structural policy change in the health-care arena almost always results from exogenous factors. This is not surprising: it is in the nature of health-care delivery systems to create powerful vested interests who are unlikely to generate internal pressures for structural change. Episodes of structural change in health care, generated as they are by factors external to the arena, arise independently of the evolution of policy ideas about health-care delivery. But the effect of these episodes is likely to be shaped very much by the prevailing climate of policy ideas. To put it another way, the "window of opportunity" for structural change in the health-care arena may be created and opened by factors in the broader political system. But that window will open onto a landscape of policy ideas that is in a constant state of evolution. The particular structural changes that result will depend in large part upon that landscape. They will also depend upon the way prevailing policy ideas are absorbed and translated within the existing structure. And in the meantime, between episodes of structural change, ongoing distributional policies will be determined by the constellation of actors and institutions that takes shape within the prevailing structure.

The period roughly from 1958 to 1971 was a watershed epoch of structural change in Canadian health care. Since then, with the exception of one or two structural amendments, policies have been largely distributional in nature, and have rested on a fundamental accommodation between health-care providers, notably the medical profession, and the state. The key question for the 1990s is whether policy will continue to be shaped by this profession-state accommodation, or whether we are entering into another era of structural change in health care. If a window of opportunity for structural change does open, it will open onto a landscape of policy ideas very different from the one that established the structure of the current system.

The relatively stable process governing distributional changes within an existing structure is inherently easier to understand and predict than is the episodic intersection of factors that results in major structural change. Because they involve changes in positions of influence and hence of status, moreover, structural policies tend to have a high symbolic content, with the volatility that symbolic politics typically entail. Given the unpredictability and volatility of structural politics, it is much easier to explain past episodes with the benefit of hindsight than it is to speculate about the future. Let me begin with the easier task.

STRUCTURAL CHANGE:
THE ESTABLISHMENT OF CANADIAN MEDICARE

The first attempt at fundamental structural change in the Canadian health-care arena occurred immediately after World War II. In 1945-46, the federal government presented a set of proposals for a cost-shared national health insurance program to the provinces, proposals that had been shaped in part by the observation of contemporary developments in Britain. At the time, there existed a remarkable consensus among medical, hospital and insurance interests favourable to the establishment of a comprehensive health insurance plan in the public sector. Viewing such a plan as "necessary ... and probably inevitable," (Taylor 1978, p. 23) these groups supported it in principle and sought to maximize their influence over its development and implementation. The sense of inevitability arose in no small part from their observation of events in Britain. Had the "window of opportunity" for fundamental change in the health-care arena been opened at that time, then, the resulting regime would undoubtedly have borne a closer resemblance to the NHS than did the scheme that ultimately resulted two decades later (Taylor 1973, p. 33; Tuohy 1989, pp. 144-145). In particular, it might well have meant much more extensive organizational change. As it was, however, the opening of the window was forestalled by forces beyond the health-care arena. The federal health-care proposals were tied to a broader package of proposals for federal-provincial fiscal arrangements that were unacceptable to the provinces, and the entire package went down to defeat.

The resulting delay gave time for private plans to develop and expand, and for various provincial governments to experiment with different models of governmental health insurance plans. It was not until the late 1950s and early 1960s that another window of opportunity for comprehensive structural change in the health-care arena opened. The opening was facilitated, as it had been forestalled in the 1940s, by the climate of federal-provincial relations. With the dawning of an era of "cooperative federalism," that climate was more favourable to the launching of a national health insurance plan. It was also facilitated by the presence of the New Democratic Party at the federal level both as an electoral threat and, after the 1965 election, as the holder of the balance of power in a minority Liberal government. The time was ripe for a broad re-thinking of social policy at the federal level.

In the health-care arena, the landscape upon which this window of opportunity opened was different than it had been in the 1940s. A substantial proportion of the population had become accustomed to relatively generous and comprehensive coverage under private insurance plans. Furthermore, opinion within the medical profession had come to favour governmental subsidization and supplementation of private plans. Although its view ultimately did not prevail, the medical profession presented a relatively united front, and could establish a policy price for its participation in the program. That price was essentially the maintenance of the existing delivery system, and the governmental underwriting of its costs on relatively generous terms. The buoyant economic conditions of the time, moreover, placed few constraints on such a design. The system was hence launched on an economic and political base favourable to more generous financing and a greater degree of medical influence than had been the case in Britain two decades earlier.

The structure of Canadian Medicare was established in two phases, each following a period of provincial experimentation. In 1958, Parliament passed the *Hospital Insurance and Diagnostic Services Act*, providing federal cost-sharing for eligible provincial plans. In the 1960s, the focus turned to medical services. The adoption of a publicly-funded medical insurance plan by the government of Saskatchewan in 1962 had a profound demonstration effect. It demonstrated the willingness of the provincial NDP to weather a medical strike to bring the program in, but also provided an example of a program that essentially underwrote the costs of the existing delivery system (notwithstanding some experimentation with community clinics) and led to an immediate rise in physician incomes. In 1964, the report of the Royal Commission on Health Services recommended the establishment of a national medical insurance plan, and by 1966, legislation establishing such a plan, the *Medical Care Act*, was passed. By 1971, all provinces were participating in the national regime. To be eligible for 50 percent federal cost sharing, provincial programs had to meet five general criteria: universal coverage (at least 95 percent of the population), comprehensive coverage of medical and hospital services, provision of coverage on uniform terms and conditions, portability across provinces, and public administration. These criteria were consistent with the "Health Charter for Canadians," that had been set out by the federal Royal Commission on Health Services. Notably, the Health Charter also included commitments to "freedom of choice" for patients in the selection of physicians and *vice versa*, and to "free and self-governing professions." While these latter two principles in the Health Charter were not specifically enshrined in legislation, they were clearly embedded in the system that resulted.

The structural changes wrought by Medicare in the Canadian health policy arena were essentially three: the role of private insurers was drastically reduced; the role of the federal government vis-à-vis the provinces was enhanced; and the role of the state as a whole was expanded.

Restriction of the Domain of Private Insurance. The advent of Medicare effectively foreclosed private insurers from covering the vast majority of medical and hospital services. A distinctive feature of the Canadian system is worth noting in this respect. The proportion of total health-care spending in Canada that flows through the public treasury, at about three-quarters, is close to the OECD average. Canada differs from most OECD nations, however, in the *pattern* of public and private expenditure. In most other nations public and private expenditures are divided on a "tiered" basis — with private alternatives to publicly-funded services within each category of service. In Canada, however, public and private expenditures are segmented. Certain segments — notably medical and hospital services — are almost entirely publicly funded; others, such as dental care, drugs and eyeglasses and other prostheses, are in the private sector. (Various provinces have plans covering drugs or dental care for certain categories within the population, such as children's dental care or drugs for those over 65. In the hospital sector, various amenities, such as private rooms, can be purchased on a private basis.) Private insurers, then, are effectively confined to certain segments of the system.

Federal-Provincial Relations. The federal government's financial leverage under cost-sharing arrangements gave it a significant steering effect on the system. Initially, by allowing provinces to cover medical and hospital services with "fifty-cent dollars," it favoured the provision of such services as opposed, for example, to home-care services. Furthermore, although the criteria for eligibility for provincial programs were very generally phrased, the requirement that services must be provided on "uniform terms and conditions" presented a potential — and, as it turned out in the 1980s, a real — constraint on the choice of policy instruments by provincial governments.

The federal government retained its financial leverage even as it decreased, over time, its share of health-care expenditures. The Established Programs Financing (EPF) arrangements negotiated in 1977 in the shadow of a threat by the federal government to act unilaterally moved from a shared-cost basis of funding to a block grant system. Federal transfers for health care (and post-secondary education) were thenceforth to have two components. One was in the form of a cash transfer conditional on the provinces continuing to meet the federal conditions of eligibility. This cash transfer was to be calculated on the basis of one-half of the per capita transfer to the province in 1975-76, escalated by the rate of increase in nominal GNP and population (not at the rate of actual health-care costs). The other "half" of the transfer was unconditional, and took the form of "tax points," essentially the revenue generated by a specified number of percentage points of the income tax yield of the federal basic tax in a given province. The actual number of tax points transferred was calculated as the number that would indeed have yielded an amount equivalent to half of the federal transfer in the base year to the two richest provinces, then Ontario and B.C. It was assumed that the growth in the yield from the tax points would outpace the growth of the cash transfer, and that eventually all provinces would be as well off as or better off than they would have been if the federal government had simply converted the entire transfer to a block grant and escalated it according to nominal GNP and population. In the meantime, a transitional payment was provided for, to ensure that no province was worse off than it would have been had that simple conversion occurred.

In the event, the economic downturn of the late 1970s and early 1980s meant that tax points were not as lucrative as had been expected, and "transitional adjustment payments" threatened to become a fixture of the arrangements. In the early 1980s, a change to the transfer formula was made that, while technical and little remarked-upon, marked the beginning of a set of structural amendments to the federal-provincial relationship in the health-care arena. The change was simply to calculate the *entire transfer* to a given province on the basis of the per capita in the base year, escalated by nominal GNP and population growth. The conditional cash component of this transfer was calculated as the difference between the yield of the tax points and the total provincial entitlement. The conditional component of the transfer, the basis of the federal government's policy leverage, hence became the residual once the tax points had done their work.

The federal government still retained considerable financial leverage in the early years of this arrangement. This was nowhere better demonstrated than with the passage of the *Canada Health Act* in 1984, reiterating the principles of eligibility for federal cost-sharing, and interpreting those principles to ban user fees and extra-billing.

Shortly after the passage of the *Canada Health Act*, however, with the coming to power of the Progressive Conservatives in 1984, the structural change implicit in the EPF formula revisions was accelerated. The Conservatives constrained the escalation of the total EPF transfers to the provinces under EPF — holding them below the rate of increase in nominal GNP from 1986 to 1990, and freezing them from 1990 onward. Since the tax point portion of the transfer continued to grow more or less in line with nominal GNP, the conditional cash transfer portion became correspondingly smaller. Various provincial governments have estimated that over the next decade the conditional portion will disappear entirely, and with it the federal government's policy leverage over Medicare.[2]

The State vis-à-vis the Medical Profession. Before speculating on the effects of these developments in federal-provincial relations, it is necessary to turn to the implications of the third structural change in the health field wrought by Medicare — the augmentation of the role of the state as a whole vis-à-vis health-care providers, and particularly the medical profession.

Under Medicare, the state became the primary bearer of the costs of hospital and medical services. And as the federal government progressively limited its share of the costs, provincial governments became entirely liable for cost increases above the rate of increase of nominal GNP and population, and finally for cost increases above the rate of population increase alone. For health-care providers, the effect of this type of change was not so much to diminish their influence as it was to change, over time, the channels through which it was exercised. In the case of the medical profession, in particular, the effect was to enhance the role of organized medicine. To understand this effect, it is necessary to understand the fundamental accommodation between the medical profession and the state that was established in the wake of Medicare, and from which subsequent distributive policies flowed.

The particular nature of that accommodation varies across provinces, for it is at the provincial level that health-care policy has been made, within broad federal guidelines. In some provinces, notably B.C. and Manitoba, the profession-state relationship has been adversarial; in Quebec it has been more "statist;" and in other provinces it has been more collaborative, albeit marked by episodes of conflict. But each of these accommodations has revolved around two pivotal trade-offs for the medical profession: one between the entrepreneurial and the clinical discretion of physicians; the other between their individual and their collective autonomy.

Almost all of the conflict between the medical profession and the state that followed in the wake of the adoption of Medicare concerned the price of medical services. Rather than paying the medical fees that were "usual and customary" in particular localities as did U.S. third-party payers, provincial governments at first agreed to pay physicians on the basis of the fee schedules set by the provincial medical associations, prorated by a given percentage. Soon, however, the schedule of payments was set through negotiations between the government and the medical association in each province. In most cases they negotiated overall increases in the payment schedule, leaving the allocation of these increases across individual items in the fee schedule to be carried out internally by the medical associations themselves. In making these internal allocations, medical associations have typically been more concerned with smoothing income differentials across specialty groups than with measuring the relative costs or benefits of given procedures. In reaching their accommodations with the state, that is, medical associations have had to manage delicate internal accommodations — a point to which I shall shortly return.

Over time, the agenda of these negotiations has broadened to include the establishment of more-or-less firmly fixed caps on total expenditures on physicians' services under the government plans. The rationale for the establishment of these limits was to take account of utilization increases. In fact, however, Lomas and his colleagues concluded after a comprehensive survey of the negotiation process in all ten provinces that the purpose of governments was to establish global limits: arguments about increased "utilization" simply provided a politically feasible way of doing so (Lomas *et al.* 1992, pp. 180-181).

As a result of these negotiations, then, the entrepreneurial discretion of individual physicians has been limited. Prices are established centrally, and the economic pay-off from varying volume and mix may bump up against either individual or global caps. But throughout this process, the *clinical* discretion of individual physicians — the ability of the individual physician to exercise his or her clinical judgement in individual cases according to professionally-determined standards — has remained virtually untouched. Financial constraints have been global and across-the-board; within those constraints, physicians experience relatively little second-guessing by third parties. Utilization review committees established in several provinces to monitor physicians' practice patterns have focused on only the most aberrant cases, identified by volume of billings.

It can legitimately be argued that the clinical autonomy of physicians is constrained to the extent that the diagnostic and therapeutic options open to them are constrained by limits on available facilities and equipment. It must be remembered, however, that the facilities subject to the greatest constraint in Canada, in contrast especially to the U.S., are those involving certain high-technology procedures;[3] and there is considerable debate among clinical epidemiologists as to the range of conditions for which such procedures are in fact indicated. As for other resources such as hospital beds and nursing staff, Canada has fewer hospital beds per capita but more employees per bed than the OECD average. (In the U.S., the bed-population ratio is even lower, while the employee-bed ratio is higher.) In a three-nation survey of physicians, Canadians were not significantly more likely than Americans to complain of a shortage of competent nursing staff (Blendon *et al.* 1993, p. 1015).

The point remains that within gross over-all constraints, the clinical autonomy of the individual physician, and of the profession as a whole, has been maintained. And in the process of making the trade-off of entrepreneurial discretion for clinical autonomy, the role of organized medicine has been substantially increased. This brings us to the second, and indeed more basic trade-off with which physicians are faced under Canadian Medicare. In order to retain some power over the price of their services, individual physicians had to cede their ability to set prices to the central association. This process was not without conflict; and each provincial association has had to manage a complex and delicate internal accommodation.

For a time, there was an option for physicians to escape these constraints to some extent by "extra-billing" their patients — that is, by billing patients over and above what the government plan would pay. Only about 10 percent of physicians exercised this option, and the amount of extra-billing was estimated at only about 1.3 percent of total physician billings under Medicare. In no province did this amount exceed 3 percent. The economic and political significance of extra-billing was increased, however, by the fact that it was "clustered" in certain specialties and localities. Even more important in political terms, extra-billing flew in the face of one of the fundamental principles underlying

Canadian Medicare — the removal of financial barriers to access to medical and hospital care.

In the early 1980s, a federal Liberal government declining in popularity and facing non-Liberal governments in each of the provinces, seized upon the issue of extra-billing as a way of symbolizing its commitment to preserving the universality of the nation's most popular social program — and, by extension, of others. It portrayed non-Liberal governments in the provinces as allowing the principle of universality to be eroded by condoning extra-billing, and passed legislation, the *Canada Health Act*, penalizing those provinces by providing for federal transfer payments to be reduced by an amount equal to the estimated amount of extra-billing in any given province — a dollar-for-dollar penalty.

In one sense at least, the federal strategy back-fired. The federal Conservatives, whom the Liberals had hoped to tar with the same brush as their siblings in power in several provinces, supported the *Canada Health Act* in Parliament. With its passage in 1984, the politics shifted to the provinces, and were shaped by the relationship between the medical profession and the government in each province. In all cases but one, the process of negotiating the ban on extra-billing was relatively non-conflictual, and the medical profession achieved substantial gains. Some of these gains took the form of fee schedule increases. Others, however, were structural, in the form of binding arbitration mechanisms for future fee schedule disputes. Even in Ontario, where the banning of extra-billing occasioned unprecedented conflict between the Ontario Medical Association and the government, culminating in a four-week doctors' strike, the dust settled by 1991 to reveal substantial structural gains for the Ontario Medical Association. A binding arbitration mechanism was agreed to, as was a "Rand formula" arrangement whereby OMA dues would be automatically "checked-off" or deducted from each individual physician's billings to the Ontario Health Insurance Plan. Finally, a Joint Management Committee of OMA and government representatives was established as a planning mechanism. In all, as of the beginning of 1993, some type of formal dispute resolution process was in place in eight provinces, and "Rand"-type dues check-offs were in place in seven.

As the agenda of health policy evolves in Canada, the various accommodations between the medical profession and provincial government that underlie the preservation of clinical autonomy will be tested. So far, these accommodations have proved remarkably resilient. This can be seen by considering the course of development of several major items on the health-care agenda of the 1990s: user fees, de-insurance, clinical guidelines and organizational change.

THE EVOLVING AGENDA

User Fees. The issue of "user fees" for insured services was put to rest for a time with the passage of the *Canada Health Act* and the compliance of all provinces with that federal legislation. The issue of user fees has reemerged, however, as the *Canada Health Act,* which bans such charges, has become increasingly toothless. With the end of federal contributions in some provinces over the next decade, the federal government's ability to enforce the provisions of the *Canada Health Act* will come to an end as well, unless funding is restored or some other enforcement mechanism is introduced.

Without the discipline of the federal legislation, it is possible that some provincial governments will reintroduce user fees. To the extent to which this occurs, it is likely to involve flat charges. (Quebec, for example, has recently announced plans to levy flat charges for certain services — such as visits to hospital emergency rooms for conditions that might be treated at community clinics. The federal government has signalled that these draft regulations will be reviewed to determine their conformity with the *Canada Health Act.*) It is highly unlikely, however, that "extra-billing" by physicians, and hence medical discretion over price, will again be permitted. That battle has been fought, and the treaties made. Any government that sought to reintroduce extra-billing would do so a great political risk, for little political or fiscal gain.

De-insuring. So far, provincial governments appear to be more attracted to the option of de-insuring some services than to the imposition of user fees as a cost control measure. This response is, indeed, more consistent with Canada's "segmented" rather than "tiered" approach to the role of the public and private sectors. The *Canada Health Act* made even more explicit the premises of its predecessor legislation: on its face, it requires provincial health insurance plans to cover fully all "medically required" physician services and a broadly defined set of "necessary" types of hospital services in order to qualify for federal financial contributions. Provincial governments, in complying with the federal legislation, have either *de facto* or *de jure* accepted "medical necessity" as the standard for coverage under their respective plans. The determination of what physician services are "medically required" and which hospital services are "necessary," however, has not been defined in legislation.

In the hospital sector, the operational definition of "necessity" has been negotiated by government and health-care providers. Through a process of prospective global hospital budgeting, provincial governments have, since the 1970s, been negotiating with individual hospitals about how many beds, imaging machines, etc. are "necessary." Differences of opinion in this regard resulted for a time in hospitals breaching their budgets to adopt non-approved programs.

The resulting deficits were tolerated and forgiven for a time by governments, but the limits of that tolerance were reached in the late 1980s.

As opposed to the question of which hospital services are "necessary" and thus must be publicly funded, the question of what physicians' services are "medically required" has until recently not been a matter of negotiation between providers and governments. As noted earlier, fee schedule negotiations between medical associations and provincial governments have generally focused on the overall percentage increase in fees, not the relative value of items and nor the scope of the services covered, which has changed little since a broad base of coverage was set up in each province upon the establishment of Medicare.

There have been, however, recent attempts to delimit the scope of coverage under Medicare. Under the letter and the spirit of both federal and provincial legislation, services can be de-insured only if they are deemed not to be medically necessary. Negotiations to identify potential candidates for de-insuring have been undertaken between the medical profession and government in a number of provinces. To date, there has been very little effect on the comprehensiveness of coverage, but the discussions around these issues are worth briefly considering here for what they can tell us about the shape of future developments.

Most of the services and procedures considered for "de-insuring" have related to cosmetic surgery, mental health and reproduction. The selection of these procedures for consideration has resulted in part from the ideological agendas of governments, and in part from a consideration of income differentials within the medical profession. In Alberta in 1985, as part of the negotiations between the Alberta Medical Association and the provincial government around the banning of extra-billing, it was decided that several services be "de-insured," including family planning counselling, tubal ligations, vasectomies, and mammoplasty. This selection was driven largely by the conservative social policy ideology of the governing Conservative party of the day. From the perspective of the medical profession, however, it focused with few exceptions on fairly lucrative procedures performed by relatively high-earning specialists. Furthermore, the de-insurance of such services freed physicians to bill for them privately at rates of their own choosing. As an internal accommodation within the profession, then, it allowed for some smoothing of differentials in Medicare earnings while allowing a "safety valve" for the specialties affected. This agreement did not survive the public protest that ensued, however, and funding for most of these services was restored. More recently, governmentally-sponsored round table discussions in Alberta proposed a policy option formed of an intersection between user fees and de-insurance that might be called "partial de-insurance." This option involves the identification of certain "non-essential" medical services to which user fees would apply.

In Ontario, a number of services are also being considered for de-insuring. In this case, the list includes some forms of cosmetic surgery, and *in vitro* fertilization (IVF) procedures. (Ontario is the only province in which IVF is a publicly-insured service.) Again, these are lucrative services and procedures performed by relatively high-earning specialists, and their de-insurance would allow them to be offered in private markets. The list also includes the annual health exam — a service whose efficacy when offered on a routine basis was first brought into question in the Canadian context by a consensus panel reporting to the federal and provincial health ministers in 1979.

The Ontario Medical Association, however, was initially less disposed to enter into this type of accommodation than its Alberta counterpart had been. The initial response in Ontario was essentially procedural. That is, the provincial government and the OMA came to an agreement on the structures through which decisions would be made about the efficacy of various procedures, through health services research; and decisions about insurance coverage would be made on that basis. As part of the wide-ranging 1991 agreement between the Ontario government and the OMA noted above, a Joint Management Committee was formed between the Ontario government and the OMA, and under its aegis an Institute for Clinical Evaluative Sciences was established, based at a Toronto teaching hospital. The process of developing a list of procedures to be de-insured went on for over a year until it became entailed in the government's broad expenditure control agenda in the spring of 1993. The unfolding of that episode casts further light on the evolving nature of the profession-state accommodation, and merits some elaboration here.

As part of a broad expenditure control package in June 1993, the NDP government of Ontario introduced legislation giving it broad powers to de-insure services, and to limit payments under the government health insurance plan on the basis of the utilization profile of the patient, the practitioner or the facility involved.[4] The OMA reacted strongly and vociferously against these provisions, accusing the government of pre-empting the Joint Management Committee process, and mounting an extensive public relations campaign. The government, for its part, stated that the legislative provisions constituted a "fail-safe" to take effect only if a negotiated agreement with the OMA could not be reached. In the result, the OMA and the government reached agreement on a range of cost-control measures, including a three-year freeze on medical fees and a "hard cap" on total physicians' billings. The JMC process for determining which services were to be de-insured was reinstated, tied to tighter deadlines, given a set dollar volume ($20 million) by which billings were to be reduced through de-insurance, and augmented by an advisory panel including "members of the public" as well as medical and governmental representatives and tied to tighter deadlines.

There are at least three points worth noting about these developments in Ontario for what they suggest about the evolution of the profession-state accommodation. First, they suggest that governments may be more willing to flex their legislative muscle to establish a "shadow" within which their negotiations with the profession proceed. Second, however, they suggest the resiliency of the profession-state accommodation even under conditions of growing fiscal constraint. And third, they suggest that the government's approach to accommodation may be shifting the balance of power within the medical profession over time. In the past, academically-based physicians were at the core of the profession-state accommodation; and the OMA played a varying role depending upon the vagaries of its internal politics (Tuohy 1992, pp. 126-127). The NDP government of Ontario has preferred, however, to deal primarily with the OMA as the legitimate "bargaining agent" for the profession. For its part, the OMA has worked its way through a wrenching internal process which has left it more open to accommodation with the state. Now for the first time a body central to the profession-state relationship, the JMC, has no academically-based medical members.

This new accommodation between the OMA and the provincial government in Ontario has not been without controversy within the profession. There is still a minority body of opinion within the profession which holds that the OMA has been too concerned with the preservation and enhancement of the power of organized medicine at the expense of the autonomy of the individual physician. The 1991 agreement, which not only established the JMC but also provided for an automatic check-off of membership dues to the OMA from each individual physician's payments under Medicare, was strongly contested by this minority.

Clinical Guidelines. The tension between the collective autonomy of the profession and the individual autonomy of the practitioner is raised even more squarely by the development of clinical guidelines. The issue of using clinical guidelines developed by professional bodies to shape the behaviour of individual practitioners has been on the agenda of Canadian health policy, to very little effect, for well over a decade. In the early 1990s, however, this mechanism has achieved greater prominence. A number of provinces have developed joint profession-government bodies to develop clinical guidelines, although the fiscal sanctions associated with the guidelines vary considerably. Ontario's Institute for Clinical Evaluative Sciences, under the aegis of the Joint Management Committee, is one such mechanism, and the status of the guidelines it is to develop is as yet unclear. An earlier initiative in Ontario in which guidelines on the use of caesarean sections were widely distributed to obstetricians was unsuccessful in modifying behaviour. In Saskatchewan, however, guidelines on thyroid tests issued by the Health Services Utilization and Research Commission resulted in a marked drop (65 to 79 percent) in the ordering of certain tests in circumstances in which the guidelines suggested they were not indicated (Mickleburgh 1993). In British Columbia, an undertaking to develop clinical guidelines backed by legislation and fiscal sanctions formed the centrepiece of an agreement negotiated between the British Columbia Medical Association and the B.C. government in August 1993. As governments and professional bodies thus move slowly in the direction of "managed care," relations between the profession and the state, and between individual practitioners and professional bodies, will be under increasing pressure.

Organizational Change. These relationships will also be strained as the system increasingly confronts issues of organizational change in health-care delivery. Such issues have been on the agenda of Canadian health policy since the 1970s, but outside Quebec there has been little action. Now these issues are gaining prominence in a number of provinces. It is worthwhile to distinguish two dimensions of policy making in this regard: one relating to changes in health-care delivery arrangements per se, and one relating to changes in the policy-making structures through which decisions about the organization of health-care delivery will be made. Provincial governments have varied considerably in the emphasis that they have given to each of these dimensions, depending on a mix of factors including the partisan complexion of the government and the degree of populism or statism in the political culture. Under NDP governments, for example, both British Columbia and Saskatchewan have recently announced plans to decentralize policy-making structures by establishing systems of local (and, in B.C., regional) health authorities with greater budgetary and managerial powers than have been granted to similar bodies in the past. In less populist Ontario, the NDP government has made a number of decisions centrally, such as the decision to regularize the practice of midwifery, that have important implications for the reorganization of health-care delivery, and has not expanded the powers of district health councils beyond their traditional advisory functions. Quebec and New Brunswick, under Liberal governments, have established or reorganized regional boards with somewhat more limited scope and more constrained powers than those proposed in B.C. and Saskatchewan. Organizational reforms in Nova Scotia, begun under a Conservative government and continued under a Liberal government, established a system of regional planning agencies with advisory powers only. In Manitoba, under a

Conservative government, proposals for a restructuring of the delivery system have emanated from the provincial government without the creation of local or regional councils (Hurley *et al*. 1993).

Most of the structural changes involving local and regional bodies are in their earliest stages; and their likely impact on the health-care delivery system remains to be seen: precursor bodies have had relatively little impact on the system. But if the scope of the authority of these or other predominantly non-medical authorities should extend to issues of the organization of medical practice, such as a re-definition of the roles of physicians and other health-care personnel, they could threaten the professional clinical autonomy on which delicate profession-state accommodations are based.

There is, then, at least in theory, considerable scope for variation across provincial plans: the definition of "medical necessity" and the structure of the health-care delivery system have been determined in the context of an accommodation between the medical profession and the state in each province. And it is true that costs, supply, and utilization vary considerably across provinces (Tuohy 1992, p. 137). What is remarkable is that the variation is not greater than it is, given the loose constraints of the federal legislation. This variation is limited because the interests of the medical profession are fundamentally similar across provinces; and, if clinical discretion is to be maintained while entrepreneurial discretion is limited, these interests militate in favour of a comprehensive and generously funded scheme.

THE FUTURE

I can now return to the question I posed at the beginning. Will the 1990s be an epoch of fundamental structural change in health care, or will we see a continuation of distributional politics within the parameters of the ongoing accommodation between the medical profession and the state?

What are the factors that might lead us to expect an epoch of structural change? Here a comparative perspective will be helpful. In the early 1990s, both Britain and the U.S. have embarked upon varying degrees of structural change in their health systems. In each case, the impetus for opening the window of opportunity arose from partisan politics. In Britain, as in Canada, ongoing distributional politics in health care have been governed by what Day and Klein have called an "implicit concordat" between the medical profession and the state. Day and Klein state the trade-off between clinical autonomy and economic discretion that underlies this concordat starkly: "[T]he state accepted the right of the medical profession to use the available resources without question, while the medical profession in exchange accepted the right of the state to set the budgetary constraints within which it worked" (1992, p. 471; see also Schwartz and Aaron 1984, pp. 52-56; and Heidenheimer *et al.* 1983, p. 61). Governmental fiscal restraint put this understanding under increasing pressure in the 1980s. Nonetheless, the impetus for considering fundamental structural change clearly derived from the broader agenda of the governing Conservative party — specifically from Prime Minister Margaret Thatcher's distrust of the power of intermediate para-public institutions such as professional bodies and from Health Secretary Kenneth Clark's adherence to market-oriented policy instruments. In this context, a set of policy ideas then current among U.S. health-care economists (notably Alain Enthoven), regarding "managed competition" in health care was particularly influential (Ham 1992, p. 147).

The result was an attempt to define much more sharply the roles of "purchasers" and "providers" within the system. Specifically, general practitioners were to be given the option of functioning as "fund-holders," with global budgets from which all services for patients on their rosters were to be published. Hospitals were allowed to opt out of the NHS to function as "self-governing trusts" to offer services on a competitive basis to general practitioners and local health authorities. In practice, these changes have, in their early stages, made for less radical change than the debate surrounding their introduction might have implied. They have in some cases shifted some clinical decision-making authority to general practitioners from consultants (specialists) in the hospitals. And they have raised the potential for a greater privatization of the system if the newly-formed hospital trusts choose to compete to an increasing extent in private markets. But at least in the early days of the new regime, observers saw the fairly rapid re-establishment of an equilibrium not far removed from what had been the case before the changes (Coulter and Bradlow 1993; Gennerster and Matsaganis 1993). Without a massive change in information technology, the multitude of fine levers of decision making about health services in Britain continue to rest in the hands of the medical profession.

In the United States, the structural changes in health care proposed by the Clinton administration are much more sweeping than were the recent British reforms; and the policy arena into which they are being introduced is much more complex than is the case in either Britain or Canada. In the absence of national health insurance, American public policy has elaborated both categorical programs and regulatory constraints. The resulting complexity has given a competitive advantage to providers with the resources to invest in understanding the system and responding strategically. Public policy has thus fostered organizational change not only directly (as in the case of HMOs, PPOs, etc.) but also indirectly (as in the case of a large multi-institutional chains, many of them for-profit, which have sprung up in response to the increasing complexity of the system).

The Clinton proposals recognize this complexity. They leave all of the existing actors in place, while introducing a significant new component upon which the functioning of the system depends: the regional health alliance. Modelled after European social insurance funds, the regional alliances are to act as purchasers on behalf of their enrollees, choosing among competing plans offered by private insurers and health-care providers. Various regulatory constraints will govern both the plans that can be offered and the premiums that can be charged — hence the label that summarizes the structure of the proposed regime: "managed competition."

The genesis of these proposed changes was in the desire in the Clinton campaign, and then the Clinton presidency, for a centrepiece for its domestic policy agenda. Twice before in the last 30 years, partisan politics in the U.S. have opened windows of opportunity for structural change in the health-care arena. In the mid-1960s, when Canada was adopting comprehensive national health insurance, the U.S. also entered into a major reform of health-care financing. Faced with implacable opposition from organized medicine, however, Democratic strategists chose to focus upon the provision of hospital and medical insurance for the elderly and the poor, and the establishment of the Medicare and Medicaid programs was the result. Then, almost a decade later in 1974, it appeared for a time that a bipartisan coalition might achieve a comprehensive national health insurance plan built upon a combination of private carriers and government programs. In the partisan manoeuvring leading up to the 1974 Congressional election under the cloud of Watergate, however, the moment was lost (Starr 1982, p. 405). In the current case, the prospects for real change are somewhat brighter. The issue is being addressed early in the first term of a president who can claim a mandate for health-care reform; and the opposition of organized medicine is much more muted and focused upon particular aspects of the plan. But the structure of the health-care arena, with its proliferation of financial interests, is much different than it was 20 and 30 years ago. The passage of the Clinton proposals through that landscape will shape the resulting plan in ways that cannot yet be anticipated.

The contemporary British and American experience, together with earlier Canadian experience, suggests that structural change in the health-care arena is likely to be triggered by partisan factors outside the arena, although its implementation is shaped by the configuration of interests in the arena. Is there reason, then, to expect that structural change in this arena will soon be triggered in Canada?

On one scenario, an era of structural change appears likely. After the period of the late 1980s in which the role of the federal government in social policy was unilaterally redefined, we can look towards an explicit renegotiation of the federal-provincial relationship. And in the next federal Parliament, it is possible that the Reform Party and the Bloc Québécois could play a role in decentralizing social policy analogous to the role played by the NDP in centralizing it in the 1960s. Even given the Liberals' firm majority, Reform and the Bloc represent strong regional challenges to the legitimacy of the Liberal mandate. Together with fiscal and political pressures within the nexus of relationships between federal and provincial governments, the complexion of Parliament could well lead the governing Liberals in a more decentralist direction.

As for the federal-provincial nexus, there is clearly growing enthusiasm in some quarters (as reflected in a number of contributions to this volume) for greater "disentanglement" between federal and provincial program responsibilities and revenue sources. There is also a growing recognition, within both federal and provincial circles, of the need to reduce provincial vulnerability to unilateral decisions by the federal government affecting transfer payments. On some of the models that have been developed for consideration, the federal government would relinquish all responsibility for Medicare, and the residual cash transfers for Medicare under EPF arrangements would be converted to tax points (Norrie in this volume).

If provinces are given greater discretion in health policy (an outcome that would occur in due course under current arrangements anyway, as discussed earlier) this will have the effect of providing ten possible windows of opportunity for structural change in health care, rather than one, that might be opened up under certain partisan conditions. And it also raises the possibility that provincial experimentation will have demonstration effects similar to the effect of Saskatchewan medicare in the 1960s.

If one or more of these provincial windows do open, it will open on a landscape of policy ideas in which "managed competition" holds great sway. Some Canadian health policy analysts have argued for some time in favour of an approach that would introduce market forces within the publicly-funded Canadian system (Stoddart and Seldon 1983). Any significant movement towards managed competition in the current Canadian context would lead to a much greater diversity in the types of coverage that Canadians enjoy than is the case today. It would also increase the transaction, and hence the administrative costs of the system. And it would reintroduce private insurers as significant political and economic actors in the medical and hospital insurance arena. In short, it would render the system, in the experience of both consumers and providers, significantly more "American," especially if the United States, by providing universal coverage through a Clinton-style plan, moves somewhat closer to the Canadian model.

This scenario is a real possibility. On balance, however, I believe that it is unlikely that fiscal decentralization in health care will progress as far as the complete vacation of the medicare field by the federal government. Furthermore, I believe that the fiscal decentralization that does occur (even if it includes the vacation of the field by the federal government) will not likely lead to extensive structural change along "managed competition" lines. My reasons for this belief are twofold.

For the first reason, I must return to the neglected "symbolic" dimension of policy to which I alluded at the outset. Polls have consistently demonstrated that Medicare is by far the most popular public program in Canada. A 1988 cross-national poll showed that Canadians were more satisfied with their health-care system than were either American or British respondents, and that they overwhelmingly preferred the Canadian system to the British or the American. A large majority of American respondents, on the other hand, preferred a Canadian-style system to their own (Blendon 1989). Subsequent polls have reinforced these results (Gallup Canada 1991). This level of public support exists not only because of the tangible benefits that Medicare yields, though that is clearly an important factor. It exists also because Medicare is a central part of Canadian public mythology. It has become an important element by which Canadians distinguish themselves from other nations, and particularly from the U.S. During the heated and wrenching public debate over the Free Trade Agreement with the United States in 1988, politicians opposing the agreement (including the then leader of the federal Liberal party) repeatedly invoked Medicare as one of the things that distinguished Canada from the U.S., and alleged that it was threatened by the agreement. Public opinion polls showed that this allegation was the most effective way of galvanizing opposition to the FTA (Johnston and Blais 1988). Given the volatility of symbolic politics, it is difficult to judge how tightly the mythological status of Canadian Medicare constraints fundamental structural change. But it is fair to say that proposing structural change in Medicare, especially in the direction of the "American" model of managed competition now gaining increasing prominence on the policy landscape, carries great political risk.

In the second place, even if structural change in the health-care arena were to be attempted, it would be conditioned, as it has been elsewhere, by the existing configuration of interests. Any attempt to introduce other administrative actors into the system as required by a managed competition model would threaten the fundamental accommodation between the medical profession and the state that underlies the Canadian system. This can most readily be appreciated through a quick comparison with the United States, where the effect of organized medicine's opposition to the introduction of national health insurance over the past few decades in the U.S. has been to preserve the economic discretion of physicians while increasingly constraining their clinical autonomy.[5] In the absence of comprehensive national health insurance, as noted above, administrative structures have proliferated. In the effort to control costs and/or to generate revenue, both provider institutions and third-party payers have elaborated systems of parameters to govern clinical decision making — systems of so-called "managed care."

Medical groups in Canada are aware of the different trade-offs that underlie the Canadian and American systems. Even in briefs critical of government policy, they typically present the Canadian system as one of the best in the world, while expressing some concerns about its future (Tuohy 1992, pp. 144-145). The twin spectres of the U.S. system (intrusive regulation, corporate dominance, inadequate coverage) and the British system (inadequate resources, excessive rationing) are frequently evoked. Attitude surveys of physicians find large majorities on balance satisfied with their conditions of practice and positively oriented towards Medicare — although sizable pockets of discontent remain. A 1986 survey of Canadian physicians, for example, found less than one-quarter dissatisfied with medical practice and less than one-third dissatisfied with the functioning of Medicare. Sixty percent believed that Medicare had positively influenced health status, but 75 percent believed that it had reduced the individual's personal sense of responsibility for health (Stevenson *et al.* 1987). A comparative survey of physicians in Canada, the U.S. and western Germany in 1991 found that although a majority of physicians in each country believed that some fundamental changes in their health systems were necessary, satisfaction with the health system was higher among Canadian and German physicians than among American physicians. When respondents were asked to identify the most serious problems with their system, the sharpest differences arose between Canadian and American physicians, whose judgements of their respective systems appeared virtually as mirror images of each other. Canadian physicians were more likely to complain of limitations on the supply of well-equipped medical facilities. American physicians, on the other hand, were more likely to identify delays or disputes in processing insurance forms and in receiving payment, the inability of patients to afford some aspect of necessary medical care, external review of clinical decisions for the purpose of controlling health costs, and limitations on the length of hospital stays as serious problems with their system (Blendon *et al.* 1993, p. 1015).

It is true that a degree of structural change, in the direction of "managed competition," has occurred in Britain even in the context of an established accommodation between the medical profession and the state based on the preservation of clinical autonomy. The effects of these structural changes seem so far to be internal to the medical profession, in enhancing the positions of "fund-holding" general practitioners. It may be the lack of the necessary information technology that has blunted the impact of change; and that the effect of the reforms will be seen only when information technology catches up with them. But by and large, the impact of the changes appears to have been blunted through their absorption into existing patterns of behaviour.

A prediction that fundamental structural change in health care is unlikely in the next decade is not, it must be emphasized, a prediction of statis. In the first place, current policy directions in health care will have incremental structural effects. As various services are fully or partially de-listed, the scope for private insurance, and hence the economic and political role of private insurers will increase. In the foreseeable future, however, this expansion of scope is likely to be marginal, and to be contained within the structure of existing provider-state accommodations. Second, as issues of technology assessment, clinical guidelines and organizational change are worked through existing policy-making structures, they are likely to yield significant if incremental change in the allocation of resources to health care and in distributional outcomes. These changes as well will vary across provinces, as they have done in the past, according to the nature of the evolving accommodations between health-care providers and provincial governments.

NOTES

1. Various scholars have wrestled with the appropriate terminology for this third dimension of policy — the terms "constitutional" (Day and Klein 1992), "constituent" (Lowi 1985) and "positional" (Aucoin 1971). In an earlier version of this chapter, presented at the conference from which this volume is drawn, I used the term "constitutional." That term, however, has specific connotations related to the fundamental law of the land. Particularly in the context of a volume devoted to issues of fiscal federalism, it is difficult to shed those connotations for analytic purposes, and I have chosen to refer instead to the "structural" dimension of policy.

2. In 1991, the federal Parliament passed legislation enabling the government to withhold *other* transfers to the provinces in the event that the "penalty" for non-compliance with the *Canada Health Act* exceeded the cash transfer thereunder. This legislation has yet to be invoked, or tested in the courts.

3. There is no doubt that the U.S. exceeds Canada in the availability of high-technology procedures. This is consistent with the general phenomenon that the diffusion of technology has been greater in systems with high proportions of specialists and less centralized cost control (Hollingsworth *et al.* 1988). As a matter of public policy, Canadian provincial governments control the diffusion of medical technology. Operating funds for certain types of equipment such as

imaging machines will not be provided unless acquisition of the equipment has been approved by the government. Furthermore, under the hospital global budgeting system, any significant change in the volume of service, including high-technology services, must be approved in order for the hospital to receive the necessary additional operating funds. A recent study based on interviews and available documentation found substantially greater numbers of MRI (magnetic resonance imaging) and radiation therapy units, lithotripsy centres, and cardiac catheterization and open-heart surgery units, and slightly more organ transplantation units per capita in the U.S. than in Canada. German ratios were intermediate between Canada and the U.S. in the case of cardiac catheterization, radiation therapy, lithotripsy, and MRI, and were below Canadian ratios for open-heart surgery and organ transplantation (Rublee 1989). Rates of coronary artery bypass surgery are much higher in the U.S., although other forms of treatment of ischemic heart disease such as other major reconstructive vascular surgery and pacemaker implantation, Canadian rates were higher (Anderson *et al.* 1989).

4. That is, payment for a given service could be reduced or denied if the number of services provided to a given patient, or by a given physician, or within a given facility exceeded a prescribed maximum during a particular time period. The legislation also granted the government broad regulatory powers to control expenditures, limit the number of practitioners, and affect the geographic distribution of practitioners and facilities.

5. The greater economic discretion of U.S. physicians does not necessarily translate into higher incomes, given the higher administrative expenses and greater incidence of bad debts associated with the U.S. system. In the decade following the introduction of Canadian Medicare, real physician fees rose much faster in the U.S. than in Canada — in Canada, indeed, (with the exception of British Columbia and Alberta) real fees declined over that period (Barer and Evans 1986, pp. 78-80). Between 1971 and 1985, real fees declined 18 percent in Canada and rose 22 percent in the U.S. (idem.). Differences in net income are less than might be expected, however, in part as a result of lower practice expenses. Because of the different specialty mixes in the two countries, income comparisons are best made by specialty. One such comparison, by Iglehart, related U.S. physicians to their counterparts in Ontario. (Ontario physicians represent about 40 percent of all Canadian physicians; and both net professional incomes and medical fees are close to the Canadian average (Barer and Evans 1986, pp. 78, 94)). In 1986, average net incomes in general practice and family practice were marginally higher for U.S. than for Ontario physicians. The differences were more pronounced in obstetrics and gynaecology, with U.S. physicians earning on average one-quarter to one-third higher than those of their Ontario counterparts. In pediatrics and internal medicine, however, the net earnings of Ontario physicians were on average marginally higher than those in the U.S. (Iglehart 1990).

BIBLIOGRAPHY

Anderson, Geoffrey M., Joseph P. Newhouse and Leslie L. Roos (1989), "Hospital Care for Elderly Patients with Diseases of the Circulatory System," *New England Journal of Medicine*, 321, 21: 1443-1448.

Aucoin, Peter (1971), "Theory and Research in the Study of Policy-Making," in *The Structures of Policy-Making in Canada*, ed. G. Bruce Doern and Peter Aucoin, Toronto: Macmillan.

Barer, Morris and Robert G. Evans (1986), "Riding North on a South-bound Horse: Expenditures, Prices, Utilization and Incomes in the Canadian Health Care System," in *Medicare at Maturity*, ed. Robert G. Evans and Greg L. Stoddart, Calgary: University of Calgary Press.

Blendon, Robert J. (1989), "Three Systems: A Comparative Survey," *Health Management Quarterly*, 11, 1: 2-10.

Blendon, Robert J. *et al.* (1993), "Physicians' Perspectives on Caring for Patients in the United States, Canada and West Germany," *New England Journal of Medicine*, 328, 14: 1011-1016.

Coulter, Angela and Jean Bradlow (1993), "Effect of NHS Reforms on General Practitioners' Referral Patterns," *British Medical Journal*, 306: 433-37.

Day, Patricia and Rudolph Klein (1992) "Constitutional and Distributional Conflict in British Medical Politics: The Case of General Practice, 1911-91," *Political Studies*, 11, 3: 462-478.

Gallup Canada (1991), *The Gallup Report*, Toronto, 1 August.

Gennerster, Howard and Manos Matsaganis (1993), "The UK Health Reforms: the Fundholding Experiment," *Health Policy*, 23: 179-91.

Ham, Christopher (1992), *Health Policy in Britain*, 3d. ed., London: Macmillan.

Heidenheimer, Arnold J., Hugh Heclo and Carolyn Teich Adams (1983), *Comparative Public Policy: the Politics of Social Choice in Europe and America*, 2d. ed., New York: St. Martin's.

Hollingsworth, J. Rogers, Jerald Hage and Robert A. Hanneman (1988), *State Intervention in Medical Care: Consequences for Britain, France, Sweden and the United States, 1890-1970*, Ithaca: Cornell University Press.

Hurley, Jeremiah, Jonathan Lomas and Vandna Bhatia (1993), "Is the Wolf Finally at the Door? Provincial Reform to Manage Health-Care Resources," Working Paper 93-12, Hamilton: Centre for Health Economics and Policy Analysis, McMaster University.

Iglehart, J.K. (1990), "Canada's Health Care System Faces its Problems," *New England Journal of Medicine*, 322, 8: 562-568.

Johnston, Richard and André Blais (1988), "A Resounding Maybe," *The Globe and Mail*, Toronto, 19 December, A7.

Lomas, Jonathan, Cathy Charles and Janet Greb (1992), *The Price of Peace: the Structure and Process of Physician Fee Negotiations in Canada*, Working Paper 92-17, Hamilton: Centre for Health Economic and Policy Analysis, McMaster University.

Lowi, Theodore (1985), "The State in Politics," in *Regulatory Policy and the Social Sciences*, ed. Roger Noll, Berkeley: University of California Press.

Mickleburgh, Rod (1993), "$1 Million to be Saved by Cuts in Thyroid Tests," *The Globe and Mail*, Toronto, 31 August, A1-2.

Rublee, Dale A. (1989), "Medical Technology in Canada, Germany and the United States," *Health Affairs*, 8, 3: 178-181.

Schwartz, William B. and Henry J. Aaron (1984), "Rationing Hospital Care: Lessons from Britain," *New England Journal of Medicine*, 310: 590-91.

Starr, Paul (1982), *The Social Transformation of American Medicine*, New York: Basic Books.

Stevenson, H. Michael, Eugene Vayda and A. Paul Williams (1987), "Medical Politics After the Canada Health Act: Preliminary Results of the 1986 Physicians' Survey," paper delivered at the annual meeting of the Canadian Political Science Association, McMaster University.

Stoddart, G.L. and J.R. Seldon (1983), "Publicly Financed Competition in Canadian Health Care Delivery: a Viable Alternative to Increased Regulation?" in *Proceedings of the Second Annual Conference on Health Economics,* ed. J.A. Boan, Regina: University of Regina.

Taylor, Malcolm G. (1973), "The Canadian Health Insurance Program," *Public Administration Review*, 33 (January-February): 31-39.

_____ (1978), *Health Insurance and Canadian Public Policy*, Montreal: McGill-Queen's University Press.

Tuohy, Carolyn (1989), "Federalism and Canadian Health Policy," in *Challenges to Federalism: Policy-Making in Canada and the Federal Republic of Germany*, ed. William M. Chandler and Christian W. Zollner, Kingston: Institute of Intergovernmental Relations, Queen's University.

_____ (1992), *Policy and Politics in Canada: Institutionalized Ambivalence*, Philadelphia: Temple University Press.

Comment: Calmness and Desperation

Greg Stoddart

I enjoyed Carolyn Tuohy's chapter a great deal, and her distinctions of distributional, symbolic and structural dimensions of policy are very useful. However, I went to the Yogi Berra School of Discussant Training and, although I can say that there is almost nothing that I disagree with, it is what the chapter does not say that I disagree with.

Reviewing some of her points, I would agree that structural policy change in the health-care arena does come from outside, that is to say from exogenous factors. I certainly would agree with the characterization of the Canadian experience of 1958-71 as the era of structural change, and her view that since then policy has largely been distributional. I also agree that it is always easier to explain the past than it is to predict the future! With regard to the future, however, I am less certain than Carolyn Tuohy that we will not see important structural changes in health-care arrangements. The likely balance of probability is against structural change, but I do have some concerns and some slightly different views.

This is a "calm" essay. It is almost a reassuring essay, or it can at least be read that way. But when I wander around the country, visiting health ministries or health-care ministries and talking to providers, I am *not* reassured. There is currently a different atmosphere, a sense of turbulence, and an atmosphere of exasperation, if not desperation.

I would like to talk about three health policy problems that fuel this exasperation. An important question is whether or not there is a federal role, fiscal or otherwise, in resolving these issues.

First, there is a sense of exasperation about having to raise revenue to finance the costs of the existing system, and this is presumably where the user charge debate comes in. Elsewhere, I and colleagues Robert Evans and Morris Barer are on record with a number of analyses of user charges, suggesting that they have very little to offer the Canadian public. There are a whole series of negative and well-known side-effects that accompany almost every form of user charge. If the intent of such charges is only to raise revenue, however, then they will probably "work," because (in an economist's language) the price-elasticity of demand for health care or medical care is very inelastic. The utilization of physician services and, in particular, hospital services is very price-insensitive. For this reason alone, user charges may prove irresistible to policymakers in the future as a source of revenue. I am not suggesting in a normative sense that I would like to see that happen. My view is quite the opposite. But there is a real chance of that happening. There is a significant group of people in Canada who would say that a user-charge policy is not a great policy but it may have to be done. There are many more forms of user charges than the flat per service charges that Carolyn Tuohy mentions, including a "tax-back" scheme whereby the value of insured medical and hospital services utilized would become taxable income. It should be noted that this scheme does not escape the problems with the other forms of user charges. Nevertheless, the issue of financing existing systems could lead to structural changes of the type that the *Canada Health Act* has played an important function in restraining until now.

Another source of exasperation is that we simply are not seeing changes in the patterns of clinical practice that are possible and warranted on the basis of the evidence we have about how to render effective and efficient medical care. Even after two or three decades of fairly extensive health services research, we still find that anywhere from 20-40 percent of the utilization of many medical procedures is either ineffective or inappropriate. We do not seem to be making a great deal of progress here. Carolyn Tuohy points out that clinical guidelines are one of the ways in which the conflict between the state and the medical profession is being accomodated. Clinical guidelines may help, but we do not have good "transmission belts" for their implementation into practice. I sense a real exasperation on the part of people committed to health-care reform that we are not moving closer to the effectiveness- or the efficiency-frontier. This is ultimately going to require reimbursement changes. But the interesting thing about these changes is that they have very little to do with fiscal federalism. They have not been prevented by current arrangements, and it is not clear how renegotiation of the arrangements will facilitate them.

On this issue there is tough work to be done at the "coal-face," at the provincial level and possibly even at lower levels. Whether or not this involves structural change of the type referred to in the paper, it may involve changes in the participation of some actors in the health-care system. One of the alternatives for addressing this problem is to challenge key institutions to show some leadership on the issue, and two key institutions would be academic health sciences centres and the self-regulating colleges, especially those of physicians. These bodies have not shown much leadership in moving the system to the effectiveness- and efficiency-frontiers by translating research studies into changes in clinical practice. In my view they should be strongly encouraged by provincial governments to assume much more active roles.

Let me go on to my third problem, the resolution of which will involve ordinary Canadian citizens. Imagine for a moment that we did reach the effectiveness- or efficiency-frontier. In economic jargon this is only a technical efficiency- or cost-effectiveness-frontier, not an allocative one. That gets us to the issue of deciding what is medically necessary. Just because something is cost-effective does not mean that it *should* be done.

There is still a consensus that needs to be formed socially about what medical necessity means. Are we talking clinically, about only the patient's capacity to benefit from a service, or are we really talking about whether or not we want to provide publicly-insured services that benefit only very small segments of the community (or large numbers of people but only in very small amounts, especially relative to their costs). We have not yet addressed this issue as a society, and I am not sure that the best way to address it is through the accommodation of medical profession-state conflict. The public is going to need to be involved but, just as in translating research evidence to clinical practice, it does not seem that we have the *mechanisms* to implement that dialogue. There may need to be some new institutions formed to do that.

This relates to the organizational change section of Carolyn Tuohy's chapter. Here I tend to differ a bit with her assessment of the likelihood of structural politics in the next decade. There is a very real possibility that the difficult decisions about which services will be provided to which groups will be dumped to a district or regional level through the creation of new decision-making bodies. The bodies may also receive some fiscal autonomy, which District Health Councils in Ontario, for example, have not had in the past. If that is the case, and if the funding is need-based there may be significant structural changes in the health-care arena, and a much greater role for the general public.

Finally, I have two more general questions to offer. The first is for those commentators who support the full devolution of health care to the provinces. What weight has been given in that discussion to the fact that the general public of Canada basically does not want decentralization, that it wants a set of national standards, and that it wants to preserve a sense (maybe even an illusion) of national unity or identity through federal-provincial arrangements for health care?

The second question concerns the nature of what we are talking about as "health." Although the topic has been billed as "health policy and fiscal federalism," it seems to me that it has not been about health policy at all; it has been about health *care* policy at the most and probably more about *sickness* care policy. There is currently a renaissance of the notion of the broader social determinants of health. Social, physical, cultural and economic environments affect health. For example, evidence is accumulating on the degree to which social support reduces your risk of mortality, for example. The health effects of early childhood development programs and other non-health care interventions and policies are increasingly being studied and found to be important. Should not *health* policy and fiscal federalism be interpreted more broadly? What is in fact the federal government's contribution to health as opposed to simply sickness care? If we look at other health-related programs, whether child development programs or tobacco programs or whatever, has there been a withdrawal, of the magnitude often alleged, of federal funding in the area of "health" policy? Perhaps we should start thinking a little more broadly if we want to have a new window on structural politics about health.

CHAPTER SEVEN

More Carrots, Please: Education, Training, and Fiscal Federalism

Judith Maxwell ·

INTRODUCTION

My topic is education and training in the context of fiscal federalism. I found that I had to write two papers — one on university and college education and the other on training. In both cases, however, the themes are bureaucratic deadlock, vested interests, jurisdictional games, and a desperate need for innovation. Oddly enough, there are more visible signs of movement in the right direction on the training side than there are on postsecondary education. But the reform of the training system is by no means guaranteed.

The main challenge in writing this paper was to figure out why reform has not taken place in the past. Certainly, there was no lack of sensible advice throughout the 1980s — by the Macdonald Commission (Royal Commission 1985), the Economic Council of Canada (1990; 1992), the Association of Universities and Colleges of Canada (Smith 1991), the Premier's Council of Ontario (1990), and legions of other task forces, scholars and policy advisers. The proposals presented here draw heavily on those documents. They are intended to replace the current permissive approach to federal funding with financial incentives to promote excellence and efficiency. Hence, my title: More Carrots, Please.

The chapter proceeds as follows. The first section begins with a discussion of what we want from education and training in the 1990s and beyond, and then a short description of the fiscal arrangements in question. Section two deals with the challenges facing universities and colleges, while the third proposes some directions for change in the financing of universities and colleges. In the fourth section, I turn to training. And the last section offers a brief conclusion.

EDUCATION AND TRAINING FOR THE FUTURE

Globalization and technology have eliminated any prospect for low-skill jobs with high pay in Canada. We had more than our share of these jobs in the postwar period because of high levels of tariff protection and the robust resource sector. In every province, there were large sections of the male population who could leave school at age 16 and expect to live a full and prosperous life working in the mines, the forests, the fishery, some parts of agriculture, and in standardized manufacturing jobs like breweries and metal bashing.[1]

Those days are gone. A young man who leaves school at age 16 today faces the prospect of a life pumping gas, flipping hamburgers, or brief seasonal work as a fishing or hunting guide. Even in the public sector, the jobs for young men who started work in the mail room and ended up as a $40,000 a year clerk with a fully indexed pension are disappearing.

A Knowledge-based Society

One way to characterize the changing configuration of employment in Canada is depicted in Figure 1. It shows the diminishing role of the goods-producing occupations in resources, manufacturing, construction occupations — in the top part of the chart — and the increasing role of service workers and knowledge workers. The knowledge and service jobs occur in all sectors — though there are only a few in primary and secondary industries.

What the figure shows is a society that is polarizing into service workers (mostly uneducated, low skill, low paid), and knowledge workers (mostly educated, highly skilled, and better paid). In other words, pay is determined by productivity. And the way work is now being organized, it is very difficult to climb the ladder from service to knowledge worker. On-the-job training will not transform a hospital cleaner into a nurse, for example.[2]

A society has two options in dealing with this polarizing trend. One is to simply accept the polarization and pay the price — which will be more poverty, crime, disease, and despair. This in itself imposes great costs in terms of public security and whatever welfare and other programs are used to moderate the poverty and despair. This is easily characterized as the American style (Maxwell 1993).

The second option is to reduce polarization by adding a learning dimension to the social contract. The original elements in the social contract were: the citizen agrees to work and pay taxes to finance the safety net, and government makes a commitment to create high levels of employment and to maintain a social safety net.[3]

FIGURE 1: Changing Patterns of Work (Share of Total Employment)

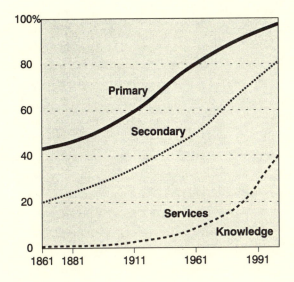

Note: U.S. knowledge workers' share of total employment

Primary	0.4
Secondary	5.0
Tertiary	<u>24.0</u>
Total	30.0
Source:	Nuala Beck.

Source: Based on Urquhart and Buckley, and Labour Force Survey.

A post-capitalist society, to use Drucker's term (1993), wants all citizens to be on a learning curve. Knowledge workers will need to upgrade, service workers need the chance to become knowledge workers, and "traditional" workers will need to adapt to constantly changing jobs in goods production. In this learning culture, there is a mutual responsibility on the part of citizens and state. Citizens have a responsibility to learn and the state has a responsibility to create opportunities to learn. Most of that learning will take place in private institutions — colleges, universities and the workplace. So the state does not deliver the education and training, though it may have to underwrite it at times.[4]

This conception of the future need for learning has two important consequences for this chapter. First, it justifies a role for government in the financing of education and training. And second, it creates a remarkable opportunity for the education and training institutions in Canada.

The rationale for the role of government in education and training rests on the externalities derived from a well-informed citizenry, a more efficient labour market, and higher levels of productivity and income. The argument is that governments are needed to ensure access for all, to facilitate the intergenerational transfer of knowledge and to build new knowledge that can be used for the benefit of all.

In the case of training, there is evidence that the private sector would underproduce training because of the risk that employees will leave in order to work for a competitor, after the employer has invested in training. For the same reason, employers will concentrate on job-specific or firm-specific training as opposed to generic training. Thus the role of government is to build institutions that will serve as bridges between general and specific training, between school and work, and between business and labour (Streeck 1990).

However, the private returns to education are also high — both for employers and for individuals (Vaillancourt 1992). So, they too should invest in education and training, and one of the key questions for the 1990s is the appropriate allocation of that responsibility.

The opportunity offered to universities and colleges by a knowledge-based society has its upside and downside. On the upside, they can expect a steady flow of students of all ages who are seeking more knowledge. They could become the chosen instrument for both social and economic policy focused on learning.

But, on the downside, universities and colleges will find that taxpayers are not prepared to throw wads of new money at the learning objective. In the next ten years, while we work through the deficit-debt issue, resources will be tight, perhaps even shrinking. Thus, new sources of financing will be essential. At the same time, students, governments and society at large are expecting innovations in teaching, in course design, and in methods of learning.

On that score, universities and colleges are on shaky ground. Universities today look remarkably like they did 400 years ago. But we know that all of the following trends are beginning to evolve (Cohen and Stanley 1993):

- It is possible to attend 12 Canadian universities from anywhere in the country by computer;

- Home computers allow us to tap into the collections of several libraries and link up with people around the world who want to discuss almost any subject;

- Lectures by the world's leading experts are available on videocassette;

- Canadian children are participating in joint science projects with children from other countries.

- Large corporations are establishing their own large scale training systems in-house because they cannot get the services they need from existing institutions.

The Fiscal Arrangements

Table 1 shows the composition of funding for universities and colleges in Canada for a representative year — 1988-89. Under the Established Programs Financing, the federal government provides cash transfers of just over $2 billion to the provinces to help them fund postsecondary education. In 1977, it also set aside tax points which by 1988-89 were worth $3.2 billion for this purpose, and there is now strong disagreement as to whether or not those tax points belong to Ottawa or the provinces. The federal government also spends another $3.3 billion on research, student assistance, and other items directly associated with postsecondary education. The formula governing the EPF was altered in the 1980s and it is now widely expected that the cash transfer will gradually shrink over the 1990s.

TABLE 1: Source of Funds for Postsecondary Education, 1988-89

	$ billion	Percent
Federal and provincial transfers[a]	8.5	71
Direct federal spending		
for research	0.6	5
for student assistance	0.5	5
other	0.3	3
Student fees	1.1	9
Other	0.8	7
Total	11.8	100

[a]Includes federal transfers to provinces of $5.4 billion; $2.2 billion cash and $3.2 billion tax points. By 1991-92, this had increased to $5.9 billion but the cash portion was beginning to decline.

Source: Statistics Canada and Secretary of State.

There is no shortage of studies which have declared that the current funding mechanisms are broken (Leslie *et al.* 1993). Cutt and Dobell (1992) show that while Canadian universities have been starved for funds in the past decade, their autonomy (i.e., academic freedom) has been better protected than that of universities in other jurisdictions. Governments do not intervene directly in the management of the universities and scholars are free to say and write what they wish. But pressures to regulate performance are mounting — Cutt and Dobell referred to the current period as the "lull before the storm."

The weaknesses identified in the literature include the following:

- The excessive generosity of the 1960s and early 1970s was not sustainable. The combination of the demographic pressure of the baby boom and the commitment to productivity growth through education created the political rationale for a flood of new funding for postsecondary education. That generosity created expectations on the part of faculty, staff, unions, and the bureaucracy that could not be sustained after productivity growth slumped so badly in the mid-1970s.[5]

- Misleading signals were built into the funding formulas of the 1970s. Al Johnson (1987) has noted that most incentives in the Established Program Financing stand in the way of reform. Peter Leslie (1980) made the point long ago in a report he did for the AUCC: "There is hardly any carrot for innovation; ... (and) there is only a very flimsy stick for inducing structural change where it is necessary, and for inventing solutions to staffing problems and program redundancy or overcapacity."

- Faulty projections of enrolments in the 1980s led to serious errors in planning with respect to funding, infrastructure, and staffing. Forecasters were looking at the demographics — the baby bust — but did not take into account the incentives in the labour market which kept young people in university longer (high unemployment) and attracted more people of all ages to attend university (skill upgrading).

- The lack of performance indicators meant that the public has taken more than a decade to realize that the quality of the system is eroding, as class sizes increase and more teaching is delegated to teaching assistants and inexperienced part-time lecturers. We may know, by osmosis, which are the strongest institutions, but the public does not know which are the strongest programs, nor does it know how little intellectual nourishment the undergraduate gets today, compared to 20 years ago. It is possible that some institutions do not know which of their programs are strong and which are weak. The first *Maclean's* article (1991) put the "cat among the pigeons," but it turns out that we do not even know how to compare institutions (Ontario. Task Force on University Accountability 1993) and some of the emerging proposals look cumbersome.

- The lines of accountability in the current funding for postsecondary institutions are confused. The best way to illustrate this is to use a diagram from Cutt and Dobell — see Figure 2. The federal government provides large amounts of funding (more than half) to the system through payments to the provinces who then distribute the money as they see fit — i.e., to education or to other purposes.

FIGURE 2: Governments and Universities: Accountability Relationships

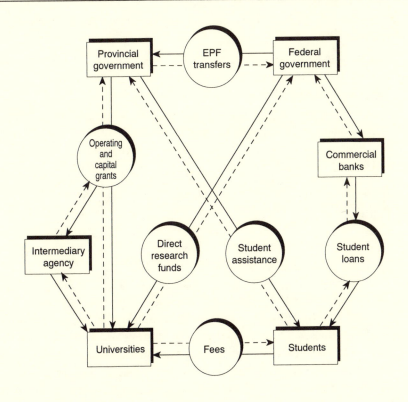

Source: Cutt and Dobell (1992).

One of the messages that shines through when we look at the fiscal arrangements is that the provinces have the jurisdiction and the federal government is paying most of the bills — 60 percent of the cost of training, 80 percent of the operating cost of universities and colleges, and 60 percent of university research funding (Cutt and Dobell 1992).[6]

This outcome is hard to explain, after the fact. Why would the federal government get itself so deeply involved in financing these activities when there is no political visibility and no accountability. The federal government has never even attempted to set standards for quality or cost-effectiveness. The other characteristic of the existing arrangements is that they were designed to create stability of funding for the provinces. The stability was achieved, however, at the price of rigidity. The system is proving to be highly inflexible in the face of a transforming society. And the provinces, which are also under fiscal pressure, have been outraged by federal adjustments to the formula intended to reduce the federal deficit. One can only marvel at the naivete of both parties to this contract which lacks both accountability and a capacity for adaptation.

THE UNIVERSITIES

Objectives

What do we want from our universities in the next few decades? Here is a personal listing.

1. A system that pays attention to the interface between theory and action. The key words are policy, empirical, and practical. (It is my impression that these are considered to be bad words in the lexicon of many university departments.) This can be achieved through cooperative education, the use of practitioners as instructors or as special guests in the classroom, university-industry cooperation, practical work assignments, and so on.
2. A system that works on the basis of teams. The key word is interdisciplinary. Society — the workplace, families, etc — works in teams. Skills are blended. Few university programs actively practice this. There is little or no cooperation across departments and faculties (the School of Policy Studies is a visible exception). Many departments do not work as a team in designing complementary courses, assignments, etc.
3. A system that offers coherent transitions from one institution to another and from one stage of study to another over a lifetime. The key words are lifelong learning, responsiveness, and articulation (recognition of credits). The typical adult will return to school several times over a lifetime. She or he should be able to get credit for previous study and for work experience.

Most institutions still treat these mature students, especially the part-time ones, as second-class citizens.

4. A system that is performance driven. The key words are excellent, efficient, and accountable. Institutions have to be able to demonstrate that there is excellence in teaching and/or in research, and that time, assets, and money are being used efficiently.

Many of these objectives are incompatible with the traditions of the university — where the focus for centuries has been on academic freedom, security of tenure, and the preservation of knowledge. Indeed, universities still look surprisingly more like the medieval institutions than the high-tech learning institutions outlined by Dian Cohen and Guy Stanley in *No Small Change*. Why has the system not adapted more swiftly to meet these objectives, and what kinds of reforms would encourage institutions to move in this direction?

There is no question that the universities have been under financial pressure to change. As Figure 3 shows, the funding per student has fallen by more than

FIGURE 3: Operating Grants to Universities per FTE Student, Canada, 1977-78 to 1991-92 (Constant 1991-92 Dollars)

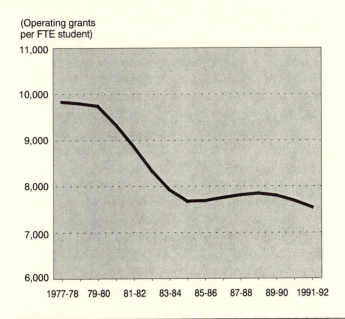

Source: Council of Ontario Universities (1992).

20 percent in real terms since 1977-78. And most provinces have cut back on the nominal level of funding in the past fiscal year. For the most part, however, universities have absorbed this financial pain by making across-the-board adjustments in budgets for all activities rather than redefining their missions, reshaping their programs, and adopting new technologies for learning.

It is difficult to determine to what degree these across-the-board cuts have affected quality of education and research. (Although stories of undergraduate courses with 800 students make many of the programs sound like mass-production, rather than structured learning systems.) The Council of Ontario Universities has produced some interesting comparisons of the sources and allocation of funds for comparable institutions in Canada and the United States (those that offer an array of doctoral programs), which provide an interesting perspective on the Canadian institutions.

Figures 4 and 5 use purchasing power parity to avoid distortions caused by short-term fluctuations in exchange rates. In these charts, we are comparing

FIGURE 4: Revenue per Full-time Enrolment at Ontario, U.S. Public and U.S. Private Doctoral Institutions, 1990-91 ($ PPP CDN)

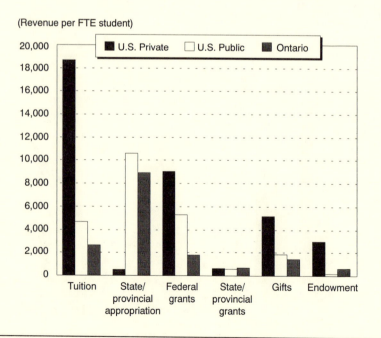

(Revenue per FTE student)

Source: Council of Ontario Universities (1992).

American state-funded universities with the publicly-funded ones in Canada like Queen's, Toronto, Waterloo, Carleton, McMaster, and Ottawa. Private institutions in the U.S. are also included for contrast.

State-funded or public institutions in the United States get more money per full-time student from tuition, state grants, and federal grants than do Ontario universities (Figure 4). In particular, the average tuition fee per full-time student in the public universities in 1990-91 was $4,658 (based on Canadian dollars, calculated according to purchasing power parity) versus $2,633 in Ontario. Recent fee increases will not have narrowed the gap by much.

On the spending side, the American public universities spend slightly more on instruction, and considerably more on research and academic support (Figure 5). They also spend more on student services and scholarships than do the ten Ontario universities.

We have no way of comparing performance of these universities in either quality or access. But, what we do see in the United States is a system that

FIGURE 5: Expenditure per Full-time Enrolment at Ontario, U.S. Public and U.S. Private Doctoral Institutions, 1990-91 ($ PPP CDN)

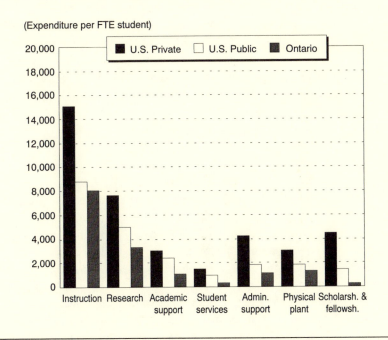

Source: Council of Ontario Universities (1992).

combines strong public support with a diverse funding base. This should strengthen the autonomy of these institutions and make them more responsive to the needs of students.

Governance

Another major source of weakness is in the governance of these institutions. Ron Watts (1992) has written that there are four ways of organizing a university:

- Professional guilds, with self-regulation by the senate and faculty.

- The political arena — such as the control that some state legislatures have over state universities in the United States.

- Bureaucratic regulation, as now happens in Europe, Australia, and more recently in the United Kingdom.

- Market systems like the private universities in the United States.

Most countries use some combination of these methods of organizing. In Canada, there is a strong emphasis on professional guilds tempered by some bureaucratic regulation. However, David Cameron (1992) has argued that the checks and balances in the self-regulation model have been eroded by democratization and by the scarcity of resources.

Cameron traces the historical pattern of governance dating back to the Royal Commission on the University of Toronto in 1906. That commission established a balance between state control and university autonomy or self-government by establishing the bicameral model. Control and management of the university were vested in the board, appointed by the governor-in-council, and academic matters were to be dealt with by the senate: "The key to holding this structure together and facilitating its efficient operation was to be a strengthened presidency, joining senate to board and holding a monopoly on recommendations concerning academic staff." This model of governance became the norm for most Canadian universities, but it has been drastically eroded over the past 30 years; first, as the faculty took control of academic appointments; then as democratic participation transformed both the management of the university, which became concentrated in committees, and the composition of the board; and more recently, as a result of external pressures such as targeted funding and employment equity regulations (Jones 1992). Cameron quotes J.A. Corry, Principal of Queen's, in 1969: "It is vital to get some things clear. Much of the substance of power has been taken out of the president's office and away from the board of governors. The members of the academic staff now have what has been taken out and they have nearly a veto on the use of what is left."

The role of the senate has also been altered, first, by the emergence of collective bargaining which subsumes many tasks that were once the responsibility of senate; and then by the development of the "global village" which means that academic standards are set by peers in other institutions — even other countries, rather than within the university community (Jones 1992).

The net effect, over time, has been to create universities without rudders. Presidents have little power to set direction or to resolve disputes. Many board members lack the analytical skills and the management background to judge whether good management systems are in place. The loyalty of the individual member of faculty shifts more and more to self rather than the university community. While the problems of the institution are recognized, there is a pervasive tendency to shrug and say: "It's not my fault."

All this leads to the conclusion that universities will not be reformed from within. Internal constraints mean that scarce resources and new demands will always be met by spreading the budget over all activities, rather than channelling resources into areas of strength or future specialization. Universities will only be able to adapt and innovate, in the positive sense, when they confront the correct financial incentives and when they have been forced to become more accountable for performance through regular transparent program reviews, and greater exposure to competition for students.

Some of the current debate on accountability is focused on the creation of a comprehensive set of performance indicators. Stuart Smith recommended several outcomes indicators which involve new data collection, and an Ontario Committee set up by the Broadhurst Task Force (Ontario. Task Force on University Accountability 1993) has done a careful assessment of a large number of performance indicators. While good data is clearly important, we should avoid burying the universities in a massive data collection and reporting exercise. The Task Force report recognized this, urging university governing bodies to focus on the purpose of a given indicator, rather than the details (1993, p. 54). It argued that over time, best practices in the use of management indicators would emerge.

It is also important to note that the data does not have to be internally generated: there is much useful system-wide information available from sources like Statistics Canada (DesRosiers). The point is that a good university will learn how to display its strengths to the community at large and it will take measures to deal with its own weaknesses. It would be folly to wait until a central agency begins to dictate what should be done with specific programs.

DIRECTIONS FOR CHANGE

It is tempting to make proposals that would completely disentangle the two orders of government — to assign the federal government the role of supporting research and low-income students, for example. However, I am persuaded that we are dealing here with a joint product — teaching and research — which makes any division of duties arbitrary. I decided therefore to stick to some practical suggestions that build on the status quo, but which are intended to create some carrots and sticks — some based on the market and some built into the funding formulae.

The general framework for the proposals is an administrative agreement between the federal and provincial governments which affirms provincial paramountcy in education but recognizes the need for a federal contribution because of the externalities described in section one as well as the tradition of sharing in the federation. This agreement would include undertakings from both parties:

The provinces would commit to:

1. Restore the autonomy and the powers of the boards of universities, and to set terms of reference which state that one of the duties of the board is to ensure that regular program reviews take place and that management makes logical decisions based on those reviews.

   To make this work well, there should be an interprovincial task force to determine the most effective criteria for board appointments. The Broadhurst Report includes draft guidelines on appointments that appear to give pre-eminence to representativity. I agree that this is important but it should not take place at a speed that risks a breakdown in governance.

2. Provide on an ongoing basis a major and increasing share of the core funding for universities, using their own revenue sources, which should be consolidated by the formal and final transfer of the EPF tax points set aside for this purpose in 1977. This is a symbolic measure but would put an end to a lot of federal-provincial wrangling.

3. Deregulate tuition fees and encourage universities to set tuition in relation to the cost of delivering specific programs. Some universities might end up charging 50 percent of total costs (roughly what the big private universities charge in the United States), others might wish to stay closer to 25 percent (not far off the current average).[7] Their decisions will be based on market choices by students and their families. But the system would offer choice of standard as well as choice of student. We would not need to homogenize standards because of fiscal restraint.

4. Establish or expand a provincial fund to provide means-tested grants or bursaries to students from low-income families. Students with lesser means would have four ways of coping: win a scholarship, choose a lower cost university or program, go into debt through the income-contingent loans (see below), and/or apply for means-tested grants.

The federal government should:

1. Formally transfer the tax points associated with postsecondary education to the provinces, and insist that the provinces are responsible for both funding and performance of the university and college systems. Using the data in Table 1, this consolidates provincial control over federal tax points worth about $3.5 billion which were transferred to the provinces in 1977.

2. Transform the remaining federal funding for postsecondary education into a much more strategic set of transfers, intended to create incentives for innovation and adaptation. Again, using the data in Table 1, the total amount would include the remaining cash payment under the EPF — roughly $2 billion — plus another $3.3 billion or more which has been used to finance sponsored research, student assistance, and other programs. These funds should be used for a combination of operating grants paid directly to the universities,[8] sponsored research grants, a reformed student loan system, and a fund to provide means-tested bursaries to students from low-income families.

3. Reform student loans to establish an income-contingent repayment system, based on market rates of interest. This fund should soon become self-financing and eventually would run a surplus as payments on outstanding loans accumulate. There should be some discussion as to the ultimate use of that surplus: Should it be used for deficit reduction? for grants and bursaries? or for supporting the growth of the institutions?

   There is a consensus in the recent literature on postsecondary education that Canada should adopt an income-contingent repayment system for student loans. Without pretending to be exhaustive, this was the conclusion of the Macdonald Commission, of the AUCC, and recently of a well-argued study by Ed West (1993) with a strongly supporting comment by Jonathan Kesselman.

4. Ideally, the funds for means-tested bursaries should be jointly funded and jointly operated in each province. This would avoid duplication and end runs and minimize administration costs.

5. Increase scholarship awards for excellent students, especially in the high-cost disciplines.

Both the federal and the provincial governments should consider a special set of incentives to promote innovation in the universities and colleges. This should be a joint program, or, if the provinces do not wish to adopt the idea, it could be a federal program designed to promote excellence in education. Whoever undertakes the program should have it administered as a peer reviewed process to avoid excessive bureaucratization and excessive intervention by governments in the management of higher education.

This University and College Innovation Program would be financed by holding back a portion of the operating grants. The funds would be used to reward universities that are clearly innovating and committed to structural change. For example, a university that actually succeeds in cutting a program that gets a poor review (against all the community and political pressure that will inevitably ensue) deserves a reward.

A holdback of 1 percent of total federal expenditures, for example, would amount to more than $50 million a year. The awards would therefore have a significant impact on the discretionary funds available to well-performing institutions. Such bonus payments could not be used to cover salaries on an ongoing basis, but they should be used at the discretion of the president and with the approval of the board to finance a chair, build a new program, etc.

Taken together, these recommendations form the instruments that can maintain the autonomy of universities while pushing them in the four directions outlined in the second section — relevant, interdisciplinary, coherent, and performance-driven.

TRAINING

Jurisdiction over and the funding of training have been one of the front-line issues in the recent constitutional epic and they continue to be a critical issue in relations between Ottawa and the provinces, especially Quebec.

To Quebecers, training is part and parcel of economic sovereignty because it is so closely tied to their linguistic and cultural distinctiveness. To many Canadians who think about the issue, the labour market is a key element in the four freedoms of the economic union — the free movement of people, capital, goods, and services. However, there are two labour markets here. French-speaking workers are not nearly so mobile as their English-speaking counterparts, and, to a very considerable extent, bilingual francophones prefer to live and work in a French-speaking environment (Economic Council 1991). Yet, while the two labour markets are distinct, they are not separate. The recent controversies over the movement of construction workers on the New

Brunswick-Quebec border and the Ontario-Quebec border illustrate the lack of complete separation.

This distinctiveness of the Quebec labour market makes a strong argument for asymmetry in the arrangements with respect to training, with the important condition that Quebec should participate in developing common training standards and then adhere to them once they are in place. This is a practical compromise which is spelled out more clearly in what follows.

Indeed, the asymmetry may well extend beyond Quebec to the other provinces, like Ontario and British Columbia, and possibly Alberta, which already have a well-entrenched training bureaucracy. They bring to the table a different set of assets from the smaller provinces whose capacity to develop and deliver training is more limited.

Background on Training

Although the provinces have jurisdiction over education, apprenticeship, industrial standards, and 90 percent of the labour force, it has been the federal government that has played the dominant role in labour markets and training since the creation of the Department of Labour in 1900. Ottawa has funded provincial employment services and training since 1918, and in 1940, a constitutional amendment transferred responsibility for unemployment insurance to the federal government.

The situation today is that the federal government accounts for 75 percent of labour market expenditures on training and other labour market programs, excluding UI (Kroeger 1993). This includes a network of 500 offices across Canada which provide front-line services to the unemployed and to employers. These offices select those who are to receive training. But the federal government does not deliver the training — it buys it from provincial institutions and from industry. Nor does it have any control over training standards, curriculum, structure of programs, etc. (Until 1985, it was buying from a single source — community colleges.[9] More recently, it has been buying places through a competitive bidding process — and private training colleges have been quite successful in bidding for these training places.[10])

In general, however, there are few training standards in Canada. Fewer than 30 occupations are certified under the federal Red Seal program, which ensures acceptance by all provinces, and those 30 are all occupations associated with construction and the old industrial economy. The apprenticeship program is equally out of date — training the wrong people at the wrong age for the wrong skills (Economic Council 1992; Canadian Labour Market and Productivity Centre 1990). And, in the current environment of structural change and high unemployment, there are too few school-to-work and welfare-to-work programs and too few training places for the people who want to upgrade their skills.

All of the provinces have their own training programs — there are 32 programs in Canada focused on workplace training, for example (Ekos 1992). So both the employer and the trainee face a confusing array of criteria and choices. Many more programs focus on training for the unemployed (Premier's Council 1990). In Quebec, the overlap and duplication extends beyond the programs to the administration, since Quebec runs its own system of employment offices for welfare recipients.

Meanwhile, there are encouraging signs of a greater commitment on the part of industry to workplace training. McMullen *et al.* (1993) found that the volume of training for a representative sample of business establishments doubled between 1985 and 1991. The National Training Survey taken in 1991 indicates that the private sector spends roughly $3.6 billion per year. Table 2 shows that private expenditure now appears to eclipse the combined total of federal and provincial spending on training.

TABLE 2: Source of Funds for Vocational Training, 1988-89

	$ billion	*Percent*
Federal[a]	2.1	60
Provincial	1.1	31
Fees	0.2	6
Other	0.1	2
Subtotal	3.5	
Employer-based training (1991)[b]	3.6[c]	

[a]Since the passage of Bill C-21 in 1990, over $1.5 billion in additional funds from the UI system are being applied to training, despite a general pattern of expenditure cuts.

[b]Government subsidies covered about 9 percent of employer expenditures on training other than apprenticeship; 20 percent of apprenticeship training was funded by governments and a further 19 percent was jointly funded by the employer and governments.

[c]The 1991 National Training Survey estimated structured training expenditures by the private sector at $3.6 billion based only on those organizations that provided actual or estimated structured training costs. The margin of error for the $3.6 billion estimate is in excess of 50 percent. Only half of the 8,000 organizations that provided detailed training information were able to provide useable information on training costs and only 13 percent of organizations providing training reported actual costs. Vocational Training Revenues by Program and Source of Funds 1988-89.

Source: Statistics Canada and CLMPC (1993).

In summary, a system exists which involves many players in the public, private, and education sectors and for whom no one is accountable. Much money has been spent on training — increasing amounts despite the fiscal restraint in Ottawa. Many program evaluations have been done. However, there is still no concrete evidence as to the program designs that work for each type of participant and there is no foundation for determining the skills that should be developed in the next decade. No standards have been developed for the occupations of the future, although there is recognition that standards are needed (Canadian Labour Force Development Board 1993; Campbell 1993). Viewed from the perspective of the unemployed, however, the system looks unresponsive, overloaded, and inefficient. The Economic Council of Canada (1992) used the expression "the worst of both worlds": a secondary school system that does not prepare young people for work and a training system that does not compensate for that failure.

Despite the problems and the immediacy of the issue, federal and provincial ministers met last January for the first time in four years. One observer comments that they spent most of the time arguing about jurisdiction (Haddow 1993). One provincial participant indicated that the provinces were not prepared to move more aggressively towards active labour market programs unless the federal government provided the funds.

Institution Building

Despite this tale of woe, there have been signs of reform in recent years. In 1989, the federal Department of Employment and Immigration launched a Labour Force Development Strategy which started with a major consultation exercise (placed in the hands of the CLMPC) and led to the formation of the Canadian Labour Force Development Board (CLFDB) in 1991.

The underlying principle was simple: transfer the responsibility for design and delivery of training to the private sector — to labour, business, and the equity-seeking groups appointed to the board. This national board was to be matched by provincial boards (which would mobilize and coordinate all provincial inputs to the training system) and by community level boards which would be responsible for determining which courses would be offered locally and who would qualify for them. The whole exercise was intended to be a vehicle for putting all the federal and provincial training resources into one pot. Eventually, it was hoped that there would be a "single window" for training, placement, and counselling at the community level.

The initial reaction to the idea was mixed. Quebec was ahead of the other provinces with its Commissions de la formation professionelle and the privately sponsored Forum sur l'emploi, but it was adamantly opposed to participating in any such federally driven initiative. Ontario was already in the process of creating the Ontario Training and Adjustment Board (OTAB), an idea that had percolated out of the Premier's Council in the late 1980s (Premier's Council 1990). The structure and design of the OTAB appeared, on the surface at least, to fit with the CLFDB concept of privatization and local delivery. New Brunswick and British Columbia soon agreed to establish their board, along the lines of the CLFDB.

Thus was launched one of the most important institution-building exercises of the 1990s — an effort to reform the training system *and* to build a bridge of cooperation between business and labour leaders. This was an ambitious task, and it is important to recognize that the pathway was strewn with institutional barriers — the ongoing federal-provincial turf war; the reluctance of federal and provincial officials to delegate their functions to a private board; and the total lack of experience of the labour market partners in working together, let alone with the equity and educational groups also participating.

Employers' and labour organizations in Canada are fragmented — there were 480 national business associations in 1980 (Coleman 1986). The labour movement had eight central union organizations in 1989 representing the one-third of the work force that is unionized (Kumar *et al.* 1990). The Canadian Labour Congress is by far the largest of these organizations but the power to organize and to bargain collectively lies mainly with the union locals. These two fragmented groups had no tradition of trust, and no practice in working together. It was obvious from the beginning that this kind of institution building would take time and a lot of dedication (Economic Council 1990; Haddow 1993). But the decision to proceed was based on clear evidence that successful training systems in Europe and Japan depend heavily on a labour-business partnership, though every country has a unique set of institutions.

It is difficult, at this stage, to discern whether the transfer of power will succeed. Some progress has been made. Individual business leaders have been participating actively both federally and in some provinces, despite some problems in creating a cohesive leadership. They have at least tacitly accepted that labour is entitled to an equal number of seats at the table. But there is not much evidence of a commitment from the business community in general.[11] Nobody expected it would be easy, and the possiblity remains that the private sector partners simply do not have the capacity to take on the powers that are on offer.

In addition, the jurisdictional obstacles are evident at every turn. Quebec, Ontario and Alberta still do not participate in the CLFDB. It is still not clear where the boundary falls between the CLFDB and Employment and Immigration Canada (now part of the Department of Human Resource Development —

HRD). The Ontario conception of the role of OTAB is rather different from the federal conception of CLFDB and its provincial partners. OTAB will have line responsibility for designing and delivering programs. It has not been designed, however, to be the channel for federal funds into Ontario. Thus, we could conceivably end up with two systems of regional or community-based committees in Ontario — one federal and one provincial. This could be avoided if both federal and provincial governments give the funds and executive responsibility to the same local boards. In contrast, the New Brunswick Labour Force Development Board appears to be designed precisely along the lines of the federal board and will be the channel for federal training funds flowing into the province.

Quebec has its own board, the Société Québécoise du développement de la main d'oeuvre. Its board includes many of the players in the Forum sur l'emploi, who are more accustomed to working together than the social partners in the rest of Canada. The SQDM has absorbed about half of the research staff of the Ministere de la main d'oeuvre, du revenu et de la formation professionelle, and is now recruiting its operating staff. The board of the SQDM voted not to accept Prime Minister Kim Campbell's offer of jurisdiction in the summer of 1993, apparently because of the condition that common standards be developed and implemented (Campbell 1993). The fear was, according to one insider, that the standards would represent a federal intrusion which would influence the boundaries of specific trades.

It is clear that we are in the middle of one of the big jurisdictional games of the century, with the roles and responsiblities of federal, provincial, and private sector partners being the main source of controversy. Out of this may come a new and improved structure for delivering training. But it could also end up as a bureaucratic jungle, with the system choking on quarrels between governments and between business, labour, and their equity-seeking partners.

My reading of federal and provincial politicians and their officials is that they all have the same goal in mind — a training system that enhances human potential. But the outcome will depend to a great extent on the ability of key leaders to nurture a new relationship between business and labour; to sustain the political will to delegate the training function to the private sector partners; to provide the partners with solid research to identify benchmarks for effective training programs; to push labour, business, educators, and public officials to get on with the job of developing training standards; and, finally, to find a way to mesh the gears of federal and provincial employment services. This is not a light agenda.

Training Needs

Table 3 provides a matrix to help frame the discussion of training needs and service delivery. The current approach to training is to pick a target group and design a program that will include some combination of income support, training courses, and infrastructure. Both federal and provincial governments aim programs at each target group, programs that establish different criteria for entry, different levels of support and so on. The contribution by the taxpayer to this system includes transfers to provinces, tax and other incentives to employers, transfers to individuals, tax and other incentives to individuals. The National Training Survey indicates that 45 percent of workplace training costs is composed of the wages and salaries of the trainees and 55 percent is actual training costs (CLMPC 1993).

TABLE 3: The Training Structure in Canada

Target Group	Training Needs	Funder	Location
Youth/Students	Basic skills Technical Apprenticeship Professional	Taxpayer	Colleges Schools University
ST unemployed	Trade specific	Employer and employee	–
LT unemployed Disadvantaged[a]	Basic skills Literacy Trade specific	Taxpayer	Colleges Schools
Unattached workers[b]	Literacy Basic skills Trade specific	Taxpayer and workers	Colleges Schools
Employed, small firms	Literacy Job specific Technical Professional	Employer? and employee	Workplace? Colleges Schools
Employed, large firms	Literacy Job specific Technical Professional	Employer and employee	Workplace Colleges Schools Universities

[a]Employable people on social assistance, for example.
[b]Mainly people in non-standard jobs with no attachment to a specific employer.

Source: Author's compilation.

Throughout this extraordinarily complex system, there are several common threads. First, all the training occurs in one of four places — the workplace, schools, colleges (public and private), and universities. Second, all the training can be reduced to four categories: literacy, basic skills, technical, and professional. Within the technical and professional categories there is an extraordinary range of occupations which require a combination of job specific and generic skills. However, it is interesting to note that in Germany, which is generally acknowledged to have the most advanced formal training system in the industrial countries, there is a shift back to generic skills and to multi-skilling, by combining the courses and standards for several occupations (Streeck 1990).

From the point of view of the client, then, what is needed is a coherent system of training programs that will permit the trainee to identify the training needed, and then move in a logical step-by-step fashion up a training ladder. Ideally, the system should have solid roots in the secondary school system, so that there are logical pathways from school to training to work.

For the most part, the literacy and basic skills programs are needed by people who are no longer in the education system and have a serious education deficit. But the technical and professional training may also be aimed at people who are no longer in the formal education system. Thus, there does not appear to be a way to clarify jurisdiction by giving part of the problem to one order of government and part to the other. We are looking at a system where responsibilities will inevitably overlap.

The key to rationalizing the system will be to establish standards and articulate the system so that someone who passes a literacy test or has succeeded in basic skills has a certificate that will be recognized in technical programs. These standards should be determined on the basis of what employers require for an effective work force — a good beginning exists in the Conference Board's employability test (1992). See Table 4.

Similarly, technical training whether it is in a college or in the workplace should be driven by standards set in consultation with labour and business. Again, the student needs a sense of achievement and a sense that the knowledge gained in one area opens the door to other training opportunities.[12] The standards are needed by every jurisdiction, and must be portable across jurisdictions. But the process can be streamlined if the provinces share the work involved in developing standards, in cooperation with business, labour, and other interested parties.

The obvious organization to coordinate this work would be the CLFDB. However, the opposition of the provinces will make this impossible. That leaves the possibility of an interprovincial commission. Whoever does it, developing

TABLE 4: Employability Skills Profile: The Critical Skills Required of the Canadian Workforce

ACADEMIC SKILLS	PERSONAL MANAGEMENT SKILLS	TEAMWORK SKILLS
Those skills which provide the basic foundation to get, keep and progress on a job and to achieve the best results	The combination of skills, attitudes and behaviours required to get, keep and progress on a job and to achieve the best results	Those skills needed to work with others on a job and to achieve the best results
Canadian employers need a person who can:	Canadian employers need a person who can demonstrate:	Canadian employers need a person who can:

ACADEMIC SKILLS	PERSONAL MANAGEMENT SKILLS	TEAMWORK SKILLS
Communicate	*Positive Attitudes and Behaviours*	*Work with Others*
• Understand and speak the languages in which business is conducted	• Self-esteem and confidence	• Understand and contribute to the organization's goals
• Listen to, understand and learn	• Honesty, integrity and personal ethics	• Understand and work within the culture of the group
• Read, comprehend and use written materials, including graphs, charts and displays	• A positive attitude toward learning, growth and personal health	• Plan and make decisions with others and support the outcomes
• Write effectively in the languages in which business is conducted	• Initiative, energy and persistence to get the job done	• Respect the thoughts and opinions of others in the group
Think	*Responsibility*	• Exercise "give and take" to achieve group results
• Think critically and act logically to evaluate situations, solve problems and make decisions	• The ability to set goals and priorities in work and personal life	• Seek a team approach as appropriate
• Understand and solve problems involving mathematics and use the results	• The ability to plan and manage time, money and other resources to achieve goals	• Lead when appropriate, mobilizing the group for high performance
• Use technology, instruments, tools and information systems effectively	• Accountability for actions taken	
• Access and apply specialized knowledge from various fields (e.g., skilled trades, technology, physical sciences, arts and social sciences)	*Adaptability*	
	• A positive attitude toward change	
	• Recognition of and respect for people's diversity and individual differences	
Learn	• The ability to identify and suggest new ideas to get the job done — creativity	
• Continue to learn for life		

Source: Conference Board of Canada (1992)

standards will be an immense task. We probably need standards for 400 occupations. In Germany, it takes about two years for the social partners to agree on the standard for one occupation. No province can afford either the time or the money required to do all 400. No country can run an effective training system without them. Why not cooperate? The actual programs being delivered will obviously vary according to the needs of each community, but once a Canadian has completed the program in Nanaimo, her qualifications should be recognized in all parts of the country.

It is important to note that the provinces have already had 35 years, since the need was first recognized, to develop these standards. And the federal government, which has no jurisdiction, has continued to fund training despite this pitiful performance. The CLMPC Task Force on Apprenticeship, composed of labour, business, and educational representatives, issued a scathing report in 1990 in which it recommended that the federal government should give the provinces three more years to develop standards for apprenticeship programs. After that, the Task Force said, federal funding should be cut off.

Delivering Services

Another thorny question is the delivery of services — the screening of applications, the placement services, counselling, and so on. Such services have to be delivered at the local level, but that can be done by a federal, provincial, or a private agency. The key challenge is to find a way for all three agents to work through a single window, so that applicants and employers do not waste time filling in forms at different offices.

One of the considerations here is the evolution of information technologies, which, before long, will permit applicants and employers to use a smart card or a network card to connect with an employment/training office from their home or from a bank kiosk. These applicants will not know or care whether the program is federal or provincial. The Department of Human Resource Development is already experimenting with these systems, and Ontario now has detailed information on training costs, availability, location of courses, etc. on computer disk. Thus, the jurisdictional debate will soon be occupied with issues of computer architecture, compatible software, etc. Let us hope that the technology gets used to simplify the debate rather than delay us for another five to ten years.

There are two possible images of this technological future. One can imagine a humane but efficient world where all the job and training openings in a community show up on a screen at home or in the local employment office. The front-line public servants would find their work transformed because all the basic information on work history, training, income, and family considerations would be on the file. The public servant would then be occupied with the more qualitative issues concerning the expectations and talents of the applicant, some counselling on job applications and interviews, a review of past successes and failures.

The other image is more Kafkaesque — like voice mail. The applicant inserts her card, gets connected to the network, is given a list of programs she does not understand, and cannot find a human being to explain them. Who knows which image will emerge?

Directions for Change

The overriding priority in the next few years must be to create a system focused on common standards and the quality of training rather than on symmetry in institutions. With continuing high unemployment and job change, there will be intense pressure on governments to come up with training programs and a delivery system that work.

The public knows that training is important and is already infuriated by the incapacity of the system to deliver. In a world where governments are broke and the public is alienated by the waste and inefficiency of the public sector, there will be big political costs if the system does not shape up soon. In the case of training, there is no statutory deadline to renegotiate the funding arrangements. However, as the major public sector funder of training, the federal government can set a deadline for resolving issues, as noted above, simply by announcing that it will withdraw funding from provinces that do not have a viable system in place in three years' time.

The specific actions required are:

1. The provinces should strike joint interprovincial task forces to establish the common standards for all the occupations or groups of occupations for which Canadians are likely to be trained in the next decade. The CLFDB and parallel provincial boards can provide useful input on the part of business, labour, education, and equity-seeking groups.

2. The provinces should also establish a task force within each province to plan the implementation of standards in the colleges, secondary schools, and workplaces where the training takes place, so that the trainers are ready to use the standards as soon as they are ready to be implemented.

3. The federal government should offer some carrots and a stick. The carrots would be, first, to help pay for the cost of developing standards, and second, to transfer federal activities in training and delivery systems to provinces that have a fully articulated system of standards in place. Not all provinces will wish to take on these activities, but the lack of symmetry should not

be a problem if the whole system is running on the basis of clearly articulated standards.

The stick would be a commitment to cut funding for all training programs in provinces that are not making clear progress in developing and implementing the standards.

4. When and if the standards are developed and in place, the federal government should hold back some of the funds that are due each year (1 percent would amount to $20 million a year), so they can be used to reward strong performance in the training system itself. The rewards should be based on criteria such as: standards are in place and regularly reviewed, innovation in course design, good articulation exists from one institution to another, employers indicate satisfaction with the training outcomes, etc.

CONCLUSIONS

The central problem with the fiscal arrangements for education and training is that the federal government has been writing cheques for services without specifying or monitoring the desired outcomes. This is a permissive kind of federalism. It may have solved jurisdictional debates in the mid-1970s when the EPF and other arrangements were renegotiated, but it has left us with an education and training system that has failed to adapt to the needs of the new economy.

This underperformance undermines the legitimacy of governments, and corrodes the nation state from within. The failure to perform breeds alienation and fosters regionalism. There are success stories buried in the education and training systems: universities with excellent programs; colleges that have built a powerful synergy with local industries (Economic Council 1992, p. 19); and training programs that have given individuals a new lease on life (Betcherman *et al.* 1990).

To make the training system work, I think we should abandon the notion of constitutional symmetry, permit institutions to develop in each province that meet the basic criteria agreed by all the parties, while using common training standards as the force that binds the country together and maintains the viability of the economic union.

To ensure that the universities adapt to the needs of a knowledge-based society, we have to build both diversity and accountability into the funding base — by deregulating tuition fees and setting the parameters for good governance.

In both cases, I am proposing more carrots. The federal government must begin to use the leverage that comes from being a major funder. To do this, it should hold back funding in ways that are specifically designed to reward good performance — to keep both training and higher education focused on our most basic goals — excellence and efficiency.

I am convinced that the capacity to deliver is there, but we need to build into the system incentives for excellence and efficiency and an ability to create the new. The risk is that the current turf wars will create a new structure that is even more rigid and less accountable than the old one.

NOTES

I wish to acknowledge helpful comments on an earlier draft by Gordon Betcherman, Robert Davidson, Arthur Kroeger, and Norman Leckie. The errors and the interpretation of the facts are mine.

1. Young women in those regions tended to stay in school longer because they did not work in the same jobs. But they, too, need more education and training in a knowledge-based society.

2. We should not accept this polarization in the definition of jobs as a matter of course. There are ways to break down the barriers. Courchene has suggested that we need to create a para-professional society — para legals, para medics, etc. (1993). Another way to break down the barriers is through contracting-out (Drucker 1993). If hospitals contract out the cleaning to a specialized firm, then the most enterprising of the low-paid hospital cleaners will be able to start a firm that can do that work efficiently. Thus, some — though not many — hospital cleaners will cross the barrier from service worker to knowledge worker, and productivity gets a boost at the same time. A third way is to use technology differently — to humanize the design and use of technology to make jobs more rewarding, whatever the pay structure (Klees and Papagainnis 1989).

3. Both sides seem to be having doubts about that contract. People are not paying their taxes and governments are not doing much about sustaining employment — but that is argument for another paper.

4. While there is a strong rationale for public provision of education and training, there is also a rationale for contracting out the delivery of these services to private institutions — to schools, colleges (public and private), universities, to non-profit organizations, and to business organizations. This can be done because there is a definable output, the results can be monitored, and there is a choice of suppliers (Purchase 1994).

5. The rate of growth in total factor productivity (the most comprehensive measure of efficiency of use of labour, capital, and materials) slowed from an average of 1.5 percent per year in the period 1962-73 to only 0.6 percent per year in the 1980s. Economists are not agreed on the reasons for the slowdown, but it appears to be connected to the energy shock of the early 1970s — which made much capital equipment obsolete and also triggered a wave of inflationary pressures. Some studies also place a lot of emphasis on the inability of institutions to adapt to the new technologies.

6. The AUCC advises that there is some dispute about these numbers.

7.   The complicating factor here is cross-subsidization of disciplines — the cost of education in health sciences far exceeds that in the arts. Arts students may already be paying close to full cost.

8.   Quebec, in particular, will probably wish to opt out of the direct payments of operating grants to the institutions. This would require some form of compensation and then raises the question as to whether other provinces would prefer to opt out with compensation, leading to a more decentralized system. If this starts to happen then it will be important for the federal government to institute a strong Innovation Program as noted here in order to ensure that the federal resources going into the system are actually being used to promote excellence.

9.   The provinces insisted on exclusive use of community colleges. It seems they were prepared to protect teaching staffs at the expense of providing relevant training.

10.   There are about 1,000 private career colleges in Canada, of which 350 have been designated by the federal government as institutions whose students are eligible for Canada Student Loans. The 350 colleges have annual tuition revenue of about $230 million. There are no comparisons of relative performance, but, in general, private colleges charge higher fees but also boast higher placement rates. They often compete effectively on the basis of compressed courses that reduce the amount of income foregone (Economic Council of Canada 1992, p. 20).

11.   The federal board is also anomalous in the sense that the public sector unions are strongly represented even though the process is aimed primarily at the private sector.

12.   The Ontario Task Force on Advanced Training documented the extraordinary lack of integration between the Ontario college and university systems (1993).

BIBLIOGRAPHY

Association of Universities and Colleges of Canada (1991), "An Overview of Selected Options for Funding University Education and Research," Discussion Document prepared for the Standing Advisory Committee on Funding, July.

_____ (1993), "A New Student Assistance Plan for Canada," a report by the Standing Advisory Committee on Funding, Ottawa, June.

Betcherman, Gordon, Keith Newton and Joanne Godin, eds. (1990), *Two Steps Forward*, Ottawa: Economic Council of Canada, Supply and Services Canada.

Cameron, David M. (1992), "Institutional Management: How Should the Governance and Management of Universities in Canada Accommodate Changing Circumstances?" in *Public Purse, Public Purpose*, ed. Cutt and Dobell.

Campbell, Rt. Hon. Kim (1993), Text and translation of letters sent to Premier Robert Bourassa and Premier Frank McKenna, Ottawa, 20 September.

Canadian Labour Force Development Board (1993), *Occupational Standards in Canada — Issues and Opportunities*, Ottawa.

Canadian Labour Market and Productivity Centre (1990), *Report of the Task Forces on the Labour Force Development Strategy*, Ottawa, March.

_____ (1993), *National Training Survey, 1991*, Ottawa: Supply and Services Canada.

Cohen, Dian and Guy Stanley (1993), *No Small Change: Success in Canada's New Economy*, Toronto: Macmillan Canada.

Coleman, William D. (1986), "Canadian Business and the State," in *The State and Economic Interests*, ed. Keith Banting, Toronto: University of Toronto Press.

Conference Board of Canada (1992), "Employability Skills Profile: What Are Employers Looking For?" Ottawa.

Council of Ontario Universities (1992), *The Financial Position of Universities in Ontario*, Toronto.

Courchene, Thomas J. (1993), "Path Dependency, Positive Feedback and Paradigm Warp: A Schumpeterian Approach to the Social Order," paper prepared for the IRPP Social Policy Roundtable, June.

Cutt, James and Rodney Dobell (1992), "Accountability and Autonomy in Canada's University Sector: Business as Usual or the Lull Before the Storm?" in *Public Purse and Public Purpose: Autonomy and Accountability in the Groves of Academe*, ed. James Cutt and Rodney Dobell, Montreal: Institute for Research on Public Policy.

Desrosiers, Edward, private communication, based on work for the Ontario Premier's Council.

Drucker, Peter F. (1993), *Post-Capitalist Society*, New York: Harper Business.

Economic Council of Canada (1990), "Towards a New Policy Framework," in *Transitions for the '90s: 27th Annual Review*, Ottawa: Supply and Services Canada.

_____ (1991), "The State of the Economic Union," in *A Joint Venture: 28th Annual Review*, Ottawa: Supply and Services Canada.

_____ (1992), *A Lot to Learn: Education and Training in Canada*, Ottawa: Supply and Services Canada.

Ekos Research Associates Inc. (1992), "Review of Federal and Provincial Programs Encouraging Employer-Sponsored Training in the Private Sector," paper prepared for the Economic Council of Canada.

Haddow, Rodney (1993), "Theme and Variation in Canada's Neo-Corporatist Training Strategy: How Much is Explained by Institutions," Department of Political Science, St. Francis Xavier University.

Johnson, A.W. (1987), *Social Policy in Canada: The Past as it Conditions the Present*, Ottawa: Institute for Research on Public Policy.

Jones, Glen A. (1992), "University Governance in the 1990s: An Issues Paper," prepared for the AUCC, February.

Kesselman, Jonathan R. (1993), "Squeezing Universities, Students or Taxpayers?" in *Ending the Squeeze on Universities*, ed. West.

Klees, Steven J. and George J. Papagainnis (1989), "Education and the Changing World of Work: Implications for Math, Science, and Computer Education in Florida," Center for Policy Studies in Education, Florida State University.

Kroeger, Arthur (1993), Notes for a lecture for a Policy Seminar on Labour Market and Social Policy Making, School of Policy Studies, Queen's University.

Kumar, Pradeep *et al.* (1990), "The Current Industrial Relations Scene in Canada, 1988," Kingston: Industrial Relations Centre, Queen's University.

Leslie, Peter (1980), *Canadian Universities: 1980 and Beyond: Enrolment, Structural Change, and Finance*, Ottawa: Association of Universities and Colleges of Canada.

Leslie, Peter M., Kenneth Norrie and Irene Ip (1993), *A Partnership in Trouble*, Toronto: C.D. Howe Institute.

Maclean's (1991), "Ranking the Universities: A Measure of Excellence," 21 October.

Maxwell, Judith (1993) "It's time to rethink the social role of government," speech to the Canadian Pensions and Benefits Conference, Montreal, June.

McMullen Kathryn *et al.* (1993), *Innovation at Work: The Working with Technology Survey, 1980-91*, HRM Project Series, Kingston: Industrial Relations Centre, Queen's University.

Ontario. Task Force on Advanced Training, Pitman Report (1993), *No Dead Ends: Report of the Task Force on Advanced Training*, Toronto: Ontario Minister of Education and Training.

Ontario. Task Force on University Accountability, Broadhurst Report (1993), *University Accountability: A Strengthened Framework*, Toronto: Queen's Printer.

Premier's Council of Ontario (1990), *People and Skills in the New Global Economy*, Toronto.

Purchase, Bryne *et al.* (1994), Government and Competitiveness Project, *Report*, Kingston: School of Policy Studies, Queen's University, forthcoming.

Royal Commission on the Economic Union and Development Prospects for Canada, Macdonald Commission (1985), *Report*, 3 vols., Ottawa: Supply and Services Canada.

Smith, Stuart (1991), *Report: Commission of Inquiry on Canadian University Education*, Ottawa: Association of Universities and Colleges of Canada.

Streeck, Wolfgang (1990), "Vocational Training: Reflections on the European Experience and its Relevance for the United States," testimony before the Governor's Commission for a Quality Workforce, Madison, WI: Center on Wisconsin Strategy, August.

Vaillancourt, François (1992), *Private and public monetary returns to schooling in Canada, 1985*, Economic Council of Canada Working Paper No. 35, Ottawa: Supply and Services Canada.

Watts, Ron (1992), "Universities and Public Policy," in *Public Purse, Public Purpose*, ed. Cutt and Dobell.

West, Edwin G. (1993), *Ending the Squeeze on Universities*, Montreal: Institute for Research on Public Policy.

Comment: The Promise of Procurement Federalism

J. Stefan Dupré

At its core, I consider that Judith Maxwell's chapter is a plea for asymmetric federal-provincial relations in matters of training and education. If this is a correct interpretation, I wish to offer her my unreserved congratulations. Before using her paper as the platform from which to sell my own brand of snake oil, I shall simply observe that I have nothing but admiration for the courage she has displayed in compiling a comprehensive catalogue of prescriptions for whatever ills — real or imagined — beset universities, colleges, occupational standard-setting, tuition fee determination, the financing of student accessibility, and any federal-provincial relations pertinent thereto. It matters not a wit that one of her prescriptions seems to fly in the face of asymmetry, to say nothing of accountability — I refer to a provincial commitment to escalate their share of core university funding at the same rate as federal funding for sponsored research and core funding. It matters even less that another prescription — the enhanced use of practitioners in the classroom — is coupled with a diagnosis that universities have been eroding the quality of education by delegating more teaching to part-time lecturers. These are mere quibbles that I raise only to prove that I did indeed read her stimulating paper and that I remain, as I have always been, an incorrigible tease.

Other chapters in this volume are also relevant to education and training. Worth framing is Thomas Courchene's characteristically trenchant observation that "with knowledge at the cutting edge of competitiveness, aspects of social policy become indistinguishable from economic policy." In the domain of education and training this says it all. Let me illustrate by framing a question concerning which I would love to hear a Maxwell-Courchene dialogue.

Consider, from Maxwell's prescriptive catalogue, the notion that provincial deregulation to permit higher tuition fees should be coupled with student accessibility to more generous loans. Even with an income-contingent repayment scheme, how well, in intergenerational terms, would the resulting educational debt-burden on the young square with a situation in which, as Courchene observes, we are already depressing the income prospects of our youth with rising payroll taxes to finance the pension benefits of an older generation whose members enjoyed the windfall of low tuition fees?

At a level that broaches less cosmic matters, Courchene's chapter, like that of his colleagues Robin Boadway and Frank Flatters, offers a bracing walking tour of that 16-year-old cornerstone of fiscal federalism in Canada: Established Programs Financing (EPF). This brings me to the snake oil remedy that the rest of my comments will try to sell: take education and training out of "fiscal federalism" and put them into what I choose to call "procurement federalism."

Where fiscal federalism is concerned, I wish to sharpen the tone of the Boadway-Flatters comment that "it is not at all clear" that the tax point component of EPF should "be considered a federal-provincial transfer at all." To me, it is crystal clear that the tax points do not represent a transfer. The tax points historically vacated by the federal government do not yield provincial revenue. What yields provincial revenue is the personal income taxes that provinces levy as a matter of their own political responsibility. Had the federal government chosen to continue to levy higher personal income taxes as a matter of its own responsibility and then transferred the yield of whatever tax points it wished to forego to the provinces in cash, the notion of a tax point transfer would have retained its relevance. As matters have turned out, the assertion that the tax points represent a transfer from the federal government comes at the top of my list of the Big Lies of Canadian public finance.

This leaves the dwindling cash portion of EPF. In the optimistic event that this portion will not be totally consumed by mounting health costs exacerbated by the mismanagement of the *Canada Health Act,* I would divert what remains to finance a policy which at long last would fund 100 percent of the indirect costs of whatever research the federal government sponsors in universities. In its research funding activities, the federal government is essentially purchasing Canada's basic research capacity, along with the applied research and development that are an indispensable component of any sensible economic growth policy. What is more, federal research grants and contracts are the outcome of a competitive awards process. Ottawa should fund the full cost of what it buys; this is a logical implication of what I call procurement federalism.

As for the realm of labour market training, procurement federalism is not new. If anything, it is the day before yesterday's approach to this activity. But when I see that yesterday's man can receive the resounding electoral mandate that has just propelled him to the prime ministership, I make no apologies for resurrecting whatever has the virtue of familiarity. What was the day before yesterday's approach to labour market training? It was Tom Kent's brainchild, the conceptually innovative program of adult occupational training launched by the newly created Department of Manpower and Immigration in 1966. Fiscal federalism was out, procurement federalism was in. The long-standing shared-cost programs that had linked the old Training Branch of the federal Department of Labour to the like-minded vocational education divisions of provincial Departments of Education were abruptly terminated. Henceforth, the federal government would purchase, at full cost, training courses for adults selected by its community-based employment counsellors on the basis of these counsellors' assessment of their clients' attitudes and future employment prospects. The desired training could be purchased either from public institutions under provincial control or from private sources.

Being myself one of yesterday's men, I was part of a research team whose work documented the unravelling of this imaginative Grand Design (Dupré *et al.* 1973). In brief, what happened was that the provincial Departments of Education interposed themselves between the federal adult occupational training program and postsecondary institutions, and forced federal officials to deal with them as "exclusive brokers" of training courses. Provincial insistence on exclusive brokerage not only hobbled private-sector trainers as potential competitors; it forced the formation of bilateral federal-provincial committees where the so-called purchase and sale of training became a negotiated, shared-cost planning process that made labour market needs subservient to provincial institutional and enrolment strategies. The federal economists, those would-be purchasers of training as a labour market adjustment tool, were trumped by the provincial educationists.

Interestingly, in that world of bilateral federal-provincial relations, the Quebec situation turned out to be *pas comme les autres*. In the Ottawa-Quebec case, the provincial side of the bilateral relationship was articulated not by educationists, but by officials of the Quebec Department of Manpower and Immigration whose professional outlook paralleled that of their federal counterparts. Recalling the times, a senior Quebec manpower official noted that the conflict between economists and educationists, which elsewhere plagued federal-provincial relations, instead emerged in Quebec as an intra-governmental conflict around the provincial cabinet table (Dupré 1988, p. 240). Whether in Quebec, Ontario or elsewhere, the problem was that a procurement approach to labour market training was viewed by postsecondary institutions and the officials responsible for their well-being as a direct threat to the planned development of province-wide community college networks.

By the 1980s, these networks had matured as planned. This mitigated, although it did not eliminate, the obstacle to a procurement approach to labour market training. The missing ingredient was a clientele behind the would-be purchasers of training that might match the political clout of the sellers. It is particularly in this light that I join Maxwell in hailing the creation of the Canada Labour Force Development Board (CLFDB) and of such provincial bodies as the Ontario Training and Adjustment Board (OTAB). It is indeed ambitious, as she points out, to link reform of the training system with building a new bridge of cooperation between business and labour leaders. Favouring as I do an enhanced labour market approach to training, I would warn against excessive expectations about the degree of business-labour cooperation that this requires. Thus, for example, I would not wish to press for business-labour consensus on such thorny issues as a grant-levy system or the use of unemployment insurance to finance training. If it is astutely managed, an agreement by business and labour to disagree on how training should be financed need not stand in the way of their joining as a strong constituency in favour of procuring training programs that have been tailored to labour market needs. Institutions are such a formidable constituency on the supply side of labour market training that they must be balanced by an equally strong constituency on the demand side if an effective buyer-seller relationship is to prevail. I need not add, but I will, that this is in the long-run interest of the institutions themselves because they have everything to gain from being adaptable and being seen so to be.

In this regard, I join Maxwell in applauding the fact that, likely thanks to their business and labour constituencies, the CLFDB and OTAB are overcoming the exclusive brokerage of the past and beginning to expose public institutions to competition from private training schools. What is more, OTAB has emitted signals that it intends to expose community colleges to competition from universities. As it has been reported to me, the initial university response belies the allegations that stigmatize these institutions as tradition-encrusted dinosaurs. The opportunity to compete in the labour market training arena will join the forces of competition that have long prevailed in the domain of research funding to differentiate the universities that organize themselves to play their strong suits. And there is more. A tough-minded, wide-open procurement approach to labour market training is precisely what can rescue the university-college interface from the wasteland it has been, especially in Ontario. To the extent that the knowledge society generates unmet demand for para-professionals or super-technologists, this need can only be met by graduates of programs that will be joint university-college endeavours. The cold cash offered by a determined buyer will do more to promote such joint endeavours than all the exhortations in all the reports that could ever be written on the university-college interface.

Admittedly, a procurement approach to labour market training remains far easier to enunciate than to implement. On this score, for example, I can contain my enthusiasm for the fact that the minister to whom OTAB reports is also the minister whose portfolio encompasses Ontario's colleges and universities. This does not augur well for what is surely vital to effective procurement practices — an arm's length relation between purchasers and suppliers. Perhaps someone at Queen's Park will note this humble opinion; in the likely event that it is not heard, let alone acted upon, I place my trust in federalism and its time-honoured role as an engine of diversity.

This is where I cannot overemphasize the importance of what I consider Maxwell's core plea that we cultivate asymmetry in federal-provincial relations. In Ontario, the influence of the CLFDB may well compensate for OTAB's regrettable reporting relationship if, as she suggests, both agencies delegate training procurement to community boards. In New Brunswick, as she points out, the New Brunswick Labour Force Development Board offers such a striking parallel to the CLFDB that it might well act as the channel for federal procurement funds. As for Quebec, the linguistic distinctiveness of its labour market and the provincial government infrastructure that has long been in place argue not only for a federal transfer of training procurement but for a transfer of the placement role played by Canada Employment Centres.

Lest this leave me to conclude on an optimistic note, I shall not stop at this point but instead indulge the morose side of my persona. Even if asymmetric arrangements can be devised to promote a suitably arm's length relation between purchasers and sellers of labour market training, it remains seductively easy to oversell the need for knowledge workers. Consider the stunning vacancy rates in office space that currently plague commercial real estate on a global scale. Are we looking at a phenomenon that is deeply structural rather than merely cyclical? It may indeed be structural if the diffusion of micro-electronic based technologies which so affected manufacturing in the 1980s is just beginning to work its way through the managerial and clerical layers of our white-collar labour force. If the so-called delayering of organizational pyramids is the wave of the future, will highly trained MBAs become a glut on the market, to say nothing of computer-literate, para-professional secretaries?

Believing as I do in a procurement approach to labour market training, I start to gag when I remind myself that effective procurement presupposes knowledgeable buyers. How facile it is to posit that the knowledge society needs para-professionals and super-technologists. How much do we know about what sectors require them with what mix of skills and in what numbers? More labour market research might help, but just as important in this mug's game are intuition, educated guesses and networking among employers, counsellors, and trainers. Have there been "good performers" in identifying emerging labour market needs among Canada's globally competitive firms, domestically oriented firms, training institutions, college and university placement offices, Canada Employment Centres? What are the secrets of their success?

BIBLIOGRAPHY

Dupré, J. Stefan (1988), "Reflections on the Workability of Executive Federalism," in *Perspectives on Canadian Federalism*, ed. R.D. Olling and M.W. Westmacott, Scarborough: Prentice-Hall Canada.

Dupré, J. Stefan *et al.* (1973), *Federalism and Policy Development: The Core of Adult Occupational Training in Ontario*, Toronto: University of Toronto Press.

CHAPTER EIGHT

Income Distribution, Income Security, and Fiscal Federalism

François Vaillancourt

INTRODUCTION

The purpose of this chapter is to examine the field of income security in Canada, and to evaluate the policy challenges and choices confronting Canadian governments, particularly as they relate to federal-provincial relations. The chapter is divided into four sections: the first two sections set the historical and factual stages; and the next two address the issues. The first section examines the evolution of the distribution of income and of poverty from 1951 to 1991-92, while the second presents the evolution of income support programs over the same period and their main features in 1993. That done, we review economic criteria that justify government interaction in this field and then examine the challenges and choices faced by Canada in the near future.

INCOME DISTRIBUTION AND POVERTY IN CANADA

This section provides an examination of the incomes and poverty of Canadians so as to allow us to better understand the relevance of income security programs. The period covered varies from table to table (starting in 1951, 1961 or 1971 and ending in 1991 or 1992), as dictated by the availability of historical data at time of writing. Table 1 tracks the growth in real per capita income in Canada from 1951 to 1991, and shows that incomes grew more quickly in the 1951-71 period than in the 1971-91 period. Table 2 summarizes the evolution of the distribution of post-transfer money income from 1951 to 1991-92 (Panel A) and of poverty from 1961 to 1992 (Panel B). Examining it, one notes that the shares of income going to the bottom and top quintiles have increased slightly from

TABLE 1: Evolution of Real Income in Canada, Various Incomes,
1950-51 to 1990-91

Income Concept	Year				
	1950	1960	1970	1980	1990
(1) Annual wages (1990 $)					
Both sexes	11,249	16,031	21,928	23,791	24,259
Men	12,843	18,477	26,196	29,871	29,757
Women	7,373	10,019	13,671	15,710	17,933
	1951	1961	1971	1981	1991
(2) Family incomes (1991 $)					
Families					
Per unit	21,172	28,116	41,054	51,756	53,131
Per member	5,601	7,136	10,919	15,496	16,761
Unattached individuals	8,169	11,226	17,209	22,723	22,514
(3) GDP per capita (1991 $)	9,638	11,988	18,072	24,746	25,030

Sources: (1) Rashid (1993); Statistics Canada (75-001), Table 1.
(2) Statistics Canada (1991, p. 25)
(3) Calculations by the author using information from *The Canadian Economic Observer*, Historical Supplement 1992/1993; Statistics Canada (11-210), Tables 51.1 (GDP), 53.2 (CPI) and 54.1 (Population).

1951 to 1991, that the Gini coefficient has remained almost unchanged and that poverty diminished substantially from 1961 to 1981 and then went down slightly from 1981 to 1992.[1]

What is the impact of the various transfer programs on the changes reported in Table 2 and, more generally, on the incomes of Canadians? This is a very difficult question to answer definitively, since one does not know how these programs affect decisions with respect to work and savings for retirement. However, Table 3 allows us to assess the importance of transfers by quintile as well as their impact on the overall income distribution from 1971 to 1991. One notes that transfers account for a decreasing share of income as one moves from

TABLE 2: Income Inequality in Canada: Quintile Shares (%) and
Gini Coefficients, 1951-91 and Poverty Rates, 1961-1991/92

	A – Income Inequality, All Units Money Income					
	Quintiles[2]					Gini Coefficients[2]
Year	1st (Lowest)	2nd	3rd	4th	5th (Highest)	
1951[1]	4.4	11.3	18.3	23.3	42.8	0.390
1961[1]	4.2	11.9	18.3	24.5	41.1	0.368
1971	3.6	10.6	17.6	24.9	43.3	0.400
1981	4.6	10.9	17.6	25.2	41.8	0.377
1986	4.7	10.4	17.0	24.9	43.1	0.390
1991	4.7	10.3	16.6	24.7	43.8	0.396
1992	4.6	10.3	16.7	24.8	43.6	N/A

Notes: 1: Nonagricultural households only.

2: The Gini coefficient is a summary measure of the distribution of income that ranges from 0, when all units have the same income, to 1 when income is concentrated in the hands of one unit. Quintiles are obtained by ordering all units, i.e., economic families and unattached individuals by income from the lowest to the highest and then dividing them into five groups of equal size. Quintile shares sum to 100 percent in each year.

N/A: Not available.

Sources: Quintile shares:
1951-1981: Vaillancourt (1985, Table 1-7); *Income Distribution by Size in Canada*, various years, Statistics Canada (13-207).
Gini coefficients:
1951-1981: Vaillancourt (1985, Table 1-7).
1986-1991: *Income After Tax Distribution by Size in Canada*, Statistics Canada, Table VIII.

B – Poverty Rates (%)			
Year	Families	Unattached Individuals	Persons
1961	27.9	49.2	N/A
1971	18.3	43.1	20.0
1981	12.0	37.8	14.7
1986	13.3	42.1	16.4
1991	12.9	40.0	16.5
1992	13.3	39.7	16.8

Notes: 1961 rates are calculated using 1961 low-income cutoffs; 1971 rates using 1969 cutoffs; 1981 using 1978 cutoffs; 1986, 1991 and 1992 rates using 1992 cutoffs. A change in the cutoffs used changes poverty rates slightly. Hence in 1991, the poverty rates calculated using 1978 cutoffs were as follows: families: 11.5; unattached individuals: 32.1 and all individuals: 14.4.

Sources: 1961-1981: Vaillancourt (1985, Table 1-12)
1986-1991: Statistics Canada (1991, p. 169).

TABLE 3: Composition of Income by Quintile and Gini Coefficients Pre- and Post-money Transfers, Canada, All Units, 1961-92, selected years

Quintiles	All Units	Quintiles					Gini Coefficients	
		1st (Lowest)	2nd	3rd	4th	5th (Highest)	Pre-Transfers	Post-Transfers
		Share of Transfers in Money Income						
1961	7.0	45.7	14.5	6.3	4.4	2.8	–	–
1971	6.6	53.3	18.2	5.7	3.4	2.0	0.447	0.400
1981	9.0	57.3	22.7	8.8	5.0	2.6	0.439	0.377
1986	11.5	60.2	32.2	13.1	6.8	3.3	0.469	0.388
1991	13.4	63.4	36.9	16.3	8.9	4.0	0.488	0.396
1992	14.0	66.8	38.2	17.6	9.3	4.0	–	–

Sources: Quintile data:
Podoluk (1968, Table 11.A.2; Families and Unattached Individuals, p. 296); Statistics Canada (1971); Vaillancourt (1985, Table 1-9, p. 14).
Gini Data:
Vaillancourt (1985, Table 1-9, p. 14); Statistics Canada (1986).

the first to the last quintile and that post-transfer Gini coefficients are smaller than pre-transfer ones, indicating that transfers play their intended equalizing role.

Two other facts are worth noting. The first is the doubling from 1971 to 1992 of the importance of transfers in the income of all Canadians, including those in the top four quintiles. Second is the increase from 1971 to 1991 in the Gini coefficients measuring inequality of pre-transfer income, while those measuring post-transfer income shows stability in the distribution. The first finding raises questions as to the targeting of transfers. The second is in agreement with the findings of Osberg *et al.* (1993), and of Beach and Slotsve (1994) who report an increasing polarization of earnings in Canada over the 1967-91 period, with differences between sexes and subperiods, but stability in the final distribution of income.

Table 4 allows us to examine the evolution of poverty in Canada since 1961 by age and since 1981 by marital status. It shows a remarkable reduction of poverty in the 65+ age group, a stable or somewhat reduced incidence of poverty in the 35-64 age bracket and an increase in poverty in the 15-34 age bracket, particularly the 15-24 age group. Part of the explanation of the reduction in poverty for the 65+ age group is the introduction in 1966 of two income transfer programs. One, the Guaranteed Income Supplement (GIS), had an immediate impact while the second one, the Canada and Quebec Pension Plans (CPP/QPP), has been gradually coming into play.

Having described the distribution of income and the levels of poverty, and having shown the importance of transfers in general, we now turn our attention to transfer programs.

TABLE 4: Poverty Rates by Age and Family Type, Canada, 1961-91

Year	Age					
	<24	25-34	35-44	45-54	55-64	65+
	Families (Age of Head)					
1961	29.0	22.1	22.1	22.1	22.2	43.9
1971	21.2	14.9	16.6	14.1	17.1	34.8
1981	22.7	12.6	10.7	9.0	10.5	14.5
1986	32.2	16.1	11.5	9.2	11.7	14.2
1991	36.6	18.6	12.9	7.4	11.8	7.9
1992	41.5	18.6	12.9	8.6	11.4	8.5
	Individuals					
1961	38.8	2.1	25.5	33.0	46.1	69.9
1971	44.9	19.5	24.9	30.8	40.8	68.4
1981	38.4	18.2	22.4	30.3	40.9	58.6
1986	54.6	27.3	25.4	30.6	45.3	58.1
1991	57.4	27.6	27.7	30.3	44.1	50.8
1992	58.8	27.2	27.3	33.7	45.8	48.4

	Family Type				
	Married Couple			*Single Parent Family*	
	No Children	+ Child	+ Child/Relative	Male Head	Female Head
1981	8.3	8.9	8.0	13.8	42.8
1986	8.1	9.6	6.1	16.4	44.1
1991	6.7	8.7	7.6	14.1	44.8
1992	8.3	9.6	7.9	16.4	47.8

Note: 1961 uses 1961 LICOs; 1971 uses 1969 LICOs; 1991, 1986, 1991 use 1978 LICOs; 1992 uses 1992 LICOs.

Sources: Podoluk (1968, Tables 8.1 and 8.2); Statistics Canada (1971); Vaillancourt (1985, Table 1-13).

CANADIAN INCOME DISTRIBUTION PROGRAMS:
EVOLUTION AND IMPORTANCE

In this section, we first recall the evolution of income security and income distribution programs in Canada, with particular emphasis on the 1946-92 period. We then present various indicators of their importance.

The Evolution of the Programs

While there was always some support by the state for the poor through such programs as subsidies to hospitals, state intervention in income security in Canada really began with the introduction of provincially provided worker's compensation insurance starting in 1913 in Ontario. Table 5 and Figure 1 present what we believe are the key elements of the historical setting. Additional details are found in Banting (1985), Johnson (1987), and Norrie (1993).

Examining Table 5 and Figure 1, one notes the following points:

• the importance of constitutional amendments in the creation of federal transfer payments to individuals (for Unemployment Insurance in 1940, and Old Age Security in 1951). Only in the case of family allowances was such an amendment not sought and apparently not required;

• in the case of unemployables, the program complexities in federal transfers to the provinces through a variety of programs gave way to consolidation in the 1960s with the introduction of the Canada Assistance Plan (CAP);

• the passage from one to four programs of income support for older Canadians from 1965 to 1975; and

• the transformation of child support from a universal non-taxed program to a targeted program in 50 years from 1944 to 1993.

TABLE 5: Origin and Evolution of Cash Income Support Programs

Program/Constitution	Pre-1946: Provider/Date(s) Initiated	Intergovernmental Relations/Funding	Evolution 1946 +
Industrial injuries and illnesses Insurance. A provincial constitutional responsibility (WCBs)	Provincial (territorial) publicly owned insurance monopolies.	Funding is through a (partially) experience-rated payroll tax levied on the employer. Boards are autonomous financial entities. There are no federal-provincial transfers. The Federal Government is covered as an employer.	Since inception, the following key changes occurred: • increased coverage of the labour force through the inclusion of initially uninsurable sectors (1950s-1970s); • increased coverage of injuries and professional illnesses (1970s-1990s); • increased real value of benefits (1980s) from 75% of gross income to 90% of net income.
Unemployment insurance (UI). A provincial constitutional responsibility until 1940. It then became a federal responsibility through a constitutional amendment.	Federal Government in 1941.	Funding is through a payroll tax levied on both employers and employees and until 1990 through a federal government contribution. There are no federal-provincial transfers. Benefits are linked to contributions which are linked to wages and period of employment.	Since inception, the following key changes occurred: • increased coverage through the inclusions of previously excluded sectors (fisheries, public administrations) (1950s-1970s); • increased real benefits (1971) then slowly eroded (1970s-1980s); • sole funding by employers and employees since 1991.
Income support (welfare) for employables and unemployables. Provincial constitutional responsibility.	• Provincial mother's pension (MP) (unemployables) were introduced in the 1920s. Other categories were reluctantly added. • Blind persons allowance (BPA) cost sharing was introduced in 1937 by the federal government (75/25).	Funding of the federal and provincial shares is through general revenues. Federal-provincial transfers occur as well as provincial-municipal transfers in Nova Scotia, Ontario and Manitoba where property taxes fund part of social assistance.	• *Blind Persons Act* (BPA) of 1951 covers blind persons aged 21+ (75% federal/25% provincial). • *Disabled Persons Act* (DPA) of 1954 covers the disabled (50/50 cost sharing). • *Unemployment Assistance Act* (UAA) of 1956 for the unemployed not covered by UI (50/50 cost sharing as of 1958). • Canada Assistance Plan (CAP) of 1966 replaces all previous programs. Until 1990, costs were shared 50/50. Since then, there is a cap on the growth of payment to Ontario, Alberta and British Columbia of 5% yielding funding ratios of 28/72 (Ontario).
Family allowances (FA). Universal payment to children aged 0-16 by the federal government using its constitutional power to spend.	Federal Government in 1944.	Funded by general revenues of the federal government.	• In 1974, allowances were increased significantly and made taxable. • In 1978, a tax credit was introduced. • In 1989, an income-based claw back was introduced. • In 1993, universality ended with the Child Tax Benefit Program (CTB).
Old age pensions. A provincial constitutional responsibility until 1951, when a constitutional amendment gave the federal government concurrent power in this field.	A federal government cost-sharing program was introduced (OAP) in 1927.	Cost shared program (50/50 then 75-25 from 1931 on) financed by general revenues. From 1951 to 1972, parts of the federal personal, corporate and sales taxes are earmarked for that program.	The *Old Age Security (OAS) Act*, established in 1951, pays pensions to Canadians aged 70+. This age was lowered to 65 in 1970. At that time, the companion *Old Age Assistance (OAA) Act*, a 50/50 transfer program for the elderly aged 65-69, was abolished. In 1966, the Guaranteed Income Supplement (GIS) was introduced and in 1975, Spouse Allowances (SA) were introduced. In 1989, an OAS income-based claw back was introduced. In 1966, the Canada Pension Plan and the Quebec Pension Plan were introduced.

FIGURE 1: Key Dates in Income Security in Canada

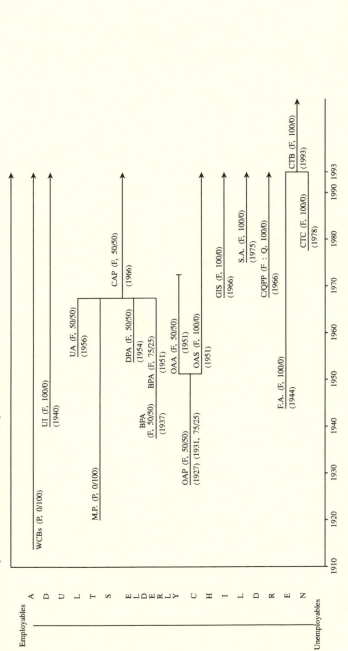

Notes: [1] Abbreviations provided in Table 5. (F: Federal program; P: Provincial program; Share paid federally/Share paid provincially when first set).
[2] OAP and OAS are for the elderly aged 70+ until 1966 when the pensionable age starts to decrease yearly in order to reach 65 in 1970. OAA is for the elderly aged 65-69.
[3] BPA 1937 is for the elderly blind people, while BPA 1951 is for blind people aged 21+.

The Importance of the Programs

While Table 5 and Figure 1 allow us to trace the evolution through time of the income support system in Canada, they do not allow us to assess the relative imporance of these programs, individually and as a whole. The most obvious measure of importance is program spending, reported in Table 6. But another dimension that may matter more from a political point of view is the size of the clientele of the major programs, which is reported in Table 7.

Table 6 shows the following trends in expenditures on income support spending in Canada:

- from 1951 to 1991, income support spending tripled with respect to GDP in Canada. Over the same period, total government expenditures increased from 21.3 percent to 46.5 percent of GDP (*National Finances*, 1991, Table 3.14, p. 3.15). Thus, income support spending also increased with respect to overall government spending;

- from 1951 to 1991, spending on children decreased from 46.4 percent to 7.8 percent of expenditures on income support. This is explained, in part, by a reduction in the number of children from 1981 to 1991 (see Table 7);

- from 1951 to 1991, payments to older Canadians increased from 25.9 percent of income support expenditures to 42.2 percent. This reflects not only the aging of the Canadian population, but also greater accessibility to income support with a reduction in age for OAS eligibility from 70 in 1966 to 65 in 1970, with increased eligibility for Spouses Allowance (SA) in 1985 and with access to (actuarially reduced) CPP/QPP pensions as of the age of 60 in the 1980s.

- from 1951 to 1991, payments to workers because of unemployment or injuries and illnesses increased only marginally from 24.1 percent of expenditures on income support to 28.2 percent. On the other hand, various welfare payments (welfare plus CPP/QPP for non-retirees) increased from 3.5 percent in 1951 to 21.7 percent in 1991, showing the fastest growth rate. In particular, note the growth in CPP/QPP non-retiree payments, which are primarily disability pensions.

TABLE 6: Expenditures on Income Support Programs in Canada, 1951 to 1991, Fiscal Year (000 000 $)

Programs	1951 $	1951 %	1961 $	1961 %	1971 $	1971 %	1981 $	1981 %	1986 $	1986 %	1991 $	1991 %
Workers' compensation	48.6	7.0	94.2	5.2	239.0	4.7	1,295.4	5.2	2,588.9	5.8	3,054.2	4.9
Unemployment insurance	118.1	17.1	409.2	22.7	901.0	17.7	5,398.6	21.6	10,639.5	23.8	14,468.3	23.3
Welfare	24.0	3.5	150.8	8.4	1,001.7	19.6	3,272.4	13.1	6,124.0	13.7	8,882.8	14.2
CPP/QPP (non-retirees)	0		0		109.7	2.2	1,241.4	5.0	2,799.6	6.3	4,648.0	7.5
OAS	178.9	25.9	625.1	34.7	1,679.3	32.0	6,140.5	24.6	9,520.0	21.3	12,705.3	20.4
GIS	0		0		526.1	10.3	2,241.9	8.9	3,451.4	7.7	3,975.7	6.4
SA	0		0		0		202.8	0.8	473.2	1.1	449.9	0.7
CPP/QPP (retirees)	0		0		83.5	1.6	2,070.4	8.3	5,054.2	11.3	9,134.1	14.7
Family allowances	320.4	46.4	520.8	28.9	554.4	10.9	2,019.5	8.1	2,534.4	5.7	2,736.0	4.4
Child tax credit	0		0		0		1,068.9	4.3	1,573.4	3.5	2,109.6	3.4
Total: $	690	100.0	1,800.1	100.0	5,094.7	100.0	24,951.8	100.0	44,758.6	100.0	62,163.9	100.0
% of GDP	3.1%		4.4%		5.2%		7.9%		8.9%		9.3%	

Note: 1990-91 as the last year for which we have data on a comparative basis.

Sources: 1951 and 1961: *Social Security Statistics, Canada and Provinces*, 1950-51 - 1977-78. Ottawa Health and Welfare Canada.
1971-1986: *Social Security Statistics, Canada and Provinces*, 1963-64 to 1987-88.
1990-1991: unpublished data, courtesy of S. Ewen, Health and Welfare.
OAS includes OAP, Welfare includes Mother's Allowance, Blind Persons Allowance and Old Age Assistance and in 1961, Unemployment Assistance and Disabled Assistance.
CPP/QPP non-pension is made up of survivors, disability and child benefits.
GDP: *Canadian Economic Observer*, Historical Supplement, 1991-92, Table 1.1. GDP is for the calendar that most closely corresponds to the fiscal year, i.e., 1990 for 1990/91.

TABLE 7: Clientele of Income Support Programs in Canada and Population/Families, 1951 to 1991

Programs		1951	1961	1971	1981	1986	1991
Workers' compensation		158,034	178,806	302,571	567,916	571,555	657,527 (1989/1990)
Unemployment insurance		617,719	722,196	584,701	710,899	1,116,360	1,200,740
Welfare		132,420	867,196	1,460,064	1,418,400	1,892,900	2,282,200
CPP/QPP (non-retirees)		0	0	88,857	628,258	902,134	1,241,309
OAS[1]		302,173	894,810	1,701,459	2,276,159	2,616,762	3,059,029
GIS		0	0	823,924	1,204,594	1,299,019	1,321,234
SA		0	0	0	81,939	111,984	119,677
CPP/QPP (retirees)		0	0	189,657	1,042,806	1,518,571	2,365,516
Family allowances:	children	4,294,500	6,317,800	6,841,040	6,857,744	6,575,347	6,700,683
	families	1,885,000	2,580,700	3,001,353	3,636,129	3,635,861	3,722,950
Child tax credit:	children	0	0	0	5,132,092	4,989,622	4,621,186
	families				2,478,158	2,476,431	2,219,190
Population (000)		14,009.4	18,238.3	21,568.3	24,341.7	25,353.0	27,000.4
Number of families		3,287,384	4,147,444	5,070,682	6,324,976	6,734,978	7,356,168

Notes: [1]Old age pensions in 1951

1951 (1): *Canada Year Book, 1955,* Chapter XVI, Table 32. This is the amount of accidents resulting in temporary disability, permanent disability or death. For Quebec, the breakdown by type was not reported: the ROC distribution was assumed.

1951 (2): *Annual Report of Benefit Years Established and Terminated Under the Unemployment Insurance Act, 1951,* Bureau of Statistics (73-201), Table 3.

1951 (3): *Canada Year Book, 1954,* Chapter VI, Table 10 for mother's allowance (families plus children); *Canada Year Book, 1952-1953,* Chapter VI, Table 7, for blind Canadians.

1961 (3): Health and Welfare, Tables 321, 331, 341, 511. The number of families on mother's allowance is transformed in the number of recipients (mothers+children) by multiplying the number of recipients in 1951 by the growth in the number of families from 1951 to 1961 accounting for a reduction in family size.

Sources: 1971-1991, *Social Security Statistics, Canada and Provinces, 1967-1968 to 1991-1992,* Health and Welfare Canada, June 1993, mimeo. 1951-1961, *Social Security Statistics, Canada and Provinces, 1950-1951 to 1977-1978 and 1958-1959 to 1982-1983 (1961-1962),* Health and Welfare Canada, November 1979.

Population:*Canadian Economic Observer, Historical Supplement, 1991/1992,* Table 11.1.

Families (census):1961-1991, *Dwellings and Households: The Nation,* Statistics Canada (93-311), 1991, Census of Canada, Table 1. 1951. *Household and Families,* Dominion Bureau of Statistics (93-514), 1961 Census of Canada, Table 43.

Turning to Table 7, one finds that:

- the number of WCB claimants increased particularly between 1971 and 1981, perhaps because of more generous access rules;

- the number of UI claimants remained below 1 million until 1986, but rose rapidly thereafter;

- welfare recipients decreased from 1971 to 1981 but increased substantially from 1981 to 1991. Over that period, the number of beneficiaries increased by more than 500,000 (138 percent) in Ontario, 60,000 in Quebec (12 percent), 75,000 in Alberta (101 percent) and by about 120,000 (91 percent) in British Columbia. Thus, national figures hide substantial differences between provinces;

- for CPP/QPP, both retirees and non-retirees have grown at a high rate from 1971 to 1991. Part of this is explained by the increased number of older Canadians, while changes in the value of the benefit (1976) and in the availability of early pensions (age 60) also played a role;

- for OAS/GIS/SA, the number of OAS beneficiaries almost doubled from 1961 to 1971 as a result of the lowering of the pensionable age and has since grown with the number of older Canadians. The number of GIS or SA recipients is not growing as fast except for SA recipients from 1981 to 1986, a fact explained by a change in accessibility in that period. This reflects, in part, the greater availability of CPP/QPP retirement pensions. Indeed, the number of GIS recipients reached a peak in 1988-89 and has since been decreasing;

- for family allowances/child tax credit, the number of children eligible for family allowances peaked in 1975-76, but the number of families receiving them has continued to increase, reflecting the decrease in family size in Canada (from 2.28 children in 1951 to 1.80 in 1991). As for the child tax credit, its take-up rate decreased from 1981 to 1991, reflecting, in part, the decrease in the poverty rate in Canada (Table 2);

- for population/families, from 1971 to 1991, Canada's population almost doubled, while the number of families almost doubled as well. Taking this into account, the increase in the number of claimants for UI is not unreasonable, while the number of welfare recipients grew much faster. Note also that in 1951, more than one family in two received family allowances: this was still (barely) the case in 1991.

The indicators of the importance of programs found in Tables 6 and 7 are aggregate indicators. In Table 8, we present evidence on their importance with respect to the income of individuals and families by reporting the value of the

TABLE 8: Value of Various Transfer Programs in $ (Current) and Relative to the Poverty Line, 1961-91

Programs	1961		1971		1981		1986		1991	
	1 Person	2/3 Persons	1 Person	2/3 Persons	1 Person	2/3 Persons	1 Person	2/3 Persons	1 Person	2/3 Persons
WCB $	2,250–4,500		4,500–6,000		11,250–18,000		14,290–30,632		17,250–31,000	
Ratio	1.5–3.5	0.75–1.5	2.24–2.98	1.12–1.5	0.93–1.49	0.79–1.27	1.34–2.88	0.76–1.61	1.29–2.32	0.73–1.31
UI $	1,404	1,872	3,692	3,878	9,828	9,828	14,850	14,850	20,400	20,400
Ratio	0.93	0.62	1.83	0.96	1.22	0.69	1.39	0.79	1.51	0.86
Welfare $	–	540–1,632	–	1,308–2,604	–	3,924–8,250	–	4,944–11,418	–	5,796–15,624
Ratio	–	0.18–0.54	–	0.32–0.65	–	0.28–0.60	–	0.26–0.61	–	0.24–0.66
OAS $	480	960	945	1,890	2,189	4,378	3,478	6,957	4,381	8,762
Ratio	0.32	0.64	0.47	0.56	0.27	0.41	0.33	0.50	0.33	0.49
OAS+GIS $	–	–	1,530	3,060	3,986	7,367	7,612	12,342	9,587	15,543
Ratio	–	–	0.76	0.91	0.50	0.69	0.71	0.88	0.71	0.88
OAS+CPP/QPP $	–	–	1,076	2,021	2,738	4,927	9,311	18,622	11,639	23,278
Ratio	–	–	0.53	0.60	0.34	0.46	0.87	1.33	0.87	1.31

Notes: In the 2/3 persons columns, calculations are for two persons for OAS, OAS+GIS and OAS+CPP/QPP, and for three persons, otherwise.

Ratio: The ratio is attained by dividing the amount of the transfer by the relevant poverty line (low-income cutoff).

For WCB and welfare, we report the minimum and maximum in a given year, since payments vary across provinces. Thus in 1984, the minimum annual WCB payment was $11,250 and the maximum was $18,000, depending on the province of residence.

Unemployment Insurance: Benefits for 50 weeks in a given year are assumed.

For 1981, 1986 and 1991, the 1978 poverty line was used to enhance comparability.

Sources: OAS/GIS and UI, 1961, 1971, 1981, 1986, *The National Finances*, (Canadian Tax Foundation, various years). For years with rate changes, a weighted average of rates was used.

WCB: *The Financing of Workers' Compensation Boards in Canada, 1960-1990*, F. Vaillancourt, Toronto Canadian Tax Foundation, in press, Tables 2-4 and D-7. 1990 data are used for 1991.

Welfare Data: courtesy of Pierre Lefebvre, Economics Department, UQAM.

benefit associated with each program. We do this both in dollar terms and by comparing it to the usual poverty measure in Canada, Statistics Canada low-income cut-offs. Such a comparison requires us to begin our analysis in 1961, the first year for which we have poverty data.

Examining Table 8, one observes that:

- insurance programs for workers are always, with the exception of UI in 1961, sufficiently generous to raise a single person above the poverty line. The apparent reduction in benefits for WCB from 1961 to 1991 is, in part, illusory, since a fair number of boards moved from benefits replacing 75 percent of gross income to benefits replacing 90 percent of net income over that period. The substantial increase in UI benefits from 1961 to 1971 (almost doubled) is the result of a deliberate enrichment of the program in 1971;

- welfare payments and disability (CPP/QPP) pensions are not sufficient to raise either an individual (disability) or a single parent family (welfare) above the poverty line. The real value of these transfers with respect to the poverty line has remained relatively unchanged from 1961 to 1991;

- universal income support for older Canadians (OAS) does not protect them from poverty. When combined with GIS, it still does not achieve that goal, but when in receipt of OAS and CPP/QPP, an elderly couple will be above the poverty line. One must note the dire impact on the income of older Canadians of living alone, often as a result of outliving a spouse.

Table 9 summarizes the main features of the major income support programs in Canada as of 1993.

As stated in the introduction, these two sections have set the historical and factual stages. Before proceeding to an analysis of the challenges and choices in income security, however, we also need to present the theoretical framework that will guide our analysis.

TABLE 9: Income Support Programs in Canada — Main Features, 1993

Programs	Main Features			
	Coverage	*Eligibility*	*Financing*	*Benefits*
WCB (provincial)	Most workers with sectoral exclusion. Varies across provinces.	Depends on accident status. No minimum contribution period. Some provinces do not pay compensation for the day of the accident.	Payroll tax levied on employers. In all provinces, it varies between industries and in some, across employers (large ones) according to the risk experience.	90% of net income (Alberta, Saskatchewan, Ontario, Manitoba, Quebec, New Brunswick (80%) and Newfoundland (80%) or 75% of gross income (British Columbia, Nova Scotia, Prince Edward Island).
Unemployment insurance (federal)	All employees. Self-employed are not covered. Maximum weekly insurable earnings ($745).	Minimum weeks (MW) required range from a minimum of 10 to 20, according to the regional unemployment rate (UR). $MW = 20-(U.R.-6)$ 10.[1]	Payroll tax levied on employees (3%) and employers (4.2%).[1] No funding from general revenues.	Depend on weeks worked range from 17 to 50 (2 week waiting period). Equals 60% (57% as of 1 September 1993) of insurable earnings: maximum $447 per week.
Welfare recipients (provincial, cost-shared)	All individuals and families.	Must meet a needs test.	General revenues of the federal and provincial governments (and municipalities in 3 provinces).	Vary across provinces.
Child tax benefits (federal)	All Canadians. Quebec has a supplementary provincial program with payments varying ranging with the age and number of children.	Depends on family income and number of children. Also affected by claim for child-care expenses and nature of income.	General revenues.	Basic amount per child from $1,020 per year at zero income to zero at $66,000 family income.
The elderly – OAS, GIS, SA (federal)	All Canadians aged 65+, OAS, GIS, or 60+ (SA).	Must have resided at least 10 years in Canada. GIS and SA are linked to income of family.	General revenues.	OAS $378.95[1] per month, GIS = 0 when single income = $10,896 (family $14,208), maximum GIS = $450.34.[1]
CPP/QPP (federal/Quebec)	All CPP/QPP contributors.	Retirees, widowers, orphans and the disabled.	Payroll tax on employees (2.5%) and employers (2.5%)	Maximum monthly retirement pension $667.36.

[1] In this formula, *all* non-integer UR rates are rounded up to the next integer.
One set of income support programs not presented here are from programs. See Treff (1992) for a summary description

REASONS FOR STATE INTERVENTION IN
INCOME DISTRIBUTION AND INCOME SECURITY

These are two strands of theoretical work that are useful in assessing the choices faced in the field of income support in Canada. The first strand is the theoretical work on federalism, particularly on federal-provincial arrangements (division of powers, transfers). Boadway and Flatters review this literature in a clear and precise manner in this volume and I will thus not address it here. The second strand is the theoretical work on state intervention in income security and income distribution, to which we now turn.

Statements about the rationale for state intervention in income security and income distribution are fairly similar, whether found in a theoretical exposition by public finance economists (Boadway and Wildasin 1984) or in more applied work (Fluet and Lefebvre 1992). Income security arguments are usually put in terms of insurance market, while income distribution arguments are usually made with reference to altruism. This does not mean that insurance programs do not have an effect on income distribution. They obviously do, but their intent is not to affect income distribution but to protect the insured from the income consequences of a given event (accident, unemployment, etc.), more (retirement) or less (accidental death) foreseeable.[2] Put differently, in a world of full employment, with perfect foresight and capital markets, one may not need an insurance/income security program, but the income distribution resulting from market force may still be judged by society to be inappropriate and to require government intervention.

Let us now examine four specific reasons for state-sponsored insurance/income security schemes linking them, when possible, to the literature on the division of powers in federal states. The first three reasons may prevent the emergence of private insurance institutions and thus lead to the introduction of government programs. The first reason is linked to costs, while the following two reasons are due to asymmetric information between the insurer and the insured.

- *High transaction costs.* If economies of scale are important in reducing transaction costs yet markets are easily entered, then it may be impossible for a single firm (or a few) to supply the market since it is not profitable to do so. A monopoly (often a public one) will be able to attain economies of scale. In a federal system, this means that programs can be administered by the federal government, by the subnational government or perhaps by agencies regrouping smaller subnational governments, along geographic lines. The best allocation depends on the number and distribution of residents of subnational governments and on the number of clients needed to attain minimum costs.

- *Moral hazard.* This occurs when the insured can modify their behaviour to benefit from the insurance program. This implies that it is difficult for private firms to offer some kinds of insurance programs. For example, it is easier to cheat on income insurance by claiming that one cannot find employment than on life insurance by claiming that one is dead. In a federal system where individuals are mobile between subnational jurisdictions, one may be better able to detect moral hazard in a federal insurance system with records more easily linked between agencies of a single government, than in a system of subnational insurance schemes where information is less easily exchanged between governments because of technological and legal barriers.

- *Adverse selection.* This occurs when potential clients do not represent the same risk for the insurer, but their degree of risk cannot be identified in advance. In that case, good risks (low claimants) will tend to underinsure and bad risks to overinsure both in terms of participation and coverage in a given insurance program. As a result, insurance premiums will not cover costs if set without taking this into account, but as they rise, good risks will insure themselves less with the possible result that only bad risks will want to insure themselves. In a federal system, mobility combined with differences in insurance programs between subnational governments could accentuate adverse selection.

In these three cases, individuals are assumed to behave in a perfectly rational way to be fully informed and so on but to be faced with deficient private markets which require government interventions. This is not so in the next case.

- *Myopic individuals.* Individuals may not plan for their future correctly. As a result, they may, for example, not save sufficiently for the future and, in particular, for old age or illnesses. This matters to society insofar as it is obligated through a moral contract, perhaps embodied in a constitutional provision such as a social charter, to prevent individuals from dying or suffering unduly from this lack of planning. If it was not so obligated, then the plight of these individuals would matter only to their families (and private charities). One should note that the existence of income security programs can lead to changes in savings behaviour which are rational and not myopic. Myopia may matter more in a federal system than in an unitary state if the power to require preventive behaviour (forced savings for retirement, etc.) does not rest with the same level of government that is responsible for making up income deficiencies.

Finally, both market and individuals can behave correctly, but there can still be a desire among members of a society for changes in the distribution of income.

- *Income distribution.* Altruism will lead members of a family to help each other, families to help one another, and people generally to care about the level of well-being of non-related individuals. In a modern urbanized, industrialized society, this desire for redistribution by potential donors, combined with the desire of recipients for increased income, will often lead to government redistribution. If income redistribution is done at the subnational level, differences in altruism between regions or differences in real benefits may reflect preferences of donors and recipients but can lead to interregional migration.

We now turn our attention to an examination of the challenges and choices faced by income support programs in Canada.

INCOME SUPPORT PROGRAMS IN CANADA: CHALLENGES AND CHOICES

In this section, we present the challenges faced by income support programs in Canada. We then examine what could be done to meet these challenges and, in particular, what rearrangement in the intergovernmental dimension of these programs (jurisdictions, overlaps, financing, etc.) could be considered.

General Challenges

Courchene (1987) identified three broad challenges — fiscal, economic-technological, and socio-demographic — that still remain today. Let us thus reexamine them.

- *Fiscal challenge.* If anything, the fiscal challenge has taken on greater urgency with a projected federal budget deficit for 1993-94 of more than 40 billion dollars, or more than 5 percent of GDP. What has changed is that this challenge has spread from the central government to most provincial governments as well.

- *Economic-technological challenge.* Various factors are transforming the work force, including globalization and an information revolution. From the individual's perspective, these changes translate into greater uncertainty in annual incomes over a lifetime profile, and a decline in the availability of middle-class jobs (Picot *et al.* 1990). The greater uncertainty associated with more self-employment and the decline in life-long employment leads to a need for more insurance schemes. The polarization in good jobs/bad jobs (Beach and Slotsve 1993) may lead to a demand for more income redistribution, although it could also stimulate greater job sharing, especially in the public sector. From a policy perspective, "in a knowledge era social policy is progressively indistinguishable from economic policy" (Courchene in this volume).

- *Socio-demographic challenge.* There are three demographic trends that matter in this context:

  - *Aging of the population.* This is a trend that increases spending on the elderly for income transfers and health. Note that tax expenditures for RRP and RRSP incurred now may reduce future income transfers but probably not by an equivalent amount.

  - *Decreasing population.* This forecasted event may lead to a demand for more immigration or more pro-natal policies as already witnessed in Quebec. If this is not the case, then expenditures on children will decline.

  - *Changing families.* Both the composition of families (same sex, single parent, blended/ reconstituted), and their stability (length of first marriage, etc.) are changing with the result that individuals are less likely to draw support from them. Taking into account the reduced number of children and the geographic mobility of individuals, people also are less likely to draw support from their extended family.

Program Specific Challenges

- *Workers' Compensation Boards.* WCBs are faced with a major fiscal challenge with their unfunded liabilities having increased from $1 billion in 1980 to $14 billion in 1992 (Vaillancourt 1993). This increase is largely the result of increases in benefits (indexing for inflation, more generous rules, etc.) imposed on WCB by provincial legislatures without a concurrent transfer of funds. They also play a role of substitute for unemployment insurance (Fortin and Lanoie 1992) (and presumably welfare) which is not surprising since they provide the highest level of benefits (Table 8). Finally, since they are entirely financed by an employer payroll tax, increases in their financial needs may in the short run increase the cost of labour and reduce employment opportunities. Thus, while WCBs are a provincial responsibility, funded by provincial revenues, issues of coordination of benefits and of impact on unemployment are intergovernmental in nature.

- *Unemployment Insurance.* Since 1990, the Unemployment Insurance Fund is to be fully funded in the long run by employer and employee payroll taxes, although short-run loans by the government are allowed for and have indeed been made. As a result, the UI fund can accumulate liabilities like WCBs and its funding can reduce employment opportunities in the short run. But while WCBs payments are either for short-term disabilities with, when required, medical and workplace interventions to ensure re-employability, or for long-term disabilities, with no set time limit as such, UI payments are for a set time limit (maximum 50 weeks) and are conditional upon loss of employment. With no experience rating of individuals or employers and a widened clientele, including seasonal workers, unemployment insurance has become less of an insurance system and more of an income support program (Kesselman 1983; Green and Riddell 1993). In particular, it does not encourage retraining and may even discourage it by its treatment of student recipients of benefits. Hence, it is not surprising that Beach and Slotsve state that "the changes and disloca-tion ongoing appear to be quite long run and now heavily established in the economy so that programs aimed at short-run safety net type of support (e.g., temporary UI benefits) won't work well ... what is called for is the creation of a flexible skill-learning environment for the labour force as a whole" (1994, p. 22). One possibility discussed since the early 1970s is a guaranteed annual income.

With respect to intergovernmental challenges, it is the interface between UI, social assistance and manpower retraining that raises the most important issues. Subsidiary ones are the offloading though short-term provincial job creation schemes of welfare recipients onto UI and the interaction with WCBs.

- *Welfare/Disability and survivor's pensions.* In analyzing welfare, one should distinguish at least conceptually between the unemployables and the employ-ables. With respect to unemployables, one must assess whether the condition is temporary (as a reuslt of child-raising responsibilities, for example) or permanent (as a result of disability or old age). In the case of disability, the issue of coordination between CPP/QPP and welfare arises. In the case of a temporary condition, one issue is the variability in norms across provinces; a second is the need to facilitate re-employment when the individual becomes employable. In the case of the employable, the issues raised in the case of UI with respect to training and offloading also matter. In addition, other issues such as the impact of changes in UI rules, or of federal immigration (Jenness and McCracken 1993) policy on provincial welfare rolls, through the admis-sion of refugees or sponsored immigrants whose sponsorship falls through, also arise.

Turning specifically to CAP, issues arise as to the appropriate matching rate for federal transfers and as to the condition that may stifle provincial innova-tions (Boadway and Flatters, this volume). But the main intergovernmental issue is the imposition in 1990 of a ceiling of 5 percent per year in the growth of CAP payments to equalization-receiving provinces. This has resulted in a loss to Ontario alone of $1.7 billions in 1982-93 and to a funding of eligible expenses of only 28 percent rather than 50 percent (Jenness and McCracken 1993, pp. 7-8). Hence, many believe that it will be impossible to go back to the standard 50/50 sharing formula on 1 April 1995, when the ceiling should end.

- *OAS/GIS/SA/CPP/QPP (Retirement).* The field of income security for older Canadians is almost uniquely federal, with only a few provincial income supplementation programs and the Quebec Pension Plan operating at the provincial level. Because of this and because of the use of the clear criterion of age to govern access to benefits, there are no important intergovernmental issues in this area. There are, however, issues of universality and of funding that are often raised. The clawback of OAS benefits certainly qualifies its universal payment structure. But one should note that individuals receiving sufficient private pension income to have their OAS fully clawed back in fact received more than its equivalent in tax expenditures for their retirement savings. Funding of the CPP/QPP is of more serious concern (Lam 1993), and changes in the Canada Pension Plan do require extensive agreement among the federal and provincial governments.

- *Child Tax Benefit.* This field is also almost exclusively occupied by the federal government with only Quebec providing provincial family allowances and birth bonuses. Issues in this area are those of universality, particularly as family allowances were received by women, and of adequacy since the child tax credit may adjust slowly to changes in economic circumstances.

Given the issues raised above, we believe that some changes are needed in the system. We first present changes to existing programs and then sketch a more radical version.

Choices — Tinkering

- *Employables*

  - *Eligibility.* All employed individuals should have access to the same pro-
    grams of income security. In practice, this would mean that the self-
    employed would have access to unemployment insurance, thus removing
    an obstacle from self-employment.

  - *Benefits.* Benefits following loss of employment should be set at the same
    level, whatever the cause of loss of employment. This would involve
    harmonizing down WCB benefits with UI, which themselves should be
    lowered to 50 percent of insurable earnings. After these benefits would be
    exhausted (40 weeks), individuals who were previously employed would
    receive welfare for employables. These payments received from the begin-
    ning by employables never employed would be associated with the obliga-
    tion to participate in training programs or public employment, and after two

years to relocate within one's province (and after five within Canada, if a federal jurisdiction is in place). Benefits would be set for individuals with a sharing reduction for couples. Children would receive supplementary allowances. The allowable earnings while receiving benefits should be substantial and the tax-back rate should be significantly less than 100 percent to encourage employment. Such a scheme could approximate a guaranteed annual income.

- *Financing.* The share of individuals should increase from 0 to 50 percent in the financing of WCBs and to 50 percent in the financing of UI. Experience rating should be introduced for UI along the lines of WCB (sectoral with partial firm-rating) as a first step.

- *Jurisdiction.* This is the area where there is exclusive provincial financing (WCB), exclusive federal financing (UI), and joint financing (welfare). One government level should become responsible. I have suggested (Vaillancourt 1991) that the reality of Canada's two labour markets, divided by language, be taken into account, with one provincial agency for Quebec and a federal one for the rest of Canada (this point is also noted in Maxwell, this volume). If this is too asymmetric, then regional units (Cousineau 1993) may be used. If this is not feasible, then this should be devolved to the provinces (Courchene 1993; Boadway and Flatters, this volume). I would favour full payment by provinces of all relevant costs with special equalization, should Ontarians still want Newfoundlanders to almost have their (real) standard of living while residing in Newfoundland. A key benefit of this is that provinces would then have a strong incentive to ensure that their microeconomic policies (minimum wages, union rules, etc.) fully promoted employment. Federal payments could also be linked in part to measures aimed at reducing data-exchange problems.

If full provincial takeover is not possible, then I would suggest that the federal government should abolish CAP and use the money thus saved to extend reformed UI benefits as welfare for employables. I thus agree with Norrie who suggests elsewhere in this volume that federal transfers should go directly to individuals. This unilateral move would at least rationalize part of the system. In this case, the federal government should adjust equalization payment for the fiscal base that could have been obtained if improper economic policies had not been pursued by the provinces. This is preferable in my opinion to a block-funded CAP (Hobson and St-Hilaire 1993) or to an expanded (net) equalization scheme (Boadway and Flatters, this volume) that finances welfare paid by the provinces to both employables and non-employables. It would also allow for an extension of training programs, in particular, if recipients of these transfers could attend post-secondary institutions for a given time.

- *Non-employables*
  - In the case of the elderly, the system works fairly well (Prince 1993). I would suggest moving CPP/QPP more towards a fully funded system (one way of reducing the debt/tax load of future generations) and requiring provinces to pay the market rate of interest (Prince 1993; Lam 1993). It may also be appropriate to better integrate all retirement income programs (Courchene, this volume), although over time the higher labour force participation rate of women will reduce the importance of the Guaranteed Income Supplement and the Spouses Allowance.
  - In the case of children, the system also works adequately if one accepts the levels of transfers as given.[3]
  - In the case of other non-employables, we have already discussed our reforms above.

Choices — Individual Economic Security Account

We would argue that it is preferable to have the federal government introduce Individual Economic Security Accounts (IESA) rather than tinker with the system. These accounts would be a forced savings scheme that would address two issues:

- *Retirement savings.* Individuals would be required to save from all sources of income for their retirement. Rates would be set to take into account the life-cycle nature of earnings (increasing with age from 25 to 50) at a level such that the account could pay real benefits equal to 50 percent of the individual's wage at retirement for a life expectancy equal to the average life expectancy at birth plus five years (as a precaution against unforeseen changes in life-saving technology). All contributions would be made by the individual. The program would be administered by private financial firms to avoid overborrowing by the provincial governments as in the existing CPP.

- *Income security savings.* Individuals would be required to save (5 percent) of income as soon as they earn income from any source. They could withdraw some monies for children or for study leave, unemployment spells, and so on. All contributions would be made by the individuals and would earn interest. Rates would depend on age, schooling, and past individual experiences.

In all cases, governments could contribute directly (and not through intergovernmental transfers or tax expenditures) to the individual's account to make up shortfalls deemed unacceptable or for specific purposes (pro-natal policy). Such an approach would have the benefits of making it clear to individuals what they are paying for and what they may expect to obtain as benefits. It is one way of implementing the transfers to individuals proposed by Norrie (this volume). Such a scheme would also significantly reduce entanglement between levels of governments. An IESA system would account for high transaction costs by being compulsory with centralized government collection and decentralized management of assets. It would do away with moral hazard and adverse selection since each individual would benefit according to contributions. It would correct for myopic saving behaviour for retirement purposes. It would allow income redistribution by governments should they wish to do some. They would do away with unfunded CPP/QPP and WCB plans and promote self-reliance. Benefits would vary in real terms across individuals, in part as a result of their region of residence. IESA should be introduced as of a given date and apply fully for Canadians aged 18 at that time, not at all for those aged 45+, and in an inversely proportional age ratio for those in between.

CONCLUSION

This chapter examined various dimensions of the distribution of income and of poverty, reviewed past and present arrangements in the field of income security, recalled the rationale for government intervention in income security, assessed the challenges faced by income support programs in Canada, and presented some choices. Our main conclusion is that there is little interaction between the federal and provincial governments in this field, but that it would be appropriate to have a single government responsible for income support for employables. This could be achieved by a federal abandonment of CAP, something that may force a more realistic attitude towards labour mobility within Canada.

NOTES

Revised version of a paper prepared for the *Conference on the Future of Fiscal Federalism*, Queen's University, 4-5 November 1993. The author thanks Keith Banting and Doug Brown for useful comments on a first version, and Stéphane Fortin for able research assistance.

1. Poverty is defined using the low-income cut-off lines of Statistics Canada which, notwithstanding that organization's denials, have by now become the measure of poverty in Canada. Other measures would yield higher (Canadian Council of Social Development) or lower (Sarlo) levels of poverty.
2. For example, Osberg *et al.* show that "unemployment insurance payments in Canada are an important source of stability in the distribution of income among

Canadian men ... substantially reducing the inequality of annual incomes." (1993, p. 42)

3.   An issue that is rarely raised is: Who should receive the payment for the children? Traditionally, it has been the mother, but in the area of charter rights and sexual equality, one may well ask the question why it is not divided equally between the two parents (guardians)? Phipps and Burton present evidence on spending patterns within families that indicates that this may matter (1992).

BIBLIOGRAPHY

Banting, K. (1985), "Universality and the Development of the Welfare State," in *Report of the Forum on Universality and Social Policies in the 1990s*, ed. A. Green and N. Olewiler, Kingston: John Deutsch Institute, Queen's University.

Beach, C. and G. Slotsve (1994), "Polarization of Earnings in the Canadian Labour Market," in *Stabilization, Growth and Distribution: Linkages in the Knowledge Era,* ed. T.J. Courchene, Kingston: John Deutsch Institute for the Study of Economic Policy, Queen's University.

Blank, R.M. and M.J. Hanratty (1993), "Comparison of Social Safety Nets in Canada and the U.S.," in *Small Differences That Matter*, eds. D. Card and R.B. Freeman, Chicago: NBER.

Boadway, R. and D. Wildasin (1984), *Public Sector Economics*, Toronto: Little Brown.

Courchene, T.J. (1987), *Social Policy in the 1990s: Agenda for Reform*, Toronto: C.D. Howe Institute.

_____ (1993), "Path Dependency, Positive Feedback and Paradigm Work: A Schumpeterian Approach to the Social Order," in *Income Security in Canada: Changing Needs, Changing Means*, Montreal: Institute for Research on Public Policy.

Cousineau, J.M. (1993), *La pauvreté et l'État. Pour un nouveau partage des compétences en matière de sécurité sociale*, Montréal: Institute for Research on Public Policy.

Fluet, C. and P. Lefebvre (1992), "La sécurité du revenu," in *Le Québec en jeu*, ed. G. Daigle, Montreal: PUM.

Fortin, B. and P. Lanoie (1992), "Substitution Between Unemployment Insurance and Workers' Compensation: An Analysis Applied to the Risk of Workplace Accidents," *Journal of Public Economics*, 49(3): 287-312.

Green, D.A. and W.C. Riddell (1993), "The Economic Effects of Unemployment Insurance in Canada: An Empirical Analysis of UI Disentitlement," *Journal of Labor Economics*, 11, 1, 2: S96-S147.

Hobson, P. and F. St-Hilaire (1993), "Rearranging Federal-Provincial Fiscal Arrangements: Toward Sustainable Federalism," Montreal: Institute for Research on Public Policy.

Jenness, R. and M. McCracken (1993), *Ontario and the Canada Assistance Plan*, Toronto: Ministry of Intergovernmental Affairs/Informetrica.

Johnson A.W. (1987), "Social Policy in Canada: The Past as it Conditions the Present," in *The Future of Social Welfare Systems in Canada and the United Kingdom*, ed. S.B. Seward, Ottawa: Institute for Research on Public Policy.

Kesselman, J.R. (1983), *Financing Canadian Unemployment Insurance*, Toronto: Canadian Tax Foundation.

Lam, N. (1993), "Fully Funded versus Pay-As-You-Go: A Projection of the Canada Pension Plan into the Future," in *Reforming the Public Pension System in Canada: Retrospect and Prospect*, Victoria: Centre for Public Sector Studies, University of Victoria.

Norrie K. (1993), "Intergovernmental Transfers in Canada: An Historical Perspective on Some Current Policy Choices," in *A Partnership in Trouble, Renegotiating Fiscal Federalism*, ed. P.M. Leslie, K. Norrie and I.Ip, Toronto: C.D. Howe Institute.

Osberg, L., S. Erpsay and S. Phipps (1993), "Unemployment, Unemployment Insurance and the Redistribution of Income in Canada in the 1980s: Provincial Results," Working Paper 93-07, Halifax: Department of Economics, Dalhousie University.

Phipps, S.A. and P.S. Burton (1992), "What's Mine Is Yours? The Influence of Male and Female Incomes on Patterns of Household Expenditure," Working Paper 92-12, Halifax: Department of Economics, Dalhousie University.

Picot, G., J. Myles and T. Wannell (1990), "Good Jobs/Bad Jobs and the Deciding Middle: 1967-1986," Statistics Canada, Analytical Studies Branch, R.P. 28, Ottawa: Supply and Services Canada.

Podoluk, J.R. (1968), *Incomes of Canadians,* Ottawa: Dominion Bureau of Statistics.

Prince, M. (1993), "Historical Analysis of Public Pension Schemes in Canada," in *Reforming the Public Pension System in Canada: Retrospect and Prospect*, Victoria: Centre for Public Sector Studies, University of Victoria.

Rashid, A. (1993), "Seven Decades of Wage Changes," *Perspectives*, Summer.

Statistics Canada (1971), *Income Distribution by Size in Canada*, Ottawa: Supply and Services Canada.

_____ (1986), *Income After Tax Distribution by Size in Canada*, Ottawa: Supply and Services Canada.

_____ (1991), *Income Distribution by Size in Canada*, Ottawa: Supply and Services Canada.

Treff, K. (1993), "Government Expenditures on Agriculture," *Canadian Tax Journal*, (41)2: 404-420.

Vaillancourt, F. (1985), "Income Distribution and Economic Security in Canada. An Overview," in *Income Distribution and Economic Security in Canada*, ed. F. Vaillancourt, Toronto: University of Toronto Press.

_____ (1991), "The Division of Powers in Canada: Theory, Evidence and Proposals for Québec," in *Economic Dimensions of Constitutional Change*, ed. R. Boadway, T.J. Courchene and D. Purvis, Kingston: John Deutch Institute, Queen's University.

_____ (1993), "The Financing and Pricing of WCBs in Canada: Existing Arrangements, Possible Changes," mimeo.

Comment: Social Policy in Winter

Susan D. Phillips

Rethinking and major restructuring, rather than minor tinkering of all of our social programs are on the agenda and, given the magnitude of the reforms that are envisioned, it is useful to revisit some first principles. While the criteria for situating fiscal federalism on a sound public finance foundation have already been well established in the literature (Ip 1993; Maslove 1992; Norrie 1993; Boadway and Flatters, this volume), it is important in assessing the feasibility of the recommendations made by Vaillancourt not to lose sight of the public policy principles specific to income security programs.

The basic premise of government expenditures on social policy that is redistributive in nature is to ensure national equity and some minimum standard of uniformity among individual Canadians (Norrie, this volume). But these individuals, as individuals, are not uniform: rather, they vary by gender, age, class, and place. For this reason, income security programs must encompass at least three basic principles: (a) intergenerational solidarity, (b) gender equity, and (c) interregional sharing. The contribution of Vaillancourt's chapter to the social policy debate is that his empirical analysis of income distribution demonstrates that these first principles are not well served by the current programs.

INTERGENERATIONAL SOLIDARITY

The long-term viability of social policy depends upon the willingness of the working age generation to support their elders once they retire from labour force participation *and* upon the responsibility of the retiring generation to provide the opportunities for them to do so by passing on favourable economic conditions and not overburdening them with debt. The dilemma of the 1990s is that for the first time the elderly are better off than the young (see also Courchene this volume). As the data presented by Vaillancourt illustrate, there has been a significant reduction of poverty among the over 65 age group, in part as a result of the income-tested Guaranteed Income Supplement (GIS) in combination with the Old Age Security (OAS) and the Canada and Quebec Pension Plans (CPP/QPP), while there has been a sharp rise in poverty and unemployment in the 15-24 age group.[1] One inherent problem in elderly benefits is related to the aging population and demographics alone will place even more onerous demands on the younger generation as the glut of now middle-aged baby boomers reaches retirement age. For example, as a recent study by Lam, Prince and Cutt (1993, p. 52) on pension reform notes, contribution rates to the CPP will need to rise to 16 percent for those just entering the labour force (compared to a rate of 3.6 to 5 percent for current contributors) in order to enjoy the same real benefits.

In examining the root problem of escalating costs for support of the older generation, Vaillancourt presents the issue as one of myopia — that people are too shortsighted to save sufficiently for their own retirement. His solution is an insurance-based forced savings plan (Individual Economic Security Accounts) that would require people to save as soon as they earn income from any source and that would be based solely on individual contributions. These accounts would provide retirement income based on rates sufficient to ensure real benefits of 50 percent of retirement wage and could also be used as income security savings, allowing withdrawals to support periods of unemployment, maternity or study leave. However, the reason that people face retirement with inadequate savings to be self-sufficient is seldom due solely to myopia; rather it relates to inadequate income from which to save as a result of marginal, part-time and interrupted labour force participation so that continuous CPP/QPP and other occupational pension plan contributions could not be sustained to ensure a living wage in retirement. The growing class divide that results from the segregation of the labour market into "good" versus low-wage service sector jobs (that seldom provide lucrative occupational pension plans) will only erode the capacity of a large segment of the population, especially women, to provide for themselves adequately through insurance-based public or private pension plans. The changing patterns of work suggest that neither privatization to an entirely insurance type system, nor to RRSPs using public funding through the regressive and expensive system of tax expenditures, will obviate the need for some kind of income security programs for those unable to make sufficient contributions over four decades of full-time employment.

As Vaillancourt notes, the field of benefits for seniors is not one in which a realignment of responsibility would bring significant rationalization or improve the level or coverage of benefits. The public policy issues lie in the programs themselves, not with constitutional jurisdiction over them and there remains a sound rationale for a strong federal presence. It is feasible, Lam and colleagues (1993) suggest, to convert the CPP into a fully funded system that would provide higher levels of benefits without unduly high contribution rates. A related concern that will have to be addressed, as Vaillancourt notes, is the growing reliance on disability benefits under the provincial WCBs to ease out older workers in their last few years of employment which has created enormous strains on these funds. But one of the most difficult issues in this area is how to balance the public and private systems and, in particular, to determine the extent to which tax expenditures should be used to provide incentives for private savings. Of course, the flip side of promoting intergenerational solidarity is to reduce the long-term debt and enhance the employment and income prospects for the younger generation through investment in training programs, reformed UI and social assistance programs, sufficient immigration to offset a declining birth rate and full employment strategies.

GENDER EQUITY

The gender equity principle is simply that social policy should not disadvantage citizens on the basis of gender. However, perhaps the most dramatic finding of Vaillancourt's analysis is that poverty is highly gendered: the poverty rate for female single-parent families is 47.8 percent compared to only 16.4 percent for their male-headed counterparts.[2] Both the number and jurisdiction of income support programs for families are diverse and, depending upon personal circumstances, may include: cost-shared CAP; federally regulated UI; federal and provincial income tax measures (including federally, the Child Tax Benefit and its earned income supplement, Child Care Expense Deduction and Equivalent-to-Married credit); subsidies for child care (provided on an income-tested basis under CAP), and provincial enforcement of child support payments by non-custodial parents. One of the most popular proposals raised in this volume is to devolve CAP (and possibly UI) to the provinces through tax points in a similar manner to the tax room that was transferred under Established Programs Financing (EPF) in 1977 to replace existing cost-shared programs. The rationale is related to enhancing the autonomy and accountability of the provinces in their own jurisdiction and the desire to create a comprehensive guaranteed annual income program.[3]

While the public finance arguments for such a devolution may be compelling, it is important to consider the policy and political arguments and, thus it may be instructive to compare this proposal with the creation of EPF. One of the reasons that EPF is called *established* programs financing is that the existing cost-shared programs related to hospitals and postsecondary education were relatively mature and autonomous programs by the late 1970s and the benefits to the federal government of a block grant greatly exceeded the administrative costs of maintaining control through direct cost-sharing, although the imposition of the *Canada Health Act* in 1984 suggests that the federal government's perspective on provincial accountability relative to health care changed somewhat.[4] In spite of its almost 30-year history, is CAP an established program in the same sense, meaning that there is relatively little change in delivery system that the federal government would want to be able to influence? I would argue that it is not, especially if we consider the gender equity issue.

First, one of the reasons that demand for social assistance under CAP grew so significantly in the late 1980s and 1990s is that Canada is undergoing an extended period of structural adjustment. Therefore, issues related to labour market strategies, social assistance (including disincentives to work), tax measures, training, and UI need to be examined as a package. Adjustment is predominantly a national issue and labour markets are becoming more national, not more local. Therefore, if we devolve CAP and UI to the provinces in the near future, we will foreclose on the opportunity to examine the bigger picture.

Second, there are several key pieces missing from family income support. One is a national child-care program tied to labour market policy. While the federal government's enthusiasm for such a program has waned due to the focus under both the Conservatives and the Liberals on debt reduction, it may become a more viable political issue if we look at inaccessibility of child care (due to both supply and cost factors) as an impediment to the entry of women to training programs or to the transition from social assistance to the work force (National Council of Welfare, 1993).[5] If we devolve CAP to the provinces now, it is unlikely that there will ever be a national child-care strategy. The other component that is missing from a truly "established" social assistance program is a nationally enforceable system of child support orders to enable custodial single parents to collect from "deadbeat" ones — who, statistically speaking, are mainly dads (Moscovitch 1993).

Although Vaillancourt's favoured position is that the full responsibility for welfare, unemployment insurance and disability rest with the provinces, his default position is that the federal government abolish CAP and extend UI benefits as welfare for employables, although the details on this are sketchy. Non-employables would be dealt with under disability (WCB), pensions and OAS/GIS, or as children under the tax system. But what would happen to single mothers and their families under this scheme? Does one simply assume they could get jobs (without training or money to pay for child care)? If they had not contributed to UI, could they access its extended benefits? Vaillancourt, like many other scholars of fiscal federalism (Courchene, this volume), would like to see support for children separated from adult or family benefits in order to better address Canada's high rate of child poverty. Ottawa would have responsibility for the welfare of children (and seniors) while the provinces would focus on adults. Although this sounds like a neat division of labour and may work providing that the child benefits are sufficiently generous, it seems to ignore the social ecology of family life. Probably the best way to enhance the well-being of children is to improve the income, training, and employment prospects of their parents.

While there may be no inherent reason not to devolve CAP funding at some point, I would argue that the timing at present is wrong. In an extended period of adjustment with a more integrated north-south economy and growing class divisions, there is good reason to take seriously Courchene's (1993) argument that social policy is the east-west glue for the country. This is not to say that CAP and other income support programs should not be touched or that there is no case for greater devolution of delivery; on the contrary, rethinking of the entire package of transfers is essential and many provinces are already engaged in innovative schemes to redesign their own welfare systems.[6] But, devolution alone or the mere separation of benefits on the basis of age of the recipient without a fundamental reexamination would be ill-timed and inadequate.

INTERREGIONAL SHARING

The third principle of social policy in a federation is that there will be some cross-regional sharing of wealth so as to mitigate the differences between the have and have-not areas of the country. This is, of course, the foundation for the formal Equalization Program and the equalization components of other fiscal federalism arrangements. My point is not to revisit the equalization issues which have already been discussed at length elsewhere in this volume, but to argue that the rethinking of social, labour market, and economic policy needs to consider more explicitly the urban dimension as part of interregional sharing. There are two reasons for this.

First, the data on income distribution (not addressed by Vaillancourt) show that, while there has been a slight nationwide decline in the incidence of poverty over the past two decades, its geographical distribution has changed resulting in a "metropolitization" of poverty (Lithwick and Coulthard 1993). Whereas in 1965, over 22 percent of the poor resided in cities over 500,000, that figure had risen to 56 percent by 1990 with an offsetting decline in poverty in small urban and rural areas.[7] This is a product not only of the ongoing industrial restructuring, especially in manufacturing, of urban areas, but of the heavy costs of geographic mobility and social dislocation borne by metropolitan areas. Increased migration, whether from Somalia or St. John's, tends to lead to Toronto (or Montreal or Vancouver), not Kingston or Kapuskasing. Many scholars would assume that this urban concentration of poverty should not be an issue in the discussion of fiscal federalism because municipalities are creatures of the provinces and because benefits flow to individuals and to municipal governments from the provinces in relation to aggregate need. However, a portion of the costs of urban poverty are borne indirectly through the education system (as additional costs related to language training for new immigrants, nutrition programs etc.) and thus are paid for not by general tax revenues, but by the less progressive property tax system.[8] My point is that the issues of poverty obviously are not uniform across the country; although urban poverty has become more acute and is being borne disproportionately by urban taxpayers, it is not yet addressed extensively in national debates.

The second reason that more attention needs to be given to urban regions in discussions of fiscal federalism relates to the new economic and social order described by Courchene (1993; this volume), among others. In a globalized, post-fordist economy, it is international cities, rather than nation states that are in direct competition for investment, footloose high-tech industries and knowledge workers. Private as well as government investment in infrastructure and in human capital increasingly will be directed towards urban regions. But, because our system of fiscal federalism is designed to deal with provinces, not cities, some reconceptualization of the principle of interregional sharing and rethinking of specific programs will be required.

CONCLUSIONS

The essence of Vaillancourt's proposals is to shift most of our existing social policies into *insurance*, rather than income *security* programs, and to devolve responsibility for social assistance and labour market strategies to the provinces. If it would not appear to be invoking too much of the "female voice," I would be tempted to call these proposals cold-hearted. Instead, I will suggest that they are like a hot sports car in an Ottawa winter: striking, but for the most part, unworkable. The recommendations are unworkable in my view because, while income support programs must be significantly redesigned for a variety of reasons and it is entirely appropriate to assume that citizens have responsibilities (as well as rights) for their own well-being, there undoubtedly will always be the need for programs of last resort and redistribution so that those who have had only marginal labour force participation will have some support. In the enthusiasm to devolve responsibility for social assistance, UI, training, and labour market policy to the provinces to comply with public finance principles, we risk overlooking political rationales and imperatives. On one hand, there are strong demands by the provinces, especially Quebec, to have such powers and we need to look seriously at accommodating decentralization and asymmetry in many policy fields. But, on the other hand, in times of major social, economic, and political adjustment, there is a political argument to be made for maintaining the federal government's presence in at least some social policy fields as glue for the nation.

NOTES

1. Elderly benefits are overwhelmingly a federal responsibility using a combination of three types of publicly-funded programs: (a) insurance-based Canada Pension Plan (CPP) which accommodates asymmetry with a separate plan for Quebec; (b) income security under the universal, but clawed-back Old Age Security (OAS) and the supplemental Guaranteed Income Supplement (GIS), and (c) tax expenditures to younger individuals to encourage private investment in RRSPs. In addition, there is a large private retirement income system through the occupational and private pensions plans (Banting 1987, pp. 19-25).

2. Women over 65 are also more likely than men over 65 to live in poverty due to less adequate pensions and the simple fact that women are more likely to out-live their spouses. However, due to space limitations, this brief comment focuses only on single mothers and family support.

3. The 1993 report of the Ontario Fair Tax Commission presents an interesting argument against a guaranteed annual income program, but this discussion is beyond the scope of this brief summary.

4. I am indebted to Martin Abrams for suggesting this line of argument.

5. One of the recommendations of the 1993 report of the Ontario Fair Tax Commission is that if Ontario were to gain control over its personal income tax system through amendments to the federal-provincial Tax Collection Agreements, it should eliminate the child-care expense deduction and use the revenue in direct program spending for child care.

6. Boadway and Flatters argue in this volume that there is no strong rationale for maintaining CAP on a cost-shared basis, in part because the federal government is at the mercy of the provinces who regulate the nature and thus establish the cost of their welfare systems. However, in the past few years, the focus of most provinces has been on cost-cutting and rationalization of their own social assistance programs, not in creating more expensive systems in response to 50 cent dollars (and due to the cap on CAP in Ontario, Alberta and B.C. these provinces now pay much more than 50 percent of CAP).

7. Lithwick and Coulthard argue that this does not merely reflect increased urbanization (1993, pp. 264-265); even as a percentage of low income in each population category, metropolitan poverty is the only population category that has risen since 1965.

8. In Ontario, 20 percent of the provinces' share of general welfare programs are paid for by upper tier government, directly out of property taxes. Due to the variability and inequities of the residential tax system, the Ontario Fair Tax Commission recommended transferring the funding of both education and general welfare to general provincial revenues from the residential tax system.

BIBLIOGRAPHY

Banting, K.G. (1987), *The Welfare State and Canadian Federalism*, 2d. ed., Kingston and Montreal: McGill-Queen's University Press.

Courchene, T.J. (1993), "Mon pays, c'est l'hiver: Reflections of a Market Populist," *Canadian Journal of Economics*, 4: 759-91.

Ip, I.K. (1993), "Putting a New Face on Fiscal Federalism," in *Partnership in Trouble: Renegotiating Fiscal Federalism*, ed. P.M. Leslie, K. Norrie and I.K. Ip, Toronto: C.D. Howe Institute.

Lam, N., M. Prince and J. Cutt (1993), *Reforming the Public Pension System in Canada: Retrospect and Prospect*, Victoria: Centre for Public Sector Studies, University of Victoria.

Lithwick, N.H. and R. Coulthard (1993), "Devolution and Development: The Urban Nexus," in *How Ottawa Spends: A More Democratic Canada...?* ed. S.D. Phillips, Ottawa: Carleton University Press.

Maslove, A. (1992), "Reconstructing Fiscal Federalism," in *How Ottawa Spends 1992-93: The Politics of Competitiveness*, ed. F. Abele, Ottawa: Carleton University Press.

Moscovitch, A. (1993), "Fiscal Federalism for the 21st Century: The Canada Assistance Plan," paper presented to the "Seminar on Fiscal Federalism" sponsored by the Caledon Institute, Ottawa.

National Council of Welfare (1993), *Incentives and Disincentives to Work*, Ottawa: National Council of Welfare.

Norrie, K. (1993), "Intergovernmental Transfers in Canada: An Historical Perspective on Some Current Policy Choices," in *A Partnership in Trouble: Renegotiating Fiscal Federalism*, ed. P.M. Leslie, K. Norrie and I.K. Ip, Toronto: C.D. Howe Institute.

Ontario Fair Tax Conunission (1993), *Fair Taxation in a Changing World*, Toronto: University of Toronto Press.

PART FOUR

COMPARATIVE VIEWS

CHAPTER NINE

A Comparative Perspective on Federal Finance

Richard M. Bird

INTRODUCTION

Economists tend, as a rule, to approach issues of federal finance from a normative perspective, deducing from first principles what fiscal system would be "ideal" from the perspective of individual citizens, on the assumption that governments are benevolently concerned to maximize the economic well-being of their citizens.[1] Even economists working in the "public choice" tradition, who assume that politicians and officials are less concerned with the general welfare than with their own, often discuss the design of federal fiscal institutions primarily from the normative perspective of their ability to constrain the presumed rapacity of the political classes.[2] Such normative analysis may provide a useful standard of reference for assessing federal finance, provided one accepts its underlying assumptions as either ethically compelling, or descriptive of reality in a particular country, or perhaps both. As a rule, however, the normative approach alone provides little assistance either in understanding why particular fiscal institutions exist in any federal country or in evaluating the likelihood, or even the desirability, of changes in such institutions.

One reason for the lack of convergence between theoretical analysis and institutional reality is that the former, for the most part, concerns "fiscal federalism" rather than "federal finance." In fiscal federalism, jurisdictional boundaries and responsibilities (tax and expenditure assignment, for example) are generally assumed to be costlessly variable, distributional concerns are focused on individuals and dominated by the central government, and the maintenance of a national common market is taken as a *sine qua non*. This situation lends itself to a principal-agent framework of analysis and implies, for example, that subnational access to source-based taxes should be restricted and that, on the whole, intergovernmental transfers should be conditional (Bird 1993). The first, if not the second, of these conclusions is common to most economic discussions of fiscal federalism.[3]

In contrast, in what I shall call a "truly federal" state, altering jurisdictional boundaries or assignments is seldom an easily accessible policy instrument; rather it is a constraint that can be altered only with considerable cost and difficulty.[4] Moreover, different distributional and other policy objectives may be legitimately pursued by both levels of government, with no necessary presumption that federal concerns should dominate even with respect to the unity of the internal common market.[5] This "federal finance" perspective suggests that the appropriate analytical framework is not a principal-agent one but rather one of negotiation among equals — in the classic words of Wheare (1963, p. 10) among federal and state governments that are "each, within a sphere, co-ordinate and independent."[6] As yet, however, the theoretical analysis of federal finance, as defined here, is not sufficiently developed to draw very strong conclusions about either the efficacy or the efficiency of particular federal fiscal institutions.[7]

The alternative approach of comparative institutional analysis may perhaps prove to be more immediately useful. At the very least, a comparative approach may help correct the apparent belief of many citizens in most federal countries that there must be a simple solution to be found somewhere else in the world that could replace the seemingly unending complexity and negotiation characterizing federal financial arrangements in their own country. In reality, there is, and can be, no such solution. Federalism is a complex multidimensional phenomenon, whose specific features depend largely upon the particular context in question. As one of the leading authorities on comparative federal studies has noted: "Federation might best be understood in terms of the problems to which it has constituted a set of historically varying answers. If we understand the problems, the understanding of structure more clearly follows."[8]

In these terms, much may be learned from studying how different federal countries arrange their fiscal affairs: the solutions reached in each may be very different, depending on the local context, but the basic problems faced are likely to be similar. A comparative approach cannot yield any clear prescription as to what should be done at any particular time in any particular country. Nonetheless, it may be illuminating both to see how different countries have dealt with similar problems and to attempt to understand the principal factors that seem to have determined both what has been done and what the effects have been in different settings.

SETTING THE STAGE

The present chapter is in this tradition.[9] Analysis of different practices in different countries is one of the few ways in which information on the effects and properties of different fiscal institutions may be obtained. In this regard, however, it is important to distinguish between decentralization and federation. Decentralization is in the air everywhere these days. Whether one looks at the developing countries of Latin America, Asia, or Africa, the transitional countries of Eastern Europe, or the developed OECD countries, decentralization is being advocated (or at least discussed) as a possible cure for many of the ills afflicting the country in question.[10] It should not be surprising that the economic literature on fiscal federalism is being drawn on for guidance in determining whether, and how, various forms of a decentralist solution may work. And indeed, as I have argued elsewhere, in the circumstances of many countries this literature may provide some help in this respect (Bird 1993).

As suggested above, however, it is less clear that there is much to be learned from this literature so far as what may be called "truly federal" — as opposed to formally federal — countries are concerned. Fortunately for economists, there are surprisingly few truly federal countries in the world: Silverman (1992), for example, lists only 17 formally federal countries. Ten of these, however, are developing countries, only two of which (India and Brazil) appear to be truly federal in the sense I use the term: that is, countries in which both central and state governments not only have formally independent powers but use them in practice.[11] Comparative analysis of federal finance must thus focus on these two countries and on the seven developed federations — Austria, Germany, Switzerland, Canada, the United States, Australia, and — since 1993, Belgium.[12]

There are, of course, wide variations among even the developed country federations, although all have high incomes and are relatively stable democracies. Four of them are relatively compact, densely-populated neighbouring countries in Europe, while the remaining three are sprawling, continent-sized countries, two in North America and one isolated in the South Pacific. One (Belgium) is brand-new; two (Germany and Austria) are post-World War II creations; three (Australia, Canada, and Switzerland) have been around for at least this century; and the last (the United States) is the orginator of federal government as we know it. Two (Canada and Australia) have parliamentary systems with little effective state representation at the central government level; the others, in different ways, have effective regional representation at the central level. Three (Belgium, Switzerland, and Canada) have important, regionally-based minority language groups; the others are more homogeneous.

Even within the small developed country sample there are thus a considerable variety of physical, demographic, political, historical, and economic characteristics.

Similarly, the two developing country federations considered briefly here, Brazil and India, are also very different, with Brazil perhaps most closely resembling the United States in its formal political structure as well as its relative cultural homogeneity and India being closer to Canada both in terms of cultural heterogeneity and its parliamentary form of government. On the other hand, the degree of regional income disparity is much greater in both Brazil and India, especially the former, than in any developed federation. Finally, the importance of municipalities in Brazil and the strong direct links between municipal and central government there are quite different from the situation in India.

Some years ago, while discussing a related topic, I suggested that there were two views of federations (Bird 1984*a*, n. 12). To keep my analogy palatable, without following the usual layer cake versus marble cake comparison, I labelled them the "Balkan" and "Swiss" varieties (thinking of yoghurt, where Balkan refers to unmixed and Swiss to mixed ingredients). At the time, I thought this was a clever play on words, since I was essentially arguing that a relatively loose and decentralized federal structure may sometimes be needed to produce Swiss-like stability in a heterogeneous country, while others seemed to see moves in this direction as a prelude to the dreaded "balkanization" (witness the disaster of former Yugoslavia!) of whatever they happened to care about. Subsequent reflection on both the nature of federations and the nature of yoghurt, however, leads me to conclude that this analogy is both inappropriate and inadequate. Its inappropriateness is obvious: after all, Switzerland is the premier example of what may be called an *unmixed* federation! So is its inadequacy: there are not just two varieties of federation; in fact, there are as many varieties as there are federations.

This point may be worth elaborating. Recently, a colleague asked me what I was working on. When told "a paper on federal finance," his immediate reaction, as a well-trained economist, was to ask: "what are your stylized facts?" I tell this little story because, in my view, one reason economists have had difficulty in dealing with issues of federal finance is precisely because there is no one set of stylized facts that tells the essential story. Federations differ in many dimensions: How many states are there? What are their relative sizes in terms of population and economic activity? How different are they in terms of per capita income? Natural resource wealth? What is the historical origin of the federation: bottom up or top down? peaceful or violent? What is its geography: compact or disperse? How homogeneous is the federation: in terms of language? ethnic groups? unifying cultural myths? To what extent do state boundaries coincide with heterogeneity in any of these dimensions? Are regional interests explicitly represented in the central political structure? How?

The answers to these and other questions shape both the nature and working of federal institutions, including fiscal institutions, so it is not surprising that it is difficult to find a set of stylized facts to represent adequately the diversity in these dimensions found in the world's few working federal countries. Each country is a separate reality and may be forced into a comparative framework only by sacrificing some of its essential flavour. Indeed, if one must, for some reason, compare federal finance to some form of food, I now think the best analogy is not to either cake or yoghurt but to ice cream — with 7, or 10, or 17, or perhaps even 31 distinct varieties on offer. Variety may be the spice of life, but it obviously makes it difficult for a brief review of a few aspects of a very diverse set of countries to reach persuasive general conclusions. Nonetheless, two general lessons do seem to emerge fairly clearly from even a superficial comparative look at some issues in federal finance.

The first such lesson is that since every federal country is both unique and in some sense constitutes an organic unity, the significance of any particular component of its federal finance system — for example, the assignment of taxes or the design of intergovernmental transfers — can only be understood in the context of the system as a whole. One cannot pick an institution from a specific setting, plant it in the alien soil of another environment, and expect to obtain the same results. Policy recommendations on intergovernmental fiscal relations must be firmly rooted in understanding of the underlying rationale of the existing intergovernmental system and its capacity for change if they are to be acceptable or, if accepted, successfully implemented. What is feasible and desirable in any particular setting depends very much upon what that setting is, and why it is that way. One size does not fit all: simple general pronouncements (even if I make them!) — e.g., that unconditional transfers are better (or worse) than conditional ones or that income taxes should always be assigned to central governments — are worse than useless as a guide to policy: they may be positively dangerous.

The second lesson I draw is rather different. It is that in the end what is more important and interesting than the precise nature of the technical solutions found to even universal problems in the different countries are the process and procedures through which such solutions are reached (Wiseman 1987; Dafflon 1977; Bird 1986a). The final section of the chapter returns to this point. First, however, I shall illustrate the first "lesson" mentioned, the need to consider each fiscal institution in context, by considering briefly what international comparisons suggest about some aspects of three of the basic fiscal problems faced in all federations: vertical balance, equalization, and tax coordination.

VERTICAL BALANCE: CLOSING THE FISCAL GAP

Two types of imbalance are frequently distinguished in discussions of federal finance. "Vertical fiscal imbalance" — or the "fiscal gap" — refers to differences between expenditures and revenues at each jurisdictional level. This concept focuses on the general assignment of expenditure and revenue functions to levels of government. In contrast, "horizontal fiscal imbalance" — often called "equalization" — focuses on differences in revenue or expenditure levels within a particular level of government. It is thus concerned with regional disparities, particularly in terms of the provision of public services.

A classic view of federal finance is that in principle "both general and regional governments must each have under its own independent control financial resources sufficient to perform its exclusive functions" (Wheare 1963, p. 93). Fiscal balance in this sense requires that state governments be assigned sufficient separate and independent revenue sources to permit them to finance the expenditures for which they are responsible without recourse to federal transfers. Only thus can states both be fully autonomous — in the sense of deciding, within their constitutionally allotted sphere, what they do — and also fully accountable to their citizens for their actions.

This argument continues to appeal to many. A 1977 report to the European Community, for example, emphasized fiscal balance in this sense, arguing that each jurisdiction should ideally have under its control and responsibility sufficient resources to enable it to finance the expenditures for which it is responsible, subject, however, to the important caveat that governments should only be able to levy taxes that burden their own residents.[13] (Commission 1977, vol. 2, p. 481.) More recently, several scholars have argued for a major reassignment of tax powers in Canada on precisely this ground — to "rebalance" federal finances.[14]

The argument begins with a numerical demonstration that at present the federal and provincial fiscal systems in Canada are unbalanced both statically and dynamically. The federal government has for several years had a budgetary surplus with respect to program spending (i.e., excluding debt service), and this surplus seems likely to grow over time. On the other hand, the provinces are currently in deficit on program spending, and their position seems likely to worsen over time given the expected growth rates of provincial revenues and expenditures. This situation arises because provincial governments are responsible for the fastest-growing expenditure areas (notably health) but most of the revenue from the largest, and fastest-growing tax, the personal income tax, goes to the federal government, which then transfers a large (though shrinking) proportion of its "excess" revenues back to the provinces. To rebalance the accounts, one proposal is that the personal income tax should become wholly provincial, while the sales and corporate taxes should in partial exchange become wholly federal, and at the same time most of the present federal-provincial transfers should be abolished.

Canada is of course by no means unique in assigning more tax revenue than expenditure responsibility to the federal government, while leaving state governments with inadequate revenue to finance the expenditures with which they are charged. Indeed, this is the situation in most federal countries: at the end of the 1980s, for example, state revenue in Brazil financed only 67 percent of state expenditure, compared to 75 percent in Canada and close to 90 percent in the United States (Shah 1991).[15] The assignment of taxes and expenditures in different countries may reflect history — perhaps the intentions of the designers of the original constitution, perhaps the accidental development of events over time. Moreover, in more heterogeneous countries in particular there may also be additional political concerns mandating central control over revenue in order to be able to damp down (buy off) potential regional secessionist movements.[16]

The usual "fiscal federalism" analysis assigns more revenues than expenditures to the centre for four reasons: (a) the centre is presumed to be a more efficient tax collector and subnational governments are presumed to be more efficient spenders; (b) fiscal redistribution is assumed to be properly a central concern (so progressive taxes should be levied at that level); (c) subnational governments are likely to distort the common market through fiscal manipulation if given too free a hand (so taxes on corporations and natural resources should also be central); and (d) in any case the central government needs "excess" revenue to carry out its allocative and distributive roles (using inter-governmental transfers both to influence state actions — to achieve "incentive-compatibility" in the current jargon — and to achieve horizontal equity throughout the nation) (see Boadway, Roberts and Shah 1993).

Each of these arguments may of course be questioned. A recent study of Switzerland, for example, suggests that extensive use of personal and corporate income taxes at the state (canton) level has proved compatible with both economic efficiency and a surprising amount of fiscal redistribution.[17] In any case, whatever weight (if any) may have been attached to these various arguments at different times in different countries, vertical fiscal imbalance in the revenues and expenditures of state and federal governments is a fact of life in all federal countries, albeit in differing degrees. Equally invariably, the resulting fiscal gap has been closed by intergovernmental fiscal transfers.

In principle, the gap in state finances could also be closed by (a) moving expenditure functions up to the central (richer) government;[18] (b) moving taxes down to the state (poorer) level; or (c) raising existing state taxes or lowering state expenditures to restore balance. Although the first of these solutions has occurred to some extent in many countries, most attention has been paid in the literature to the second, as noted earlier. Understandably, this approach has not proved very popular either with central governments — who are reluctant to give up the power their "excess" revenue bestows. It may be more surprising that they have not been popular with state governments, who seldom seem eager to accept the responsibility for levying "new" (though not additional) taxes, without any offsetting political gains from being able to expand expenditures. And, of course, even in these deficit-conscious times, no government anywhere is keen to tax more or spend less, as the third alternative to intergovernmental transfers requires.

It is thus not surprising that as a rule vertical fiscal imbalance is dealt with in federations (as in unitary states) by fiscal transfers from central to state (and local) governments, even though the result is almost invariably to break the nexus between expenditure and revenue responsibility and thus to reduce accountability to some, and often a considerable, extent. Even in the United States, where there is no general revenue-sharing or grant system and where state governments have a virtually free hand in levying taxes, federal transfers in the form of conditional grants have in recent years accounted for one-fifth of state-local expenditures: the fiscal gap in this sense is even larger in other federations, notably Australia and India.[19]

Is this a problem? It is, of course, if one thinks that the only way to achieve a satisfactory degree of political accountability in a federal system is, so to speak, by standing every tub on its own bottom, that is, by requiring each level of government to finance its own expenditures from its own taxes. In fact, however, such "tax separation" is not a necessary condition for accountability. All that is required for accountability is that, at the margin, any government that wants to increase its expenditures has to increase *its* taxes (McLure 1993*b*; see also Ip and Mintz 1992). This condition requires only that intergovernmental transfers should not be related to the expenditures of recipients, not that there should be no such transfers. From this perspective — and in contrast to the version of the "fiscal federalism" perspective adopted in Bird (1993*a*)[20] — federal transfers to states should not be conditional on expenditures but should rather be determined in accordance with a formula invariant to actual state expenditures: some other desirable characteristics of such a formula are discussed further in the next section.[21]

EQUALIZATION AND REGIONAL DISPARITY

As a rule, regional redistribution is more explicit, if not necessarily more important, in federal than in unitary states. The regional distribution of industry, employment, and income in any country at any time reflects not only market forces but also past policy decisions by both national and subnational governments. In federal states, regions that have been, or consider themselves to have been, adversely affected by past central policies are often thought by themselves, and sometimes by others, to have a legitimate claim for some form of compensatory payment. Over time, the losers and gainers may shift as the result of the relative decline of traditional industrial areas (the so-called "Rust Belt" in the U.S.) or the rise of new areas as a result of population shifts (the "Sun Belt") or natural resource developments (e.g., the move of Alberta from being one of Canada's poorest provinces to one of its richest). But in most countries, developed or developing, there appears to be a surprising degree of stability over time in regional income disparities.

By definition, federal countries are politically sensitive to such regional differences. Federal policies thus inevitably respond to such disparities, whether explicitly mandated by the constitution (as in Canada or Germany) or not. As a rule, either the poorer regions get larger explicit transfers, or federal decisions on such matters as the location of federal facilities (e.g., military bases) are biased in their direction, or both. Although it is by no means clear why richer areas are willing to go along with such favouritism even when the purely allocative effects of such decisions or transfers are unfavourable, it may be because they see it as the cost of the benefits from being part of a larger economic and political entity.[22] In any case, whether explicitly redistributive or not, to a considerable extent intergovernmental transfers in federal states thus seem best considered as part of a sort of "constitutional contract," under which regions give up certain powers and rights in exchange for transfer payments (Breton and Scott 1978). Transfers are thus one way of maintaining the political status quo in a federal setting — part of the "glue" of nationhood, as indeed has often been remarked in Canada (Courchene 1984).

Viewed in this light, regional transfers are not "subsidies" but rather payments for services rendered, either in the past (e.g., in the creation of the federation) or in the present (e.g., permitting central governments to levy income taxes) or both. Of course, this formulation best suits federations created from diverse and (either historically or potentially) separate political entities (the United States, Canada, Australia, Switzerland, Belgium, India) as opposed to those created, as it were, from above (Germany, Austria, Brazil). Nonetheless, even in the latter countries such a "quasi-constitutional" formulation seems needed to explain why quite large explicit and implicit interregional fiscal flows have so often been accepted with surprisingly little fuss by the "paying" states. At the very least, this line of argument emphasizes that it may be quite misleading to evaluate the regional effects of current policy in any country outside the historical context within which that policy evolved.

In part perhaps for such reasons, assessments of the merits or otherwise of regional transfers based on such marginally relevant (in this context) criteria as the level of national output or even the reduction of regional differentials in per capita income levels have seldom had any visible impact on policy in any country. Regionally redistributive transfers may, for example, be condemned by some as inhibiting economically desirable migration (Courchene 1970). Others, however, may view this result as indicating the success of such transfers: poor states may prefer their residents to stay put for political and prestige reasons while rich states may prefer to keep the poor in poor states rather than to have an influx of migrants.[23] In some countries at least, the continued maintenance of a relatively stable and legitimate nation state may thus depend to some extent upon policies such as intergovernmental transfers, policies that from other perspectives are clear economic losers.

The extent to which different countries exhibit what may be called a "taste" for regionally equalizing fiscal policies depends of course both upon historical experience and current reality. In one of the few examinations of this phenomenon, May (1969) suggested that regional equalization policies might be expected to be strongest either where there are strong "nationalizing" forces and no strong regional conflicts or where there are marked conflicts of interest between units, with — as suggested above — fiscal transfers being used in effect to compensate poorer regions for the supposed adverse effects of other past or present federal policies.

Germany perhaps best illustrates the first of these rationales for equalization. The federal government is constitutionally mandated to legislate as necessary to maintain "uniformity of living conditions" throughout the country (Spahn 1982), and in pursuit of this objective in many respects federal and state governments act as one. The strongly equalizing transfer system is just one aspect of the concern with individual rather than regional equality which underlies German policy. In this as in other respects, Germany (and Austria) are in a sense the least "federal" of federal states.

The second rationale for equalization may be illustrated by Canada, which would clearly be quite a different country if it were not for the critical role of Quebec as a large, relatively poor, and culturally distinct state. In all federations, as May (1969, p. 5) noted in a rather Orwellian comment "some units are more equal than others," and Quebec has certainly fit this bill in Canada. The number, the relative size, the ethnic diversity, and the wealth of the different units comprising a federation may all in principle influence its taste for equalization.[24] In practice, however, the extent of equalization in different countries does not seem to be related in any clear way either to the extent of regional disparities or to any other simple causative factor (see Commission 1977; Mathews 1981). Australia and Germany, for example, the developed country federations with the least degree of regional disparity, appear to be the most concerned with regional fiscal equalization.

As noted above, Germany is exceptional in the extent to which the concern for uniform service provision throughout the country has dominated both revenue sharing and expenditure administration, German (and Austrian) federal finance is intended to ensure that services are delivered on more or less equal terms throughout the country, although the German preference for achieving more or less "unitary" results through a federal structure is currently under severe test as a result of the incorporation of five new, and poor, states following reunification. In contrast, Canadian and Australian federal finance is intended to ensure that all states are given the same capacity to deliver services (at similar costs to state taxpayers), but is much less concerned to ensure that they actually do so. Similar arguments have become increasingly influential in India in recent years (Rao 1993). On the other hand, neither the United States nor Switzerland has an explicit general equalization program, although both incorporate significant equalizing elements into a variety of conditional grant programs.

The Swiss case is particularly interesting. Although a number of rather complicated equalization formulae are employed, their basic purpose is simply to classify the various cantons into "weak" and "strong" (Dafflon 1977; 1991). Over the years, these formulae have frequently been changed, in part it appears in order to produce more or less a constant result in the face of changes in the various factors taken into account in the formulae. As Frey (1976, p. 100) put it: "certain cantons are considered poor, and it is politically impossible to remove them from the group of poor cantons even when their economic situation has improved." Such stability in outcomes appears to be equally important in some other countries also, e.g., Canada where formula changes have usually been intended to yield constant or even increased subsidies to what is almost a pre-defined group of poorer regions.[25]

The point, of course, is that the equalization process is always and inevitably political in all federal countries. Formulae, no matter how elaborate, remain acceptable only so long as their *results* are acceptable. With little exaggeration, in most federal countries it may be said that it is not so much that the distribution of transfers reflects the outcome of a principled formula as that the formula used is the one that produces the desired distribution of transfers. As the intellectual pioneer of equalization formulae in Australia put it half a century ago: "The thing is dressed up in arithmetical terms as much as possible, and that perhaps is politically useful. But it must be admitted that in a good many instances, the actual decision as to how much allowance must be made for this or that depends, not on the strictly arithmetical computation, but on the broad judgement of the Commission as to what is a reasonable figure."[26] He did not add, perhaps because it was so obvious, that the extent to which that judgement is accepted by politicians will by definition depend upon the political acceptability of the outcome.

Despite the enormous professional literature on equalization formulae — see, for example, the discussions of India in Rao and Chelliah (1990) and Canada in Courchene (1984) — in the end regional redistribution in a federal state, whether effected through equalization transfers or in other ways, is always and inevitably the product of a political compromise. This compromise may be rationalized through mathematics, and in turn the mathematics rationalized through (more or less principled) discussion, but the fact remains that there is nothing more political in federations (or elsewhere) than who gets what. It may be desirable for many reasons to establish explicit and agreed equalization formulae for a period of time in order to obviate the undesirable effects of annually negotiating transfers. Thus the regional distribution issue is moved at least temporarily to the "constitutional" as opposed to the "in-period" decision level. But circumstances change, and, as Canada may be about to learn, equalization systems must change with them, or suffer political death or abandonment.

What matters most is thus not the details of any particular formula in place at any particular time but rather who has the power to decide what the formula should be. In this respect, there are at least three distinct models to be found in the world. In Australia and India, although in quite different form, expert commissions established by the federal government are entrusted with the primary task of establishing distributive formulae: these commissions hear representations from the state governments and report to the federal government, which normally follows their recommendations.[27] In contrast, in Germany, Austria, Switzerland, and the United States, grants are established by the federal government, but — again in quite different ways — there are formal state representatives in the federal legislature who must approve them so that state interests are generally well represented in the process. Only in Canada is the determination of the equalization formula under the control of the central government, as indeed are such other important components of federal-provincial fiscal relations as (to a considerable extent) the tax agreements and other transfer programs. It is thus perhaps not surprising that in Canada, more than in other federations, every federal-provincial issue tends to become a matter both for extended discussion between innumerable committees of federal and provincial officials and, often, for public polemics between federal and provincial governments.

The extent of concern with regional disparity and equalization is thus fundamentally a matter to be determined in the political arena. As is well known, in this game many players often find considerable virtue in obscurity and ambiguity. Nevertheless, a strong case can be made for attempting to implement a number of principles in intergovernmental transfer programs. One such principle has already been mentioned: the desirability of adopting relatively stable formulae in order to permit sounder fiscal planning at both levels of government (Bird 1990). Another principle of general applicability is that a good equalization formula should generally incorporate measures of both need and capacity (Bird 1993a), although there are of course many ways in which of these factors may be measured. Other factors may also be important in shaping the observed fiscal flows between governments, e.g., the degree of central interest in the provision of certain regionally-provided services and the need to close the fiscal gap, which may often entail returning some central taxes to the regions from which they are collected. Further discussion of these and the many other complexities that must be taken into account in developing transfer systems cannot be undertaken here, however.

TAX COORDINATION

Federal countries in which states have significant independent taxing power are usually considered to face substantial problems of tax coordination, both vertically (between federal and state governments) and horizontally (among state governments).[28] Different federations have resolved these problems in very different ways. At one extreme, Australia really has no tax coordination problem because — to exaggerate only slightly — the states really have no taxes (see McLure 1993a). They are not allowed to levy sales taxes, and they also do not levy income taxes, essentially because the federal government has pre-empted the field and has shown little interest in making "tax room" for state taxes. Similarly, tax harmonization is not much of an issue in Germany or Austria, although for quite different reasons, essentially because all major taxes are applied uniformly throughout the country, with the proceeds being divided by agreement between the federal and state governments and by formula among the states.

In contrast, in the other federations discussed here, tax harmonization is viewed by many as a serious problem, although again the situation is very different in different countries with respect to different taxes.[29] In Canada, for example, the income tax, both personal and (to a lesser extent) corporate, is basically levied on a common base and collected (for the most part) by a single administration, although each level of government levies its own rates and the proceeds are divided strictly on origin (derivation) lines. In India, the income tax is federal, but most of the personal income tax (which is not very important) is distributed to the states in accordance with the formula established by the finance commission.[30] In Brazil, the income tax is basically federal. In contrast, in both the United States and Switzerland, both state and federal governments levy both corporate and personal income taxes independently.

Concern is often expressed about the possibility of tax competition in the latter two countries (and to a lesser extent in Canada). The conventional fiscal federalism literature also tends to argue strongly for exclusive federal competency with respect to corporate taxes and federal dominance with respect to personal income taxes. In practice, however, there appear to be few serious problems arising in any of these countries from the way income taxes are currently divided.[31] Clearly, the costs of taxation are somewhat higher in a system in which more than one level of government taps the same tax base, but such costs may be considered as part of the overall cost of maintaining a federal system — a system that presumably has its own rationale, even necessity, or it would not exist. Unnecessary costs of collecting taxes should of course be minimized, but not all such costs are necessarily "unnecessary."

With respect to indirect taxes, the situation is equally varied, though probably less stable. In Australia, Switzerland, Austria, and Germany, sales taxes are federal, with the proceeds in Germany and Austria being shared with the states on a formula basis. In the United States, sales taxes are levied by the states (as, in effect, is true in the European Union also, if one wishes to think of it as a nascent federation). But in India, Canada, and Brazil, both levels of government currently levy general sales taxes more or less independently. Brazil has a form of value-added tax (VAT) at both the state and federal level, Canada has a federal VAT and, in most provinces, provincial retail sales taxes, and India has (broadly) manufacturers' sales taxes at both central and state levels. All three countries are currently considering reforms: India is considering adopting a VAT at the central level and is concerned how best to do this (Burgess, Howes and Stern 1993); Canada would like to harmonize its federal VAT with the provincial sales taxes and has encountered substantial provincial opposition in doing so (Bird 1993*b*); and Brazil is considering shifting the VAT solely to the state level (Longo 1993).

Unfortunately, no one has yet managed to work out a technically acceptable system of levying independent sales taxes at two levels of government. Broadly, four possible directions of change seem feasible in the dual sales tax countries. A first option would be to move the sales tax entirely to the state level. Such a system is clearly feasible, at least so long as the tax is levied at the retail stage, as U.S. (and Canadian) experience shows. Unfortunately, considerable experience suggests retail sales taxes are not practicable in developing countries and, for that matter, that high-rate retail sales taxes are difficult to administer in any country.[32] Pre-retail stage taxes may also be levied at the state level, as India and Brazil (like Argentina) demonstrate, but such taxes are clearly less desirable on both economic and administrative grounds. Economically, such taxes undesirably encourage shifting taxes to non-residents, and they are hard to administer on interstate sales without substantial interprovincial cooperation and central support (e.g., the so-called "clearing-house" arrangements that have been discussed — but not implemented in the EU context) (see e.g., Cnossen 1991).

A second option would be to move the sales tax to the federal level, as in Germany. In many ways, this seems the neatest solution: it is obviously technically feasible and would almost certainly substantially reduce compliance costs. In Canada, the revenue loss of such a shift could be compensated for by an increase in provincial personal income taxes (and a corresponding reduction in federal rates), although it is unclear why either level of government would be willing to make such a switch: What do they have to gain by doing so? Given the weakness of the income tax systems in Brazil and India, however, this option is probably not open to them: indeed, there does not seem to be any feasible replacement for sales taxes as the mainstay of state revenue in these countries.

A third option would be for the sales tax to become a joint federal-state tax. Such a tax could be administered by either level of government (although central administration might be better) and state and federal rates should be determined independently, but a common base would have to be agreed. Apart from the fact that the base is federally-determined, the present Canadian personal income tax arrangements illustrate such a system in operation, although it is far from clear that a similar degree of cooperation will be attainable in the sales tax field (Bird 1993b). Moreover, at the technical level, it is by no means certain how the proceeds of a VAT levied on this basis should be divided among states. Suppose, for example, that a product is manufactured in one state A and sold in another, B. In principle, State A imposes its tax on the value-added by the manufacturer and State B its tax on the value-added by the retailer. In fact, however, what happens in an invoice-credit VAT is that the tax is levied on the entire retail price, with the retailer being refunded the tax he paid when he bought the good from the manufacturer. But this would require State B to refund a tax that was actually collected by State A. Clearly, what is at issue here is precisely the problem of VAT coordination discussed by Cnossen (1991). Unfortunately, all the possible solutions he discusses in the European context appear to assume a much higher degree of reliable bookkeeping in the private sector and public trust in the political sector than seems likely in most developing countries (see also Poddar 1990). Since Canada suffers less from the first of these problems than the second, some variant of the "deferred payment" scheme that has now been adopted in the EC may work, although this question cannot be further discussed here.

A fourth, and final, option would be for both levels of government to continue to levy their own sales taxes in a more or less uncoordinated fashion, as now. So long as the perceived political cost of developing a more coherent national sales tax system exceeds the benefits, economic and otherwise, of doing so, one is unlikely to emerge in practice. As and when the costs demand some alternative solution, it may, depending on local circumstances, take the form of one or other of the options mentioned above — the Swiss solution (federal tax), the American solution (state tax), or the German solution (joint tax, with possible variations). Or it may take the form, as presently seems to be emerging in Canada, of asymmetrical agreements in different parts of the country. In Alberta, for example, where there is no provincial sales tax, there is only a federal VAT; in Quebec, the provincial retail sales tax has been altered to a form of VAT, and the provincial government also collects the federal VAT; in five provinces the provincial sales tax is levied (as in Brazil) on a base including the federal VAT, while in four it is levied (at the retail stage) on the same base (retail value excluding tax) as the VAT on goods. Such untidy and costly solutions may be part of the price that has to be paid for the Canadian version of federalism. A neater solution in some ways, though not one popular with tax experts (McLure 1987) might be for the federal VAT to be changed to a one-rate subtraction-type tax levied on an accounts basis (as is the case in Japan for most taxpayers) and administered with the federal income tax, but as yet this option has not been seriously analyzed or considered (see Mintz, Wilson and Gendron 1993; Hill and Rushton 1993). In the end, what (if anything) is done to improve sales tax coordination, in Canada as elsewhere, will depend largely upon how well, and how, the process of federal-provincial decision making works.[33]

CONCLUSION[34]

Indeed, one of the most important themes to emerge from a consideration of fiscal arrangements in a number of federal countries is precisely the central importance of the *process* of federalism, as opposed to the details of its varied products in different settings. The same lesson emerges in many other contexts also. A study of internal barriers to trade within Canada, for example, concluded that the critical factor was how federal-provincial relations were managed (Prichard and Benedickson 1983). A comparative study of political processes in federal states concluded that the essential ingredient was a set of clear procedural rules through which the necessary accommodation between governments could occur (Bakvis 1981). And a pioneering study of federal finance as a process of continual political bargaining similarly emphasized the need to work out detailed rules and policy structures — not to ensure that specifically desired outcomes emerged from the process (as in the usual normative approach) but rather to ensure that those outcomes that did emerge, whatever they may be, were the best possible given the basic constraints within which the federation operates (Dafflon 1977).

As with the various aspects of intergovernmental fiscal arrangements discussed earlier, however, simple comparisons of particular procedural features in different federations seem as likely to obscure as to illuminate reality. Consider Australia and Canada. Each has a similar historical origin from an aggregation of British colonies, and each has a similar parliamentary federal system in which many federal-state problems are resolved by an adversarial interstate approach rather than the intra-state approach that characterizes the very different political institutions in Germany and Switzerland. Each has a small number of states, and is dominated by two large states. They are also roughly similar in many other respects — size, population distribution, and level of economic development, for example. Moreover, they share a similar tradition of evolutionary rather than revolutionary change and play similar roles in the world as middle-sized industrial countries with strong resource bases. The logic of Canada-Australia comparisons seems overwhelming (Mathews 1982). For good or ill, Canadians and Australians often look at each other's experience for possible lessons.

Such looks, however, are fraught with difficulties because in fact there are some very important differences between these two countries, not least in their central federal fiscal institutions. In Australia, for example, both taxes and borrowing are far more centralized than in Canada, and intergovernmental grants are much more important as well as more equalizing in intent and (probably) result. Moreover, regional differences are much less important in Australia than in Canada, even without taking into account the most significant difference between the two countries — the existence of the important and culturally distinct province of Quebec in Canada. The game of territorial politics in Canada is more firmly grounded in socio-economic reality than it is in Australia. Australian federalism to some extent may be argued to have its basis in the simple historical fact that it was founded as a federation. In Canada, in contrast, it may be argued that a relatively loose form of federation is an essential ingredient for its continued existence as a nation state.

Similarly, Germany and Switzerland are countries that are alike in some important respects but differ sharply in others. In both countries, for example, not only are many projects jointly financed by state and federal governments but there is also extensive cooperation between the two levels in carrying out many other tasks. The significance of this "interlocked federalism" (Lehner 1982) is quite different in the two countries, however. In Germany, the result of this interdependence has been that the states have largely lost the capacity — if they ever had the desire — to decide autonomously on policies. On the other hand, in Switzerland, despite the existence of many joint and cooperative activities, the cantons continue to retain and exercise very considerable decision-making powers. Federalism in Switzerland, as in Canada, reflects current reality, while in Germany, as in Australia, in many respects it seems more a matter of history and institutional inertia. Decentralized decision making may be more economically efficient, but in itself it does not require the kind of constitutional barriers to change that characterize federations.

In the developing world, in this respect India seems more like Switzerland — albeit on an enormously larger scale — and Brazil like Germany. India contains almost a billion people living in such a heterogeneous group of states — in language, in religion, in culture, in level of development, and so on — that it is hard to see how it could possibly be governed except as a tight dictatorship (like the old Soviet Union) or a relatively loose federation. In practice, it has oscillated back and forth uneasily between these two poles but has, almost miraculously, managed to survive the vicissitudes of the last 40 years as a democratic state. Although Brazil too is so large and economically diverse that it is not clear that it could be governed, efficiently or otherwise, except in a decentralized fashion, unlike India it is more united by language and culture than divided by it, so it is far less clear that a strong federal system is essential to its survival as a nation state.

Whatever the rationale and the underlying political necessity for federalism in any particular country, a huge load is inevitably thrown on the political bargaining process in all federal countries. Federal-state conflicts, conflicts between rich and poor regions, conflicts between different interests in different states, and (except in Switzerland, with its unique coalition system) conflicts between political parties, must all somehow be accommodated in this process. The nature of the institutions within which such bargaining takes place and the evolution of those institutions thus constitute in many ways the most important characteristics of any federation.

In no country, for example, is the importance of constitutional rules more important than in Switzerland, given the exceptionally detailed nature of the Swiss constitution — which includes, for example, most major tax rates — and its cumbersome amendment procedure, requiring not only a direct popular vote but also a majority of the votes in each separate state. One might think that such a system in a diverse country (with four languages, three ethnic groups, and two religions) would virtually guarantee that no changes will be possible. In reality, however, there have probably been more constitutional amendments in Switzerland than in any of the other developed federations in which such amendments appear to be much easier. No doubt, the detailed nature of the constitution requires more such amendments to cope with changing times, but the fact is that they have been made, and the end result is that neither the growth of government nor its structure is very different in Switzerland from that in its neighbouring countries. If there is any lesson here, it may simply be that the complex Swiss system of achieving an adequate degree of political consensus and support is necessary *in Switzerland*, given its cultural and linguistic diversity, in order to achieve much the same results as in other countries, though usually more slowly.

As noted earlier, in federal countries the continued viability of the component units — the states — is generally considered an important and explicit objective of policy. The form that regional policy takes often provides a good indication of the extent to which the federal system reflects underlying socio-political realities.[35] The greater the value placed, for political or social reasons, on regional survival, the more emphasis is likely to be placed on relatively unfettered regional tax powers supplemented by equalization (as in Switzerland) or relatively unfettered and large transfers to regions (as in Canada and India). In the end, it is factors such as these, together with the institutional structure of decision making, rather than concerns about economic efficiency that have shaped, and no doubt will continue to shape such important aspects of all federations as the assignment of taxing powers, the degree of vertical and horizontal fiscal coordination, and the size and nature of intergovernmental fiscal transfers.

Fiscal arrangements invariably constitute an important component of the federal system in any federal country. Changes in these arrangements reflect, and may sometimes also induce, changes in that system, and the design and analysis of such changes is a proper subject for economic analysis. In the end, however, a federation is invariably a political creation with primarily political ends. The federal finance system existing in any country must therefore be understood and assessed within a political framework. What matters most in federal finance is who determines the rules of the game and how those rules are changed. The most important decisions affecting federal fiscal systems are more likely to be changes in the composition or role of state (provincial) representation in the federal government or the status of any new federal-provincial organs that may emerge than new arrangements for tax coordination or new twists in the equalization formula.

Of course, analysis of such formulae is important, but if such analysis is to play its proper role in the essentially political process of intergovernmental bargaining, what is needed is an institutional framework which welcomes, accommodates, and to the extent possible incorporates such analysis in the process of achieving sufficient consensus in a complex and divided society for decision making. Among the countries discussed here, only Australia and India have such a framework explicitly in place, although neither the Commonwealth Grants Commission nor the periodic finance commissions in India come close to fulfilling the ideal comprehensive and open bargaining framework set out by such authors as Dafflon (1977) and Wiseman (1987).[36] Similar, though even less structured, roles are played by other official, academic, and non-governmental institutions in most federal countries. Those who would improve the economic outcomes of the federal system in their own country would seem well advised to study these examples and to attempt to improve upon them within their local context in order to feed information into the political process and possibly to affect its outcome. In other words, to conclude on a positive note, one conclusion I draw from a comparative perspective on federal finance is that conferences such as this are a Good Thing!

NOTES

An earlier version of much of this paper was presented at the International Symposium on Fiscal Reform, Sao Paulo, Brazil, September 1993. I am grateful to Charles McLure and other participants at the symposium for helpful comments.

1. For classic examples of this approach, see the papers by Gordon (1983) and Musgrave (1983). A more recent example is the excellent review by Boadway, Roberts and Shah (1993).

2. A classic example is Brennan and Buchanan (1980). For a more recent instance, see Migue (1993). Inman and Rubenfeld (1993) make an interesting attempt to combine the standard and public choice approaches, treating political institutions as a constraint and changes in such institutions as a possible means of reform.

3. To illustrate, Boadway, Roberts and Shah (1993), although they argue strongly for what may be called "the decentralist presumption," that government activities should be carried out at the lowest possible level, conclude that subnational access to income taxes in general and source-based taxes in particular should be severely restricted both because of greater central administrative efficiency in taxing mobile factors and because of the assumed need to perfect the internal common

market. The decentralist presumption is obviously similar to the principle of "subsidiarity" which has been increasingly discussed in the European Community in recent years. It is related to, but broader than, the "decentralization theorem" propounded by Oates (1972): see Shah (1993) for further discussion.

4. In many federal countries, this statement applies only to federal-state, not state-local, relations. In some federations, however (e.g., Venezuela) even the state governments are not really autonomous in any real sense; in others (e.g., Brazil) both states and municipalities have substantial degrees of autonomy. The failure to distinguish clearly between the quite different forms of interaction between dependent (principal-agent) and autonomous ("federal") levels of government is one problem with the conventional literature, although in principle this defect could be remedied by incorporating different costs of changing political institutions at the local and the state level into, for example, the analytical framework developed by Inman and Rubenfeld (1993).

5. Some recent analyses of fiscal federalism allow for subnational distributional and even stabilization concerns, distinguishing between two quite different questions that are sometimes confused, namely, the *infeasibility* and the *undesirability* of subnational policy: see e.g., Gramlich (1987) on stabilization, and Tresch (1981) on distribution. However, few seem to accept the position argued in Bird (1989) that there is no necessary connection between the degree of unity of the internal common market and the structure of the political federation. On the contrary, concern for the purity of the internal common market motivates the conclusions of such disparate authors as Boadway, Roberts and Shah (1993); and Migue (1993).

6. On the other hand, unlike the "fiscal federalism" (decentralization) case discussed in Bird (1993a), there may be a strong case in truly federal states for unconditional interregional rather than interpersonal distributive transfers — although there is by no means agreement in the literature as to the rationale for such transfers. See Boadway, Roberts and Shah (1993) and Shah (1991; 1993) for what has come to be the accepted rationale for such transfers, essentially on horizontal equity grounds. For a different view, that such transfers may be rationalized in terms of equalizing regional fiscal capacity but not individual horizontal equity, see Musgrave and Musgrave (1993). Yet another view, common with American authors, is that intergovernmental transfers on equalization grounds can be justified only if they affect interpersonal redistribution (cf. Gramlich 1984): for a review of the (very limited) efficacy of such transfers for this purpose, see Rao and Das-Gupta (1993). Of course, others — e.g., Migue (1993) — see little rationale for intergovermental equalization transfers in any case. While the many controversies on this subject can hardly be resolved here, a somewhat different approach to equalization transfers is suggested later in the chapter.

7. See, however, the interesting analysis of Breton and Scott (1978) as well as the rather different line of analysis in Breton (1989).

8. Preston King, as quoted in Burgess and Gagnon (1993, p. 9). For other useful examples of comparative federal studies by political scientists — few of whom, however, have attempted to analyze fiscal institutions — see King (1982); and Bakvis (1981).

9. For earlier comparative studies of federal finance from this perspective, see Advisory Commission (1981); Hunter (1977); Hayes (1983); Thirsk (1983); and Bird (1986b). It should come as no surprise that portions of this chapter draw heavily on the last of these.

10. See Campbell *et al.* (1991) and Winkler (1993) in general; Bird (1984b) and Colombia (1992); on Colombia, and Shah (1990) on Brazil, for examples; see Economic and Social Commission for Asia and the Pacific (1991); see especially Silverman (1992) on Africa; see Bird and Wallich (1993) for a preliminary survey of the transitional countries of Eastern Europe, as well as Wallich (1992) on Russia; see Bird (1993a) on OECD countries.

11. To illustrate in the Latin American context, Venezuela and Mexico are formally federal; yet neither is in practice as "federal" as Argentina, let alone Brazil. Of course, many developing countries such as Malaysia (Gandhi 1983) and Papua New Guinea (Bird 1983) also have some "federal" characteristics, but on the whole — at least in a short essay like this — I shall simply assert that they are not "really" federal. For a more generous view, see Shah (1993).

12. For recent reviews of federal finance in these countries, see on Canada — Boadway and Hobson (1993); on Germany — Spahn (1991) and Fiedler (1991); on Switzerland — Dafflon (1991) and Kirchgassner and Pommerehene (1993); on Austria — Thoni (1991); on the United States — Advisory Commission (1993); on Australia — James (1992); and on India — Rao (1993) and Sury (1992). In addition, see Shah (1990) and Oliveira and Velloso (1991) on Brazil, as well as Gandhi (1983) for an interesting comparison of Brazil, India, Nigeria, and Malaysia, and Shah (1993) for a more general comparison. I am not aware of any study of federal finance in Belgium.

13. The case for restrictions on tax exportation (to non-beneficiaries) is further developed in Bird (1993). See also Walsh (1992) for further discussion of this "correspondence" (or "equivalence") principle.

14. See Ruggeri, Howard and Van Wart (1993). Somewhat similar, though less drastic, suggestions for change are made by Ip and Mintz (1992). For further discussion, see Bird (1994). Interestingly, much the same discussion is currently going on in the very different environment of Russia (Wallich 1992), though I hesitate to draw any parallels between the two countries.

15. Shah (1993) updates and extends this analysis: for a skeptical view of all these measures of "balance" in a federal setting, see Bird (1986a).

16. For an early analysis of the relation between rising political tension in the Canadian federation and the decline in federal capacity to "buy off" dissenters, see Bird, Bucovetsky and Foot (1979, chaps. 8-9).

17. See Kirchgassner and Pommerehne (1993): the arguments in this paper may be disputed, but they are broadly compatible with the view expressed in Bird (1986b) to the effect that Switzerland, like the U.S., seems to have paid a surprisingly low price for allowing state (local) governments far more fiscal leeway than suggested by the conventional fiscal federalism analysis. The low level of mobility may explain the Swiss outcome to some extent, but obviously the same explanation cannot hold for the U.S.

18. Although it is not possible to discuss expenditure assignment here, it should perhaps be noted that it is generally misleading to speak of a clear "assignment"

of a particular expenditure function to a particular level of government. In practice, most major expenditure functions in most countries are shared among different levels of government (and the private sector) in different ways, with respect to regulation, to finance, and to service delivery, for example.

19. The U.S. data is from the Advisory Commission (1992); for other countries, see e.g., Bird (1986b); and Shah (1991; 1993). Incidentally, the impressionistic statements in the text may be more meaningful than the false precision of quantitative comparison of fiscal balance in different countries. In particular, although attempts to calculate a precise coefficient of "vertical fiscal imbalance" have been popular since Hunter (1977) — see e.g., Shah (1991; 1993) — such calculations are inherently so suspect on both conceptual and empirical grounds (see Bird 1986a) that they are not attempted here.

20. Bird argues that, in the principal-agent framework, the relevant accountability for local government expenditures financed by central transfers is to the central government rather than to the local taxpayer.

21. The formula suggested in Bird (1993) (and developed in more detail in e.g., Bird and Slack 1983) is essentially a variant of a so-called "foundation" approach: it also permits states to lower their taxes if they wish to provide fewer public services. (This discussion excludes from consideration the traditional economic argument for intergovernmental transfers in the case of jurisdictional spillovers of benefits, as well as the arguments for such transfers to induce states to spend in accordance with central government priorities. For further discussion of such arguments, see Bird (1993a); as well as Boadway and Hobson 1993.)

22. This is a rather glib assertion about a phenomenon that has been little studied. Indeed, in general the allocative effects of regionally redistributive transfers (or other policies) are not well understood. From the early controversy on this matter between Buchanan (1952); and Scott (1952) to the latest papers by such authors as Oates (1993) it is clear that the relationship between federalist policies and regional and national economic growth is far from clear in any country, although this complex theme cannot be further discussed here. For an interesting discussion of this issue, including extensive reference to Canada, see Higgins (1981).

23. An analogy with foreign aid may be suggestive: rich countries may prefer to give aid to poor countries rather than to accept their (competitive) products, let alone their people.

24. See Inman and Rubenfeld (1993) for an interesting preliminary attempt to incorporate the number of states explicitly into a political-economic model of federalism.

25. See Courchene (1984) for a discussion of changing equalization formulae in Canada. Gil Diaz (1990) noted a similar phenomenon of what is often called "grandfathering" (maintaining the status quo) in Mexico with respect to the coefficients of VAT shares, i.e., the proportion of revenues from this tax going to different states. McLure (1993b) specifically cites the Mexican case as an example of what should not be done: technically, he may be right, but he is almost certainly wrong politically.

26. L.F. Giblin, quoted in May (1969, p. 63). The "Commission" mentioned in this quotation is the Commonwealth Grants Commission, an expert agency established in Australia before World War II to determine equalization grants to states.

27. In India, the Constitution requires the government to accept these recommendations, although it should of course be remembered how freely the central government in India replaces state governments with which it disagrees. In the early 1980s, for the first time since the Australian Commission was established, the federal government refused to accept its recommendations. Although this refusal led to considerable uproar in Australian academic circles (e.g., Groenewegen 1983), what is surprising is that for so long the Commission was able to defuse the potentially explosive politics of regional redistribution by recourse to its increasingly arcane and pseudo-scientific formula approach.

28. Note that this way of putting things assumes that there is a need to coordinate: for a more skeptical view see McLure (1993b); and Bird (1984a). This issue has been extensively discussed also in the European context in recent years (see, e.g., Cnossen 1991; and Kopits 1992). As argued in Bird (1989), in a number of respects the "harmonization" issue is rather different in a common market and a federal state, but this point cannot be further discussed here.

29. It should perhaps be noted again that I have no information on the situation in Belgium.

30. The fact that revenue sharing in India is concentrated on the personal income and central excise taxes has the unfortunate effect of biasing central tax policy decisions: since the central government gets to keep all of an increase in customs duties or corporate taxes, but only (say) 15 percent of an increase in personal income tax, its interest in the latter is correspondingly reduced. To avoid such bias, a desirable feature of revenue-sharing schemes is to state them in terms of a share of all central revenues (as in Colombia, for example) rather than as a share of particular taxes.

31. See Thirsk (1993) for a recent overview of the tax competition literature, which again cannot be further explored here. As mentioned earlier, Kirchgassner and Pommerehne (1993) provide support for the "it doesn't matter much" view stated in the text. See also McLure (1993b) for the argument that tax competition is, from the citizen's perspective, basically a good rather than a bad thing.

32. In Canada, for example, a "joint" federal-provincial retail sales tax would have a rate of 14 percent or more, that is, higher than any such tax in the world, and above the level at which even well-ordered homogeneous countries such as Norway found it necessary to change to a VAT (Bird 1970).

33. More research is needed with respect to the relative efficiency of alternative coordinating mechanisms. Migue (1993), for example, makes a strong case in principle for relying on market, or at most "club," coordination rather than a centralized hierarchial structure, but offers no evidence that this is the best way to proceed. Boadway, Roberts and Shah (1993), on the other hand, prefer to put their faith in central benevolence. A movement from faith to knowledge seems necessary to make any progress in this area though it seems unlikely to happen soon: indeed, I made a rather similar remark nearly 30 years ago (Bird 1966)!

34. The argument in this section (as in some of the preceding text) largely repeats points made in Bird (1986b), since subsequent experience has given me little reason to change my mind on these matters.

35. Analyses of fiscal federalism (e.g., Boadway and Hobson 1993) often ignore regional policy concerns on the grounds that they are unrelated and better pursued

in other ways. Unfortunately, while analytically neat, this approach flies in the face of reality. In every federal country, the fact is that regional development concerns and federal fiscal arrangements are inextricably linked.

36. Another example of such an institution may be found in Papua New Guinea, which shows the influence of both the Australian and Indian examples: see Bird (1983) for further discussion of this case.

BIBLIOGRAPHY

Advisory Commission on Intergovernmental Relations (1981), *Studies in Comparative Federalism*, Washington, DC.

_____ (1992), *Significant Features of Fiscal Federalism: Revenues and Expenditures*, Report M-180-11, Washington, DC.

_____ (1993), *Significant Features of Fiscal Federalism: Budget Processes and Tax Systems*, Report M-185, Washington, DC.

Bakvis, Herman (1981), *Federalism and the Organization of Political Life: Canada in Comparative Perspective*, Kingston: Institute of Intergovernmental Relations, Queen's University.

Bird, Richard M. (1966), "Regional Policies in a Common Market," in *Fiscal Harmonization in Common Markets*, ed. C.S. Shoup, New York: Columbia University Press.

_____ (1970), "The Tax Kaleidoscope: Perspectives on Tax Reform in Canada," *Canadian Tax Journal*, 18: 444-78.

_____ (1983), *The Assignment of Taxing Powers in Papua New Guinea*, Port Moresby: Institute of National Affairs.

_____ (1984a), "Tax Harmonization and Federal Finance: A Perspective on Recent Canadian Discussion," *Canadian Public Policy*, 10: 253-66.

_____ (1984b), *Intergovernmental Finance in Colombia*, Cambridge, MA: Harvard Law School International Tax Program.

_____ (1986a), "On Measuring Fiscal Centralization and Fiscal Balance in Federal States," *Environment and Planning C: Government and Policy*, 4: 389-404.

_____ (1986b), *Federal Finance in Comparative Perspective*, Toronto: Canadian Tax Foundation.

_____ (1989), "Tax Harmonization in Federations and Common Markets," in *Public Finance and Performance of Enterprises*, ed. Manfred Neumann and Karl W. Roskamp, Detroit: Wayne State University Press.

_____ (1990), "Intergovernmental Finance and Local Taxation in Developing Countries: Some Basic Considerations for Reformers," *Public Administration and Development*, 10: 277-88.

_____ (1993a), "Threading the Fiscal Labyrinth: Some Issues in Fiscal Decentralization," *National Tax Journal*, 46: 207-227.

_____ (1993b) "Federal-Provincial Taxation in Turbulent Times," *Canadian Public Administration*, 36, 4: 479-476.

Bird, Richard M. and Enid Slack (1983), "Redesigning Intergovernmental Transfers: A Colombian Example," *Environment and Planning C: Government and Policy,* 1: 461-743.

Bird, Richard M. and Christine Wallich (1993), "Fiscal Decentralization and Intergovernmental Relations in Transition Economies," WPS 1122, Policy Research Department, World Bank, March.

Bird, Richard M., Meyer Bucovetsky and David Foot (1979), *The Growth of Public Employment in Canada,* Montreal: Institute for Research on Public Policy.

Boadway, Robin W. and Paul A.R. Hobson (1993), *Intergovernmental Fiscal Arrangements in Canada,* Toronto: Canadian Tax Foundation.

Boadway, Robin, Sandra Roberts and Anwar Shah (1993), "The Reform of Fiscal Systems in Developing Countries: A Federalism Perspective," paper prepared for Conference on Fiscal Reform and Structural Change, New Delhi, August.

Brennan, Geoffrey and James M. Buchanan (1980), *The Power to Tax,* Cambridge: Cambridge University Press.

Breton, Albert (1989), "The Growth of Competitive Governments," *Canadian Journal of Economics,* 22: 717-750.

Breton, Albert and Anthony Scott (1978), *The Economic Constitution of Federal States,* Toronto: University of Toronto Press.

Buchanan, James M. (1952), "Federal Grants and Resource Allocation," *Journal of Political Economy,* 60: 208-217.

Burgess, Michael and Alain-G. Gagnon, eds. (1993), *Comparative Federalism and Federation,* Toronto: University of Toronto Press.

Burgess, Robin, Stephen Howes and Nicholas Stern (1993), "The Reform of Indirect Taxes in India," London: Suntory-Toyota International Centre for Economics and Related Disciplines, London School of Economics.

Campbell, Tim, George Peterson and Jose Brakarz (1991), *Decentralization to Local Government in LAC,* Regional Studies Program, Report No. 5, Washington, DC: Latin America and the Caribbean Technical Department, World Bank.

Cnossen, Sijbren (1991), "Co-ordination of Sales Taxes in Federal Countries and Common Markets," paper prepared for Seminar on Fiscal Federalism in Economies in Transition, Paris: OECD.

Colombia (1992), *Colombia: descentralizacion y federalismo fiscal,* Informe final de la Mision para la Descentralizacion, Bogota: Departamento Nacional de Planeacion.

Commission of the European Communities (1977), *Report of the Study Group on the Role of Public Finance in European Integration,* Brussels.

Courchene, Thomas J. (1970), "Interprovincial Migration and Economic Adjustment," *Canadian Journal of Economics,* 3: 550-576.

_____ (1984), *Equalization Payments,* Toronto: Ontario Economic Council.

Dafflon, Bernard (1977), *Federal Finance in Theory and Practice with Special Reference to Switzerland,* Bern: Paul Haupt.

_____ (1991), "Assigning Taxes in a Federal Context: The Experience of Switzerland," paper prepared for Seminar on Fiscal Federalism in Economies in Transition, Paris: OECD.

Economic and Social Commission for Asia and the Pacific (1991), *Fiscal Decentralization and the Mobilization and Use of National Resources for Development*, Bangkok.

Fiedler, J. (1991), "Assigning Taxes in a Federal Context: The Experience of Germany," paper prepared for Seminar on Fiscal Federalism in Economies in Transition, Paris: OECD.

Frey, Rene L. (1976), "The Interregional Income Gap as a Problem of Swiss Federalism," in *The Political Economy of Fiscal Federalism*, ed. W.E. Oates, Lexington, MA: Lexington Books.

Gandhi, Ved P. (1983), "Tax Assignment and Revenue Sharing in Brazil, India, Malaysia, and Nigeria," in *Tax Assignment in Federal Countries*, ed. Charles E. McLure Jr., Canberra: Centre for Research on Federal Financial Relations, Australian National University.

Gil Diaz, Francisco (1990), "Reforming Taxes in Developing Countries: Mexico's Protracted Tax Reform," paper prepared for World Bank.

Gordon, Roger H. (1983), "An Optimal Taxation Approach to Fiscal Federalism," in *Tax Assignment in Federal Countries*, ed. Charles E. McLure Jr., Canberra: Centre for Research on Federal Financial Relations, Australian National University.

Gramlich, Edward (1984), "A Fair Go: Fiscal Federalism," in *The Australian Economy: A View from the North*, ed. R.E. Caves and L.B. Krause, Washington, DC: The Brookings Institution.

_____ (1987), "Subnational Fiscal Policy," *Perspectives on Local Public Finance and Public Policy*, 3: 3-27.

Groenewegen, Peter (1983), "Tax Assignment and Revenue Sharing in Australia," in *Tax Assignment in Federal Countries*, ed. Charles E. McLure Jr., Canberra: Centre for Research on Federal Financial Relations, Australian National University.

Hayes, John (1983), *Economic Mobility in Canada*, Ottawa: Minister of Supply and Services.

Higgins, Benjamin (1981), "Economic Development and Regional Disparities: A Comparative Study of Four Federations," in *Regional Disparities and Economic Development*, ed. Russell Mathews, Canberra: Centre for Research on Federal Financial Relations, Australian National University.

Hill, Roderick and Michael Rushton (1993), "Multi-stage Sales Taxes and Interprovincial Trade: Lessons from Europe," in *Symposium on the Simplification of the Federal/Provincial Sales Tax System*, Toronto: Canadian Tax Foundation.

Hunter, J.S.H. (1977), *Federation and Fiscal Balance: A Comparative Approach*, Canberra: Australian National University Press and Centre for Research on Federal Financial Relations.

Inman, Robert P. and Daniel L. Rubinfeld (1993), "The Structure of Taxation for Federalist Economies: An Overview," paper prepared for International Seminar in Public Economics, Linz, Austria, August.

Ip, Irene and Jack M. Mintz (1992), *Dividing the Spoils: The Federal-Provincial Allocation of Taxing Powers*, Toronto: C.D. Howe Institute.

James, Denis W. (1992), *Intergovernmental Financial Relations in Australia*, Sydney: Australian Tax Research Foundation.

King, Preston (1982), *Federalism and Federation*, London: Croom Helm.

Kirchgassner, Gebhard and Werner W. Pommerehne (1993), "Tax Harmonization and Tax Competition in the European Community: Lessons from Switzerland," paper prepared for International Seminar in Public Economics, Linz, Austria, August.

Kopits, George, ed. (1992), *Tax Harmonization in the European Community: Policy Issues and Analysis*, Washington, DC: International Monetary Fund.

Lehner, Franz (1982), "The Political Economy of Interlocked Federalism: A Comparative View of Germany and Switzerland," Ruhr-Universitat Bochum, August.

Longo, Carlos Alberto (1993), "Federal Problems with VAT in Brazil," revised version of paper prepared for International Conference on Tax Reform, New Delhi, December 1992; July.

Mathews, Russell, ed. (1981), *Regional Disparities and Economic Development*, Canberra: Centre for Research on Federal Financial Relations, Australian National University.

_____ (1982), *Public Policies in Two Federal Countries: Canada and Australia*, Canberra: Centre for Research on Federal Financial Relations, Australian National University.

May, R.J. (1969), *Federalism and Fiscal Adjustment*, Oxford: At the Clarendon Press.

McLure, Charles E., Jr. (1987), *The Value-Added Tax*, Washington, DC: American Enterprise Institute for Public Policy Research.

_____ (1993*a*), "Vertical Fiscal Imbalance and the Assignment of Taxing Powers in Australia," Hoover Institution Essays in Public Policy, Stanford.

_____ (1993*b*), "The Tax Assignment Problem: Ends, Means, and Constraints," paper presented to the International Symposium on Fiscal Reform, Sao Paulo, Brazil, September.

Migue, Jean-Luc (1993), *Federalism and Free Trade*, London: Institute of Economic Affairs.

Mintz, Jack M., Thomas A. Wilson and Pierre-Pascal Gendron (1993), "Sales Tax Harmonization: The Key to Simplification," in *Symposium on the Simplification of the Federal/ Provincial Sales Tax System*, Toronto: Canadian Tax Foundation.

Musgrave, Richard A. (1983), "Who Should Tax, Where, and What?" in *Tax Assignment in Federal Countries*, ed. Charles E. McLure Jr., Canberra: Centre for Research on Federal Financial Relations, Australian National University.

Musgrave, Richard A. and Peggy Musgrave (1993), "Tax Equity with Multiple Jurisdictions," paper prepared for Ontario Fair Tax Commission, Toronto, January.

Oates, Wallace E. (1972), *Fiscal Federalism*, New York: Harcourt Brace Jovanovich.

_____ (1993), "Fiscal Decentralization and Economic Development," *National Tax Journal*, 46: 237-243.

Oliveira, Joao do Carmo and Raul Velloso (1991), "Intergovernmental Fiscal Relations in Brazil: Trends and Issues," paper prepared for Seminar on Intergovernmental Fiscal Relations and Macroeconomic Management, New Delhi, August.

Poddar, Satya (1990), "Options for a VAT at State Level," in *Value Added Taxation in Developing Countries*, ed. Malcolm Gillis, Carl S. Shoup and Gerardo P. Sicat, Washington, DC: World Bank.

Prichard, J.R.S. and J. Benedickson (1983), "Securing the Canadian Economic Union: Federalism and Internal Barriers to Trade," in *Federalism and the Canadian Economic Union*, ed. Michael Trebilcock *et al.*, Toronto: University of Toronto Press.

Rao, M. Govinda (1993), "Indian Fiscal Federalism from a Comparative Perspective," New Delhi: National Institute of Public Finance and Policy, New Delhi.

Rao, M. Govinda and Raja J. Chelliah (1990), "Survey of Research on Fiscal Federalism in India," New Delhi: National Institute of Public Finance and Policy.

Rao, M. Govinda and Arindam Das-Gupta (1993), "Inter-governmental Transfers as an Instrument to Alleviate Poverty," New Delhi: National Institute of Public Finance and Policy.

Ruggeri, G.C., R. Howard and D. Van Wart (1993), "Structural Imbalances in the Canadian Fiscal System," *Canadian Tax Journal*, 41: 454-472.

Scott, Anthony D. (1952), "Federal Grants and Resource Allocation," *Journal of Political Economy*, 60: 534-536.

Shah, Anwar (1990), "The New Fiscal Federalism in Brazil," WPS 557, Country Economics Department, World Bank.

_____ (1991), "Perspectives on the Design of Intergovernmental Fiscal Relations," WPS 726, Country Economics Department, World Bank.

_____ (1993), "Perspectives on the Design of Intergovernmental Fiscal Relations," paper presented to the International Symposium on Fiscal Reform, Sao Paulo, Brazil, September.

Silverman, Jerry M. (1992), *Public Sector Decentralization*, World Bank Technical Paper Number 188, Washington, DC: World Bank.

Spahn, P. Bernd (1982), "Financing Federalism: West German Constitutional Issues and Proposals for Reform," Reprint 49, Canberra: Centre for Research on Federal Financial Relations, Australian National University.

_____ (1991), "Financing Federal and State Governments: The Experience of Germany," Paper prepared for Seminar on Fiscal Federalism in Economies in Transition, Paris: OECD.

Sury, M.M. (1992), "Centre-State Financial Relations in India: 1870-1990," *Journal of Indian School of Political Economy*, 4: 15-54.

Thirsk, Wayne (1983), "Fiscal Harmonization in the U.S., Australia, West Germany, Switzerland and the EEC," in *Federalism and the Canadian Economic Union*, ed. M.J. Trebilcock *et al.*, Toronto: University of Toronto Press.

_____ (1993), "Fiscal Sovereignty and Tax Competition," Government and Competitiveness Project Discussion Paper 93-08, Kingston: School of Policy Studies, Queen's University.

Thoni, E. (1991), "Designing Revenue-Sharing and Grant Mechanisms in Federal and Unitary Countries: The Experience of Austria," paper prepared for Seminar on Fiscal Federalism in Economies in Transition, Paris: OECD.

Tresch, Richard W. (1981), *Public Finance: A Normative Theory*, Plano, TX: Business Publications, Inc.

Wallich, Christine (1992), *Fiscal Decentralization: Intergovernmental Relations in Russia*, Washington, DC: World Bank.

Walsh, Cliff (1992), "Fiscal Federalism: An Overview of the Issues and a Discussion of their Relevance to the European Community," Discussion Paper 12, Canberra: Federalism Research Centre, Australian National University.

Wheare, K.C. (1963), *Federal Government*, 4th ed., London: Oxford University Press.

Winkler, Donald R. (1993), *The Design and Administration of Intergovernmental Transfers*, Regional Studies Program, Report No. 29, Washington, DC: Latin American and the Caribbean Technical Department, World Bank.

Wiseman, Jack (1987), "The Political Economy of Federalism: A Critical Appraisal," *Environment and Planning C: Government and Policy*, 5: 383-410.

Comment: The Value of Comparative Perspectives

Ronald L. Watts

INTRODUCTION

The two major themes of Richard Bird's chapter are ones with which I find myself in strong agreement. The first relates to recognizing both the limitations and the value of the comparative perspective. The second is his emphasis, as a result of his comparative survey, upon the essentially *political* character of the issues in federal finance. His essay is an excellent survey and overview of the major patterns of federal finance and of the similarities and differences in the major federations. It is a pity, however, that time and space limitations resulted in his deliberately not going into as much depth as he might have on some of the specific issues facing the current review of Canadian federal finance.

THE VALUE OF COMPARATIVE ANALYSIS

Richard Bird's chapter has important things to say, with which I agree, about both the limitations and value of comparative analysis.

Generally speaking, Canadians seem to be reluctant to undertake comparative analysis. Indeed, on the first day of this conference I noted just two brief references to experience elsewhere: Tom Courchene referring to disparities within Australia and Richard Simeon to the problems in Germany with joint decision making. Many Canadians seem to think of comparative studies as simply excuses for foreign travel by self-indulgent members of Parliament and sabbatical scholars or as shameful acceptance of the pretention of foreigners. As a result the largest portion of Canadian comparative work tends to focus on our obvious closest neighbour to the south and underestimates the value of comparisons with other federations which, because of their parliamentary institutions or their socio-cultural and ethnic diversity, may be more relevant to the Canadian political context and problems.

Richard Bird draws attention at a number of points in his chapter to the importance of recognizing the limitations of comparative analysis, and he is right to do so. There is no single pure model of federalism or of federal financial arrangements that is applicable everywhere. The basic notion of federalism, involving the combination of shared-rule for some purposes and self-rule for others within a single political system so that neither is subordinate to the other, has been applied in different ways to fit different circumstances. Federations have varied in many ways: in the character and significance of the underlying economic and social diversities; in the number of constituent units and the degree of symmetry or asymmetry in their size, resources, and constitutional status; in the scope of the allocation of expenditure responsibilities; in the allocation of taxing power and resources; in the character of their central institutions and the degree of regional input to central policy making; in the procedures for resolving conflicts and facilitating collaboration between interdependent governments; in their procedures for formal and informal adaptation and change.

One cannot, therefore, just pick models off a shelf. Even where similar institutions are adopted, different circumstances may make them operate differently. A classic illustration of this is the operation of the similar formal constitutional amendment procedures in Switzerland and Australia. Both involve referendums for ratification requiring double majorities, i.e., a majority of the federal population and majorities in a majority of the constituent units. In Switzerland there have been over 90 formal constitutional amendments since 1874 (over three-quarters of those initiated by Parliament and submitted to referendum) which have met this requirement, but in Australia of 42 attempts since 1901 only eight have succeeded.

Richard Bird is also right in emphasizing that as long as these cautions are kept in mind, there is genuine value in undertaking comparative analyses. Many of the basic problems of federal finance are common to virtually all federations, particularly the four aspects examined in Richard Bird's essay: correcting vertical imbalance, pressures for equalization, the need for tax coordination, and the importance of the political context, institutions, and processes. Moreover, comparative studies may help to identify options that might be overlooked, identify consequences that might not be foreseen likely to flow from particular arrangements, and through similarities or contrasts draw attention to certain features of our own arrangements whose significance might otherwise be underestimated.

In this latter respect two particular features not emphasized by Richard Bird but which do affect intergovernmental fiscal arrangements in Canada are the parliamentary form of our federal institutions, and the character of our constitutional distribution of powers. Other parliamentary federations such as Australia, India, and Germany, by contrast with the United States and Switzerland which incorporate the separation of executive and legislative powers within their central institutions, share with Canada second chambers which are not symmetrical with the popular chamber in their powers, and a tendency for executive predominance leading to executive federalism as the predominant form of intergovernmental relations including the processes relating to intergovernmental financial arrangements. In the constitutional distribution of powers, most other federations emphasize interdependence more and include large areas of concurrent jurisdiction, where our own constitution emphasizes the exclusive jurisdiction of each order of government. Some like Switzerland and particularly Germany even constitutionally de-couple legislative and administrative jurisdiction in many areas centralizing the former and decentralizing the latter. These differences not only affect media interpretations and public attitudes about intergovernmental relations which in Canada emphasizes the competitive and zero-sum character of these relations, but have important implications for appropriate arrangements relating to federal finance. Thus in Canada we hear repeated calls for disentanglement while the focus in other federations is often more on how to make joint decision making more effective.

THE IMPORTANCE OF THE POLITICAL CONTEXT

In all federations, the financial arrangements have invariably constituted an important, indeed crucial, aspect of the political operation of the federation system. Their importance derives from the fact that the relative financial resources play a large part in determining the relative roles of the different governments within a federation, are a major means for flexibility and adjustment, and shape public attitudes about the costs and benefits of the activities of different governments. This political significance places federal-provincial financial arrangements at the heart of the processes of intergovernmental relations. Federal financial arrangements are therefore not simply technical adjustments but inevitably the result of *political* compromises. It is important, therefore, to understand the two-way interaction between the intergovernmental financial arrangements and the political institutions and processes of political bargaining which is typical of all federations.

In an earlier chapter Richard Simeon raised the question of whether our political institutions have the capacity to resolve the current problems in federal finance facing Canada, and expressed some doubts. Put in the context of the issues raised by Richard Bird's chapter, the question becomes, can experience elsewhere help us in improving our institutional capacity? At this point there is one ironic example to which I cannot resist bringing attention. The 1991 proposals of the Government of Canada for constitutional reform, *Shaping Canada's Future Together: Proposals*, advocated an intergovernmental Council of the Federation as one instrument for improving intergovernmental collaboration with a view to strengthening the economic union. However, in the subsequent deliberations that notion was abandoned because of the fears of some provinces that it would contribute to federal government dominance and because others saw it as redundant for regional input to central policy making if a Triple-E Senate were also created. Yet shortly afterwards, in Australia, which has had a powerful Triple-E Senate since its inception in 1901; a Labor federal government together with the states decided in May 1992 to adapt to its own uses the Canadian proposal for a Council of the Federation by establishing a Council of Australian Governments that has as its primary objective the strengthening of the economic union. This illustrates how we in turn can learn from experience elsewhere of political institutions and processes designed to facilitate the adjustment of federal financial arrangements while recognizing that that experience must be adapted to our own needs.

THE ISSUES OF VERTICAL BALANCE, EQUALIZATION AND TAX COORDINATION

A central portion of Richard Bird's chapter deals with the three sets of issues relating to federal finance common to virtually all federations: closing the gap in vertical imbalance, equalization arrangements to deal with regional disparities and tax coordination. Each of these are areas relevant to the impending review of Canadian fiscal arrangements and each would warrant going into considerable depth. Given space limitations, however, I will simply limit my comments to three specific points.

First, while identifying the importance of the issue of closing the gap between the revenue capacities and expenditure responsibilities of each order of government, especially in a period marked by the federalism of scarcity, Bird's chapter does not draw out how closely this issue is tied to responsibilities for the provision of social services. The significance of a vertical financial imbalance for the provision of social services is not unique to Canada. It is an underlying contemporary problem in most federations today and reductions of federal transfers leading to accusations of offloading responsibility for social programs are common elsewhere. We may be able to learn in this area from how other federations have attempted to deal with this problem. In the United States, for example, it has been argued that such offloading has in fact led to creative innovations in some states in the provision of social services.

Second, another issue that is related to that of correcting vertical imbalance is the application of the principle of financial responsibility. Some of the earlier discussions in this volume have already drawn attention to the principle of financial responsibility, i.e., the notion that to achieve political accountability the government that has the nasty job of raising taxes should control how the proceeds of those taxes are spent. This principle has figured prominently in the theoretical literature on fiscal federalism, and it has been especially emphasized in the United States with the constitutional separation there between the executive and legislative branches within each government. It should be noted, however, that in parliamentary federations, where the executive is directly responsible to and accountable to its own legislature, this provides an alternative mechanism of accountability through the legislature to the electorate. It is not surprising that this mitigating factor has meant that, broadly speaking, within parliamentary federations there has been less insistence upon conditional grants and more acceptance of unconditional transfers since there is another mechanism of accountability for their executives.

In Richard Bird's section on equalization, particularly useful is his identification of three models for deciding upon equalization formulae: (a) expert commissions (as in Australia and India), (b) the federal government with regional input through central institutions, e.g., the second chamber (as in Germany, Austria, Switzerland, and the United States), and (c) the federal government without regional input through the central institutions (Canada being the sole example). Given Canada's uniqueness here, and the failure of all efforts to date to reform the Canadian Senate, the first of the three alternatives adapted to Canada's needs and circumstances may well be worthy of serious attention. Alternatively, if that is not acceptable, we may need to consider renovation of the mechanisms of executive federalism to facilitate the process for adjusting the equalization formulae.

CONCLUSIONS

As Canadians face the review of our federal-provincial financial arrangements, of major importance is the capacity of our political institutions and processes to carry out that review effectively. An important part of the review, therefore, will be considering ways of improving those political institutions and processes. In this task, keeping in mind the limitations of comparative analyses, we may still have a considerable amount to learn from the experience of other federations in terms of the recognition of intergovernmental interdependence within federations and in terms of both positive and negative examples of political mechanisms that may facilitate intergovernmental financial arrangements.

Looking ahead to the final section of this volume where a panel reviews the options and considers whether Canadian fiscal problems will require for their resolution a "big bang" or merely "tinkering," the two themes emphasized in Richard Bird's chapter will be particularly relevant. First, if the political context and processes are so crucial to resolving issues of federal finance, to what extent are our political institutions equipped to achieve effectively a "big bang" reform, or is their capacity limited to "tinkering"? Second, while evolutionary development is less risky, if we have reached a point where such an approach is clearly no longer sufficient and a more radical transformation is necessary, then the positive and negative lessons from alternative approaches elsewhere may be particularly worthy of careful consideration in order to understand the practical and possible unintended consequences of the radical options that are contemplated.

Part Five

THE FUTURE

CHAPTER TEN

Big Bang or Quiet Tinkering:
A Round Table

A Tridential Strategy

Peter Leslie

My theme is risk, or coping with risk: as one contemplates the reform of Canadian social policy, how to calculate the risks involved, and how to contain them. This is a subject that is implicitly evoked in the title of this session, which asks whether to go for a "quiet tinkering" approach or to engineer a "big bang." Tinkering involves a series of minor, experimental changes; none can do much damage to the pre-existing structure, and any that turn out badly can be reversed, or at least counterbalanced by other little innovations as need be. But with a big bang — perhaps a controlled nuclear reaction is a better image, since there is no big bang unless things go awry — once you start, there is no going back.

Several contributors have already opened up the question of caution and risk. Some have proposed a wholesale, multifaceted remake of Canadian social policy, while others have warned of the perils of opening up new policy controversies in politically explosive times.

My own view, publicly argued, is that the present system of federal-provincial fiscal arrangements is programmed to self-destruct in a short time, that nothing less than wholesale revision will avoid their collapse, and that significant changes to social programs must be part of the reform package (Leslie 1993). Tom Courchene's chapter has approached the subject from the opposite direction. He surveyed the shortcomings of the present social policy mix in Canada, and argued for their redesign — and for adapting or recasting federal-provincial fiscal arrangements to finance the new system (substance first, means later). This approach is perfectly logical, and I support it. I only add, addressing those who would like to shelve the reform of social policy until forseeable political turbulence is out of the way (if it ever is), that the imminence of a fiscal crisis of Canadian federalism makes postponement of social policy reform unrealistic. In other words, fiscal crisis will compound the political turbulence that many, myself included, expect to result from the Quebec election of 1994. My general point is this: whether one starts with the reform of social policy and redesigns the fiscal arrangements to suit, or launches a reform of the fiscal arrangements and undertakes, in this context, the redesign of our social programs, the effect is the same: reforms must take account of fiscal realities and substantive policy reforms. As Richard Bird notes in his chapter, every part of a system of fiscal arrangements is linked to every other part. Thus, whenever you open up one issue — as must be done, in the context of social policy reform — you have the makings of a big bang.

It is wise to go into this process with one's eyes open: to recognize the risks. Of these, I propose to discuss three.

UNINTENDED CONSEQUENCES OF REFORM: THE UNFORESEEN VICTIMS

The redesign of government programs, perhaps especially social programs, is always risky in the sense that it is hard to tell what the consequences of major change will be. It is clear, though, that reform will have its victims, and that some of the effects are unlikely to have been anticipated. This is the simple fact that makes caution, or a long process of quiet tinkering, look like the best option. Incrementalism, a rose by any other name.

My rejoinder, though, is that incrementalism is not exactly the same thing as muddling through, or endless short-term improvisation. The best approach, in my opinion, is to set goals and principles for a fundamental redirection of policy, and to strike out in the desired direction through a set of phased-in changes. Have a good sense of where to go, and move with deliberate speed. Phased-in change reduces the risk of unforeseen consequences, and, if there is time to introduce counterbalancing measures when unintended effects become manifest, may reduce adverse political fallout.

The problem, of course, is to put these generalities into practice. For this I propose — here I address the federal government — a new approach to the conduct of federal-provincial relations, involving a four-stage process.

- The first is to identify a set of aims or objectives, non-fiscal ones, for example, as in the statement on the social union in the Charlottetown Accord. "Charlottetown" was not the final word, and did not purport to be, but it did at least attempt to establish some benchmarks for what an adequate social policy would accomplish; it went beyond verbal formulae such as "equity" or "social justice." Complementing a statement of substantive policy objectives there could reasonably be a statement of fiscal targets, goals, or limits.

- The second step is to float various options for achieving the desired goals: not to commit to a specific policy, but to discuss alternative approaches. For this, a fairly detailed discussion paper would be appropriate; unlike the federal proposals for constitutional reform, as released in September 1991, the discussion paper should contain some information. It should review, tentatively, pros and cons of various options. On this basis, the government would be able to test the waters with the relevant policy communities and with provincial governments. More input, more information, better decisions.

- The third step is to involve Parliament, by striking a committee to hold public hearings. This would offer a creative role for the government's own backbench MPs, and would be an educational experience for newer MPs from all parties. It might even, to some extent, smoke out opposition parties' views on difficult issues. Most important of all, it would generate greater public understanding of the dilemmas that face policymakers. This could help build support for a redirection of policy.

- The final stage would be to open negotiations or consultations with provincial governments. Negotiations are needed where policy change demands complementary action from both orders of government. Consultations are needed where federal policy alone is involved, but should take account of what provincial governments are doing and want to do, and of their fiscal circumstances. Too often in the past this "final stage" has come first. One result has been public outrage against executive federalism, its *faits accomplis*, and its inherent secrecy; another has been that the federal government has ceded strategic advantage to the provinces — whenever you get 11 or 13 government representatives in a room together, the federal government sets itself up for being outvoted. In my opinion (I advance this as a general rule, applicable far beyond the realm of social policy), Ottawa should routinely build a constituency for what it wants to accomplish, before opening negotiations with provincial governments. If it were to do this, it would invert past practice, and put the conduct of federal-provincial relations on a new footing entirely.

AGENDA OVERLOAD

A second area of risk arises from the sequencing problem, or the agenda-overload problem. Earlier, Keith Banting remarked that no government in its right senses would want to start a three-front war, simultaneously (a) remaking the fiscal arrangements, (b) redesigning social policy, and (c) altering the assignment of federal-provincial responsibilities, if not actually reallocating legislative powers under the constitution. Someone responded by saying that the federal government may have no choice about all this; it may try to control the agenda, but it will not be able to do so.

I must say, that latter response rings true to me. I have seen too much of Ottawa's attempting to control the public agenda, to channel and focus public discussion to suit a timetable or a sequence that the government would find convenient. Every time, it has merely succeeded in ensuring that the issues it wanted to postpone or suppress would be opened up by others, in circumstances that were highly unfavourable for the government and indeed, I believe, for Canada. There seems to be rather little a government can do to keep issues off the public agenda, if various powerful players want to put them there.

In particular, I think it would be dangerous self-delusion to suppose that one could deal, in some "phase one," with a set of big political issues, and then open up a "phase two" in which matters like the fiscal arrangements (the category of issues that René Lévesque used to describe casually as "the plumbing") were tidied up. On the contrary, I am inclined to think that fiscal crisis, and, equally, the policy concerns that Tom Courchene, Carolyn Tuohy, François Vaillancourt, and others have expounded, will force a set of dangerously controversial issues out into the open, and that this will happen just at the time that Quebec is gearing up for an election that may well bring an *indépendentiste* government to power. These problems will be further compounded by the fact that the opposition in Parliament consists of two regional parties of equal strength and diametrically opposed objectives.

Certainly this is a frightening prospect. To some it suggests, as I infer it has done for David Milne (among others), that extreme caution is called for. The problem I see with this is that it merely confirms what Parizeau and Bouchard have been saying for some time, that Canada has become ungovernable because its internal divisions have paralyzed it. Innovation will have been shown, again, to be impossible. Federalism will be shown to be a system that does not and cannot work, at least not in Canada.

For this reason I conclude that, while the risks of a three-front war cannot be ignored, the biggest risk of all may be to say that nothing much can be done, or should be attempted. More than that, there are two strong reasons (in addition to those of substance, already reviewed throughout this volume) for undertaking a major initiative now. One is that it will show some sign of movement, and that change on things that do matter a great deal need not await formal constitutional amendment. The other is that a big package offers opportunities for trade-offs that single-item changes cannot.

I enter a plea, then, for calculated risk-taking, that is, for opening up new issues — but not in a way that every criticism of possible policy options turns automatically into an attack on an entrenched federal position.

CONFLICT: COQ AND QUEBEC

The third area of risk to which I wish to refer follows directly from the preceding one. If major policy changes are proposed, or even floated, it may quickly become obvious that the only changes acceptable to Canada outside Quebec (COQ) are anathema *within* Quebec, or at least to the Quebec government. Assume, for example, that Ottawa proposes taking on a more direct responsibility for those with low or unstable incomes, beyond the responsibilities it already has under the unemployment insurance program, old age security, and the Canada Pension Plan; and assume further that it proposes diverting some of the monies now paid to provincial governments to finance the new federal income security system. This would amount to a policy change under which transfers to provincial governments were replaced by transfers to persons. Depending on the specifics, this shift in policy might be attractive in most of COQ, but vehemently denounced by the Quebec government.

In that case, it would be necessary for the federal government, and for the whole of Canada, to face once again the asymmetry issue. If one province, presumably Quebec, wants to gain added constitutional powers and policy responsibilities — and of course claims the fiscal resources needed to fulfil those responsibilities — while elsewhere in Canada those powers, responsibilities, and fiscal resources are considered appropriately vested in the federal government, then what is to be done? At the very least, this poses a difficult policy dilemma for Ottawa, which will want to manage or minimize the risks inherent in a debate over asymmetry.

On this, two strategies seem worth consideration:

- One is to avoid raising the asymmetry issue, but to develop contingency plans for responding to demands by a PQ government and by the Bloc Québécois, that Quebec should become a sort of associate member of the Canadian federation. These plans would have to include a strategy for facing a PQ government that had won a referendum on sovereignty; equally, they would have to include a review of possible responses to demands from the Reform Party and others (including, certainly, within the Liberal Party) that Quebec should be forced into line, or if it refuses, that it should be forced to get out of Canada. I do not know what, in substance, to propose; but I do know — to take a recent case — that failure to develop fallback positions as part of the strategy for securing the ratification of the Meech Lake Accord was ultimately very costly for Canada. I hope that the same absence of contingency planning does not afflict the Privy Council Office today. Given that Quebecers will soon be going to the polls, to neglect or suppress the asymmetry issue would be foolhardy.

- The second strategy is a mildly pre-emptive one. It would involve raising the asymmetry issue (playing with fire, I admit), but in a form that is aimed at making hardliners on both sides — the sloganeers — back down a little, and take a more nuanced position. Or, if this is a pipe-dream, then at least the attempt could be made to provoke a discussion on what constitutional out-comes are thinkable and what ones are not. For example, if Quebec votes for sovereignty, are the rest of us going to say, "If you want to be part of the economic union, you have to be part of the sharing community too." In this context, I have wondered from time to time whether it would be a good idea to float "radical asymmetry" as a constitutional option, at least to think about. Under this option, the whole of the income security system — including pensions and unemployment insurance — would fall within the purview of the Quebec government, while elsewhere the responsibility for attaining or ensur-ing income security goals would be, as it is now, shared in some way between Ottawa and the provinces. Tax transfers of course would be necessary; equalization payments would no longer be made to Quebec; and some institu-tional changes (Quebec representation in Parliament, or Parliament's conduct of its business) might be necessary. If there is to be asymmetry, it would certainly have to be "asymmetry without privilege."

The main purpose of spelling out what asymmetry might involve, or of identifying its institutional and fiscal preconditions, would be to help Que-becers realize what sovereignty would actually mean in practice. It is not at all clear that Quebecers who profess themselves sovereigntists have, in their own minds, opted for withdrawal from the sharing community: that all existing federal programs for income security and social services, whether federally-administered or merely financed in part from federal taxes, would disappear, and that the Quebec programs replacing them would have to be financed entirely from Quebec tax revenues. Nor is it clear that sovereigntists recognize the institutional implications of the option to which they have apparently assented; many, for example, in 1980 did not know that "sovereignty-association" entailed losing the right to send MPs to Ottawa. The prospects for achieving real clarity on such issues are small indeed, but any marginal increase in public awareness of the scope of constitutional adventurism that the PQ and the BQ are proposing, can only be salutary. Unfortunately there is a real prospect that Quebecers will take some irrevocable constitutional step without realizing what they are actually committing themselves to. Anything that can reduce the likelihood of their doing so helps to limit risk for everyone.

CONCLUSION

I have put forward a *tridential strategy* for managing risk in the reform of social policies and the fiscal arrangements. The first prong of the trident is to adopt new techniques for the conduct of federal-provincial relations, introducing a more open process that involves less commitment to entrenched positions from which it is an embarrassment to withdraw. The second prong is to take a calculated risk in opening up a combination of issues, aiming for fundamental redesign of social policies and the fiscal arrangements; this will lead ultimately to a bargaining process in which there will be multiple opportunities for trade-offs. The third prong is to face the asymmetry issue in one of two ways: to prepare contingency plans for the day that a PQ government demands sovereignty together with economic association, or to adopt a mildly pre-emptive strategy by nudging forward a public debate on the meaning and preconditions of radical asymmetry.

BIBLIOGRAPHY

Leslie, Peter (1993), "The Fiscal Crisis of Canadian Federalism," in *A Partnership in Trouble: Renegotiating Fiscal Federalism*, ed. Peter Leslie, Kenneth Norrie and Irene Ip, Toronto: C.D. Howe Institute.

Delaying the Big Bang

Robert Normand

INTRODUCTION

It is very difficult to come up with new ideas on fiscal federalism and I would like to thank the academics who decided to dive into a pool that was reserved too long to a bunch of civil servants and technicians who thought they were the only ones to be able to swim in the muddy waters of fiscal federalism. I appreciate their valuable contributions that shed new perspectives on a very complicated field of activities that is also so important to all the citizens of Canada.

The analysis is there and it is good: substantial changes are needed not only in the field of fiscal arrangements, which are due to be renegotiated shortly, but also in the public policies that justify the existence of these arrangements. These changes must be made in the name of rationality, efficiency, and equity.

The refrigerator is full; all the ingredients and the recipes have been sorted out; it is now up to the politicians to decide what they want to put in their sandwich.

But, I agreed with Richard Simeon and André Blais: substantial political changes are not made in the abstract for the sole reason that they are necessary. They can only be implemented if the political context makes it possible to do so and I submit, at the risk of being a party pooper at this late hour, or looking a bit cynical, that Canada is not ready to accept all the important fiscal changes that are necessary, and that the next fiscal arrangements will not be very different from the existing ones, unless they are shoved down the throats of the provincial authorities by the federal government.

MAJOR CHANGES? NOT NOW!

I am of the opinion that Canadians may accept, but with reluctance, the transformation of the GST, if the operation is done with beneficial or at least neutral effects; but I submit that Canadians are certainly not ready for other substantial changes in our fiscal regime and our costly social programs, for the following reasons.

First, we have been going through a severe economic crisis for the last three years and we are not out of it yet, no matter what the Conference Board or other crystal ball readers may say. The rate of unemployment is still too high and has been up for too long. The housing starts are low at a time when the interest rates would normally stimulate the demand. Consumers are afraid of what tomorrow may bring, and are reducing their spending to a minimum. Inventories are low and are being kept there. So, the taxpayers want to keep what they still have and can hardly accept major reductions in the existing social programs; they would be afraid of jeopardizing their already unsafe situation.

Second, the recent federal election has shown that the voters have not accepted the Progressive Conservative proposals to reduce the level of the federal deficit and to shave the social programs. On the contrary, they have rather favoured more government spending, job creation, and the maintenance of the costly security nets that prevent them from falling lower.

Third, governments, at all levels, are impaired by a very serious fiscal crisis. Revenues are lower than expected, while expenditures are not lower. Deficits are too high. The burden of the public debt is too heavy; interest charges are so high (one-third of its revenues for the federal government) that governments have no more fiscal room to stimulate the economic development. So, the federal government will be inclined to reduce even further its transfer payments to the provinces. But the latter are going to resist strongly, especially after having lost $40 billion in the last few years, as pointed out by Tom Courchene in his chapter.

Fourth, the presence of two strong regional parties in the House of Commons will limit the capacity of the well-established Liberal government to manage in a rational way. If Jean Chrétien wants to reduce the existing federal benefits to the province of Quebec, or in the west, he will then only fuel the Parti Québécois in *La Belle Province* and consolidate the possibility for the Reform Party to take the place of the Progressive Conservatives elsewhere.

Fifth, and I should not say this publicly, but it is obvious to me that Canada cannot solve its problems, but always shovels them forward and piles them one on top of the other. Canada has been wrestling for more than 25 years with constitutional problems that are getting more and more sour, without generating the will to find a proper solution; and it is not by refusing to talk about it that the situation will get better: it gave birth to two regional parties recently that are echoing the frustrations of a large number of Canadians.

The problems of Native Peoples are also left unsolved; even though we spend, each year, amounts in the order of $6 billion to buy band-aids, that only makes it necessary to increase the medication each year.

And in a more and more competitive world, Canada has lost its place at the top and is losing its previous position of former years without being able to do what is required to regain its place.

Therefore, for these reasons, I do not believe that Canada is ready for substantial changes in its fiscal regime and in its social programs. This is bad because we are only making even tougher the adoption, at a later date, of measures that are required now. In other words, we are following the path of New Zealand and Argentina instead of the tough, but progressive approach adopted by Sweden. We are not yet deep enough in the mud to develop a strong will to react properly.

TUG-OF-WAR OR K.O.?

My second point is that the next fiscal arrangements will either be similar to the existing ones, or be substantially different. But they will then have to be imposed by the federal government upon the provinces in a manner similar to the methods used by Trudeau 15 years ago.

The name of the game, in the discussions to come, will be "figures," not principles. "Who gets what," as Richard Bird said. All parties to the discussions that are going to take place in the coming weeks will be very cautious as to the costs involved and the monetary advantages or inconveniences that they could derive therefrom.

Both the federal government and the provinces will be demanding something, since the budgetary situation of the federal government is intolerable, while the provinces cannot accept more cuts in transfer payments without having to reduce the level of services to their citizens or having to pass the buck again to the municipalities.

So, normally, in a typical Canadian fashion, the potential clash should be resolved by a draw, i.e., the maintenance of the existing arrangements. Or, and this is also a possibility, Chrétien could very well come out with the abolition of the GST and its replacement by a new tax system, as Fred Gorbet pointed out, relying on the strong mandate that was given to the Liberals, and thus, imposing these new arrangements on the provinces together with substantial changes in the financing of the established programs and transfer payments.

I cannot rule out that possibility, even though I believe that the political context is not favourable for that type of approach. The provinces with NDP governments, Quebec and Alberta, would have to react strongly if the changes are not financially advantageous. More tensions would then be created on the political scene and the net results would not necessarily be the ones that were contemplated at the beginning of the process.

So, at best, the provinces can expect the renewal of the fiscal arrangements more or less as they are now.

EPILOGUE

But over and above these fiscal arrangements, what is seriously needed now is a political will, at all levels of governments, to give a good haircut to our fiscal regime and our social programs and not wait until the head itself would have to be chopped off. At the federal level, we all know that Chrétien does not have more than 18 months ahead of him to do what must be done; because after that, the electoral preoccupations will again take precedence.

If we hope to protect these security nets, we must maintain the deficit at a reasonable level and therefore, we must work on a framework that would limit the possibility for the federal and the provincial governments to keep on passing the costs of these programs to the future generations. If Chrétien decides to do so and succeeds in doing so, then he will have been a really great prime minister. And I would have two suggestions to make in that respect that are nothing more but adopting here, what has been done by our neighbours down south.

First, I see as an absolute necessity, the adoption of a constitutional amendment by Parliament and by all the legislatures to require that each borrowing of money by a government be authorized, specifically by a special act of the legislative body or bodies involved. This is already done at the municipal level in Canada and by the state legislatures in the United States. Furthermore, I believe that this measure would be strongly supported by all Canadian citizens since it brings more transparency into the use of their borrowing powers by the governments. But no other constitutional amendment should be dealt with at the same time. No language solution. Nothing for Native Peoples.

This single measure would also bring about some side-benefits by restoring public credibility to the constitutional amendment process and by relaunching the possibility of serious constitutional discussions for the future, on a footing that would be acceptable by all those concerned.

Second, the adoption, by Parliament and each provincial legislature, of the equivalent of the Gramm-Rudman Act, which was enacted by the U.S. Congress some six or seven years ago and which imposed on the body that adopted it, a five-year plan setting the maximum level of deficit that could be reached during each of those years. Of course, this type of legislation can always be changed by the body that adopted it, but the taxpayers are then made aware of the behaviour of their government and, unless the measures are an absolute necessity and well explained, the government that decides to change the plan, faces the possibility of having to pay a high price for the change, in the ballot box! And fear is a good start for wisdom!

But here again, my cynicism on our collective incapacity and will to really solve our problems, stimulates my pessimism.

CONCLUSION

So, to come back to the topic: "Big bang or Quiet tinkering?" I would say that a position in the middle of the road would be advisable, but that we will probably follow the typical Canadian tinkering route, thus building the necessity for a real Big Bang in the years to come.

Fiscal federalism can only reflect the type of political federalism that we want and in that respect, we do not yet know what we really want. Or when we think we do, as in the case of Meech or Charlottetown, we cannot implement our solutions.

So good luck to all of us.

Not So Quiet Tinkering

Katherine Swinton

The reform of fiscal federalism is a daunting task. On the one hand, it presents difficult and often divisive questions about financial arrangements in the federal system, requiring decisions about the tax sources to which governments should have access, the need for and desirability of revenue equalization across provinces, and whether there should be limits on governments' ability to spend and borrow. While these are questions that economists and finance department officials may see as their domain, major social and economic policy issues are implicated in the solutions proposed, since access to financial resources affects the levels of social assistance, child care, training, health care, and postsecondary education available to citizens throughout the country.

Recognizing the complexity of this area of federal-provincial relations, an effort to forecast whether there will be a "big bang" or "quiet tinkering" in Canadian fiscal federalism leads to the conclusion that no solution can be quiet in these times of fiscal constraint, governmental competition for limited financial resources, and citizens' demands for empowerment and insistence on their rights. While the reality of fiscal constraint should push us towards major reforms in many policy areas over the next decade, the lesson that I draw from the chapters in this volume, and other considerations outlined below, is the importance of the process towards major reforms. A "big bang," in the form of major change, may well be needed, but there are dangers of failure if those changes are unilaterally imposed by the federal government or achieved through federal-provincial bargaining without careful efforts to educate the public on the need for restructuring and the rationality of the choices proposed. If something beyond tinkering with existing programs is required, the process will not be quiet, since there will be winners and losers. However, success is more likely if the process is not left solely to bargaining among experts, but also engages a public educated to understand the debate and aware of the distributive implications of restructured social and economic policies.

This volume presents a wide range of options for the reform of fiscal federalism. Some require constitutional amendment; others call for increased federal use of conditions attached to spending; others emphasize the importance of provincial control over social policy and even equalization. As a lawyer among many political scientists and economists, my comments reflect my interest in the choice of instruments and processes by which change will occur and the effect of legal instruments, such as the *Canadian Charter of Rights and Freedoms*. Therefore, I address three issues: methods of constitutional change in relation to fiscal federalism and social policy, the impact of citizens' rights, and the process for reform.

METHODS OF CONSTITUTIONAL CHANGE

Canadian federalism literature contains many references to the ways in which the constitution has been adapted since 1867. With respect to the distribution of legislative powers, formal amendments have been few. Yet there has been significant evolution through more informal methods, most particularly, the federal spending power that underlies programs such as equalization, Established Programs Financing, and the Canada Assistance Plan. In addition, changes in the functions and relationships of federal and provincial governments have come through tax policy, administrative delegations and intergovernmental agreements. The received wisdom is that these instruments of change have contributed to the immense flexibility and adaptability of the Canadian constitution.

This volume contains arguments that the current distribution of functions in the area of social and economic policy requires formal changes — for example, the allocation of unemployment insurance to the provinces or the transfer of social assistance to the federal government. While theoretically interesting, such proposals seem an impossible dream in the current political climate for a variety of reasons, including constitutional fatigue in the country, the complexity of the amending formulae demonstrated in the last two unsuccessful constitutional rounds, the impossibility of limiting the size of the agenda, the high symbolism (and, therefore, the great risk) associated with constitutional amendments, and the resistance to decentralization in Canada outside Quebec and to centralization within that province.

More importantly, I am not convinced that the proponents of change have proved the need for the amendments sought. Those who make such a significant proposal have an obligation to consider in detail the reasons for such change, as well as the practicality of carving up new watertight compartments in this era of governmental interdependence. For example, there are several proposals for the transfer of unemployment insurance to the provinces, yet it is not clear that this is a sensible solution. There are many ways to improve the UI program within the current power structure, and, indeed, many of the criticisms of the current system, such as hidden regional subsidies, unjustified departures from insurance policies, and individual dependency, can be addressed by the federal government alone (if the political will is there) or through cooperation with the provinces. Moreover, while UI policy has important links to provincial social assistance or workers' compensation, it also has important connections to the federal role in promoting a healthy economy through worker training.

Similar observations can be made with respect to the argument for federal control of social assistance, or at least federal responsibility for children. The value of provincial jurisdiction is not addressed — for example, possible diversity in policy responses — nor is the interaction with ongoing provincial policy areas such as workers' compensation or family law.

The lesson, then, is to avoid formality. However, it must be acknowledged that from some perspectives, there is declining efficacy and flexibility associated with the more informal mechanisms of Canadian constitutional change. In periods of growth, the federal government could use its spending power and the tax system to affect policy in areas within provincial legislative jurisdiction. During the last two constitutional rounds, many emphasized the importance of this federal spending power to achieve national standards (although, in fact, very few national standards are found in the major social programs, while those set out in porgrams like the Canada Assistance Plan are at very broad levels of generality).

Kenneth Norrie and Judith Maxwell suggest ways in which the federal spending power can continue as an important policy instrument, for example, in the form of federal vouchers to individuals for postsecondary education, or the use of "carrots" in the allocation of funds to educational and training institutions. Clearly, political considerations may mute the willingness of the federal government to use the spending power in ways perceived to be "illegitimate" or unconstitutional by the Bloc Québécois in Parliament or a Parti Québécois government in Quebec.

Yet it is important not to give up too quickly on the spending power as an instrument. Fred Gorbet has noted the importance of a federal leadership role in setting national standards: continued spending in provincial areas of jurisdiction, such as health care, gives the federal government a legitimate claim to participate with the provinces in jointly setting nationwide objectives. More importantly, in some areas, described by Stefan Dupré as "procurement federalism," federal spending with conditions attached continues to be a legitimate and important policy tool. This is especially true in relation to training initiatives, where funding can be directed to programs that meet prescribed occupational standards. Federal legitimacy here derives partly from its constitutional responsibility for unemployment insurance, but also comes from the facilitation of worker mobility, an objective underpinning the economic union sought by the 1867 constitution and also guaranteed in section 6(2) of the Charter of Rights. Thus, in the future, federal spending with conditions is most likely to occur in relation to the purchase of services, while the pursuit of national objectives in areas of provincial jurisdiction will come through joint federal-provincial action, especially as the federal cash contribution under EPF or the Canada Assistance Plan declines.

A third lesson emerges from the discussion about instruments of constitutional change. While it has long been assumed that tax and spending policy are instruments of flexibility, the ongoing debate about the significance of the transfer of income tax points from the federal government to the provinces in 1977 under EPF, described by Kenneth Norrie, may signal the need to qualify that assumption. While some commentators assert that those tax points should be characterized as a continuing federal contribution to EPF, others argue strongly that this is misleading, since the transfer was a one-time vacation of tax room to the provinces, and not tied to spending on EPF programs. One need not decide which group is correct. Norrie notes that both have a rational basis for their conclusions. The more important lesson is that transfers of federal income tax points constitute an important and at least semi-permanent allocation of power to the provinces, which cannot effectively be recaptured when the provinces have taken up that room. Therefore, in the current discussion of fiscal arrangements, the (in)flexibility of proposed changes is an important consideration.

RIGHTS TALK

Many in this volume address the concerns of federal and provincial governments in meeting their policy objectives. Their focus on regional considerations is not surprising, given the traditional territorial focus of federalism. But the discussion of fiscal federalism is also centrally about social and economic policy, and many groups will demand that it be recast to focus on distributive considerations, particularly the interests of the poor, women, those with disabilities, or those with inadequate workplace skills. Major changes to the funding of the Canada Assistance Plan (e.g., a shift to block funding or federal withdrawal from the Plan) would affect those groups in significant ways because of offloading — not only in the levels of their direct financial assistance, but also in access to support services such as daycare subsidies. Similarly, the call for a negative income tax to help children must not ignore other important family issues, such as child-care support for working parents.

The concerns of these groups will affect the process in a number of ways. First, some will actively support more national standards and a strong federal role in social policy, which may be a political asset to the federal government. Second, if these groups do not feel that their concerns are adequately addressed in the political process, they are likely to resort to litigation. In recent years, the Supreme Court of Canada broadened the rules of public interest standing in *Finlay* to allow a recipient of social assistance to challenge federal payments to Manitoba under the Canada Assistance Plan on the basis that the province did not comply with the conditions in the federal statute and federal-provincial agreement, when Manitoba deducted overpayments from his benefits. Subsequently, he lost his case on the merits in a 5 to 4 decision in the Supreme Court, which held that Manitoba had not violated the conditions of the Plan.[1]

There are two lessons here: one, interest groups and individuals are increasingly litigating in areas which federal and provincial governments thought were their preserve; second, governments must be careful when they import conditions and standards into fiscal arrangements, since others may come forward to enforce them, even when governments might be willing to ignore breaches for political reasons. An obvious area for future litigation is in relation to the *Canada Health Act*, if provinces try to reduce funded medical procedures.[2] In some cases, this might be challenged as a failure to provide medically necessary hospital services in accordance with section 2 of the Act or a failure to provide a "comprehensive" health-care insurance plan in accordance with this and other criteria set out in sections 7 through 12. Whether such litigation will succeed is open to question. *Finlay* did lose under a statute that was more explicit in its criteria than the *Canada Health Act*, and judges will understandably be wary about embarking on a detailed determination of what is "medically necessary."

Even in the absence of statutory standards, individuals and interest groups may resort to the Charter of Rights to prevent the erosion of social programs, although in many cases this will not be a useful instrument. Section 6(2), the mobility rights section, provides some protection against provincial discrimination in labour policy, although it does not prevent different occupational standards in provinces if these are aimed at ensuring quality of service, rather than discriminating against those from other provinces. Section 6(3)(b) also allows the imposition of reasonable residency requirements as a qualification for the receipt of publicly provided social services. Section 15 of the Charter, the equality rights guarantee, has been interpreted to apply only to those grounds listed (e.g., sex, disability, race) and to analogous grounds (i.e., those that have led to a history of disadvantage in our society, such as sexual orientation).[3] Therefore, section 15 might permit a challenge to the decision not to fund tubal ligations or abortions as a form of sex discrimination, or a rationing of heart transplants on the basis of age as discrimination, but it would not likely be available to attack refusal to cover in vitro fertilization or user fees. Finally, section 7 of the Charter, the right to life, liberty, and security of the person and the right not to be deprived thereof except in accordance with principles of fundamental justice, has not been interpreted to confer positive rights to economic security, despite the hopes of poverty groups and some academics. Finally, section 1 of the Charter makes all the rights set out in it subject to reasonable limits.

Overall, then, while a Charter challenge is possible, the likelihood of success is questionable in many areas, since the judges will often be reticent to intrude into complex debates about the allocation of public funds among competing social interests, as in the design of publicly funded medical care systems or social assistance.

The Charter is not the only rights document that may come into play. Activists are also working in international forums to affect domestic policy. A recent example is the report of the United Nations Committee on Economic, Social and Cultural Rights examining Canada's compliance with the *International Covenant on Economic, Social and Cultural Rights.* Not only was concern voiced about Canada's failure to alleviate poverty, but there was express reference to the federal government's reduced contributions to shared-cost programs.[4]

Thus, courts will be called into the disputes about fiscal federalism and the design of social policy with greater frequency. While they may be reluctant to challenge the role of the legislative branches in this area, this will not prevent interest groups from resorting to the judiciary when other routes for political change seem deficient.

THE PROCESS OF REFORM

Several authors in this volume have emphasized the salience of deadlines for the reform of fiscal arrangements and described a scenario of federal-provincial negotiations to work out a new sharing of revenues. Both Fred Gorbet and Peter Leslie contemplate broad agendas for this round of negotiations so as to allow room for trade-offs. The danger in such a scenario is, as Richard Simeon noted, that the interests of fiscal federalism will trump the policy challenges in areas such as social assistance or postsecondary education.

This may well trigger a negative reaction from citizens, who will see this as yet another "deal" worked out by governments without a coherent policy analysis. Unsuccessful efforts at constitutional reform should teach us that the more dramatic the changes to be wrought, the greater the need to involve the broader public in the process. This should not be read as a call for numerous public hearings or rounds of consultation like those in the constitutional process. Rather, it is a call for openness in the process, public education about the trade-offs that must be made, and informed debate about the choices being taken — in short, my call here is for political accountability. Without the information and discussion that governments owe to citizens, the major reforms in this area that are needed can only come with a "big bang" — but it may well be in the form of public resistance and reaction that will undermine effective restructuring of finances and programs.

NOTES

1. *Canada (Minister of Finance) v. Finlay* (11986), 33 D.L.R.(4th) 321 (S.C.C.); *Finlay v. Canada (Minister of Finance)* (1993), 101 D.L.R.(4th) 567 (S.C.C.).
2. R.S.C. 1985, c. C-6.
3. *Andrews v. Law Society of British Columbia* (1989), 56 D.L.R.(4th) 1 (S.C.C.).
4. United Nations Committee on Economic, Social and Cultural Rights, "Consideration of Reports Submitted by States Parties under Articles 16 and 17 of the Covenant — Canada," 10 June 1993 (E/C.12/1993/5).

The Case for Cutting the
Public Sector Payroll

John Richards

In the spring of 1993, Vancouver school teachers launched a strike over their demands for higher salaries, smaller classes, and more help with foreign-language students. With well over half Vancouver children using English as a second language, I have some sympathy with the third demand; as for the rest, none! When first they came to power in British Columbia, the NDP had rewarded teachers with a handsome salary increase. Given the provincial deficit, given teachers' job security and relative salary levels, given other education needs such as vocational training in rapidly expanding suburban communities, the provincial Cabinet quite reasonably included only minimal salary increases when constructing the 1993-94 education budget. On their side, the teachers feared "falling behind," and struck on behalf of their demands. Caught between its obligation to manage an efficient education system and partisan loyalties to a powerful interest group within the NDP, the provincial Cabinet procrastinated. As the strike dragged into its third week and risked jeopardizing student completion of the school year, public hostility to the teachers mounted and, reluctantly, the government legislated them back to work. To be fair, the strike was not universally unpopular: 100,000 children enjoyed a three-week holiday during a gorgeous West Coast spring.[1]

At the risk of being dismissed for using an unrepresentative anecdote, I begin with this story. It illustrates two fundamental ideas. We Canadians value the European-style welfare state constructed since World War II. It creates a more equitable society, and it supplies a range of services more efficiently than could a private market alternative. But it can only sustain these achievements if public sector managers — politicians, deputy ministers, local school boards — actually exercise discretion over budgets, and reallocate public revenues to meet changing needs as defined in terms of some broad conception of the public interest. If public sector managers identify primarily with narrow interest groups intent on constraining that discretion, realizing the benefits of the welfare state becomes problematic.

A second idea is that the public sector *inescapably* operates under an ill-defined, but nonetheless real, budget constraint because citizens want simultaneously to maintain a large private sector. The provincial Cabinet concluded — correctly in my opinion — that provincial citizens are near their current maximum willingness-to-pay for social programs, and hence the Cabinet could not avoid politically painful trade-offs by simultaneously granting the salary increase, funding new programs and raising the required funds by a combination of tax increases or increased borrowing.

In general terms, most people probably agree with these two ideas. The purpose of this essay is to go beyond the general, and discuss some pragmatic implications.

To anticipate the end point, I arrive at four policy recommendations. First, federal and provincial governments should balance their aggregate accounts by no later than the end of the current Parliament, and do so subject to the present ratio of taxes to the gross domestic product (GDP). Such an exercise requires expenditure cuts. If we accept the first recommendation, the obvious question arises, where to cut? The second recommendation is that a major component of the required cuts — in the order of 50 percent — should derive from reductions in the public sector payroll. The third recommendation is that, since the provinces have a far greater potential than Ottawa to reduce payroll expenditures, Ottawa should share in provincial savings via reduced transfer payments. Finally, in order to maintain public support for fiscal restraint, governments must pay close attention to the redistributive impact.

A PRIMER ON RECENT CANADIAN FISCAL HISTORY

After that bald introduction, let me step back. We cannot hope to discuss future options intelligently unless we understand the historical forces that produced the present, a situation in which more than one-half of Canadian GDP is now allocated directly by government, or passes through government in the form of government-designed transfers. Table 1 provides summary data (in terms of percentage shares of GDP, and on a national income accounts basis) for selected years since 1961. As a primer on the past three decades of Canadian fiscal history, here is a five-point summary:

1. *Expansion of social spending derived primarily from provincial governments (municipal governments and hospitals are included in this category).* They increased their spending by nearly 7 percentage points of GDP from the early 1960s to the mid-1970s. Since then, aggregate provincial program

spending has been roughly constant during normal economic conditions; it increased during recessions in the early 1980s and 1990s.

2. *Recessions aside, federal program spending net of transfers to the provinces has remained remarkably constant.* The Mulroney government reduced spending in the late 1980s from levels induced by the early 1980s recession, but in 1989 it was within one percentage point of the level of Trudeau's government in 1981 and of the average of Diefenbaker's governments in the early 1960s.

3. *Federal cash transfers to the provinces increased dramatically between the mid-1960s and mid-1970s and, thereafter, grew slowly until peaking in the mid-1980s; since then, a slow decline has occurred.* From the mid-1960s to mid-1970s, Ottawa made extensive use of conditional transfers to encourage provinces to expand social programs. Cash transfers increased during the recession of the early 1980s, less so in the more recent recession of the early 1990s. Intergovernmental transfers comprise approximately one-quarter of federal government program expenditures and are a legitimate target, as will be discussed later, for budgetary restraint.

4. *Federal and provincial own-source revenues grew from the early 1960s until the early 1980s — by 2 and 8 percentage points respectively — but thereafter remained roughly constant until the 1990s recession. Revenues never increased sufficiently to balance the aggregate public sector, which has been in deficit in every year since 1974.* Gross debt charges have risen dramatically since the 1970s, and now constitute over 9 percent of GDP (on a national income accounts basis).

5. *Aggregate program spending increased significantly during both the early 1980s recession and that of the early 1990s — respectively by 4 and 6 percentage points of GDP. Constrained by rising debts, both levels of government accompanied their spending increases in the early 1990s with tax increases, a phenomenon that did not occur during the previous recession.* Having failed to realize any surpluses in the boom of the late 1980s, governments faced pre-recession debt charges nearly 3 percentage points of GDP higher in 1989 than in 1981. Total public spending by 1992 was 5 percentage points higher than the average during the previous recession. Despite tax increases, aggregate public sector deficits were by 1992 as large as in the early 1980s.

TABLE 1: Trends in Public Sector Revenue and Expenditure, 1961-92
(as a percentage of gross domestic product)

	Average, late Diefenbaker years, 1961-63	Trudeau Years			Mulroney Years		
		Middle, 1975	Late, 1981	Average, 1982-84 Recession	Early, 1985	Middle, 1989	Late, 1992
Revenue							
Federal	15.9	18.5	18.3	17.3	17.4	18.3	20.0
Provincial							
Own sources	9.4	14.4	17.6	18.4	18.0	19.4	20.5
Federal transfers	2.6	4.5	4.0	4.4	4.5	3.9	4.3
Total	12.0	18.9	21.5	22.8	22.6	23.3	24.8
All government	27.9	37.4	39.8	40.1	40.0	41.6	44.8
Expenditure							
Federal							
Programs net of transfers to provinces	12.3	14.1	12.5	14.6	14.3	11.8	13.9
Transfers to provinces	2.6	4.5	4.0	4.4	4.5	3.9	4.3
Debt service	1.9	2.2	3.9	4.5	5.2	5.7	5.7
Total	16.8	20.8	20.3	23.5	24.0	21.5	23.8
Provincial							
Programs	15.2	21.9	22.5	24.5	24.1	23.8	28.1
Debt service	1.0	1.7	2.4	3.0	3.3	3.2	3.7
Total	16.2	23.6	24.9	27.5	27.3	26.9	31.9
All government							
Programs	27.5	36.1	35.0	39.1	38.4	35.6	42.0
Debt service	3.0	3.8	6.3	7.4	8.4	8.9	9.4
Total	30.5	39.9	41.3	46.6	46.8	44.5	51.4
Deficits (+)/Surplus (-)							
Federal	1.0	2.2	2.1	6.1	6.6	3.2	3.8
Provincial	0.8	0.3	–0.6	0.3	0.2	–0.4	2.8
Total	1.8	2.5	1.5	6.4	6.8	2.9	6.7

Notes: All figures are based on national income accounts definitions. Public accounts definitions vary among governments; small discrepancies in some totals are due to rounding. Provincial data include local, school, and hospital sectors.

Source: Calculations by author, from data in Canada (1993a).

THE NEED FOR "CREATIVE DESTRUCTION"
IN THE PUBLIC SECTOR

Social program initiatives over the last three decades have realized important successes — notably in improving average Canadian health status and in lowering the incidence of poverty among the old. But many social problems persist more-or-less unchanged, and others have worsened.

Large interregional government transfers have lowered the regional dispersion of per capita post-transfer income, but per capita earned income inequalities have narrowed only slightly. As measured by the ability of provincial governments to raise revenues with equal taxing effort, the ranking of provincial governments has changed little over the last three decades. The three "have" provinces remain Ontario, Alberta, and British Columbia; the four Atlantic provinces remain the poorest of the "have nots." Continued low earned incomes, high regional unemployment and high poverty rates in particular provinces have become, as Courchene (1993, p. 17) puts it, "a policy-induced equilibrium, not a disequilibrium."[2]

Average Canadian unemployment rates have risen over the last three decades, and have been high relative to other G7 countries (Economic Council 1990). In explaining this trend, some weight can be attached to factors beyond the ken of public policy. The rise in single-parent families has probably increased learning difficulties for children which in turn is reflected in unemployment statistics. Inadequate aggregate demand during recessions also explains some of the increase. But much of the increase is probably due to the working of labour markets in the context of inefficient government policies. As with regional inequality, persistent high unemployment seems less an aberration than a "policy-induced equilibrium." We have, for example, restricted labour mobility via interprovincial trade barriers, devoted most of our labour market expenditures to passive income support for the unemployed, used unemployment insurance as a permanent subsidy to low-productivity seasonal industries such as the fishery, allowed the elementary and secondary education system to drift with inadequate testing of student performance, and neglected the training needs of those entering the work force without the advantage of professional postsecondary education (Economic Council 1992a).

Two glaring concentrations of poverty and psychological distress in Canada are aboriginals and single-parent families. Despite some improvements — for example, rising average education levels — distress among aboriginal families has probably worsened. The incidence of poverty among single-parent families has declined, but the proportion of families in this category continues to increase (Economic Council 1992b).

The minimum conclusion from all this is that, despite a massive increase in the absolute and relative size of the Canadian welfare state over the previous quarter century, serious social problems persist and in some cases have worsened. But two other conclusions seem inescapable. First, its successes indicate that the welfare state has the potential to be a more efficient institution — than is the market — in supplying a broad range of services that comprise the core of the welfare state, or in subsidizing individuals to purchase the relevant services. But this is true only if politicians retain the discretion to undertake Schumpeterian processes of "creative destruction" to redesign social programs as publicly defined social needs change. Second, a larger public sector is no guarantee of better social policy. "Bad" social policy, such as our present UI program and Canada Assistance Plan, has induced dependency. Individuals and governments have adapted to generous, but inefficient, programs. In such cases, it requires ever-larger incremental public expenditures to reduce indices of social distress, and over time the stress from "withdrawal" of such programs becomes progressively more acute.

Besides the obvious desire to improve outcomes, the impetus for redesign of social policy comes from the fact that the proportion of Canadian voters consciously demanding a reduction in the size of the public sector is growing and, however convoluted the process may be, fiscal policy will ultimately reflect public preferences. Early signs of a new "fiscal realism" have already appeared at the provincial level.

Newfoundland Liberals and Alberta Conservatives won re-election in 1993 with campaigns based on promises to cut aggregate public spending. Popular opposition to increases in public sector spending and taxation by the Ontario and British Columbia governments persuaded these NDP Cabinets to undertake the extremely painful exercise of reversing their early spending patterns, alienating thereby their natural allies, in particular public sector unions.

The case of Saskatchewan displays a certain irony: a nominally conservative government allowed provincial finances to degenerate in the 1980s from fiscal health to the bottom of the provincial debt league; a nominally socialist government has since 1991 undertaken necessary, but politically painful, fiscal restraint.[3] A Conservative provincial administration presided over the decline of provincial economic fortunes during the mid-1980s, when the international grain subsidy war dramatically lowered farm incomes. The Conservatives attempted to offset the terms of trade effect by deficit spending. (The federal Conservatives also contributed via generous agricultural subsidies.) The Saskatchewan NDP returned to office in 1991, and has in three budgets reduced real program expenditures by 9 percent, increased provincial revenues by 14 percent, and reduced the deficit by four-fifths (Saskatchewan 1992; 1994).

The government has been able to accomplish this wrenching, by Canadian standards, fiscal adjustment while maintaining if not majority, at least plurality, support among the electorate.[4] One explanation for public support has been the care devoted to assessing the redistributive implications. The provincial government has been fairly careful in targeting its expenditure reductions — the public sector payroll being among them. Simultaneously, it has undertaken numerous initiatives to increase the progressivity of the tax system: the introduction of a "deficit surtax," an increase in child tax deductions for low-income families, and, an increase in a wage subsidy for low-income workers.

At the federal level, fiscal federalism will also prevail, but not yet.

A significant minority of Canadians west of the Ottawa River voted in the 1993 general election for the Reform Party, whose major promise was the equivalent of East European shock therapy: expenditure reductions sufficient to balance the federal budget in three years. While a significant minority voted for fiscal restraint, a plurality obviously voted for a party whose leaders maintained throughout the election campaign a studied ambiguity on the controversial issues of fiscal policy. During the years of Conservative rule, the Liberals enjoyed support from interest groups frustrated by modest Conservative spending constraints. The dynamic of interest group politics plus an ideological predisposition towards government activism led most Liberals, while in opposition, to minimize the significance of Canadian public sector deficits.

The dynamic of governing is very different. The severity of federal fiscal problems very quickly came to the fore. Within a month of assuming office, the new Minister of Finance announced that the 1993-94 deficit would be 35-40 percent higher than the $32.6 billion estimate contained in the spring 1993 budget.[5] Martin talked realistically of the growth of the underground non-taxpaying economy, of "hundreds of thousands of otherwise honest people who have withdrawn their consent to be governed, who have lost faith in government." He insisted that a prerequisite to re-establish lost faith is to "restore control over the nation's finances." (Canada 1993*b*, pp. 3-4).

The 1994-95 federal budget unfortunately did not break with federal fiscal trends of the last two decades. The new government intends to increase program spending modestly, from $121.1 billion in 1993-94 to $123.3 billion in 1994-95.[6] This is a 1.8 percent nominal, or 1.0 percent real, increase (based on the economic assumptions of the budget). The Liberals intend to increase revenues from $114.7 billion in 1993-94 to $123.9 billion in 1994-95, a 8.0 percent increase. Eliminating non-recurring revenue effects (such as accelerated tax return processing), the budget estimates that revenues will grow by 5.1 percent. This revised figure is still above the 3.9 percent projected nominal GDP growth.

Hence, while the budget contains no major tax increase, it does intend a modest further increase in the federal tax-GDP ratio. Making one adjustment (described in the endnote), the Liberals expect to lower the federal deficit, on a public accounts basis, from $45.0 billion to $40.4 billion.

The government has made some explicit spending reductions, notably in defence. It has also tentatively sought to cut expenditures, or curtail their growth, in the major areas of potential savings:

- public sector payroll (by extending the Conservatives' salary freeze until 1996-97);

- intergovernmental transfers (by requiring that, after this round of social policy reform, the aggregate of transfers net of Equalization not exceed 1993-94 levels);

- pensions (by reducing the generosity of income tax treatment for the old);

- unemployment insurance (by slightly increasing work requirements before qualifying, and slightly reducing duration and level of benefits).

Given the accounting complexities, any brief assessment necessarily sins by omission. But, in summary, it is fair to say that the aggregate fiscal adjustments of the new budget are trivial relative to what is required to eliminate the federal deficit during the life of the present Parliament. To realize even the modest goal of reducing the federal deficit below 3 percent of GDP by 1996-97 will require a more aggressive combination of spending cuts and/or tax increases than are contained in this budget.

Table 2 provides some — far from conclusive — evidence in support of the idea that voters in modern industrial countries have converged in how much public spending they want, and hence, on how large they want their respective welfare states to be. The desired range of public spending appears to be between 40 and 50 percent of GDP.[7] Governments that allow the public sector to rise above 50 percent are electorally punished; conversely, voters will support interventionist politicians in countries where public spending is below 40 percent. Canada under the Conservatives exceeded the upper end of the range, as did the French socialists and the centre-left coalition in Italy. All three of these governments lost power in 1993. These defeats occurred for many reasons but, in all three cases, public opposition to the relative size of the public sector was a prominent issue.

Two major outriders have been Japan and the United States, but even here, convergence may be occurring. The OECD (1993, p. 148) projects a continued slow increase in the Japanese public spending-GDP ratio over the next several years. In the case of the United States, the new Democratic administration may

TABLE 2: General Government Outlays (Percentage of GDP)

	1979	1984	1989	1993
United States	31.6	35.5	35.7	38.7
Japan	31.6	32.9	31.5	34.9
Germany	47.7	48.1	45.5	50.8
France	45.0	52.0	49.1	54.2
Italy	41.7	49.4	51.3	54.8
United Kingdom	42.6	47.2	40.7	47.0
Canada	39.0	46.8	44.9	51.5

Source: OECD (1993, p. 33).

well push that country's public sector above 40 percent by implementing broad health insurance reform.

As welfare states have grown in the major industrial countries, their governments are now engaged in running "subeconomies" larger than the pre-1989 command economies of the communist countries of Eastern Europe. And, not surprisingly, some of the analysis developed by East European economists in the last generation applies equally to the welfare state.

An example is the Hungarian economist, Janos Kornai (1992), who summarized much of his work with the idea of "soft budget constraints." Central to Kornai's analysis is that command economies — and by extrapolation the welfare state — generate powerful interest groups with quasi-property rights in the status quo. These groups come to exercise immense political pressure against reallocation of resources between government and the private sector and within the public sector itself. Even when certain governments like Hungary introduced market socialist reforms to encourage efficiency-enhancing reallocations based on financial performance, these governments could not in practice impose "hard" budget constraints on state-owned firms. In the event of financial losses, interest groups of workers, managers, and local politicians exercised sufficient influence to obtain subsidies and prevent bankruptcies. For similar reasons, new firms seeking entry into established industries faced severe barriers.

The analogue in the welfare state is that its growth has been accompanied by the growth of interest groups intent on defending specific programs. Their effect is to render extraordinarily difficult the exercise of Cabinet discretion — at either the federal or provincial level — in the field of social policy.

The relevant interest groups in this process can be usefully categorized:

One category of groups is *public sector unions/associations of contracted workers*. Those whose primary source of income derives from provision of a particular social program have a strong interest in preserving and increasing relevant budget allocations. Despite the incentive of worsening deficits, Canadian governments have been unable over the last decade to reduce the premium of public over private sector wages. As is discussed below, the overall premium appears to have increased.

A second category of groups are those *representing beneficiaries of major transfer programs*. This category contains many examples. Old age security is a rapidly growing category of social spending that ministers of finance want to constrain. For understandable reasons, organizations representing senior citizens constitute a powerful lobby against any modification of pension benefits. In particular industries, such as seasonal-employment forestry and fishery, UI benefits constitute an important source of income to employees. Without UI, employers would have to pay higher wages; competition to minimize cost increases would impose further use of labour-saving equipment, and employment in such industries would decline. Representatives of employers and employees in such industries quite logically organize to resist reallocation of labour market budgets that entail serious cuts to UI payments. The power of such interest groups derives from the universal and visible nature of the benefits they defend, and the large number of voters who, potentially, can be mobilized.

A third category of groups is *regional alliances in "have-not" provinces*. As already discussed, interregional transfers have increased post-transfer per capita incomes but done little to bring market-based per capita earnings in "have-not" provinces up to the national average. Such results strongly suggest the desirability of political entrepreneurship to redesign programs such as UI, a process which means attaching more benefits to individuals and fewer to regions. (An obvious example is an increase in training grants to the unemployed that could be spent anywhere, paid for by elimination of regional extended UI benefits.) This in turn would encourage outmigration from "have-not" provinces. But outmigration poses losses to a broad swath of interest groups with fixed assets in "have-not" regions. The threatened fixed assets range from the obvious (commercial real estate in communities of declining population) to the subtle (the "style-of-life" value placed on farms by people wanting to live in stable rural communities, or attractive civil service jobs many of which would disappear with outmigration).

For a generation, politicians in Atlantic provinces and other "have-not" regions have built broad alliances based on these three groups — public sector unions, immediate program beneficiaries, and those with fixed assets threatened by change in social policy. These alliances have been a formidable obstacle to any would-be political "entrepreneurs" advocating change. In the long run, however, "have-not" regional alliances are unstable; countervailing alliances arise in "have" regions.

WHY INCUR THE PAIN OF BALANCING THE BUDGET?

If federal and provincial governments do seek to balance their aggregate accounts, as is recommended here, there will inevitably be some — perhaps severe — dislocation costs. Why incur such costs? The answer is that extrapolation of present fiscal policy probably poses worse costs. The costs from pursuing "as is" fiscal policy range from the almost certain (such as the increased cost of servicing public debt because lenders now impose a risk premium on government bonds) to the probable (rising political conflict over distribution of government transfers and taxes) to the speculative (disruption of credit markets for the debt of one or more provinces, or even for Ottawa). It is always possible that a prolonged economic boom and stable public expenditures will allow us to grow our way out of the present fiscal mess without serious fiscal restraint. But that prospect is becoming increasingly unlikely.

Bill Robson (1994) has recently conducted an exercise in simulating fiscal prospects for Canadian governments over the life of the present Parliament. He concentrates on four outcomes: (a) change in the interest burden of the public debt as a share of GDP; (b) change in national savings as a share of GDP; (c) change in foreign debt as a share of GDP; and (d) change in provincial debt service costs as a share of provincial tax revenues. As opposed to using point estimates for independent variables, such as GDP growth and interest rates, he assumes these variables are random, obeying normal distributions about his baseline estimates. Running many simulations with realizations of the random variables generates an experimental distribution of outcomes.

One key conclusion is that small changes in parameter estimates produce dramatic differences in outcomes. To illustrate, Robson employs two sets of baseline estimates — "rosy" and "gloomy." The latter employs slightly lower baseline potential GDP growth (2.5 percent compared to 2.75 percent), slightly higher real interest rates on public debt (5 percent compared to 4 percent), and a smaller present output gap (5 percent of GDP as opposed to 6 percent). Both sets of parameter values lie within the range of current conventional wisdom. Under the "rosy" scenario, 27 percent of the simulation runs lead to a worsening (1997 relative to 1993) of two or more of the outcomes. Under the "gloomy" baseline assumptions, by contrast, 67 percent of the runs result in a worsening of two or more outcomes.

My conclusion from Robson's and similar exercises is that pursuit of "as is" fiscal strategies poses significant costs. Many of these costs are uncertain, but they are the benchmark against which to measure the more tangible adjustment costs posed by pursuit of fiscal restraint.

If governments agree to pursue fiscal restraint, what should be the target variable — deficit, debt-servicing costs, primary surplus, net debt-GDP, federal values only or federal-plus-provincial? And what should be the target value for the target variable? These are interesting questions, but of secondary importance. It is possible to state most targets in terms of alternate variables; the fundamental issue is to recognize the value of fiscal restraint, given the various risks posed by extrapolating present fiscal policy. Pragmatically, I believe the target of balanced provincial-plus-federal accounts, at 1993-94 tax-GDP ratios, by the end of the current Parliament (i.e., by 1998-99) is a reasonable criterion to determine whether Cabinets can reassert credible control of their respective budgets.

If we accept this first recommendation, the next question is, where to cut?

It is possible to undertake a case-by-case examination of government programs and find candidates where, by any reasonable assessment, costs exceed benefits. The federal Department of Fisheries and Oceans (DFO), for example, offers a long list of suitable programs for cutback (Vastel 1994). Overly generous unemployment insurance is a major candidate. Another candidate is extremely generous present pension policies (Walker and Horry 1993). They are creating a social division between the old, who enjoy the present generosity, and the working age population which is beginning to appreciate the implications of a rising dependency ratio and the actuarially unsound basis of the Canada/Quebec Pension Plan (Lam *et al.* 1993).

But the answer to the question, where to cut, is far more complex than the above paragraph suggests. Passive income support under UI is indeed too generous, but there is a need to expand training and apprentice programs. Hence, overall, labour market programs should not be expected to contribute to deficit reduction. However ruthlessly DFO spending is trimmed, it is a small "fish" in the ocean of red ink facing Canadian finance ministers. One major source of spending reduction worth identifying is the public sector payroll.

Identification of the public sector payroll as a source of spending reduction is warranted for three reasons. First, the wages of public and quasi-public employees are too large an item to ignore: in the order of 15 percent of federal program spending net of transfers to the provinces; 60 percent of provincial program spending.[8] Over a range of reasonable fiscal assumptions, a 10 percent cut in the aggregate federal-plus-provincial payroll would provide between one-third and two-thirds of all required expenditure reductions.[9] (If inflation continues at 2 percent annually, governments could achieve a 10 percent real cut by freezing the nominal aggregate payroll until 1998-99.) Second, the compensation advantage of public sector over comparable private sector wages has become unjustifiable given the need for budgetary restraint. Precise estimation of this advantage is fraught with controversy, but it is now probably close to 15 percent.[10] The compensation advantage occurs primarily among lower skilled employees and in the form of better deferred benefits, such as pensions (Gunderson and Riddell 1993; Quebec 1993). Third, comparative compensation studies do not take into account the benefit — a truly dramatic one during the recent recession — of greater public sector job security.[11]

A pragmatic argument to consider here is that concentration on the public sector compensation advantage reduces the short-run employment disruption caused by fiscal restraint. Payroll reduction may take the form of reduced public sector employment, in which case employment is obviously directly affected. In summary, if the Ontario NDP government concluded that deficit reduction requires reduction in the public sector payroll, it is a safe bet that the matter warrants close attention! See Ontario (1993).

The provinces have a much greater potential than does Ottawa to reduce their deficits by payroll reductions. Were federal transfers to the provinces to remain at their present level — cash transfers are approximately 4 percent of GDP — resort to a significant cut in the public payroll would place the provinces in surplus while Ottawa continued with a large deficit. This brings me to my third recommendation. Ottawa should share in the potential provincial savings from payroll reductions by a significant reduction in intergovernmental transfers. If Ottawa and the provinces want to eliminate their combined deficit by 1998-99 via a significant payroll cut, then cuts in intergovernmental transfers serve to equalize the percentage cuts required in other non-salary program expenditures at the federal and provincial level.

This argument does not replace, but supplements, other arguments for reducing intergovernmental transfers. Many analysts have concluded, for example, that an increased federal tax credit for children would be a more equitable and efficient program than the present Canada Assistance Plan. Redesign of social policy in an age of fiscal restraint cannot ignore the brute fact that intergovernmental transfers currently constitute approximately one-quarter of federal program spending.

The final recommendation is that governments pay close attention to the redistributive impact of restraint. This injunction is second nature to most practising politicians; academic analysts are wont to forget it. As proof of its importance, I remind readers of the earlier discussion of Saskatchewan's deficit-cutting exercise.

CONCLUSION

Having started off with the anecdote about the Vancouver teachers' strike, and having insisted upon deficit reduction by expenditure cuts, I am open to the charge of harbouring a general hostility to the public sector. I plead innocent. A generous welfare state is one of the major achievements of industrial society in the twentieth century. It must co-exist, however, with a market economy, and that implies serious analysis of the appropriate limits to be placed on each.

In summary, I could state the thesis of this chapter as follows: do not confuse the case for a generous and efficient welfare state with the case for extrapolating the past quarter century's trends in public sector expenditure growth and, *a fortiori*, do not confuse the case with extrapolating trends in public sector collective bargaining.

NOTES

1. This essay contains revised passages from a recent essay written for the new C.D. Howe series on social policy (Richards 1994).
2. Tom Courchene discusses these interregional trends in detail in a forthcoming volume of the new C.D. Howe series on social policy. See also Peter Leslie's article in Leslie *et al.* (1993).
3. As measured by the magnitude of the provincial tax-supported debt-GDP ratio, Saskatchewan had become by 1992 the most debt-ridden province of the country, including Newfoundland. For comparative data on provincial deficits and debts see Saskatchewan (1993).
4. According to one poll in the fall of 1993 the Saskatchewan NDP enjoyed 41 percent voter support; the provincial Liberals enjoyed 25 percent, and the former governing Conservatives only 16 percent (Roberts 1993).
5. The Conservatives implemented several dubious accounting changes in their spring 1993 budget to minimize the deficit estimate in a pre-election budget. The new government has reversed these changes, and made some dubious accounting decisions of its own. The effect of the Liberal changes is to shift expenditures into the 1993/94 fiscal year and hence increase the deficit base against which to assess its own deficit-reduction performance (Canada 1994). Despite these accounting distortions, however, four-fifths of the deficit increase reflects a genuine fiscal deterioration relative to early 1993 expectations, primarily in lower-than-expected revenues.
6. The expenditure figures are derived from Table 17 of the 1994-95 budget (Canada 1994) — with one adjustment. I have reallocated the $700 million "restructuring charges" arising from cancellation of the helicopter contract and closing of military establishments to the 1994/95 fiscal year, instead of the 1993/94 fiscal year as reported. The revenue figures are contained in Table 16. The summary economic assumptions are in Table 1.
7. While approximately two-thirds of public spending in wealthy OECD countries is devoted to social programs, interpreted broadly, the proportion of non-social

spending differs among countries and hence the relative size of national welfare states is not strictly proportional to aggregate public spending data. Some spend more on defence (Canada spends less than average); some spend more on debt charges (Canada among them).

8.   These estimates derive from personal communications with senior officials in the finance ministries of federal and provincial governments. One source against which to gauge these estimates is Statistics Canada (1993) which compiles data on public sector employment and remuneration under several definitions of varying scope. For purposes of this exercise the most relevant definition is "government employment," which includes the civil service plus health, education, and social agencies; it excludes government business enterprises. Unfortunately this definition also excludes several important categories of workers who derive most of their income via salary or fees negotiated with government. Two such categories are universities and independent health-care providers (primarily physicians). For fiscal 1991/92, federal remuneration of "government employees" so defined was 18 percent of federal program expenditures net of transfers to the provinces; the analogous provincial statistic was 23 percent. This latter statistic is a serious underestimate. The majority of local public sector employment (e.g., teachers) is financed by grants from provincial governments. University employees and health-care providers absorb in excess of 10 percent of provincial program expenditures.

9.   This conclusion is derived from an exercise, similar in spirit to Robson's (1994), in which Ottawa and the provinces reduce program spending sufficiently to eliminate the combined federal-provincial deficit (on a public accounts basis) by fiscal 1998/99. The key assumptions are (a) that real GDP grows between 3 and 4 percent annually, (b) that government tax revenues rise at the same rate as GDP, and (c) that average real interest rates on public debt decline somewhat. See the article by Richards (Brown et al. forthcoming).

10.   For a future C.D. Howe Institute study, David Brown (Brown et al. forthcoming) has compared wages in the public sector (defined broadly to include those in health, social, and educational institutions) and private sector. The ratio of wages in the public sector to those in the industrial aggregate rose from 1.1 in 1983 to 1.14 in 1993. There are many difficulties in comparing public versus private sector compensation accurately. This ratio measures average wages and salaries. It takes no account of wage determining characteristics of employees and jobs (skill levels, work conditions, security of tenure) that can be expected to influence competitive market pay levels; nor does it include deferred benefits (e.g., pensions) that tend to be more generous in the public sector.

11.   Between 1990 and 1992, employment in the broadly defined public sector grew 2.3 percent; total employment declined 2.6 percent, and employment in the private sector declined by 4.0 percent (Brown et al. forthcoming).

REFERENCES

Brown D., J. Richards *et al.* (forthcoming), *Social Policy and the Fiscal Crisis* (working title). The Social Policy Challenge: a series on social policy, no. 3, Toronto: C.D. Howe Institute.

Canada. Department of Finance (1993*a*), *Economic and Fiscal Reference Tables*, Ottawa: Department of Finance (August).

_____ (1993*b*), Statement by Minister of Finance in Montreal, 30 November 1993, Ottawa: Department of Finance.

_____ (1994), *The Budget Plan*, 1994/95 budget document, tabled in House of Commons 22 February 1994, Ottawa: Department of Finance.

Courchene T. (1993), "Path dependency, Positive Feedback and Paradigm Warp: A Schumpeterian Approach to the Social Order," in *Income Security in Canada: Changing Needs, Changing Means*, Montreal: Institute for Research on Public Policy.

Economic Council of Canada (1990), *Transition for the '90s*, 27th annual review, Ottawa: Supply and Services Canada.

_____ (1992*a*), *Education and Training in Canada*, Ottawa: Supply and Services Canada.

_____ (1992*b*), *The New Face of Poverty: Income Security Needs of Canadian Families*, Ottawa: Supply and Services Canada.

Gunderson M. and C. Riddell (1993), "Competitiveness and Public Sector Wages and Employment," Government and Competitiveness Project Discussion Paper 93-17, Kingston: School of Policy Studies, Queen's University.

Kornai J. (1992), *The Socialist System: The Political Economy of Communism*, Princeton, NJ: Princeton University Press.

Lam N., M. Prince and J. Cutt (1993), *Reforming the Public Pension System in Canada: Retrospect and Prospect*, Victoria: Centre for Public Sector Studies, University of Victoria.

Leslie P., K. Norrie and I. Ip (1993), *A Partnership in Trouble: Renegotiating Fiscal Federalism*, Toronto: C.D. Howe Institute.

OECD (1993), *OECD Economic Outlook*, 54 (December), Paris: Organization for Economic Co-operation and Development.

Ontario (1993), *Jobs and Services: A Social Contract for The Ontario Public Sector*, Toronto: Government of Ontario (5 April).

Quebec (1993), *Quebec's Public Finances: Living Within our Means*, Quebec: Ministère des Finances.

Reform Party (1993), "Look at the national debt hole Canada is in," four-page flyer, Calgary: Reform Party of Canada.

Richards J. (1994), "The Social Policy Round," in *The Case for Change: Reinventing the Welfare State*, ed. D. Brown, J. Richards and W. Watson, Toronto: C.D. Howe Institute.

Roberts D. (1993), "Saskatchewan Liberals return to the fold," *The Globe and Mail*, 8 November 1993, p. A4.

Robson W. (1994), *Digging Holes and Hitting Walls: Canada's Fiscal Prospects in the Mid-1990s*, Toronto: C.D. Howe Institute.

Saskatchewan (1992), *Rebuilding Saskatchewan Together: Budget Address*, Regina: Department of Finance.

_____ (1993), *Addressing Saskatchewan's Debt Problem*, Regina: Department of Finance.

_____ (1994), *Delivering the Promise: Budget Address*, Regina: Department of Finance.

Statistics Canada (1993), *Public Sector Employment and Remuneration 1992*, 72-209, Ottawa: Statistics Canada.

Vastel M. (1994), "Les vrais poissons ne sont pas ceux qu'on pense," *L'Actualité* (February).

Walker M. and I. Horry (1993), "March's solution: Effective federal spending cuts," *Fraser Forum*, (March).

Contributors

Keith G. Banting is Professor of Political Studies and Director of the School of Policy Studies at Queen's University.

Richard M. Bird is Professor of Economics at the University of Toronto.

André Blais is Professor of Political Science at Université de Montréal and Co-Director of the Canadian Election Study Team.

Robin Boadway is Sir Edward Peacock Professor of Economic Theory and Associate Director of the John Deutsch Institute for the Study of Economic Policy in the Department of Economics at Queen's University.

Douglas M. Brown is Executive Director of the Institute of Intergovernmental Relations at Queen's University.

Thomas J. Courchene is Jarislowsky-Deutsch Professor of Economic and Financial Policy and Director of the John Deutsch Institute for the Study of Economic Policy at Queen's University.

J. Stefan Dupré is Professor of Political Science at the University of Toronto.

Frank Flatters is Professor of Economics and Associate Director of the John Deutsch Institute for the Study of Economic Policy at Queen's University.

Claude E. Forget is Senior Vice-President of the Laurentian Group Corp.

Frederick W. Gorbet is Executive Vice-President of North American Life Assurance Company and former Deputy Minister of Finance, Government of Canada.

Paul A.R. Hobson is Associate Professor of Economics at Acadia University.

Peter Leslie is Professor of Political Studies at Queen's University.

Judith Maxwell is Associate Director of the School of Policy Studies at Queen's University.

David Milne is Professor of Political Science at the University of Prince Edward Island.

Robert Normand is Vice-President, Corporate Affairs of Groupe UniMédia Inc.

Kenneth Norrie is Professor of Economics at the University of Alberta.

Lars Osberg is Professor of Economics at Dalhousie University.

Susan D. Phillips is Assistant Professor in the School of Public Administration at Carleton University.

John Richards is Professor of Public Policy in the Faculty of Business at Simon Fraser University.

Richard Simeon is Professor of Political Science and Law at the University of Toronto and Vice-Chair of the Ontario Law Reform Commission.

Greg Stoddart is Professor of Clinical Epidemiology and Biostatistics at McMaster University and Fellow of the Population Health Program at the Canadian Institute for Advanced Research.

Katherine Swinton is Professor of Law in the Faculty of Law at the University of Toronto.

Carolyn Tuohy is Professor of Political Science and Vice-Provost at the University of Toronto.

François Vaillancourt is Professor of Economics at Université de Montréal.

Ronald L. Watts is Professor of Political Studies at Queen's University.